❖

No Stranger to Tears

NO
STRANGER
TO TEARS

A Surgeon's Story

WILLIAM G. CAHAN, M.D.

RANDOM HOUSE   NEW YORK

*Grateful acknowledgment is made to the following for permission
to reprint previously published material:*

HARPERCOLLINS PUBLISHERS INC.: Excerpts from "Natural History"
from *Poems and Sketches of E. B. White*. Copyright 1929 by E. B. White.
Reprinted by permission of HarperCollins Publishers Inc.

MCA MUSIC PUBLISHING: Excerpts from "Fat Man Blues"
by Zeke Manners and Bill Cahan. Copyright 1946 by MCA Music Publishing,
a division of MCA, Inc., New York, NY 10019.
Copyright renewed. Reprinted by permission. All rights reserved.

THE NEW YORK TIMES: Excerpt from an article about William Cahan
from February 13, 1969. Copyright © 1969 by The New York Times Company.
Reprinted by permission of *The New York Times*.

Library of Congress Cataloging-in-Publication Data
Cahan, William G.
No stranger to tears: a surgeon's story/by William G. Cahan.—1st ed.
p.   cm.
Includes index.
ISBN 0-394-56518-5
1. Cahan, William G., 1914–   .   2. Surgeons—United States—Biography.
3. Oncologists—United States—Biography.   I. Title.
RD651.C34   1991
617'.092—dc20
[B]   91-52690

Manufactured in the United States of America

9   8   7   6   5   4   3   2

First Edition

Book Design by Lilly Langotsky

To Amazing Grace,

and for

my genebearers

Surgeons must be very careful
When they take the knife
Underneath their fine incisions
Stirs the culprit—life!
—EMILY DICKINSON

Humanity is all.
—ALBERT EINSTEIN

For a compassionate man, nothing human is
alien; no joy and no sorrow, no way of living and no way of dying.
—HENRI J. M. NOUWEN,
THE WOUNDED HEALER

ACKNOWLEDGMENTS

In 1986, Arthur Gelb, then managing editor of *The New York Times,* heard me mention that my son was doing surgery at my hospital. He thought it would make a good story and assigned Samuel Freedman to write it. "In His Father's Footsteps" appeared in the June 1, 1986 *Times* Sunday magazine, and spawned the idea for this book.

During its long gestation there have been several midwives without whom it would not have seen the light of day.

My wife, Grace, who inspired me by her own remarkable example of creativity and diligence.

Beatrice Arbaiza, my secretary for twenty-two years, who had an added burden of helping me with endless details while still maintaining my complicated practice.

Other "without whoms" for whose suggestions I am sincerely grateful: Sigrid Nunez, Joan Sanger, Ric Frede, Larry White, Nan Talese, Alice Trillin, Leo Lerman, Murray Schumach, MaryAnn Eatz, and the late Phyllis Atkinson.

A major "without whom": my infinitely patient—but not always—editor, Samuel S. Vaughan.

CONTENTS

PROLOGUE

OPERATION (PHASE I)

I stood watching over the young surgeon's shoulder, waiting for him to begin.

The night before, he had called and said, "I'm ready for you. Could you be there tomorrow morning at eight?"

We met in the locker room and changed into green scrub suits, caps, masks, and shoe covers. As we walked together to Operating Room number 4, he briefed me about his patient, Mrs. Robinson, a sixty-three-year-old woman who, while bathing a few weeks before, had found a lump in her right breast. A subsequent physical examination and mammogram indicated that it was probably malignant.

The surgeon said that he had discussed various options—lumpectomy versus mastectomy—beforehand with the patient and her family. If cancer were found, he had explained, options were limited because of its large size—over two inches. This would necessitate removing a large segment of the breast to provide safe margins around the growth.

The family told the surgeon to use his judgment, and do what he thought best.

Entering the O.R., we were warmly greeted by the surgeon's assistants, the anesthetist, and two nurses: the rotating, "unsterile" one and the other, the "sterile" instrument nurse. They welcomed him by his first name and me by my last, presumably in deference to my age.

The surgeon had instructed the anesthetist to withhold anesthesia until he could see and talk with the patient. He went to her side and took her hand. She smiled up at him as he, with mock formality, introduced himself much as a father might formally introduce himself to his daughter. Then, as he nodded to the anesthetist, he leaned over the patient and, in a gentle voice, said, "Don't worry, I'll be with you all the way." Sodium pentothal was injected into the intravenous tube attached to her arm and, within seconds, she was asleep.

I smiled to myself. Years before, I had told him: Remember, patients are friends in trouble. They are frightened and feel very much alone, particularly in the operating room. Greet them by name. Relax them with some sort of light humor. Most important, be sure to hold their hands. This bridge, this contact between you, reassures them. Someone they know, someone who cares, is there.

The anesthetist gently opened the patient's mouth and introduced an airway tube into her windpipe. Then she attached the tube's free end to a plastic hose that led to the automatic respirator. She recorded the time on a form, where blood pressure, pulse, respiration, and other details of the operation would also be entered.

As I stood off to one side, it was difficult to believe that here, in this room, where I had been operating for more than forty years, I was no longer the key figure. The nurses with whom I had worked sensed how strange and even pained I must feel. The rotating nurse whispered that I was missed and brought me a high stool to sit on while waiting.

Somehow, these loving, caring, well-intentioned gestures, the concern the staff were showing—as if for a patient—made me feel the bystander's role even more keenly; they knew I was now thought to be out of things, isolated, abandoned, shelved.

For my part, it was not that I yearned to do the operation myself, for I had long since reached the etceteras of surgical life. Instead, it was just that I had hoped that one day, I would be able to operate with this young surgeon.

The nurse untied and removed the patient's gown and the surgeon, indelible pencil in hand, drew a large "V" between the patient's breasts. He turned to the nurse.

"Is that about right?" he asked.

"Perfect," she said.

He explained to his assistants that if the biopsy were positive, necessitating an extensive excision, he would be careful to keep the incision outside the "V" so that later the patient could wear a dress with a low neckline or a bathing suit and not show a scar. Another lesson well learned.

As the surgeon and his assistants left the O.R. to scrub, I thought of the extraordinary changes that had taken place since the thirties and forties, when I was a medical student, intern, and resident. For one thing, the speed and ease with which the patient was anesthetized were a far cry from the time when ether was dripped from a can onto a gauze-covered metal-screen cone—the "tea strainer"—held over a patient's nose and mouth with instructions to breathe deeply. Ether required many minutes before inducing sleep. Later, quicker-acting nitrogen oxide, then commonly called laughing gas, was used to begin anesthesia. However, nitrogen oxide was no laughing matter, because as patients became unconscious, some went through an "excitation" phase when they might thrash about so violently that they had to be strapped down to avoid injuring themselves or others who were trying to restrain them.

As the surgeon scrubbed, he kept glancing through a window over the sink at the patient's cardiac monitor screen to be sure that all was well.

After the rotating nurse adjusted the overhead lights, she painted the area of the patient's breast with a water-based iodine antiseptic. In pre-antibiotic days, surgeons were haunted by the specter of postoperative infections. To reduce these, the section to be operated on was first vigorously washed with green soap, rinsed, then painted with tincture of iodine followed by alcohol, a combination that could leave burns. Surgeons themselves scrubbed a minimum of ten minutes with stiff bristle brushes and a mixture of lime, salt, and baking soda, after which they dipped their hands and forearms up to their elbows in a vat of alcohol. If this procedure was repeated two or three times a day, their skin became brawny, red, and inflamed. By contrast, these young doctors had to scrub only five minutes, using soft plastic brushes and sponges with a nonirritating antiseptic soap.

When the timer at the sink sounded, the surgeons finished scrubbing, rinsed away the soap, and with hands held high, backed into the O.R. They paused before the patient's mammograms (we had none), mounted on an X-ray viewing box on a wall. The surgeon pointed to the suspicious sign: a white, stellate smudge that stood out clearly in the otherwise translucent breast tissue.

I watched the surgeon dry his hands, proceeding from the more sterile to the less sterile areas: hands first, forearms next, elbows last. (At least some things hadn't changed.) Then the instrument, or "scrub," nurse gowned the three of them by first holding open green paper gowns (ours were made of white cloth), then rubber operating gloves, snapping them into place over the surgeons' cuffs.

The surgeon and his assistants took their places on opposite sides of the patient. The instrument table with its precisely arranged clamps, retrac-

tors, suction apparatus, and gauze pads was wheeled into place, and the instrument nurse stood in readiness.

The surgeon held out his hand for the scalpel. Just before making the incision, he looked over his shoulder at me and nodded.

In surroundings as familiar to me as my own living room, I was nevertheless uneasy in an observer's role—yet fascinated by the still-surprising drama unfolding before me. And I couldn't help marveling at the chain of events that had led to this treasured moment, watching this particular young surgeon about to begin a major operation. I wondered: What was I doing here? How did he—and I—get here? How and when did it begin?

❖
No Stranger to Tears

❖

CHAPTER I

Epiphany

═══════════

───────────

In July 1928, when I was almost fourteen, my parents rented a two-story gray shingled house for the summer, at the seashore in West End, New Jersey. It had a large, shady porch with rockers and a hammock. Around it lay a wide green lawn, separated by hedges from neighboring houses. One hot day in July, my mother and I were waiting for my grandmother, Fanny Gomperts, who was coming down for a respite from the baking New York City streets.

My mother's mother was the heart of our family. Sadly, she was an "old" sixty-five: obese, diabetic, and hobbled by swollen legs covered with varicose ulcers that I had often dressed. Still, we adored her for her warmth, her easy laughter, her quickness to forgive—and not least for her cooking. We looked forward to having her with us to enjoy the comfort of shady trees and cool sea breezes. Her son, my uncle Robert, was to accompany her. He called as they were about to leave the city by taxi. The trip would take no more than two hours.

When three, and then four, hours passed and there was no sign of them, we grew more and more apprehensive. My mother began pacing restlessly up and down the porch. I would run across to the lawn's edge and look down the road in the direction of New York. Finally, the yellow taxi drew up to the curb. My mother and I ran out and flung open the door with joy and relief.

We were met by the familiar aroma that surrounded my grandmother: a strange bouquet of lilac water and Burow's antiseptic

SAMUEL CAHAN

The grandmother whose illness touched off a spark

solution. Our delight quickly vanished when we saw Grandma leaning against my distraught uncle, panting, looking flushed, bathed in perspiration. Scattered around them were straw fans, pillows, paper bags filled with dressings and bottles of antiseptic. Grandma could manage only the feeblest, loving smile.

My mother and uncle eased her forward to the edge of the seat and slowly rotated her so that one swollen leg at a time touched the ground. I crawled in on the seat behind her to assist as they pulled her to a standing position. Then we lowered her into a chair and my uncle, the cabdriver, and I carried her to the porch. We paid the driver, who had lost his way, and he left.

Once on the porch, my grandmother could not seem to get comfortable. She looked extremely anxious, continued to gasp, and could hardly speak. We fanned her, applied cold, wet wash-clothes to her forehead, and told her what a wonderful rest she would have now that she was at the shore.

After a while, Grandma whispered to my mother that she had to use the bathroom. My mother urged her to use a bedpan right there on the porch, because the only bathroom was on the second floor. However, Grandma was too modest to do so, and she insisted that we take her upstairs.

Uncle Robert and I carried her in the chair to the foot of the stairs. To lift her, my uncle supported her under the arms and I held her legs. It took all our strength.

As soon as we started, my grandmother closed her eyes and began moaning and grunting. While we strained to move her upward, I kept reassuring her: "Just four more steps, Grandma—just three more—"

And then she went limp.

We struggled up the last steps to a bedroom and onto a bed. My mother and uncle were panic-stricken. They slapped her wrists, sprinkled her face with cold water, all the while crying, "Mamma! Mamma!" But she did not respond. Then I remembered a Boy Scout first aid maneuver used for fainting and propped her feet up on a pillow. Uncle Robert frantically asked a telephone operator to send a doctor. Horrified, I knew we had to get help, any help, and ran downstairs and out of the house. In my desperation, borne aloft with anxiety, I leaped over the hedge I had always thought was insurmountable. I rang a neighbor's bell, but no one was home. I tried the neighbor on the other side but without success. Dreading what I would find, I returned to our house to find my beloved grandmother just as I had left her: staring silently and not breathing.

I had never before experienced such helplessness.

I had never before witnessed death.

Alone with my grief in the days that followed, I was haunted by one fact above all: *I had not known what to do.* On the third day, I experienced a kind of epiphany and vowed that never again as long as I lived would I feel helpless and ignorant while someone I loved was in acute distress. Years later, I learned that my grandmother's grunting as we lifted her up the stairs was probably a sign of impending heart failure. We should never have tried to move her from the porch, modesty or not, until a doctor came.

Any retrospective search for childhood experiences that helped shape a life decision risks simplifying or overinterpreting or reading overmuch significance into one event. Yet, without question, the episode with my grandmother gave direction to what had been a vague, ill-defined, subliminal leaning.

In hindsight, it is not too farfetched to detect the start of a pattern in that moment as well as in other painful experiences of my childhood. I had a lion's share of mishaps.

Pain can leave its boon behind, serving as a harsh teacher. To an accident-prone boy, it taught much, including reason to be grateful to and admire those responsible for its relief.

I was not quite seven when I was severely burned following a fall into a bonfire. A few years later, on July 4, a Roman candle I was holding backfired up my sleeve. My mother smeared those burns with butter, which was thought to be the thing to do at the time. I still bear their scars as well as one on my forehead resulting from the fall I took on a stone step. I can still see myself running down 142nd Street, blood streaming into my eyes from what I soon was calling the hole in my head. And to stop my frequent nosebleeds, my parents stuffed a wad of tissue paper under my upper lip and put a cold key at the back of my neck.

As one of the boys of summer, I walked through the smoke of a brushfire in which poison ivy was being burned and, for endless days and nights, every inch of my miserable young body was covered with agonizing itchy eruptions.

At eight, after I had a strep throat, my urine was grossly bloody; this heralded the onset of acute nephritis. Once this kidney condition subsided, my parents were advised to have my tonsils removed. This nightmare was performed in a doctor's office under ether-drip anesthesia; following it I lost a great deal of blood and couldn't swallow or speak for days.

I was about ten when a piece of metal dust became embedded in my cornea, causing one eye to become markedly inflamed. My anxious father took me at night to the emergency room at St. Luke's Hospital. I had never been in a hospital before. The combination of the hospital odor, mysterious dark corridors that, at one point, echoed with a child's wailing, plus the sound of an ambulance siren winding down, terrified me. But soon I relaxed, fascinated, when an intern, having assured me that all would be O.K., dripped a local anesthetic into my eye and painlessly removed the fragments with a shiny metal instrument.

He smiled.

Relieved and grateful, I smiled back. One day could I be like him?

It is not difficult to imagine how panicked my parents became each time their only child appeared, exhibiting the latest calamity. After they got over their immediate fright, and comforted me with loving reassurances and primitive first aid, one would say: "Quick, get Rheinthaler on the phone!" Once I knew that Dr. Rheinthaler was on the way, it meant that the current catastrophe would soon be relieved.

Dr. Rheinthaler was in his late sixties and talked with a slight German accent. He always wore a navy blue suit and peered at me through pince-nez suspended from a black ribbon. I vividly recall his gleaming baldness, his thermometer in its silver case, his chilly stethoscope, and a mysterious pungent odor that, years later, I would associate with hospitals and healing and Dr. Rheinthaler.

Constantly kind and gentle, he apologized for hurting me, always "for your own good," like the tetanus shot he administered in my lower abdomen (God only knows why there!) after I had plunged a rusty Civil War sword into my foot. The pain from the shot was worse than the wound. But he never left me without first reaching into his black bag and bringing out a lemon lollipop that, after he told me how brave I'd been, had remarkable calming and curing powers.

His office was in a Gramercy Park brownstone, in a large room with mullioned windows, rich mahogany chairs with worn black leather seats, and fumed oak walls decorated with diplomas of age-yellowed paper or parchment, with indecipherable writings, red and gold seals, and ribbons. Faint antiseptic smells mingled with fumes from the lighted alcohol lamp in its silver base, over which he shook a test tube with my urine sample, looking for albumen. I will never forget the jubilant look on his face when it finally tested negative, signaling the end of nephritis.

Needless to say, my parents idolized Dr. Rheinthaler and the respect with which they spoke his name made a deep impression on me.

Less dramatic events foreshadowed my professional future, conceivably. In recalling these dust-covered scraps from the attic of memory, I am guilty of giving them far more importance than they had, magnifying and romanticizing them. For example, could the manual dexterity I would need, and of which I was so proud, have come from doing a little crude carpentry? Or was there a clue in the fact that during my many illnesses or convalescent periods, I asked for a box of buttons and amused myself for hours by sewing them onto a cushion? (Thus earning for myself the nickname Billy Buttons.)

Or when I joined the Boy Scouts, starting as a Tenderfoot and

Author's father, age 11 (1887), as a newsboy before he made sidewalk
drawings of the sinking of the battleship *Maine*

shooting all the way through the ranks up to Second Class Scout,
I took the Scouting motto seriously, particularly the "daily good
deeds" idea. For a while, I did all the standard ones: volunteering
to run errands (ones I couldn't have avoided anyhow); pushing
crumbs on overfed pigeons; offering to help hapless "older people" (most were about thirty-five) across the street. These small
services made me feel virtuous: Doing good seemed satisfying.
When asked "What do you want to be when you grow up?"—*if*
I grew up, given my propensity for injuries—I said I wanted to
be a fireman, adding, with sickening sweet solemnity: "to save
lives."

I suppose that every doctor secretly or overtly longs to have at
least one child who will study medicine. My father looked for any
leaning I might have toward drawing or painting. Contrary to
myth, he would have been proud to proclaim, "My son, the
artist . . ."

In my early teens, my father was elated when, yielding to his urging and, anxious to please him, I began a watercolor. The trouble was that I chose a very difficult subject: a multiplaned iridescent art moderne vase. This problem was compounded by my choice of that most difficult medium, watercolor; in my inexperienced hand the paints flowed into each other and came to look like a design for batik. Nevertheless, I gamely struggled on and, even discounting the adoring praise of my father for what it was, the result was not too bad for a first try. However, the estates of Winslow Homer and John Singer Sargent had no need to be concerned: That was my first and last experience at producing art, a source of disappointment to my father.

So far as is known, there was no physician on either side of the family.

In 1886, the Statue of Liberty was just being finished, and my grandmother Sarah brought her six-month-old son Samuel to

Peddler on New York's Lower East Side, by Samuel Cahan.
Author with Buster Brown haircut in foreground

America. My grandfather Simon who had preceded his family in an exodus from pogrom-prone Lithuanian Russia, got his first look at his third child when all were united at Castle Garden.

Castle Garden is located on the Hudson River basin at the southern tip of Manhattan, at the edge of Bowling Green. Originally, it was an opera house, in which Jenny Lind sang. In the latter part of the nineteenth century, before Ellis Island opened, it became a place of entry for European immigrants. Later, it was New York's Aquarium and, today, is a marine museum.

Like many other immigrants, the family settled in that famous finishing school called the Lower East Side, exchanging free living space in a tenement for Sarah's work as a janitress. Simon did everything to keep his family from starving, from selling shoelaces to tutoring other immigrants in what little English he had learned. They had eight children: four boys and one girl survived infancy. As soon as they were old enough, the boys were sent out on the street to sell newspapers at two cents per copy.

Dramatic headlines helped. In 1898, the battleship *Maine* was blown up, setting off the Spanish-American War. My father, tired of walking barefoot near Park Row shouting "WUXTRA! WUXTRA!" decided to stack his papers outside a busy restaurant and, to attract attention and business, drew a picture of the *Maine* disaster in colored chalk on the sidewalk.

As happens in such stories, which cynics insist are only folklore, the art editor of Joseph Pulitzer's daily newspaper the New York *World* came out of the restaurant, saw something in the drawing, and suggested that the newspaper seller apply for a job as an office boy at the *World*. My father had to borrow shoes from one neighbor and a shirt from another, but he got the job at two dollars a week.

In those days, sketches were the photographs for newspapers. After studying at the National Academy of Design, my father was still in his teens when he became the paper's staff artist. Soon, his drawings of personalities as well as major news events appeared regularly. He illustrated stories by O. Henry and Sholem Aleichem and other well-known writers in the *World*'s Sunday magazine, as well as many scenes of the Lower East Side. He was to remain on the *World* until it was sold, thirty-four years later, to the Scripps-Howard newspaper syndicate to become the *World-Telegram*—now extinct.

My father first saw blond, blue-eyed Flora Julia Gomperts, a

The author's father, artist Samuel Cahan,
at his drawing board at the New York *World,* 1915

native New Yorker of English and Dutch descent, when she was appearing in an amateur musical at a theater in Harlem. She was seventeen. For six years he courted her. For most of those years, Flora's parents refused to allow her to give Sammy Cahan her hand until he was, in their eyes, earning enough to support her. My father never forgot that, rather than take his word for it, the Gomperts insisted on seeing his bankbook. (Years later, I would encounter such scrutiny myself when I wanted to marry the daughter of a famous actress.)

They were married on October 16, 1913, at the Martinique Hotel on Thirty-second Street. On their honeymoon, they cruised to Panama. Because I was born a little over nine months later, my father always said that I began the trip with him and came back with my mother.

On that very hot Sunday, August 2, 1914, at 603 West 140th Street, while my mother was in labor, my father paced up and down anxiously in the next room. From the courtyard below came the sounds of two pianists trying to drown each other out, one playing the "Marseillaise," the second, "Deutschland Über Alles": France and Germany had just declared war.

My father was so deeply disturbed by my mother's labor, that he vowed never to put her through that torment again. So I was to be their only child. Although there would be moments when I wished for the company of a brother or sister, I had a happy childhood.

In 1916, my father, age thirty, was asked to do a portrait "from life" of President Woodrow Wilson. The sketch, which was signed, was distributed through America and became the official campaign portrait during Wilson's bid for a second term in the White House. My father could never get over this. "Imagine," he used to say, "in just eighteen years, a twelve-year-old barefoot newsboy from the streets drew a portrait, *in person,* of the President of the United States!"

When he sketched some prominent person for a *World* feature story, he would ask that the subject sign the original. The signed original of the one he did of Margaret Sanger, the pioneer birth-control activist, my father kept after it had been printed on the *World*'s front page as part of a story on her crusade.

Many years later, while Dr. Grant Sanger, one of her sons, and I were interning at New York's Presbyterian Hospital, he asked if my father would give him the sketch. But my father demurred. When Grant asked if he would donate it to the Margaret Sanger

The author's mother, drawn by his father. He sketched on anything everywhere, as here on hotel stationary.

Library Room at Smith College, my father was glad to do so, and it is there at present.

After work, my father always found time to do what he loved most: sketch and make etchings. Later, as a teenager, I was always ecstatic when he asked me to help. Using a diamond-pointed needle, he transcribed his pencil sketches onto wax-coated copper plates. When the plate was dipped into a bath of nitric acid, the acid bit into the copper only where the needle scratches had perforated the wax coating. When printed, etched lines are sharp and distinct.

My father had his own etching press in our apartment. Inked copper plates were centered on slightly dampened Japanese rice paper and fed between two steel rollers. These were turned by a hand crank that I helped him rotate. What emerged magically was often a thing of beauty. After each print, the plate was inked anew, so prints varied slightly from one another. When the ink and paper dried, my father signed each print in pencil at its bottom and numbered it in series: e.g., 12/50. (Years later, Paloma Picasso and I reminisced about how we helped our fathers turn the cranks of their etching presses, and what suspense and excitement we felt as a beautiful print emerged at the other end.)

Some of my father's drawings, etchings, and drypoints hang on the walls of our home today. They include portraits of bearded rabbis, of Lower East Side peddlers, of my mother, of my father's mother, of me at the age of three months and again as a medical student characteristically sick with "la grippe."

Although not drafted during World War I because he was over thirty and had a child, my father drew posters for Victory Bond drives and, after work, would help paint camouflage on the sides of destroyers. Wartime spirits ran high and were infectious. My mother insists that when I was a toddler, and she served me a fried egg, I would jab the yolk with a fork and cry, "Right in the kaiser's eye!"

When I was four, we moved to 644 Riverside Drive, at 142nd Street where I immediately befriended a neighbor, Morton Kanner. Mort was one year behind me at PS 186. He was stout, clumsy, very bright, unsociable, and bad at games. Mort was always the last one taken when we chose up sides and was assigned to the position on the field where he could do the least harm. As his best, and only, friend, I often had to coax other kids into letting him play with us.

Mort's family was religious; mine was not. My father's teenage idol was the "Great Agnostic," Robert Ingersoll. Mother believed in God and prayed to Him in gratitude or for some special favor. Her religious observances were limited to burning a yahrzeit candle on the anniversary of her father's death and fasting on Yom Kippur to atone for her "sins." Not from conviction, but for the challenge, I joined her in fasting. I usually lasted only to lunch time because of my mother's concern about "weakening" me. Somewhat guiltily, we would break our fast with tea and toast. Although we did not observe the Jewish holy days, I took off from school on the high ones. I went to Sunday school once; Mort talked me into it. When I was thirteen, I agreed to go through with a bar mitzvah, for I was told it would please my grandmothers.

Washington Heights, where we lived, had just begun to be peopled by Jews who were financially able to move from Lower East Side tenements. Some moved to the Bronx; others to Brooklyn; and those who could afford it, to Washington Heights. When I was a kid, most of my neighborhood friends were Catholics. Instead of attending public schools as we did, they were enrolled in parochial schools, the local one being Our Lady of Lourdes.

I suppose I was first made to feel different and separate from Gentiles when a Catholic friend asked me to show him my penis. He explained that he wanted to see what a circumcision looked like because the priest in his school talked about Jesus having had one.

On rare occasions, in the middle of a fistfight brought on by a close call in a game, a few hotheads would scream compliments at each other: "sheenie" or "kike" or "Jew bastard" or "dirty Irish mick." After a few punches had been traded, we'd separate the combatants and continue the game as if nothing had happened.

Solely because they loved seeing the joy of children at Christmas and Easter, my parents made these into festive holidays. On Christmas Eve, I was allowed to sleep in my parents' bed, and awoke in the morning to find the stocking beside me filled with nuts, fruits, and candies. In my bedroom stood a tree that had been decorated while I slept. Beneath it were all the toys I could hope for. Invariably there was some dirty water in the bathroom sink, and a soiled, crumpled towel on the rack. Each year, my mother would show these to me, then sigh and say: "Santa used one of my best towels again."

At Easter, baskets filled with my father's splendid hand-painted eggs rested on the dining room table. Black "rabbit" tracks—made by fingers dipped in candle soot—led from the windowsill across the floor, up, and across a white tablecloth to a plate holding a half-gnawed carrot. I have preserved these traditions by passing them down to my children and grandchildren.

My parents socialized largely with Jews, probably because they felt more comfortable doing so, as many Jews still believed that America was run by a somewhat hostile, Gentile-dominated society. When my father invited a Gentile artist home, usually a friend from the *World,* my mother felt somewhat awkward and apprehensive. She would shine up the house and cook her best, but as the evening wore on, she was surprised and delighted at how harmoniously it was going and, as everyone became more comfortable with each other, my father would embark on his repertoire of funny stories told with a remarkably faithful imitation of a Yiddish accent.

I grew up comfortably; my parents adored each other and lavished such vast amounts of affection on me that I had a difficult time not being spoiled. They made every effort to give me a cultural education: My father often took me to the Metropolitan Museum of Art; my mother insisted that I take piano lessons, played songs from musical comedies we'd seen, and took me to concerts.

I remember how on one memorable occasion, after a concert, she dragged me backstage at Carnegie Hall to meet the soloist. Sergey Rachmaninoff's lined face was topped by cropped gray hair; he looked gravely down at me as he took my hand in his damp, long-fingered one and slowly pumped it up and down. It didn't rub off.

Other things did. My career as a budding scientist was given a boost when my uncle George, my mother's youngest brother, gave me a battered second-hand microscope for my thirteenth birthday. Examining a drop of water from a vase of faded flowers, I saw *miracles:* teeming microscopic life. Fascinated, I looked for other things to study—hair, saliva, grains of yeast. Blood from one of my own frequent nosebleeds, smeared on a glass slide, offered my first view of red corpuscles. Over the years, peering down the barrels of more sophisticated instruments, I would never lose that sense of wonderment.

Once after combing my hair, I held the rubberized comb in a beam of sunlight. To my amazement, dust particles kept jumping on and off the teeth of the comb as if they were alive. (No, there were no legs on them.) I couldn't imagine what was happening. Nor could my parents explain the phenomenon. Puzzled, I repeated the experiment many times. When I told my pal, Mort, about it, he described the phenomenon of static electricity. At age twelve, he had already acquired an impressive basic education in science.

Perhaps some ill-defined awakening of a different sort showed itself when I was learning the anatomy of a lobster. Besides discovering what lobsters have known all along—how to tell a male from a female—when we dissected the lobster in my biology class, I discovered the location of its brain.

When Mother bought lobsters for dinner and plunged them alive into boiling water, I cringed, haunted by my own burns. Perhaps, I reasoned, they might feel it less were I to pith them beforehand. My mother indulged me in what she felt was a merciful gesture, but hurriedly left the kitchen first.

I was never sure whether the lobsters appreciated this gesture, but I felt the better for it.

Yet another experience might indicate the healer-in-embryo. Every summer, my father suffered from ragweed-induced hay fever. As there were no air conditioners or antihistamines in those days, the poor man had the classic torments—irritated eyes, running nose, frequent sneezes, and sleepless nights. I had heard that hay fever came from inhaling pollen. If that were the case, I thought, why not partially plug each nostril with thin, wet cotton pledgets and screen out the pollen?

To indulge me, my father followed this suggestion. To his surprise, and my immediate satisfaction, the severity of his symptoms was reduced. Although not cured, my "first patient" was at least relieved. Needless to say, my father boasted inordinately about this miracle to his friends.

Like father, like son. As part of my self-adulation I am not above a bit of boasting about sons myself.

With their diverse interests in art, music, and journalism, my parents attracted an interesting and varied assortment of guests. I was allowed to stay up late to meet and listen to them. I can remember Frank Harris, Oscar Wilde's biographer, reciting as he wrote in our guest book an excerpt from Swinburne:

From too much love of living,
From hope and fear set free,
We thank with brief thanksgiving
Whatever gods may be
That no life lives forever;
That dead men rise up never;
That even the weariest river
Winds somewhere safe to sea

Other frequent guests included the author Konrad Bercovici; the singer Paul Robeson; the painter Buck Warshawsky; Dudley Nichols, chief correspondent of the *World;* and Rabbi Stephen S. Wise.

In high school, I had my own circle of friends who wrote poetry and short stories. Having had piano lessons and some elementary instruction in harmony, I began composing short ballads, which my delighted mother described as "filled with longing." (I didn't remind her that *all* Russo-Semitic music is filled with longing.)

It was a time when Edna St. Vincent Millay, Eleanor Wylie, Emily Dickinson, Robinson Jeffers, and T. S. Eliot wrote for and to us, articulating our romantic selves. I can still recall four of five love sonnets, memorized from Millay's *Fatal Interview,* which, at one time or another, I murmured to the girl I was romancing at the time.

Love is not all: it is not meat nor drink
Nor slumber nor a roof against the rain;—etc.

When my family moved to 380 Riverside Drive at 110th Street —a building designed by Stanford White—I enrolled in PS 165. I had skipped two grades, so I was not quite thirteen when I graduated and went on to DeWitt Clinton High School.

For fun, I played at sports along Riverside Drive, read the adventures of the Rover Boys, Tom Swift, Frank Merriwell. I also liked *Amazing Stories* magazine, the Fu Manchu and S. S. Van Dine mysteries, and was especially fascinated by the dramatic text and drawings of Robert Ripley's "Believe It or Not!" Ripley's widely syndicated feature, with its "Stranger Things on Heaven and Earth" quality, opened my eyes to the fact that highly improbable and singular events can and do occur.

Then, in my teens, a major influence was added to affect my future: I fell in love.

During the last year of high school, I met my uncle George's new and beautiful wife, Malvina, who was a professor of physiology at New York University. Malvina was a liberated woman, way ahead of her time. As a "Lucy Stoner" she insisted on keeping her maiden name after she married. She didn't want to have children; it was she who first explained to me what a pessary was.

Malvina was of medium height, had brown hair tied back in a bun, high cheekbones, and blue eyes that hid behind half-closed lids when she smiled or laughed, which she did readily. She had good legs and a full figure that undulated as she strode—not walked—from place to place.

Knowing of my interest in science, she invited me to her lab to observe her experiments on cats. The smell of ether, the rotating kymographs recording each cat's respiration and heartbeat, and the stunning Malvina, masked, gowned, gloved, and smeared with cats' blood—all cast a powerful spell on me. A flirtation with the idea of becoming a doctor flared into a passion.

Malvina undoubtedly added an aura of mystery and glamour to the study of science, and her perfumed presence catalyzed my ambitions of several kinds.

I was desolated when, after I left to go to college, she and my uncle were divorced. Later, Malvina married Erno Balogh, the accompanist of the great soprano Lotte Lehmann. We lost touch with each other until decades later. In the early 1970s, I was scheduled to give a lecture in Washington, D.C. Malvina, who was teaching there, happened to see a poster announcing the lecture. I was surprised and delighted when she telephoned. We had a long talk filled with reminiscences, ending with her promise to come to hear me.

Before and after my talk and during it, I looked for her in the crowd, but never found her. I'm sure that she was somewhere in the hall and had disappeared after my last slide was shown, before the lights came on. I've always wondered what kept her from our meeting. Perhaps, remembering how I obviously worshiped her, she was reluctant for me to see the changes that forty years had made. I never tried to solve this mystery, nor did I ever hear from Malvina again. (Perhaps if she reads this, she might call.)

❖

CHAPTER II

Enter to Grow in Wisdom

ENGRAVING OVER THE GATE TO HARVARD YARD

By the time I applied to college and was accepted by NYU in 1931, I knew that I was going to be a doctor. I longed to go to an out-of-town college, but was reluctant to leave New York: All my friends were here and, since I was an only child, my departure would be painful for my parents. Then, too, the Depression had begun, and my father's limited income had to be taken into account.

Wall Street's bleak October of 1929 provided the beginning of a slide into the Great Depression. The *World* building was close to Wall Street. When my father heard the news that the market was crashing, he ran down to the Stock Exchange and, from its balcony, drew a picture of the pandemonium below. The drawing was printed the next day across the front page of the *World*.★

The Crash took a great deal of my father's hard-earned money with it. He was able to keep working on the *World* until 1932, when it was sold to the Scripps-Howard newspaper chain and became the *World-Telegram*. When the *World* stopped publishing, he felt that "a mother had died."

Although our family's finances were precarious, they were never desperate. My father managed to find work illustrating pulp magazines like *Argosy* and *True Detective*. At night, he retouched photographs for *The New York Times*.

During these harsh times, on his only day off—Sunday—he

★ The original is in the Museum of the City of New York.

and I would take long walks, during which we saw many men dressed in oversized, threadbare overcoats, wearing shoes stuffed with straw or lined with newspaper, selling apples on street corners for a nickel apiece. Clusters of shanties set up by the unemployed in any area where there was a clearing were nicknamed Hoovervilles, after the President, who was felt to be both responsible for the Depression and unsympathetic to those hardest hit by it. These shelters were made from wooden packing cases or planks with corrugated iron roofs. Their inhabitants cooked in tin cans held over fires whatever they had been able to scrounge.

In my sophomore year at NYU, I became restless, felt unfulfilled, dissatisfied with the curriculum, which I felt was not stimulating or challenging. I also had to commute each day by subway to NYU's Heights Branch in the Bronx. My uncle George, who was like an older brother, and I decided that it was time for me to get out of the nest (or, as George said, from under smother love). He took it upon himself to persuade my parents that it would be a good idea. To our surprise, they readily agreed.

I applied to several colleges; when I was accepted at Harvard for entrance in my junior year, I was ecstatic.

Although 1933 was the depth of the Depression, one would never have known it at Harvard; signs of affluence were everywhere. It seemed as if everyone dressed and ate very well and owned open touring cars or roadsters. At first, it was not easy for me, a transfer student, to fit in with my better-off classmates, many of whom came from wealthy families and had gone to the "right" prep schools. I felt like an outsider looking in. But I soon found a group who shared my interests in music, science, and Chinese dinners.

For many of us, life at Harvard was pure luxury. I lived in Leverett House, in a roomy suite: a living room with a fireplace, a bedroom, and a bath. Our rooms were tidied by maids and we were served by waitresses in the wood-paneled dining room. Add to this the wonderful cultural resources Harvard had to offer, the beauty of Cambridge in all seasons, and my first taste of independence, and I was happier than I had ever been.

Not everything was picture perfect. Although my parents had to struggle, they never uttered a word of complaint. They assured me, when I raised the subject, that educating me was ample reward for any hardship they had to endure.

Tuition then was three hundred dollars a year, and room and board cost about the same.

Things were so precarious at home, what with money so scarce, that I refused to accept six dollars from my father for bus fare to come home for the Thanksgiving and Easter holidays. Fortunately, a friend, H. Vose Greenough, Jr., invited me to his family's attractive home in Brookline, Massachusetts, for those holidays. Eventually, I got to know the Greenoughs well; they made me feel like one of their family.

Harvard was predominantly Gentile; however, the only overt instance of anti-Semitism I recall was when a girl with whom I had been having a romance broke it off when she learned I was Jewish. Furious after she made an anti-Semitic slur, I began a poem: *Thin pale words on thin pale lips / cacophony of hate and fear.* Minorities accepted the fact that the exclusive "eating clubs," like Porcellian or The Fly, had never been known to admit Jews or blacks to their halls. However, the Hasty Pudding Club did not discriminate and accepted anyone with wit and talent, particularly if he could contribute to their famous annual show: for example, Alan Jay Lerner.

I took basic pre-med courses: biology, physics, biochemistry, comparative anatomy, and German. It was a grind, especially physics, and I had to study harder than ever before. At the end of my first semester, I was put on the probation list because I had two C's and two D's. By resisting many of Harvard's distractions —trying out for athletic teams; girls; endless listening to Vose Greenough's records; girls; Chinese dinners in Boston; and girls —I survived academically, successfully finishing the year with all B's.

Whenever I could, I leavened pre-med courses with those in philosophy and music appreciation. I sat in on George Lyman Kittredge's classes on Shakespeare and Alfred North Whitehead's on philosophy. I listened to Robert Frost "say" his poetry and will never forget his gravelly reading of "Stopping by Woods on a Snowy Evening," which ends with the line "And miles to go before I sleep."

My tutor stimulated me to do research. (Each undergraduate was assigned his own tutor.) Dr. Roy Whelden, a botanist, and I discussed scientific problems for hours. He started me doing research on fertility with Gregory Pincus, who was studying the reasons why rabbits were so fertile. Years later, Dr. Pincus's research would become a major factor in the development of the Pill.

Harvard introduced me to a world that had seemed far out of

reach, unattainable. I soon discovered that being a "Harvard man" lent one an aura that, deserved or not, conferred an extra dimension of distinction that was often the envy of lesser mortals.

Most of my friends were liberals; some were members of the Young Communist League. However, liberal as I was, when they asked me to join the YCL, pointing out the harshness of the Depression and the treatment of blacks and other minorities by uncaring "capitalists," I could not bring myself to do so. I cared —but not for communism.

But there were other connections to the outside world. In 1935 my mother, full of excitement, called to say that my father was going to Princeton to do a sketch of Albert Einstein. After he returned, I pressed for details. When my father met Einstein, the great man was dressed in an old leather jacket, baggy tan pants, and sneakers without socks. He was eating an ice cream cone.

My father found a good light in the pit of a teaching amphitheater. He tried posing Einstein this way and that to catch the

Sketch by author's father at Princeton, 1935

best lighting. At one point, Einstein volunteered to sit on the floor if that would help. My father finally found a satisfactory light and began drawing.

About an hour later, a pupil of Einstein's appeared and, apologizing for intruding, asked if he could talk to the professor about a troublesome equation. In German, Einstein asked my father's permission for the student to use the huge blackboard to write out the problem. For the next ten minutes, the student filled it with numbers. Finally, when he had finished, Einstein again excused himself to my father, looked up at the blackboard, and, in a few seconds, said, "Und ein Viertel" ("Add one quarter").

The student had to erase everything and refill it with figures once more. This time when Einstein looked at them, he nodded and said, "Ja." The student left and my father worked on.

The Einstein experience loomed large in our family. Einstein signed the original pencil drawing, which now hangs in our library. His letter inviting my father to come down to make the sketch is framed and hangs nearby. Einstein also signed several drypoints my father made from his sketch, most of which were auctioned off at fund-raising dinners to benefit refugees from Nazi Germany. On one occasion while Einstein was signing these, Fiorello H. La Guardia, then mayor of New York City, leaned over and added his signature. My mother was incensed—a rare reaction in her—and gave that print away, much to my everlasting regret.

Einstein received an honorary degree from Harvard at our commencement in 1935, and my father introduced me to the great man. He looked every bit the genius, his huge head and bushy hair protruding from beneath a precariously perched mortarboard.

As a pre-med student, I did my first dissections, isolating the organs of worms and grasshoppers, and progressing to dogfish and cats. As the time for applying to med school neared, I began wondering what it would be like to operate on a human being. To satisfy my curiosity, I persuaded a friend, Jack Nelson, a student at Harvard Medical School, to arrange for me to watch an operation. Nervous but excited, I joined his class in the surgical amphitheater at Peter Bent Brigham Hospital. It was a huge room with at least fifteen rows of seats, steeply banked so that spectators would be as close as possible to the operating table. I borrowed a white coat so as to appear to be one of the students, and was elated just putting it on.

I sat discreetly in the very top row of the amphitheater, just in case I should become a bit queasy or, God forbid, faint. I need not have worried, for from the moment the patient was wheeled in I was far too absorbed in the drama to be sick. Not even the smell of ether could put me off, redolent though it was of my own tonsillectomy. I felt as if I were watching a religious ceremony. It began with the ritual of the anesthesia; the painting of the skin with antiseptic; the gowning and gloving of the surgeon and his assistants; then came the climax: the incision. As the surgeon repaired an inguinal hernia, he seemed commanding and self-possessed, like a high priest with his acolytes about him. He described each step with such clarity that even I could understand it. When the operation was completed, I was irrevocably committed: I would be a surgeon.

In spite of pre-med's demands, I managed to find time to buy a cheap upright piano. My high school piano teacher had arranged for me to study harmony with the composer Lehman Engel. (Lehman used to invite me to musical soirées at his Greenwich Village studio, where I met, among others, Aaron Copland and Martha Graham.) I took advanced harmony with Walter Piston. When I wasn't studying the anatomy of the dogfish, I was trying to write short, original compositions for Professor Piston. Soon the piano keys were stained yellow with formalin. For my own amusement, I wrote a silly tune called "Preludes and Dogfish."

As a member of the Harvard Glee Club, I felt exalted (and gloried) in being able to learn the chorus of Bach's B Minor Mass and his *Passion According to St. Matthew*. Harvard and Radcliffe students performed these together, along with Serge Koussevitzky and the Boston Symphony Orchestra.

Lady loves had I three, all wooed with syrupy ballads I'd written. With my allowance of two dollars a week, it was difficult to take them out, so for entertainment I took them in. After the football season was over, we would sit before my fireplace on a Saturday afternoon and listen to the Metropolitan Opera on the radio.

To entertain a female guest in one's room in those days, one needed permission from the housemaster, and we were warned that our young ladies had to be out by seven P.M. sharp. No sooner had the bells of a nearby church struck that hour when the house security man struck the door. His banging was enough to chill anyone's ardor.

One of the rewards of being in Cambridge was that my childhood friend Mort Kanner was nearby at MIT. He was, as anticipated, a superb student, getting the highest grades in all courses. We saw each other regularly and traveled back to New York together during major vacations. By this time, Mort already knew that he was headed for a career as a physicist and we often speculated on how our separate interests could complement and reinforce each other.

The time was coming to apply to medical school. I hoped to return to New York, as I was virtually certain that I was going to make my life there. Besides, I wanted to be near my parents.

I applied to Cornell, Columbia College of Physicians and Surgeons (P&S), and Harvard. Cornell and Harvard turned me down, so it was with trembling fingers that, one day, I opened an envelope and was overjoyed to see an acceptance by P&S. P&S was, and still is, one of the best medical schools in the country, and I felt it would be a privilege to study there. The tuition: three hundred dollars a year. Again, my father managed somehow.

There were 110 students in our class. All were white; a half-dozen were women. On our application, we were asked to state our sex, religion, and color, and to enclose a photograph. It was understood, if not openly acknowledged, that P&S—along with most medical schools—had a quota for Jews (I think there were ten of us) as well as for Catholics. Blacks, Hispanics, and Asians were a rarity at "white" medical schools. So I was one of the beneficiaries of a dubious quota system.

I entered P&S in September 1935. Anatomy class began the very first day. This class, in which we were expected to plunge in and work on cadavers, can cause some students a great deal of anxiety and trepidation. In fact, faced with the experience, a small number drop out. When one of my classmates hanged himself later that week, the rumor was that anatomy class had caused his acute depression.

Four students were assigned to each stiff (as we called the cadavers), two to a side. As was customary, a coin was tossed by each team to decide which of us would begin; I won. The first dissection involved exposing the muscles of the shoulder.

I cannot explain exactly why, but making that first incision, I felt absolutely comfortable. Every day after that, I couldn't wait for my turn to dissect. By the end of the year we had dissected every part of the body, down to the finest blood vessels and nerves. We were also given a "box of bones"—the complete human skeleton—to study at home.

The first year at P&S, or at any other medical school, is undeniably the toughest: a period of punishing memorization of hundreds of anatomical and other medical terms. In addition to learning the names of every body part, one had to know how each functioned and be able to locate and dissect them.

As we went beyond that first dissection, I could observe the eons of modeling for survival that nature had fashioned—for example, the logic of the muscles' attachment to bones and the "intelligence" with which their nerve sources are protected in grooves and pathways. Swirls of these structures fit together like interdigitating or interlocking jigsaw pieces, each making room for, or accommodating, their surrounding neighbors so that they can work in harmony. One can go on at length about the base of the skull, for instance, with its apertures craftily placed to protect and accommodate the passage of vessels, the spinal cord, and nerves. I found myself almost persuaded that all of this was the result of a deity's artistry, that an all-seeing eye and celestial hand had fashioned these minute details. The complexity, beauty, and function of the eye have often been used as evidence of a Supreme Being at work. Believers say: "How could it possibly exist without a God/Nature/whatever—a supreme schemer, who thought it up and did it all?" Yet, as has been asked as many times, can this same Supreme Being be capable of fashioning so much treachery, or remain so seemingly indifferent to the frequent violations of innocents and so many tragic endings?

There is something comforting about this Nature/God, call it what you will, who knows when to stop and who, like a true artist, has the good taste to do so before life becomes too tedious, lengthy, boring. Mother may "know best"; Mother Nature knows better.

Frankly, if you believe, as I do, that there is no beginning *and* no end, it is unimportant to insist that such intelligence must come from a deity rather than an ageless force.

Whatever our beliefs, we went ahead into the marvels and mysteries of the body, and toward a sense of revelation from which I have never recovered.

Competition among students was fierce, and I got caught up in it. We were not given grades, but were told every few weeks in what percentile of the class we stood. I managed to stay in the top I–II for a semester before slipping to III–IV. Although I excelled in anatomy, I did less well when we got to biochemistry and physiology.

I didn't dare take time off, not even weekends, for fear of falling behind. Occasionally, for a break, I'd sit on the terrace of P&S's dormitory, Bard Hall, which overlooked the Hudson River, and watch the progress of the George Washington Bridge, then under construction. I forced myself to stay in shape by running, swimming, and playing squash.

Sometimes, late at night, I'd descend to the common room and listen to a fellow student play jazz on the concert grand piano that had been donated to Bard Hall by Rachmaninoff. The composer had signed his gift inside the cover, but when I looked for it years later at a class reunion, I was told to my horror that someone, perhaps an overzealous cleaning woman, had washed this "scribble" away.

Toward the end of that first year, I began dating a student nurse who lived in the nearby nursing school dormitory. With nowhere else to go at night, we would sneak into one of the lecture amphitheaters and, with overcoats as a mattress, make love on the floor. I had classes in this room. Remembering the night before and looking forward to the night ahead added an extra dimension to physiology. Reveries made it difficult to concentrate on the day's lectures. (Perhaps *that* was one reason I slipped in the class standing.) Ah, the tumescence of spring and youth! Buffeted by the fragrances of budding trees and flowers that wafted across the Hudson River from New Jersey, and by romantic fantasies borne aloft by the soulful sounds of a classmate's repeated playing of Bruch's violin concerto on his phonograph, I had to struggle not to succumb to the turbulence they stirred in me. It was a wonder that I got through the final exams. But sweet release finally came: Exams were over. Never was a vacation more welcome, and I indulged myself only in forbidden fruits: sleeping late; going to the theater and movies; playing sports; and, of course, constant female companionship.

When I returned to school in the fall, seriousness returned too. Unlike today's med students, who see patients in their first year, we had to wait until the end of the second year to do so. At P&S,

the majority of patients for teaching rounds came from the charity wards and clinics at Presbyterian Hospital, which was connected directly to the medical school. There were many examples of pneumococcal pneumonia, rheumatic fever, poliomyelitis, advanced syphilis, and malaria. Some of these diseases, such as polio and rheumatic fever, commonplace then, are rarely seen today and, thankfully, may well be on their way to becoming extinct.

To observe patients with infectious diseases, we made special trips downtown to Willard Parker Hospital, a somber building on the west bank of the East River; there we had our first views of scarlet fever, measles, chicken pox, typhoid fever, and, though rarely, leprosy. A bus carried us to Seaview Hospital on Staten Island, which housed many patients with tuberculosis, whom we saw as rich sources for learning about the physical diagnosis of the lungs. We wore masks so as to reduce the possibility of getting TB ourselves.

Years later, in the early fifties, Seaview, along with other TB sanitaria such as Trudeau (Gary-the-cartoonist's grandfather) at Saranac Lake, New York, would close because tuberculosis patients who no longer needed bed rest could be treated effectively by drugs.

The last two years of med school were a delight. Instead of concentrating on abstract knowledge and absorbing facts by rote, we were finally dealing with patients. All the logic, rationale, and wisdom of the earlier basic studies came together and prepared us for making diagnoses and for treatment. No longer were we confined to cold texts; now, the struggle to master anatomy, physiology, biochemistry, and microscopic tissue analysis had relevance to human ills. Patients were books to be read—some like short stories; others like novels; and many, alas, like unsolved mysteries.

At first we were shy and tentative with patients, but in time we became more confident and began to feel the healer's power. To our immense satisfaction, we saw that our reasoning and deductions began to resemble and coincide with those of our teachers.

Although the patients knew we were students, they always gave us an instant field promotion by calling us Doctor. They even listened attentively when we discussed their problems with them. When one is twenty-three or twenty-four, this can be heady stuff. No wonder hyper-inflated egos are one occupational hazard of being a physician; it is so easy to be corrupted by such absolute power . . . and so early in life.

Over quick snacks and coffee in those early clinical days, we excitedly exchanged anecdotes and case histories. Like philatelists talking over a rare stamp, we boasted to each other about what unusual conditions we had seen. We consulted textbooks to read in detail about each disease we encountered. Our pockets bulged with copious notes, crumbs of wisdom from the lips of our mentors which we filed for future reference and, of course, for exams. We felt that what we were learning was for keeps, to be harvested when one day in the far future we went out into the world to practice on our own.

Those were frantic, golden days, and they blurred by. We spent two to three weeks in each specialty: ear, eye, nose, and throat; dermatology; urology; and so forth, and were assigned for longer periods to general medicine, obstetrics, pediatrics, and general surgery.

In the late thirties, surgery was far riskier than it is now: There were no antibiotics, blood banks, or cardiac monitors. Intravenous fluids were not yet used. Fluids were given by hypodermoclysis—that is, through a long needle placed subcutaneously—so as to be slowly absorbed into the circulation.

Infections accounted for many deaths, particularly of patients with ruptured appendixes, who died of peritonitis. Infections of the skin led to cellulitis (and erysipelas, which could be fatal). This took a dramatic form on the face, where severe infections resulted from squeezing a pimple. Some of these, despite all treatment, were fatal. As vascular surgery had not been developed, amputations for diabetic and arteriosclerotic-caused gangrene were common.

Although a large majority of patients survived surgery, postoperative complications and mortalities were much more prevalent than today.

Pneumonia often resulted when patients were immobilized in bed for extended periods after surgery. Hernia repairs were common but, unlike today, patients were kept in bed for as long as ten days with the leg on the operated side propped up on a pillow. Small wonder that there were complications such as phlebitis and pulmonary emboli. Today, patients walk almost immediately after hernia surgery, and some go home within hours. Surgery was not recommended for "older" patients unless absolutely necessary. I remember a chapter in a textbook of the day that began: "It is immoral to perform major elective surgery on anyone over sixty."

Primitive as those days may sound, operations of considerable magnitude were successfully performed: partial gastrectomies (removal of part of the stomach) for cancer and ulcers, colon resections for cancer, thyroidectomies, and radical mastectomies were frequent. Dr. Allen Oldfather Whipple, our professor of surgery, had perfected a very complicated method for removing cancer of the head of the pancreas. The procedure became known as the Whipple operation.

Lung surgery, however, was still in its earliest stages and was used mostly to drain infections of the chest cavity and to collapse lungs in an effort to heal tubercular cavities. As the first successful pneumonectomy (lung removal) for lung cancer had been done only a few years before, in 1932, by Dr. Evarts Graham, many physiological and technical features of it were still being refined.

Students were encouraged to "scrub in" on operations. When I was the third assistant at a thoracic operation, the surgeon, a Southerner with a heavy drawl, was tentatively picking his way through the procedure, attempting to remove a lung cancer, and he became more and more hesitant. Suddenly, to our astonishment, he stopped operating. He sat down in a corner of the operating room and began to moan softly, "Ah just don't know where Ah am and what to do next." It was our first experience with surgical fear—and stress.

Minutes later he regained his composure and finished the operation.

During my third year, I was eager, even impatient, to begin interning. I was given permission to take time away from the school's curriculum to substitute for a vacationing intern at Bellevue Hospital.

In contrast with the largely elegant Presbyterian Hospital, Bellevue, a city hospital, was at the other end of the socioeconomic scale. Presbyterian's ordinary wards had a maximum of sixteen beds lined up in two neat rows opposite each other. The rooms were well lit and the bed linen immaculate, and curtains could be drawn around each bed to provide privacy. In sharp contrast, Bellevue teemed with patients. Its larger wards had at least fifty beds each. Patients were tightly clustered, separated by just the width of tiny bedside tables. There was always an overflow, so that beds extended out into the corridors and down the hall, just short of the elevators.

The attendants and nurses did wonders to keep the wards clean, but it was impossible to be immaculate at all times as the patient population was largely drawn from the indigent, including a number of derelicts who (though one must be sensitive about saying so) often brought with them their own menagerie of bedbugs and fleas.

For med students hungry for as much clinical experience as possible, Bellevue was a wonderful museum of pathological conditions. In spite of the relatively primitive surroundings, the medical and nursing care was excellent. Interns worked like Trojans, performing many of the functions that are nowadays done by technicians—drawing blood for chemical analysis, doing urinalyses, blood counts, typing, and cross-matching for transfusions; taking and developing emergency X rays. As substitute interns, not yet M.D.'s, we were denied the wonderful experience of being able to "ride the bus." Dressed in white coats and black peaked caps, interns used to ride ambulances to tend the city's acutely ill who could not make it to the hospital. In good weather, some would take up a romantic position on the ambulance's back step, holding onto its railings as it screamed through traffic.

Beloved Bellevue, your huge, dark, dank interior swarming with people! I will never forget that within your walls I performed my first operation and helped a person. While I was assisting a resident one day, he suddenly said, "You do this." Then, step by step, he guided me in the removal of a lymph node from a patient's neck. To my chagrin, I, who had always had such confidence in my dexterity, who had tied countless knots skillfully on bedposts, instantly became all thumbs. As I tentatively followed the resident's instructions—"Cut here, clamp there, tie this"—a group of fourth-year P&S students, who were assigned to Bellevue that semester, came in to the O.R. to observe. They did not recognize me in my mask and operating garb, and stood silently watching. When I had finished, they thanked us and left.

Back at school, I did not reveal that it was I they had been watching, but I wondered whether, after seeing such an amateurish performance, any of them who were budding surgeons decided to switch to another specialty.

My early fascination with my future specialty began during the first year of medical school when, in histology class, I saw cancer cells under the microscope. I wondered then about the malicious mischief latent in the beautiful patterns and colorful swirls beneath the lens. Over the next few years, although we saw patients with cancers in various sites of the body, we did not feel the weight of its ominous presence as we do today. But we were soberly impressed when told how slim the chances were of curing many of them.

In our fourth year, our class spent two days of intensive cancer instruction at the old Memorial Hospital at 106th Street and Central Park West, where we saw more cancer patients than we had ever seen. In those days, relatively few cancers were detected early. As a result, patients were often in far-advanced stages, either because they had brought their problems late to the doctor, or as the sad result of delay caused by a mistaken diagnosis. They were often too late for surgery or, when surgery was done, it required extensive and complicated procedures. Because these operations often distorted anatomy and were physically deforming, particularly in and about the head and neck, and involved great risk, radiation therapy was the main method of treatment. Although irradiation was undoubtedly curative in some instances, it was beginning to be apparent that the treatment could produce side effects that at times were worse than the disease.

It was impossible not to pity these people, and more than with most diseases I had seen, I felt an intense desire, a compelling need, to help. One thing that impressed me deeply in the two days we spent at Memorial was the dedication of its physicians and nurses. Yet, skillful and compassionate as they were, it was clear that something better than what medicine then had to offer was desperately needed. So little, too, was understood about the causes of cancer that the adage "Prevention is better than cure" simply did not apply. I cannot recall any lectures in my four years at medical school that dealt with the subject of carcinogenesis more deeply than a mere warning about overexposure to radiation.

During a quiet period in medical school, I took my father up on the offer he had made many times: to take a sentimental journey through "my Lower East Side," as he called it. I had always professed an interest in seeing his old haunts and, one spring night, we walked through streets lined on both sides by pushcarts, picturesquely lighted by wires strung from nearby tenement houses or by gasoline or kerosene lamps. To me, it was pure poetry, perhaps because the scene reminded me of several of my father's drawings and etchings. Our route included Hester, Delancey, Broome, Henry, and Orchard streets. Each street awakened memories for my father of episodes I had never heard him mention before. "This is where my sister was run over and almost beheaded by a horse cart in front of my mother's eyes!" "This is where my public school stood and I was expelled for punching a teacher after she rapped my knuckles with a wooden ruler."

I had come straight from school to meet him, and was carrying several heavy medical textbooks. I was so absorbed in what was going on about us that I did not realize how intensely I was clutching them. After walking for hours, when we sat down for a glass of tea at Katz's Delicatessen on Houston Street, I could hardly move my right arm. No matter: The look on his face and the zest with which he sketched in the details of his boyhood caused me, who had always been close to him, to love him all the more and to appreciate vicariously what it must have meant to him to be able to emerge from these surroundings. Colorful and picturesque and evocative though they were, they were also a documentary of poverty and striving and strife—and, for some reason, success.

In my third year at P&S I met Arthur Ross, then an official at General Electric's Schenectady plant. For some reason, possibly because GE made fluoroscopes, he and I talked about how careful one had to be while using these instruments and what protective devices were essential. He told me, with some pride, that GE was very conscious of these hazards, and he described, as an example, the cable-manufacturing section of their plant. As the finished cable rolled beneath a fluoroscopic screen, workers checked whether the wire was centered in its insulation. To protect those employees who stood behind the screens (for forty hours a week), GE made sure that they wore lead aprons and lead gloves, and viewed the fluoroscopic image through leaded glasses. They also had blood counts at regular intervals to make sure that their bone marrow was not being affected. Ross said that the walls enclosing the area were also lead-lined.

I asked him about the floor beneath the fluoroscopes. Was that lead-lined, too? Was anyone working on the floor below?

He thought for a moment and said, "The floor is *not* insulated." And his eyes widened as he added: ". . . Oh my God, there's a secretarial pool down there!"

GE instituted further protective measures soon thereafter, I trust, although some companies—for example, those whose workers were exposed to asbestos—turned out to have been notoriously indifferent to workplace hazards until forced (by catastrophe and/or law) to take stringent precautions and institute strict safeguards.

This conversation could have been a harbinger of things to come in my own career—of corporate responsibility and long-distance diagnosis.

One knotty problem in my preparation for a life in surgery began not at Harvard but in the Boy Scouts. My meteoric ascent from Tenderfoot to Second Class Scout meant that certain knots had to be mastered and either demonstrated to the scoutmaster or mounted on a board with labels: granny, square, hangman's noose. The square knot, with its appealing symmetry, also had instructions with a certain poetic symmetry: "Over-and-around-and-behind, and then under-around-and-behind." From the first time I saw surgeons tie knots, I longed to be able to do as they did. For the most part, surgeons use square knots to encompass a blood vessel. They tie first one knot, and then lay a square knot on top of it, until finally a third knot is added for security (what I later called the slumber knot—the patient could sleep, and so could I). Watching, I felt I had to master these graceful gestures, so I began looking for manuals that might help me do so. The "How To Tie Knots" section of a general surgical textbook left me confused. I managed to convince interns to give me basic instruction. There was a certain urgency to this; we were approaching the time when we students would be assisting in the operating room.

Spools of cotton were obtained and hundreds of knots tied on bedposts, others' fingertips, drawer pulls, anything that could serve as a hitching post. We tried tying knots on substitutes for living tissues, like the tufts of Turkish towels. One of us would grasp a tuft with a hemostat clamp while the other, acting as "first assistant," would place the first knot and cinch it securely. After the hemostat was removed, a second knot was placed, then a third. The assistant gave a tug on the knot to see if it held. With a professional flourish, he would use scissors to sever the two strands just above the knot. We practiced these maneuvers hundreds of times, so that the towel soon became speckled with black dots. Then, one graduated to using pieces of raw meat;

some, surreptitiously, went to the anatomy class to try tying knots on real blood vessels. Even strands of a beloved's long hair were tied, and served as painful reminders when caught at the next combing.

The ultimate challenge was to tie knots deep in a hole, thus simulating surgery done on layers deep within a chest or abdomen. The "hole" in this case was an empty can, open at both ends. At the bottom of the can was a towel, whose tufts stood in for "bleeders," which required two instruments to tie off. Once they were mastered, it was show-off time, demonstrating dexterity to friends.

Finally, the moment of truth arrived. As a third assistant, on that never-to-be-forgotten day, you were handed a spool of thread or catgut. At which point all previous practice on bedposts, towels, and human heads came into play, and a few dexterous flourishes should have completed the knot. Instead, chaos! Fingers trembled and deserted you. The rubber gloves were sticky, and you developed ten thumbs. Meanwhile, the surgeons paused and patiently waited for you to complete your maneuvers. Their quiet did not help. Standing silently, they seemed for all the world like vultures, birds of prey, circling and ready to pounce. Miraculously, after you finally completed the knot, the thread ends were casually cut, and the operation proceeded.

Some time later, a compassionate surgeon provided me with a second opportunity. This time I was a little more confident, a young bird just learning to fly. After a while knotting became second nature. Once that point had been reached, the exhilaration was not to be believed. Never had you felt such pride in an accomplishment, comparable to that of a young soloist giving a first concert: The notices may not have been great, but you got through the performance. In the meantime, whenever you left the O.R., you thought: *Back to the bedposts.*

◆

CHAPTER III

Ladies in the Dark

During the summer vacation of 1938, Warren LaPierre, a P&S classmate, and I sailed on the *Queen Mary* ($225 round trip, tourist class), on our way to a bicycle trip through England, then to the Continent to tour France by rail. As it turned out, our stateroom was next to the door that led to first class. We often found it unlocked and would ascend to the elegant ballroom (forbidden territory) to dance the Lambeth walk, the dance that was the rage in England that year (and the set piece of the recent hit musical *Me and My Girl*).

On the last night of the voyage, we met another P&S student who *was* traveling first-class, and he introduced us to Pamela Gordon-Howley, an English girl on her way home from a visit to her mother, who was living in New York. The four of us stayed up partying most of that night. Next morning, the ship docked at Southampton. As we were waiting on the lower deck to disembark, I glanced up and saw Pam many decks above, waving a white-gloved hand and clearly signaling us to wait for her on the dock. We did, and arranged to meet again in London after our cycling tour.

Pam was vivacious, had a great sense of humor, a charming English accent, and a love for art and music. She told me that she desperately wanted to live in America. I was attracted to her from the beginning.

After Warren and I returned, Pam and I kept up a lively correspondence. A year later, anxious about England's involvement in

HORST

Gertrude Lawrence: The author married the daughter of the great stage star and found he had married into show biz, for better and for worse.

the war, her mother sent for Pam. To my delight, she called me at medical school one day, saying that she had gotten a job as a guide at the 1939 World's Fair in Flushing, Queens. By then, I had learned that Pam's mother was the celebrated actress Gertrude Lawrence, then appearing on Broadway in Samson Raphaelson's *Skylark*.

I first met Gertrude—she was called Gee—and Richard Aldrich, a theatrical producer, at her luxurious apartment at 17 West Fifty-fourth Street. She had heard that Pam and I were "serious" and decided that the four of us should attend a Sunday night

Actor's Equity benefit performance of *The Little Foxes.* It was a marvelous show, and Tallulah Bankhead gave a superb performance. Afterward, we went backstage to meet her and then went on to dinner. I knew I was under scrutiny and, what with the awe in which I held the great star of *Skylark,* I was, for once, unusually shy and silent.

It did not take long to see that Gertrude was a star off, as well as on, the stage. She knew how glamorous she was and that her aura always made her the center of attention, a role she acted to perfection. She didn't just walk, she strode everywhere like a greyhound. With her boyish figure, she was a sleek clotheshorse. Her clothing, made for her by Molyneux, Mainbocher, and Valentina, hung and moved beautifully. Her mobile face, her English accent, and her infectious laugh mesmerized everybody, including me.

I'm sure that in the tradition of such matters, a mother of a girl of marriageable age must scrutinize the daughter's "steady." I was never quite sure that Gertrude approved, particularly as my income was fifteen dollars per month, but when we met on social occasions, she was always cordial and made a point of introducing me to her many gilded friends.

When Pam and her mother were together, one could see their physical resemblance, particularly nice upturned noses and high cheekbones. Both had good legs and although, like Gee, Pam was not classically beautiful, one forgot this when she turned on the personal charm.

Pam's childhood had the usual mixture of the handicaps and some of the advantages of always being referred to as "Gertrude Lawrence's daughter." A classic irony: Three of Gee's hit plays—*Susan and God, Skylark,* and *Lady in the Dark*—all had similar themes: the impact of a dynamic, glamorous mother on a daughter.

In Pam's preteens, she was sent off to elegant boarding schools in England (Roedean) and later to Switzerland (Brillantmont). Summer holidays were spent with her mother, her mother's current lover, and their circle of friends, characters like Noel Coward, Somerset Maugham, and Douglas Fairbanks, Jr. Once the holidays were over, Pam returned to school and aloneness. She had been virtually orphaned by the theater.

Since Gertrude saw Pam infrequently, one could not fail to get the impression that she did not relish Pam's presence particularly;

she had a procession of intimate men friends, and Pam served to remind her both of her past indiscretion—marrying an obscure theater manager—and of her own getting on in years. So Pam felt more resented than loved. She yearned for affection and, especially, to be loved for herself. I decided that, if nothing else, I would try to boost Pam's ego and encourage the strength of her own personality—for, more than her mother, she was genuinely cultured and generous.

Several months after I met Gee and Dick Aldrich, they were married in Dennis, Massachusetts, where Dick was managing the Cape Playhouse. Pam was not invited to the brief ceremony, but her mother called by phone soon afterward to tell her the news just before it broke in all the newspapers.

Although I practiced no religion actively, I was always sensitive to any evidence of anti-Semitism, anyplace and anytime.

Granted, in keeping with the prevalent mood of those days, Jews had subliminal and overt reminders of discrimination. Although many became somewhat paranoid on the subject of anti-Semitism, unquestionably, there was gross and subtle evidence of its omnipresence. For example, Jews were not admitted to many country clubs (still aren't!), certain businesses, and even some apartment houses. Real estate ads, after describing a house and its location, intimated anti-Semitism by adding phrases such as "churches nearby." And minority quotas were an accepted part of medical school applications.

Even though there was never any clearcut incident or expression of anti-Semitism at medical school, we couldn't help but notice that there were no Jews—nor had there ever been—on Presbyterian's surgical staff, and only a rare Jew was spotted here and there on the staff of other services. Surgeons, in general, seemed united in an untouchable, unassailable old-boys' network. Using today's jargon, those at P.H. would be designated WASPs. To their credit, however, they never displayed by word or gesture any prejudices whatsoever.

A member of an older class, "one of us," made it, becoming first an intern, then a resident at P.H. This was a break—and a breakthrough. To be sure, he was bright and handsome and spoke with a well-modulated prep school baritone. These were qualities, we theorized, that made him "pass," made him an easy fit. Although never denying his religious background, he seemed to keep a somewhat lofty, aloof attitude toward us, one that those who secretly envied him sardonically referred to as subacute goyitis.

Many years later, after he had been added to the surgical attending staff at Presbyterian, he confessed to me that although there had been no overt reminders or humiliations, he had nevertheless suffered from innuendos and well-veiled slights, that he felt were examples of the staff's "gentlemen's agreements." Whether this was real or imagined, fact or paranoia, he was never invited to his colleagues' homes, and only rarely did other staff members refer patients to him. He also saw his slow promotion to higher academic rank as an expression of the same attitude.★

On the other hand, I was made to feel reverse discrimination by my mother. When I brought a Gentile girlfriend home for dinner, my mother was always outwardly gracious and courteous, but I could sense that underlying her hospitality rows of icicles were dangling from her otherwise warm heart. My father couldn't care less and usually charmed my dates, much to my admiration. After these meetings, my mother would step up her campaign, foisting daughters of Jewish friends on me. After having had a couple of parent-inspired dates that were clinkers, I grew wary, particularly when my mother began by saying, "So-and-so's daughter is lovely—and she has such beautiful teeth and smile." As soon as I heard incisors and molars introduced, I *knew* that beneath or behind the dazzling display of straightened, pearly-white teeth there lurked a man-eating personality and/or an anatomic disaster.

(Years later, some of my mother's candidates became my patients. They turned out to be quite attractive, and we laughed as we reminisced about the secret matchmaking that went on.)

The major concern of fourth-year medical students is getting a good internship, an important stepping-stone to their future. Those at the top of the class usually have their pick of appointments at the better hospitals. Those with middle-level or lower standings have to rely on interviews and luck and must be willing to settle for less than superior locations. Fortunately, P&S's rep-

---

★ When the first black, Dr. Charles Drew, an ex–Olympic athlete, was admitted to Presbyterian's staff, notes were circulated to the other staff members asking them to make an effort to treat him cordially and with respect.

utation virtually guaranteed its graduates better-than-average appointments.

When the time came to apply for internship, once again Jews were reminded of barriers ahead: We were being asked to designate our religion. We knew that it was almost futile to apply to certain hospitals that had notoriously rigid racial policies, particularly for surgical internships. We heard that even Mount Sinai had its own version of discrimination, consistently admitting students of German-Jewish origin while seemingly reluctant to accept their "poor cousins" of Russian, Polish, and Hungarian descent.

In spite of these barricades, some Jews kept trying to breach these sacrosanct bastions, for most were otherwise splendid places of learning and highly esteemed in the world of medicine. Encouragement to persevere surged when Al Levy, a student in the class ahead of us, became the second Jewish surgical intern accepted by Presbyterian Hospital. Then, mirabile dictu, a classmate of mine, Henry Mayer, was accepted by Lenox Hill Hospital (formerly the German Hospital), and Henry Janowitz, of Russian-Polish background, made it into Mount Sinai, both as medical interns.

Just before starting my fourth year, I took another substitute internship for four weeks at New York Hospital. Toward the end of this tour of duty, I was told by my attending surgeon that if I applied for an internship there I would be accepted. So assured, I submitted my application to New York Hospital and did not apply elsewhere. On the application, I listed details of my background—including religion.

At that time, 1938, there was an American Indian swastika at the top of New York Hospital's twenty-five-story smokestack. That swastika was used as a decorative scheme. However, with the public outcry about the Nazi implications of such a symbol, even though it was reversed from the Nazi version, New York Hospital paid to have a bricklayer hoisted up to fill in the bent arms, converting the swastika to a simple cross.

Unfortunately, New York Hospital's concern about the swastika and its symbolism was not an expression of or a metaphor for changing attitudes. While others were receiving their acceptances from various hospitals, a dismaying letter arrived from the surgeon who had been my chief supporter. He explained that "because of certain hospital policies," my application had been turned down. He apologized at length, saying that he would be glad to write a strong letter of recommendation for a position elsewhere, and so on.

This was a severe blow. I should have been wiser and applied to other hospitals as well.

Unfortunately, by that time those to which I could have applied had filled their staff appointments. I would have to wait six months at least.

To tide me over, I accepted a residency in surgical pathology at Presbyterian Hospital. This was a fortunate choice, for it offered the opportunity to examine numerous surgical specimens, fresh from the operating rooms, and to view their microscopic appearance. My appointment at Presbyterian was to begin on July 1. In the meantime, in early June, our commencement exercises took place.

The graduates of Columbia's schools were scattered through the huge space before the statue of Alma Mater on the steps of Columbia's Low Library. I sat listening to the oratory and the handing-out of degrees, thinking back on the days when my father and I, on one of our many strolls, used to walk to this area from our home just a few blocks south, and recalled how fascinated I had been as a child by a five-foot high polished marble ball that reflected the campus about it, including the spot in which I was now seated.

Although we were part of an enormous group, our particular moment came when, in mortar boards and gowns, we stood for the Hippocratic oath, led by our dean. My parents were there, and, after the ceremony they embraced me. My mother said, with shining eyes, reflecting my father's as in that polished marble ball, "*Doctor* Cahan!"

"*Doctor* Cahan," they both murmured, again and again.

During the six months in surgical pathology, the more cancer specimens I saw, the more I kept asking myself the same questions that had puzzled scientists for centuries: What causes normal cells to become malignant? Why do some cancers spread and others not? Why does cancer usually occur in one of a pair of organs such as the kidney, the breast, or the lung; or, if it does occur bilaterally, why does it not always do so simultaneously? Above all: How can cancer be prevented?

The chairman of the surgical pathology department was the

world-famous Dr. Arthur Purdy Stout. On many occasions while I was working on specimens in the lab, I would hear his special phone ring, and I knew that he was being summoned to the operating floor. I made a point of accompanying him whenever possible. He would stand outside the entrance of an operating room, the door slightly ajar, and a nurse would hand him a gauze-wrapped specimen of tissue. The surgeon would call out the name of the organ it came from. Dr. Stout would rush down the hall, me at his heels, to a special cubicle where, using carbon dioxide gas, he would freeze a section of the suspicious specimen. After slicing a thin section of it and then staining and examining it under the microscope, he would race back to the operating room, open the door a crack, and inform the surgeon: "Malignant" or "Benign." Dr. Stout's finding could mean the difference between, say, removing a benign breast lump and going ahead with a radical mastectomy.

As a result of working there, I began to understand why even the most radical surgery could fail to control the spread of cancer. Time and again, we examined "gross" specimens in which the cancer was surrounded by a wide margin of normal tissue. One could be misled, if one looked at them alone, into thinking that the patient's future was bright. However, a few days later, when the microscopic slides made from the specimen were reviewed, they might show that cancer cells had, in fact, invaded tiny blood and/or lymph vessels. This meant that they could travel by these routes and implant themselves in different parts of the body. Clearly, one could not always rely on controlling cancer locally, whether by surgery or radiation therapy. What was needed was a method to seek out and destroy far-flung cancer cells. But this was 1939, and the possibility of a method of doing so seemed a distant dream. In those days, one heard it said that a "cure" for cancer would probably *never* be found.

After six months at Presbyterian, I began a two-year surgical internship at the Hospital for Joint Diseases (HJD), then at 1919 Madison Avenue (at 124th Street) in Harlem.

HJD was primarily an orthopedic hospital, but because it was located in a densely populated area that had only three other hospitals (Sydenham, Harlem, and Wickersham), it had to cope with all kinds of emergencies. Compared to Presbyterian, it was dingy and overcrowded, but the care, especially the orthopedic care, was good, and interns gained enormous experience treating a parade of emergencies.

In those days, the atmosphere of a hospital was far different from that of today. For one thing, there was a distinctive, unmistakable "hospital smell"—a mixture of ether and carbolic-acid antiseptic that could be detected blocks away. It permeated one's hair and clothes and lingered even after washing. I used to call it Bellevue N° 5. As interns, we even took a secret pride in this smell. We smelled like doctors. After a while we didn't notice it, but other people did. They complained, especially at meals.

Interns at HJD were provided with uniforms: white pants, a white tunic that buttoned down the neck and the side, à la Dr. Kildare and Ben Casey; room and board; and the aforementioned fifteen dollars a month. (At Presbyterian, I worked for a little less: nothing.) In spite of this chicken feed, we were expected to be grateful for the privilege of training—and, in fact, we were. I worked a minimum of five and a half days a week and was on call every other night and every other weekend, or about seventy hours a week. I loved it.

Back then, hospital lighting was depressingly dim, and walls were usually institutional gray, brown, or some other cheerless shade. The noise level was high. Today's hospitals are quieter, not only because of better acoustics but also because the public-address paging system has been largely replaced by beepers. Now the PA is used mostly for emergencies. But though beepers are more efficient, I confess I used to get a kick out of hearing my name announced.

There was no air-conditioning, so in summer fans were used and doors had to be kept wide open. This brought some relief; it also let in noise, dust, and fumes. On the hottest days, all but emergency surgery had to be canceled, for patients lost excessive amounts of salt and water through perspiration, and in the days before intravenous feeding, this could be dangerous. If we absolutely had to operate, we had no choice but to keep windows open, which meant letting in unfiltered air. Although we used screens, a fly would occasionally manage to get in—and then what a circus it was trying to keep it away from the table. We sweltered in our O.R. gear, and nurses constantly had to mop our foreheads (as they are still seen doing in movies). In spite of their efforts, and to our dismay, sweat occasionally did drip onto sterile areas.

Recovery rooms and intensive-care units did not exist. Patients went straight from the O.R. to their beds in their rooms or the wards. I shudder when I remember this, and am amazed to think how, with so little monitoring, we managed to pull most patients through, including those who had undergone major surgery.

We handled in-hospital emergencies as well as we could, given the few resources available: manual artificial respiration; oxygen; a few resuscitative drugs—a major difference from today's trained emergency teams who are expert in CPR, intracardiac stimulants, shock paddles . . . One life-saving device used extensively was the oxygen tent. These were noisy and cumbersome, with walls of heavy-duty celluloid. The machine was attached to a hose, through which humidified oxygen was propelled into the tent. The opening for the oxygen was near the patient's head, around which a towel or sheet was wrapped for protection from the chill vapors.

To examine a patient in a tent, the doctor had to unzip a small window and insert the upper half of his body through it. If he used a stethoscope, he had difficulty hearing because of the humming of the machine and the *whoosh* of oxygen flow. Worst of all, the system would occasionally malfunction: The machine went on humming, but the oxygen flow had been exhausted. More than once, I had to rip open a tent to save the patient from asphyxiation.

About eighteen years ago, it was found that oxygen delivered through a face mask or nasal catheter is just as efficient as a tent and far easier and simpler to use.

The patients at HJD that I remember most vividly were those with osteomyelitis—infections of the bone and bone marrow. Among them were veterans of the Abraham Lincoln Brigade: American volunteers who had fought with the Loyalists in the Spanish Civil War. Their bone infections came from shrapnel or bullet wounds. They were a genial group, who liked to joke together and who bore their suffering with stoical pride. They used to shake the walls with thunderous renditions of Brigade songs.

Patients with osteomyelitis suffer from high fevers, pain, and swelling, usually of an extremity. As antibiotics did not exist, a surgeon had to drain the infection by making an incision down to the marrow and leaving the wound open to heal from the bone up to the skin. Recovery was slow and such patients required extended inpatient hospital care. Several methods were used to encourage more rapid healing, some of them startling to recall. Besides removing dead bone and necrotic tissue, we used irrigations and antiseptic dressings. Astonishingly, maggots were used to clean up the slough of dead tissue that covers the wound, and were kept in place, covered with gauze. Once they began sprouting wings (and became flies), they were removed. The first time I saw this, I could not believe my eyes. I added maggots to my medical menagerie that included bees held in a container to enclose an arthritic joint! (The bee stings relieved the joint pain by counter-irritation.) It was not uncommon either to use leeches to reduce the swelling and bruising of black eyes and to help dissolve clots in veins affected by phlebitis. Cats' corneas had just begun to be used to replace scarred human ones.

Bizarre as some of these may seem, I had seen even stranger practices. One was akin to football, at least in language. At the time, plastic surgeons, desperate to cover raw areas caused by widespread burns, began investigating whether pigskin could be grafted onto patients. They felt that young pigskin resembled human skin closely enough to give it a try.

Once the pig was anesthetized, a flap of its skin was stitched to one edge of skin bordering a raw area. The other half of the graft was left on the pig, so as to maintain a blood supply to the graft until it took. This meant that the piglet had to be kept alive—and sedated to prevent it from becoming rambunctious.

Needless to say, the patient-pig pairing made for an odd couple indeed, presenting many interesting nursing problems, among others. It was quite a sight to see these patients walking the halls with their "Siamese pigs" close to them. You'd think at first it was a swaddling infant—then you'd see the snout and hear an occasional plaintive oink.

The pig-patient experiment was a failure and has not, to my knowledge, been repeated, although lately drugs are being tested that could overcome the problem of host-graft rejection.

At HJD I performed many surgical procedures for the first time. Under an attending surgeon's guidance, I learned to do appendectomies, thyroidectomies, hernia repairs, cholecystectomies, and even circumcisions. I treated many head injuries and stab and gunshot wounds. I was on duty when one of the first Harlem riots erupted. Our E.R. and all the surrounding corridors looked like a wartime battalion's aid station, with wounded civilians and police everywhere. That was my first experience with triage: making the hard, poignant, but necessary choices about who would have priority care. Sobering as it was, I would be grateful for this training a few years later in the Pacific.

At HJD, assisting at cancer operations, I learned that this type of surgery often involved complicated, intricate work and required an exceptional amount of ingenuity and patience. In spite of standing for four to six hours for a single operation, and the heavy demands of postoperative care, somehow I was always eager to be part of any cancer surgical team. Whenever possible, I traded my gallbladder, hernia, or appendix operations for fellow interns' cancer cases.

Near the end of my internship at HJD, I decided to specialize in cancer surgery. Knowing that the best place for such training was at Memorial Hospital, I applied in the spring of 1941 for a one-year assistant residency there. As usual, the application blank had a space for religion. I swallowed hard. A few weeks later, I was granted an interview with the admissions committee at Memorial.

Understandably, I approached this meeting with trepidation, for just two years before, I had had the unhappy experience across the avenue at New York Hospital. However, my interviewers, Dr. Cornelius "Dusty" Rhoads and Dr. Lloyd Craver, put me at ease. Apparently they were impressed by my fervor about wanting to specialize in cancer, for about a week later, I was informed that I had been accepted.

Once inside Memorial, I never felt any ethnic bias. However, I recall one attending surgeon who, upon being introduced to me in my early months there, bluntly asked, "What kind of a name is that?" I told him, and for a moment he eyed me intently. Then he said, "Oh," and walked away.

Taking Harry Ehrlich, another Jew, and me, reflected, I'm sure, a change in Memorial's policy when Dusty Rhoads became its director. Dusty's liberal policy was a quantum leap from that of the previous director, Dr. James Ewing, who was rumored to be strongly anti-Semitic, and whose son, James, Jr., was outspokenly so.

When after my fellowship, I was chosen to become a staff member, I was the second Jew in the hospital's sixty-four-year history to do so. Norman Treves (né Tannenbaum) was the first many years before.

Times have changed in more ways than medicines, procedures, and equipment. At present, the president; the head of Sloan-

Kettering Institute; the heads of radiation therapy, internal medicine, colorectal, and thoracic services are Jews. Women, blacks, Sikhs, Asians, Hindus, and more abound; the hospital halls are adorned with yarmulkes and turbans. *That* is progress—and in solving the riddle of cancer, prejudice can play no part.

On December 30, 1940, *Lady in the Dark* opened at the Shubert Theater in Boston. Pamela and I were invited by Gee Lawrence to the opening night. The show was a rare combination of fine writing and direction, lyrics and music. And why not—with Moss Hart, Ira Gershwin, Kurt Weill. The cast was perfect, and Harry Horner's sets were not only a delight to behold, but also astonished everyone by how rapidly the scenes could be changed, thanks to Horner's converting the stage into rotatable sections.

Gertrude was an ideal choice for Liza Elliott, the glamorous, dynamic fashion editor (ironic in light of my later life) of a *Vogue*-like magazine. She embodied all those qualities of a star in Oscar Hammerstein's later description of her in *The New York Times:*

> In every great theatrical artist there is ambition and industry. These qualities beget craftsmanship. In every great theatrical artist there is a capacity for human understanding and sympathy. In a star—in a true star—of the theater, there are all these things . . . and one thing more! And that one thing is mystic and intangible. It cannot be learned or imitated. It belongs to its owner and to no one else. It's a kind of a glow that emanates from one, and communicates itself to all. It is just as unearthly as the glow of a heavenly star and just as hard to explain—harder perhaps, because astronomers and mathematicians have learned more about stars in the sky than producers or authors or critics have been able to learn about stars in the theater.

He went on to say that Gertrude cheerfully dedicated her own life to a series of elaborate and glorious "imitations of life"— imitations that were just a little better, a little brighter than life itself. This was her fun. This was her "mission."

I had reservations about my future mother-in-law, but there was no question that when she was on the stage, no one else seemed to matter, no one else could be watched.

The first act ended and, at intermission, people buzzed with excitement about what was obviously a big hit. Besides the show itself, an extra drama occurred in the second act. Moss Hart had used a young comedian, fresh from the borscht circuit in the Catskill Mountains, to play Russell Paxton. The young actor was reddish-blond; he moved like a ballet dancer, alternatively swishing and sashaying, as he acted the part of a petulant, ill-tempered, effeminate photographer to perfection. In the second act, there was a beautiful dream sequence. Earlier, Liza, under psychoanalysis, has recounted one of her dreams, in which all the characters and the conflicts of her life appeared. She is also having a crisis of indecision about whether to choose the "Easter" cover or the "Circus" cover for the next issue of her magazine. The stage was made up as a fantasylike circus, and the characters in Liza's life appeared dressed in typical circus costumes. The photographer, in the uniform of a lion tamer, sang his only aria, in which forty-nine Russian composers are named at breakneck speed. That number, "Tschaikowsky," stopped the show and brought down the house. That night, Danny Kaye became a star.

Gertrude was to follow him with a solo in a few minutes. Great stars do not relish being topped or upstaged, particularly by newcomers. So she used all the tricks of her eventful stage life and pulled out all the stops. What made her performance so remarkable was that she was making up many of these flourishes as she went along, in inspired response to Danny's challenge. She strutted like a stripper, complete with grinds and bumps, and it titillated everyone to see this lady, fresh from drawing-room comedies with Noel Coward, suddenly bringing in raw hints of the earthy. This interpretation gave an extra edge to the lyrics of "Jenny"—a combination that couldn't be beat. The ovation that followed her performance topped that given Danny's and stopped the show for twice as long.

At the final curtain, Pam jumped to her feet and yelled "Bravo! Bravo!"

Three weeks later, *Lady in the Dark* came to New York where it was triumphantly received and ran for years.

When it was clear to my parents that I would probably marry Pam, they tried to dissuade me from doing so, pointing out what I already knew: I had no income or capital to support her. Besides, although she was undoubtedly a "nice girl," she was, after all, a fatherless child of a famous star and therefore, at risk of being unstable.

Although Gertrude had real reservations about her daughter

marrying a penniless medical apprentice, she apparently thought that Pam's courtship had gone on long enough. One day before a matinee of *Lady in the Dark,* she took me to lunch at the Italian Pavilion. As soon as we were seated, she began. It was the equivalent of asking whether my intentions were "honorable." I felt pressured, and we soon wound up raising our voices and stalking single-file out of the restaurant as other diners gaped. Very theatrical, you might say.

A few months later, I did what I had planned to do all along: I asked Pam to meet me on the steps of the pediment supporting the Statue of General Sherman at Fifty-ninth Street and Fifth Avenue, and there I proposed. She paused for a count of three, then accepted.

Once we were engaged, my parents did everything to make Pam feel part of the family and, in time, became almost parental with her.

Pam and I were married in June 1941 on the lawn of Gertrude and Richard's home in Dennis, Massachusetts. Besides my parents and my uncle Robert I had invited only two friends—Mort Kanner, and a P&S graduate and distant cousin, Mike Gomperts. At the time, Mort was doing postgraduate work in atomic research at Princeton. The nature of his work, he explained, involved "bombarding deuterons with other deuterons." When I realized that this meant that he was constantly exposed to radiation, I became alarmed and warned him to protect himself. But Mort shrugged off my fears, saying that he had a blood count done every month and that whenever his white blood corpuscle count fell, he stopped working for a while until it rose again.

This precaution struck me as inadequate and made me very uneasy.

Pam and I moved to 405 East Fifty-fourth Street and, with some help from Gee, managed to make ends meet. Pam was working with the British-American Ambulance Corps, a group raising money to buy and ship ambulances to England, which was in a full-scale war with Germany. My contribution to our household budget consisted of my whole salary, raised now to a whopping twenty-five dollars a month.

One Sunday, as Pam and I were having lunch with my parents, who lived three blocks away on Fifty-seventh Street, Gertrude called and told us to turn on the radio at once. We did, and listened in stunned silence to the report of the Japanese air attack on Pearl Harbor.

My acceptance at Memorial meant that I was to begin working there on January 1. When I volunteered for the Air Corps, I requested that I be allowed to finish at least one year of residency before being called up for service.

CHAPTER IV

Mort

On New Year's Day, 1942, I began a one-year appointment as an assistant resident in surgery. Memorial—America's first cancer hospital—was founded in 1884. In those days, many women with cancer were denied entrance to general hospitals, particularly to New York's Women's Hospital. The reason given by hospital officials was that cancer patients required too much nursing care, thereby draining the hospital's resources. Besides, there was a lurking fear that cancer might be contagious. Consequently, apart from city hospitals and a few private institutions, women with cancer had no place to go.

This inhuman attitude stirred two women—Elizabeth Cullum and Mrs. John Jacob Astor—and a friend, John E. Parsons, to build a structure that had long been a dream of Dr. J. Marion Simms. Together they formed the New York Cancer Hospital. Its first—temporary—location was in a building at the present site of the Waldorf-Astoria Hotel, at Fiftieth Street and Park Avenue. (The hospital later became known as Memorial Cancer Hospital, and was later changed to Memorial Hospital for Cancer and Allied Diseases. Now it is known as the Memorial Sloan-Kettering Cancer Center (MSK).

The first site was too small, so that, with funds provided by the Rockefeller family, the cornerstone of a new hospital was laid in 1884, at 106th Street and Central Park West. The building, which still stands, is a French Gothic structure of Belleville sandstone with dark red pressed-brick walls that make it fortresslike. "The Bastille's" corners were rounded to bring more light into the wards and to make the patients more accessible to the nurses at the ward's hub. There was only one very large operating room, where several operations could take place simultaneously.

Memorial's prestige slowly but steadily increased and was given great impetus when the renowned pathologist Dr. James Ewing became its head. The hospital attracted not only women but men with cancer, who felt they could be best served in an institution that specialized in that disease.

The new building, at Sixty-eighth Street and York Avenue (where we work now) opened its doors in 1938. It is fourteen stories high and has a light red-brick façade embellished with architecturally interesting details. Memorial's interior was well lit, brightly colored, and quiet—the antithesis of the old site on Central Park West. Two lower floors had twelve-bed wards at either end. The four floors had one-, two-, and four-bed rooms. The ninth and tenth floors, the "Gold Coast," had spacious, mahogany-doored private rooms. Memorial was the first hospital to devote a wing to pediatric cancer.

We residents had rooms on the eleventh floor; on the twelfth floor were six operating rooms, some of which had balconies where visitors could view procedures or, alternatively, see a splendid panorama of Manhattan, the East River, and the Queensboro Bridge.

The attending staff was small, about twenty-five in all—twenty-three men and two women—and composed largely of graduates of Memorial's residency program. The staff was so closely knit that it created an intimate, almost clublike atmosphere. The facilities even included a private dining room and waitresses. Attending staff members had outside private offices and used the hospital for surgery and to care for very sick patients. Once or twice a week, attendings "paid their dues" by donating their services to charity patients in the outpatient clinic and teaching surgery to the house staff in the operating rooms.

Surgical services were divided by anatomic regions: breast, head, and neck; gastric and mixed tumor (melanomas, sarcomas); urology; gynecology; bone; colorectal. Each service was headed by a chief surgeon who, along with his staff, concentrated on the diagnosis and treatment of benign and malignant tumors of one region of the body. The majority of attendings had been trained as general surgeons first but, by specializing in tumors of a particular area, had become expert in their management.

Memorial had established itself as a prestigious institution even when it was on Central Park West. In its new location on Sixty-eighth Street, its reputation rapidly increased, attracting patients from all over the world. For a young surgeon to be able to care for a large number of cancer patients who often required major, complex operations, expertly performed by renowned surgeons, was like entering a surgical nirvana. In a single day at least four or five operations were performed, each of which was of such magnitude as to be considered a major event in a general hospital. As a result, in one month I saw more cancer patients and assisted at more extensive operations by far than I had in my entire two-year internship. In addition, I was introduced to special surgical procedures that I had never known existed.

Assistant residents also spent a month on nonsurgical services: pediatrics, lymphoma, and the outpatient clinics. For two months we were also assigned to radiation therapy. Memorial insisted that in order to provide cancer patients with the best possible care, their physicians should be familiar with the value and limitations of both surgery and radiation therapy. With that familiarity, they could select the method, or combination of methods, that would be best for their patients.

Although we were surgeons-in-training, we were fascinated by the remarkable world of Memorial's radiation therapy department; probably the most sophisticated in the world, it was monitored by a special department of radiation physics. It also had the first millon volt X-ray machine, and was one of the first to start using tiny gold seeds that contained something called radon, the gas formed by the disintegration of radium. The seeds were inserted through needles directly into a cancer. On one of the hospital's floors were two lead-lined rooms, into the walls of which radioactive material sources were inserted. The theory behind this was that patients who had systemic cancer, such as leukemia or lymphomas, would be bombarded by total body irradiation. This technique proved ineffectual and was discontinued.

The heart, core, soul of any hospital are its patients and once again I was struck by the extraordinary range of their needs and unsolved problems. I found time away from my surgical duties to read all I could, attend lectures, and take courses in radiation physics. My first assignment was in the head and neck service, and I spent long hours at night dissecting at nearby Cornell Medical College's anatomy lab, reacquainting myself with the intricate structures of that region.

Although I had seen cancers in various areas of the body, I was not prepared for those that extensively involved the face, jaw, tongue, scalp, eyes, and nose. It was quite a shock, therefore, to see patients in whom one or all of these structures were missing as a result of surgery performed in an attempt to cure or curtail their cancers.

The chief of the head and neck service, Dr. Hayes Martin, had been chosen in 1938 over Dr. Douglas Quick, a radiation therapist. Because Dr. Martin was a surgeon, this symbolized a shift in emphasis away from radiation therapy in treating cancers of the head and neck. Martin was a born leader, aggressive and innovative. He published many articles, had a huge influence on the course of head and neck cancer surgery, and became a world-class authority on the subject. He was a member of that school of surgeons, all too prevalent in those days, who were autocratic, short-tempered, and, on occasion, even rough with patients. Not infrequently, I would stand by, wincing, as he upbraided patients who were slow in following his commands. In spite of this gruff treatment, he saw them daily and they respected his ability and felt secure in his hands.

One of Dr. Martin's patients, Joseph Lerner, founder of the Lerner Shops which sold women's clothes, had over forty operations for recurrent cancers of his tongue, mouth, and lower jaw. As a result, he had lost his entire tongue, jawbone, larynx, and upper esophagus (gullet). He breathed through a tracheostomy tube and was fed by a tube inserted into the remnant of the upper end of his esophagus. Nevertheless, wearing a veillike mask that covered his "Andy Gump" deformity, he was otherwise charming and presentable, and wrote long and interesting notes on a pad he carried with him at all times. Even in his state, he purportedly had many lady friends. Eventually, Lerner's cancer eluded surgical and radiation therapy efforts to control it, and it killed him. He had been a smoker. Eventually, his son—and my friend —Alan Jay Lerner, a genius of musical comedy, another smoker, would become a patient at MSK too.

Joe Lerner's problems were just another example of the extensive and often distortive surgery being done then for cancer of the head and neck. Dr. Martin added the dental and plastic surgical services to combine their special talents to relieve or reduce the patient's disfigurement. Thereafter, facial reconstruction at Memorial was done in a more artful, sophisticated way. Plastic models were fashioned that uncannily resembled the patient's original facial structure. These were carefully tinted to resemble their natural skin tones. If an ear was removed, another was made by matching the existing one on the opposite side. New noses—often combined with cheekbones—made of silastic rubber, were held in place by special glue and supported by being attached to eyeglass frames. Within the oral cavity, ingenious devices filled defects caused by the loss of the hard and soft palates, so the patient could swallow and phonate.

These devices may sound like makeup for a science-fiction movie, but they made possible a more normal, fuller life for patients who might otherwise have gone into hiding. Under Dr. Martin's guidance, and because of the vast range of his methods and techniques, plus the capability of its staff, the head and neck service became the foremost one of its kind in the world.

Surrounded by such a wealth of fascinating material and individuals, and stimulated by the spirit of the place, I plunged into this new world with such enthusiasm that I often skipped taking scheduled nights and weekends off, which meant that Pamela was often left alone. From the start, I was anxious to contribute something of my own. At one of our weekly conferences, Dr. Martin presented a patient who had had a radical neck dissection—the removal from the side of his neck of lymph nodes containing cancer that had spread from a primary cancer within the oral cavity. At the end of his presentation, Dr. Martin said he wished that someone would summarize the service's enormous experience with neck dissections for a comprehensive article on the subject. After the conference, I took him aside and said I would volunteer to do so.

To tabulate the data, I used large sheets of white cardboard and lined them so that I could see at a glance each patient's name, age, sex, primary cancer site (lip, tongue, larynx, floor of mouth, gum, tonsil . . .), type of operation, pathology report, and length of survival following surgery—either cancer-free or with recurrences.

Hundreds of patients had undergone neck dissections, so my room was soon stacked high with charts that I pulled from the hospital's record room. I became obsessed with the project, knowing that my time at Memorial would soon be shortened by entry into the armed forces. I set a goal of analyzing at least six charts per night.

While assisting Dr. Martin in the operating room one day, I was introduced to a great coloratura soprano. She stood in the viewing balcony in the O.R., having asked Dr. Martin if she could watch him perform a laryngectomy. After the voice box was removed, she asked to see the specimen and to have the vocal cords pointed out to her. There was something eerie, even surrealistic in seeing Lily Pons, our leading coloratura, peering intently at the tiny membranes that formed the vocal cords with which she used to reach high E above C. She was probably wondering at the two bits of gristle in the throat that can transmit, can transubstantiate, words into music, matter into spirit.

Although Dr. Martin knew I was working on the neck-dissection paper, he asked me to figure out the answer to another, surprising, offbeat question: how to determine, once and for all, whether the characteristic, telltale breath of those who had eaten garlic was due to "local" causes—garlic coating the oral cavity and teeth—or of systemic origin.

In a few weeks, I had an answer. As I examined a patient who had had a total laryngectomy (voice-box removal) and permanent tracheostomy (an opening in the neck that leads to the windpipe), I detected the unmistakable odor of garlic fumes as he exhaled. As a total laryngectomy disrupts the anatomic continuity between the trachea and the esophagus, the garlic he had eaten twenty-four hours before must have entered his circulation, been excreted into his lungs, and exhaled. No garlic odor was detectable within his mouth. Not exactly Nobel Prize–winning—but instructive.

Each Wednesday morning, there was a hosptial-wide conference in the auditorium. Attendance was mandatory for the attendings and the entire house staff. There was always one seat reserved in the first row at the right side of the auditorium for Dr. James Ewing. Ewing was one of the world's great pathologists, a man who had earned his reputation through an encyclopedic knowledge of cancers and a remarkable skill at making microscopic diagnoses. He had written a scholarly book on cancer pathology and was the first to recognize and describe a specific bone cancer, one that was then named Ewing's sarcoma.

Dr. Ewing had first come to Memorial in 1913 as its chief pathologist as well as its director. Ewing's dedication impressed philanthropists such as John D. Rockefeller, Jr., and James Douglas, who provided the grounds and much of the funding for the new building on York Avenue. Now that he was in his seventies, his opinion was sought by pathologists from all parts of the world. They would bring or mail to him glass slides containing puzzling tumor tissues.

One of my attending surgeons received slides from a Russian colleague who asked if he would get Dr. Ewing's opinion. The surgeon asked if I wanted to accompany him to meet the great man. As Dr. Ewing was a legendary figure, I jumped at the opportunity.

We found him in a tiny office in a corner of the pathology laboratory, seated before his battered old microscope. The surgeon knew what an arch-conservative Dr. Ewing was, so as he handed over the slides, he began apologizing for the fact that they were from Russia.

Dr. Ewing took the slides, placed them under his microscope, and said, as he started to study them: "Stop the nonsense, Frank; Communists get cancer, too."

In addition to receiving clinical instruction, I was beginning to adopt the sometimes grisly, sometimes shocking, frequently bawdy surgeon's sense of humor. During one summer vacation, I sent a postcard to Dr. Martin from the Piazza della Signoria in Florence that reproduced Cellini's statue of Perseus holding the head of Medusa. I wrote: *They also do radical surgery here.*

Six months into assistant residency, I was informed that I had been selected to continue in the three-year residency program at Memorial. Good news. But two months later, there was another notice: Report to duty with the army air force medical corps on February 17, 1943. Sobering news—but fair. This meant that I would be able to complete only one month of the three-year residency before I left. However, I was assured that after the war, making the usual assumptions about surviving, I could resume my interrupted training.

Realizing that the days at Memorial were limited, I worked even harder to complete the paper on neck dissections. Each night I stepped up my quota of charts, and I managed to complete the data on 350 patients before leaving for the military. I arranged with Dr. Harry Ehrlich, who was classified 4F, to continue the project in my absence. Later, during the war, another co-author, Dr. Bernardo del Valle, a Guatemalan, was added. By 1946, they had completed the data on 620 patients. Illustrations showed each step of a classic radical neck dissection. Such a long, detailed paper required many drafts and rewrites until finally it was published, five years later, in the journal *Cancer*. Dr. Martin's name headed the list of authors. "Neck Dissection" is still considered to be a classic.

My friend Mort Kanner had gone from Princeton's Institute for Advanced Study back to his alma mater, MIT, where he was doing research of a highly secret nature.

We were used to speaking frequently on the phone, and he began to complain of a nagging abdominal pain, which physicians in Boston thought was from a stomach ulcer. Once or twice he called from a military airport just before taking off for England on missions he was not free to describe. Then, one day, he called to say that he was going to have an exploratory abdominal operation at Massachusetts General Hospital because "something other than an ulcer" had been found. He asked if I could be there.

As I watched the operation, I saw the situation all too clearly and to my despair: Mort had far-advanced lymphosarcoma. As the surgeon uncovered the abdominal mass and looked up at me, I thought, *My God, what will I tell his mother?*

Once Mort recovered from surgery, I arranged to have him brought to Memorial for treatment. To treat such a large abdominal tumor, it was necessary to irradiate a wide area, so Mort had to be hospitalized to care for his radiation sickness. I visited him daily, and occasionally would run into military guards standing outside his door. I would wait until his visitors emerged; some of them had attaché cases chained to their wrists. I could not contain my curiosity, so one day, while sitting with Mort as he waited his turn on the million-volt X-ray machine, I asked him what all this secrecy was about. He walked to his dressing cubicle, fogged the mirror with his breath, and with his forefinger wrote: "RADAR."

As the time to leave for the Air Force approached, I could see that Mort's cancer was not responding to radiation and that he was wasting away. It broke my heart to see him that way and to have to tell his parents threadbare white lies in order not to deprive them of all hope. On the second of February 1943, I visited Mort in his home, knowing it would be the last time I saw him. He knew it, too. As a farewell gift, he gave me our favorite symphony—Beethoven's Seventh the second movement of which is a funeral march. I remember—and still have—the card he enclosed: "Speed the parting Cahan!"

SAMUEL CAHAN, 1944

Morton Kanner, Ph.D., who made important, secret contributions to the war effort—and who later lost his life to that cause and that research

Each time I called, first from Florida and then from Texas, I heard his voice grow weaker. Soon, too soon, there was a letter.

Dear Bill,
    Always glad to hear from you. Our friend, Mort Kanner, although still able to get about, is rapidly approaching a terminal stage and will enter the hosptial in a few days. Craver plans to feed him heptaldehyde (secret)—something that Kensler has been playing around with and has given some encouraging results in the test tube. He has been a bit depressed because nothing is done about his ever increasing ascites, but the idea of coming into the hospital for some new treatment has cheered him up a bit. He's a sweet person and I feel terribly sorry for both him and his poor mother. I'll let you know how things go.

Subsequent letters from his physicians gave ominous reports. One day while I was at Sheppard Field in Texas, my mother called, in tears. Mort was dead.

Mort Kanner was twenty-eight years old. Only after the war was over could the nature of his work be fully revealed. He was lauded by U.S. General "Pete" Quesada for his important contributions to the victory of the Battle of Britain and the Allied cause. Together with Isidor Rabi and Luis Alvarez, Mort had helped in a major way to evolve the Microwave Early Warning System. They tested it secretly from the roof of MIT by tracking commerical planes flying in and out of the Boston airports.

Years later, both Rabi and Alvarez received Nobel Prizes for their major scientific work. What none of Mort Kanner's eulogists mentioned was that his many exposures to irradiation during his research years had probably cost him his life.

The loss of my closest friend, my oldest but very young friend, was devastating. Mort's sacrifice turned out to be crucial to one major undertaking that still lay ahead: a battle to alert people to radiation's dangers.

Forty-five years later, Isador Rabi himself became a patient at MSK. I caught up with Rabi in the holding area of the operating room, where he was awaiting surgery. I explained that we had a friend in common and asked the famous scientist if he remembered Mort Kanner. Although eighty-nine years old and sedated, the great man brightened. "Oh yes, I remember Mort well. In fact," he said, "I remember that he won a limerick contest at MIT." He then proceeded to recite the award-winning entry in its entirety:

> We hear tall tales about spies
> That the walls and doors are all eyes
> That maids dark and handsome
> Peek over the transom
> Trying to make us poor guys.

> It is all a packet of lies
> There just ain't any beautiful spies
> We would trade information
> For a slight titillation
> And be shot uttering rapturous cries.

♦

CHAPTER V

High on the Wings of Victory

After six weeks of Officer's Training School in Miami Beach, I was assigned to Sheppard Field, Wichita Falls, Texas. The station hospital cared for about 50,000 air cadets and other army personnel. On some days that summer, the mercury registered 132 degrees in the sun. With the excuse that he was preparing the men for desert combat, the commanding general sent them out to drill at high noon. As a result, the hospital was swamped with men suffering from heat- and sunstroke. It was only after repeated appeals by us physicians that the general agreed to limit drills to the cooler hours.

My first duty as a surgical officer of the day (though, in fact, it was the middle of the night) was to deliver the baby of a soldier's wife. It was a breech birth, one procedure I had never performed —or even observed.* At the critical moment, I remembered the relevant passage in our obstetrics text: "Deliver each leg separately, following the normal joint action. Then, deliver the buttocks. Pass your hand up to the shoulders and bring each arm down separately. Place one forefinger firmly along the cervical spine in back of the head to splint it and prevent hyperextension, and gently, with the other hand on the infant's chin and a finger in its mouth, ease the head out anteriorly, occiput up."

---

* These are even rarer today, for when a breech fetal position is established by sonograms, at term, the baby is delivered by cesarean section.

For once, I followed orders. The baby was a boy, a fact that was clearly evident minutes before he was born.

A colonel who had been a surgeon in a Southern state and was not well trained in general surgery headed the surgical department of the station hospital. He had achieved that elevated position by having accumulated service credits in the peacetime army reserve corps. To hide his inexperience, we found, some of us would have to guide him through various elective operations that he insisted on doing.

I was not a favorite of his. For one thing, I was outspokenly critical of his ruling that black soldiers must be segregated in the wards. Each time we violently disagreed, he relegated me to the dispensary (the "coal mines"). Then, when he needed help with some operation, I would be reinstated. During one of my banishments, I heard that while doing a varicose-vein operation, the colonel accidentally severely damaged a major artery, causing a soldier to lose his leg. A few days later, while doing a hysterectomy on an enlisted man's wife, he damaged the ureter, causing her to lose a kidney.

A formal investigation was scheduled. We were told that high-ranking air force inspectors would be coming to the hospital, and that all of us should be available for questioning. On the designated day, all medical officers, minus the colonel, assembled in the hospital's meeting room. At the command "Attention!" we jumped to our feet. To my surprise and pleasure, Colonel Bradley Coley and his aide, Lieutenant Colonel Norman Higinbotham, both of whom I had known when they were attending surgeons on the bone service at Memorial, entered the room. When they spotted me, their greetings were effusive. Soon they said that they would like me to be one of the witnesses in the formal investigation. In short order, the colonel was relieved of his duties and shipped to another post.

As medical officers, one of our tedious duties was to examine droves of enlisted men before they began their special training to become crew members, i.e., gunners and navigators. This involved their going through basic training, a major part of which required marching and drilling while carrying rifles. Not infrequently, a worried soldier would appear at sick call with a painful lump beneath the nipple of his left breast. Some physicians who saw this for the first time became alarmed, feeling that the lump could be cancerous and, knowing my background, consulted me.

However, I reassured them that they were examples of gyneco-mastia (*gyneco-*, "woman"; *mast-*, "breast"; together the word means "womanlike breast"). This condition can result from glandular disorders, but when it is unilateral it is usually a response to chronic irritation of the nipple. In these young soldiers, friction occurred when they were carrying rifles, the strap of which frequently passed over their left nipple. Gynecomastia is remedied by eliminating the source of the friction. We suggested that each soldier pad his nipple with a soft cloth or cotton ball secured with tape while he marched. It would also help if he hooked his left thumb beneath the rifle strap to hold it away from the nipple. In civilian life, I am consulted by men with this condition. When they point to the site of the lump, I ask if they usually carry anything in the shirt or coat pocket on that side. In the majority of instances, they bring something out: a wallet, a cluster of pens and pencils, an eyeglasses case, or even a hearing-aid battery. When these are shifted elsewhere, the lump and tenderness begin to disappear within a few weeks; within a year, they are usually gone. (However, in middle-aged and elderly men, these lumps might, in fact, be breast cancer, and if there is any suspicion that cancer may be present, a mammogram and biopsy are indicated without delay.)

Cancers are uncommon in such a relatively young group of air force men and women. Nevertheless, we would, at times, find testicular cancers, lymphomas, or melanomas; in older officers, colon and stomach cancers; in WACs, benign and malignant breast and uterine tumors. As tumors could be easily overlooked in mass examinations, I felt that I should alert other medical officers to this possibility. "Cancer in the Armed Forces," my first published paper, appeared in *The Military Surgeon* in 1944.

One day in September 1943, while proofreading the galleys of the article, I was handed orders to "proceed" to New York City, where I was to be attached to a unit of the Army Emergency Relief Fund. This organization helped servicemen finance emergency furloughs on, for example, the serious illness or death of a parent, or the birth of a baby. As few government funds were available for these personal emergencies, it was hoped that a new Broadway show might be put together to raise money for the purpose. The show was to be called *Winged Victory* and it was being written and directed by Moss Hart. David Rose, a romantic, wrote the music. The splendid jazz pianist Joe Bushkin was one of the orchestra conductors, and Sergeant Harry Horner (of *Lady in the Dark* fame) designed the sets. Along with several wives of soldiers in the cast, Pam appeared in crowd scenes.

It was my mother-in-law who had arranged for my transfer. When Gertrude heard that Hart needed a doctor for his company of about three hundred air force soldiers-actors-singers-stage-hands, she suggested me.

The show first opened in Boston. Heartened by our reception, though the play was by no means a sure thing, we moved three weeks later into the 44th Street Theatre in New York, where I set up a dispensary in a star's dressing room backstage.

I had to hold sick call backstage before each performance, as the cast was scattered about the city in various hotels and apartments. I had one other facility to work in for a certain purpose.

Army regulations stipulated that soldiers had to have a "short arm" inspection by a medical officer once a month. This inspection was limited to the pubic area and its purpose was to detect venereal disease or unwanted tiny visitors, "crotch pheasants." *Winged Victory* used the 92nd Street YMHA for physical exercise and lectures. It also used the Y's stage for these monthly inspections. My three assistants and I would sit in one of the backstage

MORRIS BLECHMAN

Moss Hart, author, producer, director of *Winged Victory,* an Air Corps show that took off

The Slate Brothers on stage, wigs left and right, with (far left) Zeke
Manners on accordion and in the middle, Red Buttons

wings while the cast lined up in single file across the stage. A
spotlight was focused on the appropriate area and each soldier
would step up to it, drop his trousers, and—once we had given
him a clean bill of health—readjust his clothing. Inevitably, this
became an occasion for horseplay and, as actors, and sometimes
artists, the soldiers worked it for all it was worth. We learned to
expect surprises and tried to keep a professional tone as we were
treated to drawings on abdomens and thighs of Dr. Seuss–like
collections of crabs, lobsters, tigers, mermaids, giraffes, and other
members of a menagerie. There were signs on skin: USE ONLY IN
EMERGENCY, or FIRE EXIT, or NO SMOKING, or HANDLE WITH CARE.
Some of the homosexual members wore mistletoe in their navels,
which was particularly festive at Christmas time. Usually someone, like radio personality Sgt. Zeke Manners, would use the
piano in the orchestra pit to play "I've Got You Under My Skin"
or "A Pretty Girl Is Like a Melody," a favorite number for bur-
lesque strippers.

At one of these inspections, the stage door opened suddenly and a woman looking like a char, with a bandana wrapped around her head, appeared. She held a feather duster in her hand and without looking up, went around dusting backstage objects. All of us on the staff and all the half-clad soldiers were transfixed and nervously waited to see what else she would go after. She never looked up and left by the same door, followed by roars of laughter. She was, of course, put up to it by one of the soldiers. Interestingly, given the notorious love life of actors, there was not a single instance of VD in the year I was associated with the show.

On the night *Winged Victory* opened in New York, an age-old theatrical superstition was tested. To put a hat on a bed, or to see a bird (or even mention birds) is said to be bad luck for a play. That night a pigeon walked around on the window ledge outside the dispensary, and not one, but three hats happened to be placed on the double-decker bed we had installed for emergencies. When this became known, there was lots of clucking and grave head-wagging—by both the actors and the pigeons. Perhaps these om-

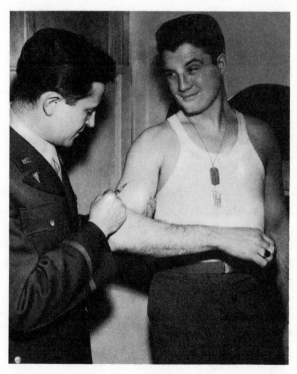

Could this shot have turned George Reeves into Superman?

inous omens canceled each other out. One of the ranking critics, Ward Morehouse, wrote, in part:

> The American theater rose to magnificence Saturday evening when, upon this island and in this town, [with] "Winged Victory's" . . . premiere performance. Here is a thrilling show, a combination of play and spectacle that dwarfs all else in the current season. . . .

That was a rather nice opening paragraph. But Morehouse did not stop there.

> "Winged Victory" is Mr. Hart's finest contribution to the Broadway stage. It is of the stature of Irving Berlin's "This Is the Army," but it has far more emotional strength. For it's a play, catching the spirit of the Air Forces, that takes young men from the comfortable homes and back porches of midland America and sends them on the big hop to the steaming and tangled jungles of the South Pacific, where war is in disguise and hovering on every side . . .
> . . . Hart, with great warmth, poignancy and understanding, writes of the young men, drawn from all walks of civilian life, who are the cadets and combat fliers of this hour and of this war. . . .
> "Winged Victory" is exalted stuff. It is a memorable evening.
> . . . It brings to Moss Hart a new and enormous prestige and pays its tribute to the glory of the Air Forces.

Morehouse concluded by saying that the show was probably the greatest "single build-up of the flying machine since the Wright Brothers . . ." *Winged Victory* ran for seven months to standing-room-only crowds, and stopped its Broadway run in order to be made into a Hollywood movie.

Winged Victory's cast had been culled from the cream of air force talent and was hand-picked by Moss Hart and Lieutenant Irving "Swifty" Lazar, later a mega-agent. It was Lazar who had hatched the idea for the show and sold it, first to Air Force General "Hap" Arnold and then to Moss. Hart and Lazar traveled to many airfields looking for talent. The degree of their success is attested to by the roster of those who went on to become better known— Edmond O'Brien, John Forsythe, Red Buttons, Peter Lind Hayes, Karl Malden, Gary Merrill, Barry Nelson, Lee J. Cobb, Anthony Ross, Kevin McCarthy, George Reeves, and Ray Middleton, to name a few.

Moss was proud of his show and of his cast, and when digni-

Members of the *Winged Victory* cast included (left to right) Don Taylor, Mark Daniels, Edmund O'Brien, Peter Lind Hayes, (on ladder, top) Karl Malden, Martin Ritt (below), George Petrie, Alfred Ryder.

taries such as General George Marshall, General "Hap" Arnold, and Eleanor Roosevelt attended, he would invite them to come backstage after the show and address the all–soldier cast. One night, Moss welcomed a famously talented figure of the theater by saying: "And now let me introduce the Moss Hart of the British empire: Noel Coward."

PFC Mario Lanza's glorious voice was buried in the fifty-man soldier chorus. From time to time, however, we would be treated to its astonishingly natural beauty when he sang solos at private gatherings.

At that time, Mario (Alfred Cocozza) weighed 265 pounds. He had invited his parents, who lived in Philadelphia, to see the show and, mortified by his enormous girth, asked me to put him on a crash diet. But, without telling me, he went far beyond what I had prescribed, putting himself on a complete fast, and drinking water and tea for days, nothing more.

Mario lost fifty pounds in a few weeks; each night before the

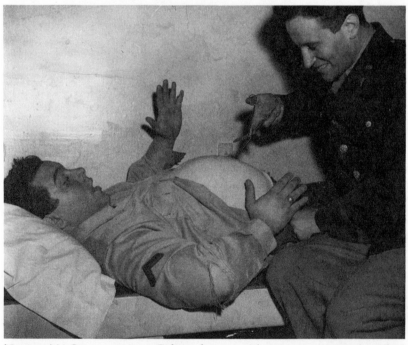

Young Air Corps surgeon Cahan clowns with young, supremely gifted singer named Mario Lanza. But Lanza's protuberant belly becomes no laughing matter when the two met again after World War II.

performance he would come to our backstage dispensary and proudly show us the new notches on his belt as he tightened it. The night his parents were slated to see the show, Mario was so weak that we could barely get him on the stage, indeed were only able to do so with the help of stimulants. The next day, after his parents left, he sat down to a twenty-four egg omelette and was off on a calorie binge ("calorgy") once more.

In 1959, after Mario had become a superstar, I visited him and his family in his enormous mansion in Rome, which had been once the home of Mussolini's general Marshal Badoglio. Mario was there in self-imposed exile from the U.S. Internal Revenue Service. He was about to make a movie in Italy, and once again was trying to reduce, this time by taking Benzedrine as an appetite suppressant. Not many weeks later, he suddenly died at the age of thirty-eight, for reasons which were said to be obscure.

During our run, several cast members who only appeared in crowd scenes, and who felt that their talents were buried, wanted to display them. Martin Ritt assembled and directed a group of them to perform Sidney Howard's play *Yellow Jack*. *Yellow Jack* dramatized the conquest of yellow fever and the heroic role of Dr. Walter Reed during the building of the Panama Canal. The cast included John Forsythe, Whit Bissel, Gary Merrill, Olive Deering, Karl Malden, Phil Bourneuf, Alfred Ryder, and, oddly, me.

To shorten the play for purposes of time, Ritt replaced the first act with a simulated medical-corps lecture. I laced my talk with descriptions of the symptoms of yellow fever, adopting the tone of someone struggling with the epidemic among those building the canal. As I neared the end of the talk, lights dimmed, and the music, especially written by Norman Leyden, bridged to the beginning of the second act.

Yellow Jack was to have its only performance one afternoon at the 44th Street Theatre before an audience supposedly composed of just *Winged Victory* cast members and Moss Hart. However, word got around, so the theater was also packed with friends and relatives. Mrs. Sidney Howard, the playwright's widow, and her two daughters, Sydney and Jennifer, were in the audience.

Yellow Jack was a huge success and, luckily for my stage nerves, I did not know that it was being reviewed by the critics of several New York newspapers. Very favorably, as it turned out. After the war, Marty Ritt tried to repeat its success on Broadway, using some of the actors who had been in this production. However, the revival did not succeed. Undaunted, Marty returned to Hollywood, where he directed a number of fine movies, including *Hud*.

While *Winged Victory* was playing onstage, I had little to do in my backstage dispensary. Frequently, I went to the nearby Stage Door Canteen to help wait on tables and wash dishes. The Canteen became world-famous as a center where soldiers and sailors of the Allied nations could go for free meals and to be entertained. There was always music playing, and hostesses volunteered to dance with the soldiers and sailors. All in all, it was a colorful, romantic place, made even more popular by the Irving Berlin song "I Left My Heart at the Stagedoor Canteen."

It was romantic and especially colorful for a young doc, still new to show biz and the military. One night a sailor asked: "Hey, Lieutenant, where's the head?" I thought for a second, then pointed out the woman in charge. He stared at me in disbelief. I didn't know that "head" was navy talk for the men's room.

It was during its successful Broadway run that *Winged Victory* was bought by 20th Century Fox. When the company boarded the troop train for Hollywood, I went with them. Although Pam's and my marriage was beginning to show signs of strain, in part because of her attachment to a member of the *W.V.* cast, its condition had not become critical, so she joined me in California.

The movie version of *W.V.* was directed by George Cukor and took five months to film. I set up a dispensary in a high school playground in Santa Monica, where most of the cast was bivouacked in improvised barracks.

In 1944, Inga Arvad, a Hollywood columnist, visited our Santa Monica "camp" to do a story about *Winged Victory*.

Inga was Danish, and before the war, as a Danish newspaper correspondent, had covered the 1936 Olympics. There, she was introduced to Hitler, who invited her to sit with him in his box. Although she despised him, she thought it might make a good news story. According to Joan and Clay Blair's book *In Search of JFK,* Hitler called her "the perfect Nordic beauty"—and that she was.

Not only was I struck by her blue-eyed, blond-haired beauty, but some atavism in me must have been at work, for I was enthralled by the way her zygoma met her maxilla—O.K., her high cheekbones.

History eventually revealed, but I was unaware at the time, that

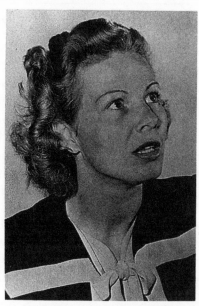

Inga Arvad, whom Hitler called "The Perfect Nordic Beauty,"
adored by John F. Kennedy and the author

four years earlier Inga had been involved in an affair with a young
U.S. Navy lieutenant. Because of the well-known incident with
Hitler in Berlin, she was believed to be a Mata Hari, so their trysts
were subjected to eavesdropping by the F.B.I. Although the suspicions were apparently unfounded, their romance was broken off
as a result of pressure by the lieutenant's domineering father, Joseph Kennedy, then U.S. ambassador to the Court of St. James's.

During what turned out to be Inga's and my romance, Lieutenant John F. Kennedy came to Los Angeles for a few days, and
Inga arranged for us to meet at her apartment. He and I talked
Harvard, football, show business, and so on. After a while, however, it became clear that one of us would have to leave. To my
great relief, he did.

My affair with Inga continued for the five months it took to
complete the film. Although Pam and I lived under the same roof
and were cordial with each other at all times, we seemed to have
reached a plateau in our marriage and stayed together probably
more for convenience than from devotion. At that stage, whatever could be salvaged of our crumbling relationship was not
helped by my affair with Inga, I realized.

Nevertheless, I did try to shield Pam from my infidelity. This was not difficult. I left early in the morning for sick call in my dispensary at Santa Monica and returned in time for dinner in the house we shared with another couple in the Hollywood Hills.

Oddly enough, Inga may have revealed a clue, a "whisper of nature," that was not to be part of medical knowledge until twenty-five years later. After making love, she would often comment that her painful rheumatoid arthritis was dramatically relieved. How much of this was due to psychological factors and how much to a sudden surge in her adrenal hormones (of which cortisone is one), was hard to say. Although I am unaware of any careful research on the subject, such observations must have been made by others, at least informally. Years later, I saw a pillow in a friend's house whose needlepoint read SEX CURES ARTHRITIS.

At the end of September, as the filming of *Winged Victory* was drawing to a close, plans were being made for the show to tour American cities. I had not done any surgery for a year and missed it, so this seemed to be an appropriate time to request a change to more active duty. Consequently, I wrote to the Air Surgeon in Washington to this effect, and was soon sent to a staging area in Salt Lake City.

As if in a scene out of a B movie, while I was reading my orders to go overseas, "The Star-Spangled Banner" was played over the PA system, signaling the end of the workday. "O.K.," I thought, standing. "Let's go."

Pam had returned to New York. Knowing I would soon be gone, Inga joined me for a few days at the majestic old Hotel Utah, where, a week before Christmas, we exchanged presents before a tiny Christmas tree that I had found. Inga returned to her journalist's job in Los Angeles, and, just before Christmas, a group of us marched to a train while a military band played the air corps song. The next day I detrained at Pittsburg, California, where, with thousands of others, I waited to be sent to the Pacific.

I spent Christmas Day with hordes of soldiers and stood in line for hours behind others who were also telephoning their homes. It was a dismal day—yet, as I wrote in the diary I had just begun, I couldn't have been in better company.

On New Year's Eve, 1944, from a pier near Fisherman's Wharf, we boarded the troopship *General A. E. Anderson,* and while celebrations were beginning in San Francisco, sailed with five thousand soldiers under the Golden Gate Bridge into the Pacific, headed for Destination Unknown.* But we had company. Until dusk, we were escorted by a navy blimp on the lookout for submarines.

* During *Winged Victory,* Pam and I had written a corny but heartfelt song that was sung on national radio by Don Richards, who was in the show and later became a star of *Finian's Rainbow.*

"DESTINATION UNKNOWN"

Destination unknown
I must leave at dawn for
destination unknown
and I'm so forlorn for

It's at a time like this
that I recall
our one last loving kiss,
your troubled eyes—and that's all.

When the victory is won
dreams will all come true, dear,
days of laughter and fun
they will start anew, dear,

Someday we will return
to reap the harvest we've sown
someday, from destination unknown.

CHAPTER VI

A Touch of Shangri-La

To confuse enemy submarines, the ship followed a zigzag course across the Pacific. One night the seaman lookout on night watch thought he saw a distant track of phosphorescence. In those southern Pacific seas, this could have been caused by a submarine. The ship stopped moving so as not to create her own giveaway trail. We were rousted out of our bunks and stood on the deck in total darkness in our Mae West life jackets. The navy crew manned the few gun stations on board. The ship's PA system announced: "the smokin' lamp is out." No one was allowed to smoke on deck because even the tiny glow of a cigarette might be visible to the enemy. At daybreak we resumed our zigzag course and were comforted later that day to see one of our planes criss-crossing ahead of us; after a few hours, it wigwagged and dipped its wings as it flew off. About a week later, there was another nighttime alert, but still we saw no enemy subs—and weren't sad to miss the opportunity.

During the last nights of our trip, as we made our way along the north coast of New Guinea, we could see bonfires on the distant shore, probably started by natives for cooking. These could be dangerous: If an enemy submarine were on the open-sea side, our ship would be silhouetted against them.*

---

* One week after we landed, we heard the Japanese radio propaganda personality Tokyo Rose announce that our troop-laden ship had been sunk—just how she got its name is a mystery.

Seventeen days after leaving San Francisco, we sailed into the battleship-filled harbor in Hollandia, New Guinea. There I was assigned as medical officer to the 322nd Troop Carrier Wing of the Far Eastern Air Service Command. The 322nd was used both for reconnaissance and to transport troops in and out of combat areas. It also served as a supply line to bases in Australia. From time to time, I soon learned, its transport planes, called Fat Cats, unofficially provided such luxuries as Aussie beer and gin, and, even more precious, the fresh cow's milk that soldiers never seemed to get enough of.

My aides and I set up our dispensary at the edge of the jungle where our unit was bivouacked. It was a crude structure constructed with upright two-by-fours and covered with a corrugated-iron roof. At sick call each morning, we usually saw not only our enlisted men but a number of natives, who were employed by the air corps for malaria control. To improve the deplorable mouth and skin conditions of most of them, I prescribed vitamins. The mouths they opened to receive vitamin pills were

The author's dispensary and ambulance, New Guinea, 1945

stained bloodred—from chewing betel nuts, I was told. After a time, some showed their gratitude by giving me gifts of beautifully crafted masks, spears, bows, and arrows. Recognizing their value, I shipped several pieces back home to the States. Unhappily, they never arrived.

Duties in the dispensary for our outfit were usually over in the morning, so I volunteered to do surgery at the nearby 51st General Hospital. Its O.R.'s were housed in semipermanent structures with wood sidings, screens, and corrugated-tin roofs. There were rows and rows of wards in vast tents, holding at least a hundred beds each. Although some of the beds were occupied by soldiers with routine medical problems, the majority were filled with the wounded. Some were not seriously injured and returned to combat. The more gravely wounded were treated until they were able to withstand the flight back to hospitals in the States.

We were kept busy by the large population of soldiers whom we cared for, attending to such emergencies as appendicitis, burns, injuries, and infections. Then, following a major battle in the Philippines, we would be deluged by the wounded, who arrived by plane and hospital ship, and we would work around the clock. Given the relatively crude operating conditions, the recovery rate we achieved was remarkably high. This reflected both the youth of the soldiers and the excellent frontline care given by those who were in immediate contact with them: the medical corpsmen and those at the battalion aid stations. The low incidence of infection could also be attributed, in part, to the fact that the soldiers, as well as medical corpsmen, had been trained to sprinkle sulfa powder into fresh wounds and cover them with sterile dressings. (Although penicillin was beginning to be used, it was not yet readily available.)

I never tired of accompanying an air corps senior officer each week as he walked from bed to bed in the huge wards for the touching ceremony of awarding the casualties Purple Hearts.

In Hollandia, my P&S and Memorial training turned out to be useful in another way. I sat through a meeting presided over by our commanding general, not knowing what it was about, and perhaps my attention wandered. But it was soon seized by the face of the general's sergeant, who was sitting beside him. There was a suspicious mark on the sergeant's cheek, on which I focused —and the result was an instance of what might be called a curbstone diagnosis. I persuaded him to have it removed. One of the results, the least important, was an introduction to the wonderful world of military citations.

That little action hardly needed or deserved all the military fuss and feathers that ensued, but it did provide a postscript in a letter to my parents. Many years later, being a good Samaritan would backfire. But for the moment, the military was pleased with me.

In a letter—I wrote to my parents regularly—there were other bits of local color, not all expressed in the language of diplomatic cables:

> Just heard that we bombed the daylights out of Osaka, one of the chief industrial cities of Japan, and so on until those bastards are enlightened the hard way. All sorts of estimates of when this thing will be finished over here run from Christmas of this year to Christmas of next year. Me, I give a good big damn but don't know. My guess is another 12 months from now, for which I will settle indeed. [Given that the letter was written on June 16, 1945, you can see that I was not exactly in on the secret of the atomic bomb.]
>
> I am sitting opposite Joe, the parrot, whom the boys have adopted and whom I am keeping for a nurse friend of mine to carry north with us when we leave. He is a riot of color and humor and likes nothing better than walking up my arm, sitting on my shoulder (so far only a few near misses; I'm lucky) and giving me a big horny-billed kiss. I guess I am Bill and he is Coo. . . . I keep reading books and surgical texts. We can buy grapefruit and canned orange juice for ten cents a bottle. Tomorrow of all things, they have a parade. So off we go in a dazzle of Atabrine yellow and khaki.
>
> Stay well, beloveds, and cool. I pity you the hot summer: no tourists down here, no Sunday drivers, no crowded hotels, no screaming babies, no crowded trains or hot pavements. Poor civilians. When are you taking your vacation and where?
>
> Your,
> Sojer

And I included the citation, knowing my parents would relish hearing this:

> At a recent visit to this office you recognized and called to the attention of one of my men, Sergeant ———, a cancerous growth on his face and recommended immediate medical attention. As a result, prompt action was taken and the growth successfully removed at the 51st General Hospital, probably saving the man's life. The medical officers of the General Hospital have expressed high

commendation for your interest and action in this case. Sergeant
———was evacuated to the U.S. shortly afterwards.

At his request, I wish to express his undying gratitude for your
interest in him and seeing that he received the prompt medical
attention necessary. I feel that the personal interest shown in the
welfare of this man—who was not seeking medical advice and who
was not a member of your organization, is outstanding and worthy
of the highest commendation—a credit to the Medical Corps of the
Army. Let me add to those of Sergeant ———my sincerest thanks
and best wishes.
Signed,
his Commanding Officer,
General ———

This was the first of several unasked diagnoses about which I
felt compelled to speak up and to warn unsuspecting individuals.
As we'll see, such unsolicited advice can be both rewarding and
humbling.

One day, making rounds at the hospital, I was introduced to
Louise, a blond and vivacious nurse, with whom I felt an immediate kinship, for she wore the pin of New York's Presbyterian
Hospital. I also met Billy Likoff, a Philadelphia cardiologist, and
his friend, a nurse named Alice. We soon formed a closely knit
foursome, and used to spend our evenings listening to music,
going to outdoor movies and to occasional parties, and even writing poetry. On our off-duty days, we explored hidden parts of
the jungle and at night went to "clubs" set up by the hospital.

One of the many advantages of being in the Medical Corps was
that ambulances could be used not only for transportation, but
also, where privacy was at a premium, as motels.

The American military population in New Guinea was made
up of 250,000 troops and nine hundred women—nurses and
WACs. The official rule was that commissioned officers could
date only other commissioned officers, which reduced the few
women companions available to enlisted men by about one-quar-
ter. (Nurses were second lieutenants.) Security regulations required that officers with dates would (a) have to carry an
automatic pistol and (b) go out with another couple. These measures were less for protection against any Japanese who still lurked
in the area and more to shield women from our own troops who
might be driven by desperation and lose control.

Proposals of marriage overseas occurred in epidemic proportions. Not only that, but the brides-to-be, although praiseworthy for having served their country, were often twice the age of their suitors. Nevertheless, they received anywhere from two to ten proposals of marriage per week. Before the situation got out of hand, our commanding officer mandated that all serious proposals must be reviewed and that no marriage could take place without the approval of the committee he appointed.

However, permission for certain marriages was automatically granted, of necessity. On these occasions, the four of us were often called upon to act as witnesses for a military wedding. "Military" in both senses of that word: it was of the shotgun variety. This usually involved a pregnant nurse or WAC, and her lover. Although dating between an officer and a noncommissioned officer was against regulations, love can find a way—or, *amor* can *vincit* not only *omnia* but the army, as well as its endless regulations. At one such wedding between a nurse and a sergeant in the medical corps, the bride's gown was fashioned by her pals from white parachute silk, the wedding music was played on a harmonica, and our commanding officer gave the bride away, as the chaplain of appropriate faith officiated.

Afterward there was a party, complete with Australian sherry, gin, and beer. For three days following the ceremony, the couple was given a "honeymoon tent" discreetly set aside from the others. Following this, the bride was shipped stateside and honorably discharged.

The groom remained where he was.

In one shipment of casualties from the Philippines, there was a group of injured Filipino civilians, including a woman with her infant. When the nurses saw that baby, the first they had seen for years, all their maternal instincts surfaced. That baby had fifty instant mothers. It was necessary to program the infant's care, they all wanted to do it so badly.

Once each batch of wounded was cared for and there was a lull between battles, we looked for ways to relieve our daily routine. From time to time, I flew to Australia and experienced the culture shock of going in a few hours from deep jungle to civilized society with its stores, hotels, good food and drink, and lovely ladies in dresses instead of khaki trousers.

On an inspection visit to one of our wing's squadrons in Sydney, purely by chance I read in a newspaper that Inga was engaged to a wealthy man in California. The article showed pictures of the happy couple. I was frantic, for although she and I had not made any promises about our future together, I had not only kept up a regular correspondence with Pam and with my parents, but a steady, affectionate correspondence with Inga. Somehow I found a way to send her a cable that read WAIT. THE WAR IS NOT FOREVER. LOVE, BILL. When I returned to Hollandia, I eagerly waited for a letter from Inga. There was none.

I was just about reconciled to this loss when she wrote that she had broken her engagement.

Some of our air force top brass patients arranged for me to visit the jungle mansion that General Douglas MacArthur had had constructed on a mountaintop in Hollandia. It required Seabees and their equipment to carve the miles-long road, and army engineers to construct a large, ranch-type house. When news of this extravagance leaked back to the States it raised eyebrows. However, what scandalized those in the army hierarchy was evident to those who stood on the veranda of MacArthur's house: A few hundred feet below were two small cottages separated a short distance from each other by an orderly pathway. One was occupied by an American lieutenant general, the other by his Australian mistress, whose husband was in the Australian army in India.

The Australian woman had been given a "field promotion" to lieutenant colonel in the WACs. When this tidbit reached Washington, the amorous general was recalled to the States and the lady stripped of her rank and returned to Australia.

One new diversion was provided by our commanding officer, Colonel Ray Elsmore. While looking for a shorter supply route from Australia to the Philippines to replace the long way, going around the eastern end of New Guinea, he flew across an area just east of sixteen-thousand-foot-high Mount Wilhelmina (now Trikora). On looking down, he saw a valley that the Dutch government map described as "Unknown Territory." Fascinated by the enormous number of terraces that ran up the sides of the eight-thousand-foot mountains rimming the valley, suggesting an ancient civilization, he pinpointed his position and, a few days later, flew some of us into the area. As we circled over the valley, we could see clusters of grass-covered huts; animals resembling pigs; and a river that had a bridge across it.* The welcoming committee

---

* Nelson Rockefeller's son, Michael, explored the area after the war and met his death at the mouth of the river that ran south through the valley and emptied into the Coral Sea.

was uninspiring: When we flew low enough to photograph them, natives who seemed at least seven feet tall flung spears at us. I named the place Shangri-La, and thereafter anyone who flew over it was given a diploma designating him or her a member of the Shangri-La Society.

Shangri-La became a favorite Sunday outing for many air force units. But one day a plane loaded with eight WACs and sixteen soldiers did not return. Dozens of planes immediately began a widespread search. Finally, the plane's wreckage was found on the side of a mountain, three thousand feet above the valley floor. There were only three survivors: two soldiers, and a WAC named Hastings.

All manner of supplies—including walkie-talkies, rifles, beads, and Kotex—were dropped by parachute. Chaplains were flown over the wreckage to say prayers for the dead. The story of the crash hit the world's news, and we were besieged by reporters.

To effect the rescue, gliders had to be brought in from other Pacific installations (there were no helicopters available then). As our units were unfamiliar with gliding technique, practice runs were made on how to "snatch" them up to get them airborne. Meanwhile, we heard from the survivors that a tribe of pygmies had walked in on them. Using sign language, the friendly pygmies indicated that they were in constant dread of the valley giants: They were headhunters. Philologists were fascinated by this group and recorded their dialect. The women of the tribe stirred restlessly and became something of a problem when the chief was too overtly fascinated by, and kept ogling, the blond Hastings.

After a bulldozer, a battalion of Philippine paratroopers, and a couple of Seabees had been dropped into the area, a landing strip was carved out of the jungle. Forty-seven days after the crash, a glider landed and, with the survivors on board, was picked up. As it took off, its bottom was ripped off by the underbrush, and the passengers had to straddle struts all the way. They were safely towed to our Santini landing strip in Hollandia. I waited for them with an ambulance and was relieved to see that they appeared to be in remarkably good health. WAC Hastings was shipped home and became the center of attention, which culminated in an article on her experiences that was published in the November 1945 *Reader's Digest*. Its title was "A WAC in Shangri-La."

In any war, there are constant narrow escapes. Medical officers are less likely to have these as a result of combat, but we had our moments. One occurred in Australia: Our B-25 was just about to land when an enormous cloudburst so drenched our wings that the weight of the water was forcing us to the ground short of the runway. Colonel Elsmore, a former air mail pilot, sharply banked the plane so the water slid off the wings, enabling us to regain altitude and wait for the weather to clear. In another, an unarmed C-47, in which I was returning from inspecting dispensaries and medical equipment of the wing's scattered squadrons, also had fifteen replacement nurses on board. The pilots, showing off their flying skills to the nurses, accidentally flew over a pocket of Japanese resistance near Wewak in northern New Guinea. The Japanese began firing at our lumbering plane, one that had a top speed of only 165 miles an hour. We made an agonizingly slow retreat and managed to get the hell out of there while, at the same time, radioing the Japanese position to a nearby fighter squadron. Within a short time, P-38 fighter planes appeared and began strafing the Japanese gun emplacements. It was too good a show to miss so we circled the area, watching and at times cheering. Then we continued on our way. We were twenty minutes short of landing when the pilot came back and asked if anyone aboard happened to have a monkey wrench: They needed to tighten a bolt to prevent hydraulic brake fluid from leaking out. We looked around as if they were crazy. Then, to everyone's astonishment, one of the nurses reached into her bag and produced a wrench. Just why she was carrying it was a mystery. I thought it was probably for self-protection. (Although everyone admired her, they would probably give her a wide berth thereafter.) The date was April 12, 1944: a date fixed in memory, for my sergeant, coming out to meet us in a jeep, said that President Roosevelt had died.

Oddly, the most harrowing episode of all occurred after our unit moved to Manila in the spring of 1945. The Pacific War ended in August, soon after the startling news that something called an atom bomb had been dropped on Hiroshima. Relieved of most of our responsibilities, some of us, including Billy Likoff and my friend, Louise, decided to take a trip to the now-famous Corregidor. We hitched a ride on a PT boat that carried us across Manila Bay, where we were sobered by the sight of the stacks of several sunken ships protruding from the water.

When we arrived, a sergeant in a jeep offered to take us to see some of the smoldering ammunition dumps and other places of interest. Louise, another officer, and I sat on the jeep's rear seat. We saw hundreds of Japanese prisoners barricaded into an area in front of the huge cave in which, three years before, U.S. troops had sought refuge after their historic march from Bataan.

As we were descending a steep road, the jeep began to accelerate at an alarming rate. The sergeant-driver yelled that the brakes were not holding. In his panic, we careened back and forth from the edge of the road, which bordered a dizzying hundred-foot drop into a wooded valley, to a steep wall with a drainage ditch. We could see ahead that at the bottom of the hill, the road took a hairpin curve high over the rocks in Manila Bay. We kept going faster and faster until, in desperation, the sergeant slammed the jeep into the wall. We overturned: The three of us, who were sitting on the top of the backseat, were fired like a salvo down the road. I can still see the ground rushing up to meet me, and recall trying to save myself by using the old football trick of rolling in the direction of severe impact. (A movie camera I had been carrying was apparently triggered as it whirled through the air and, when the film was viewed after the war, it showed a wildly gyrating landscape and a close-up of the road as the camera spun to earth.) After a dazed moment, and although my back hurt, I was able to get up and run toward the cries of Louise and the other officer, who had been flung forty to fifty feet down the road. Though shaken and severely scratched, they were, miraculously, not seriously injured. The driver, however, was in agony and lying beneath the overturned jeep, which was dripping gasoline on him.

Several soldiers who had witnessed the accident ran to help us, and together we lifted the jeep and extricated the sergeant. I commandeered a passing jeep for the injured man and me, and another for Louise and the other officer. When we reached the PT boat, we radioed for an ambulance to meet us at the dock. Racing across Manila Bay, Billy Likoff (who had not come on the jeep ride) helped me give what medical assistance we could with the PT boat's first-aid kit. A few hours later, at the 51st General Hospital, the sergeant had an operation for his dislocated hip.

In the midst of the excitement, I gave my back pain scant attention and, although it nagged me, in a few weeks it went away. I was to wonder, years later, whether a collapsed thoracic vertebra that was found on a lateral chest X ray could have been caused by that accident. But we had been lucky. We all, in a manner of speaking, walked away from it—and from the war.

The conflict over, all thoughts were directed one way: returning to the United States. Louise, Billy, and his nurse friend, Alice, had been overseas longer than I, so their rotation came earlier than mine. We had a tearful farewell as the three of them boarded a bomber that had been converted and refitted to carry military personnel back to the States.

I waited. There was still work to do, and I also went to the first concert given by members of the Manila Symphony Orchestra since the Japanese occupation. The musicians had been scattered during the war, but reassembled bearing their beloved instruments—violins, violas, cellos, horns, drums—which had been secreted, even buried, during the Japanese occupation. At this first postbellum concert, I sat enthralled. As I listened to Brahms and Tchaikovsky, I thought what a symbol, an expression, an affirmation this was of the power of beauty and of people's innate need for freedom of expression. Composers and musicians are spokesmen for the soul. The same feeling echoed forty-five years later, in 1990, when Leonard Bernstein conducted Beethoven's Ninth—"Peace"—Symphony at the Spielhaus concert hall near the recently demolished Berlin Wall. It, too, sweetly symbolized the triumph of the human spirit over brutality.

Finally, on Thanksgiving Day, 1945, I boarded an old Liberty ship, the S.S. *Latimer,* and sailed out of Manila Harbor bound for San Francisco. En route we were forced to stop several times when free-floating mines were sighted. Antiaircraft guns were fired at them until they exploded. At night, we wondered about the mines we could not see.

Mines were on my mind, but Inga was more so. I had the ship's radio operator send her the name of our ship and the approximate date that we would dock. A few hours before dawn on the day we were scheduled to arrive, a group of us collected about the ship's radar screen and saw the Golden Gate Bridge outlined about twenty-five miles away. On December 14, 1945, we entered San Francisco Bay. As we came into dock, a solitary figure was standing there. It was Inga. In this scene, she was a silhouette out of some sentimental wartime movie, and as I rushed down the gangplank, I gave in to the surge of feeling in that moment. If that script had been followed, she and I would have walked, arms around each other, into the sunset. However, a continent would soon divide us.

Inga had made a reservation at the St. Francis Hotel, where, for the first time in a year, I had the luxury of a hot tub bath (and room service).

The next day, Inga returned to Los Angeles and her job, and I boarded a troop train that took six days to cross America. I arrived at four A.M. at Fort Dix, New Jersey, where, within hours, I was officially discharged. It was four days before Christmas. In my one clean tropical-weight uniform, new major's leaves clipped to my collar, I took a train to New York. Although I had called Pam when we arrived at San Francisco, I did not know exactly when I would get to New York.

When Pam opened the door of our apartment, we embraced— and it was good, but it was the embrace of friends. In the days that followed, I wondered if we could salvage our marriage after the long separation, particularly with the adventures we had had apart from each other. It was peacetime, and New York was resplendent and festive for what would be like the first Christmas.

It was truly a great moment when, complete with hugs, kisses, and tears, I saw my father and mother again.

A few months later, there was another and a secret reunion. Inga came east to discuss "our future." This seemed a reasonable idea until we really confronted it. In the interval since San Francisco, I had become so caught up in work at Memorial that we had spoken only sporadically, and less and less frequently, by phone. Resuming my training and returning to friends and family and to a settled domesticity with Pam had given me (for a time) a semblance, an illusion of solidity.

Inga and I reminisced about our wartime love affair—then faced facts and the future. We talked frankly about the obstacles to our marriage. Inga had a well-established career, a home, and an elderly mother to take care of in Los Angeles; I had a wife and a three-year residency to complete, with a salary far too small to support us. In a particularly poignant moment, we realized that this was probably the last time we would meet.

As Inga and I kissed farewell, and not like old friends, I found myself haunted somehow by *Casablanca*'s theme song, "As Time Goes By." Even now, when I watch a revival of that classic film or hear the song, I see myself leaving her hotel room at the Plaza, and recall that long corridor outside, down which I walked not daring to look back.

Several months later, I read that Inga had married Tim McCoy, who was a popular cowboy movie star of the pre-war period. Each Christmas she would write, wishing me well, and she soon began writing about her two sons. Then we lost touch.

Years later, on the bitter cold day of John F. Kennedy's inauguration, while seated in front of the inaugural stand at the Capitol, I thought back on our meeting in Inga's apartment. Then he had been a young, handsome, brightly uniformed naval officer; now, almost twenty years later, he was on his way to being an inspiring president of the United States. I was touched, too, to hear Robert Frost reciting ("saying") his poetry, which brought back memories of my college years.

Some time later, I read that while JFK was participating in a Harvard commencement exercise, an FBI agent who had known him and had been one of those who listened to a wiretap conversation between JFK and Inga, was in a group watching the parade of dignitaries. As Kennedy passed, the agent whispered to him: "Whatever happened to Inga?" To which JFK muttered, staring straight ahead, "You son of a bitch."

So she continued to haunt him and, to an extent, me. In 1989, a television show about J. Edgar Hoover's reign as FBI director described in some detail the liaison between JFK and Inga. In it, a voice was heard, purportedly from a tape of their bugged conversations and trysts, a voice that could well have been Inga's. Photographs were flashed, of Kennedy and a woman who resembled Inga getting in and out of limousines.

In the August 1991 issue of *Mirabella,* an excerpt from a book about J. Edgar Hoover again dealt in some depth with JFK's and Inga's romance and featured a picture of her. The magazine's editor, my wife, had never heard me mention Inga up to that point, so I told her of our relationship.

As the article suggests, nothing was ever proved that justified the FBI's suspicions that she was a spy. Certainly, at no time had I any reason to believe this. To me, in places intimate or formal, she was a stunningly attractive woman who responded to men and they to her. In any case, I knew no military secrets. *She* was my secret.

Recently, when her name came up in a conversation between old, mutual friends of ours, they told me she had died in 1973. Of breast cancer.

Operation (Phase II)

The surgeon made an incision over the suspicious lump. Almost immediately, he encountered a grayish-white, gritty, hard area that was distinctly different from the soft, fatty breast tissue surrounding it. He excised a small sliver from it for a biopsy, placed it on a gauze pledget, and gingerly handed it to the rotating nurse. She wrapped the specimen in wax paper, labeled it with the surgeon's and the patient's names, and sent it by vacuum tube to the pathology laboratory.

Meanwhile, the surgeon stitched the edges of the small incision together, and in tying knots his fingers darted in and out, making a little ballet of their own—a pas des doigts. The wound was sealed with a colloidinlike liquid to prevent cancer cells from seeping through its edges.

Minutes later, through the intercom, the pathologist's "voice of doom" broke the silence. First, he asked for the surgeon by name, then announced: "The biopsy of the right breast of your patient, Jane Robinson, shows carcinoma."

The pathologist's verdict set several activities in motion: The surgeons changed their gowns and gloves lest cancer cells from the biopsy cling to them and be inadvertently seeded in the next incision. The patient was readied for a modified radical mastectomy; the rotating nurse removed the original drapes and repainted the breast and a wide area about it with antiseptic. When she redraped, she left a space about the breast, exposing the armpit. The patient's arm was wrapped separately in sterile bandages, so that an assistant could move it during the procedure to facilitate dissection beneath the pectoral muscles.

A much larger instrument tray than that used for the biopsy was rolled into place over the patient's feet. The instrument nurse stood in readiness; the surgeons returned to their positions; and I moved behind the surgeon.

Once again, just before asking for the scalpel, the surgeon turned and briefly glanced at me; then he began an elliptical incision started at the armpit and curving diagonally downward. The edges of the incision left a margin of skin around the nipple and the previous biopsy area. At its lowest angle, it stopped just short of the "V."

CHAPTER VII

The Surgeons

One week after Christmas, on January 1, 1946, my postponed dream was realized: I was back at Memorial to take up my interrupted residency—and I was thirty-one.

Coming back to the hospital was like returning to my family. Veterans were warmly greeted by those who, as a skeleton staff, had somehow managed to keep things running. For those of us who had been treating the acute, emergency surgical conditions of the young in the military, it took time to adjust to the chronic problems of cancer in the middle-aged and elderly. But we brought back with us at least two major innovations. One was penicillin, which was found to be more effective than sulfa drugs in treating infections. Because of its impact on a much broader spectrum of bacteria, it would be invaluable in reducing the hazards of major surgery. With such an ally, new surgical procedures, which otherwise might have been plagued by postoperative infections, were made possible.

The second innovation was revolutionary: Rather than prolong bed rest following surgery, it was found that early postoperative ambulation reduced complications, improved healing, and hastened recovery.

With the war behind us, we were anxious to make up for the precious time lost in our battle with cancer. One great war had ended; great ones lay ahead. We were caught up in a pervasive sense of optimism; a new era in cancer was beginning. Exciting ventures were begun in every discipline.

One phase of this promising new world was that cancer "came out of the closet." Newly arrived immigrants still held the old-country belief that cancer was an automatic death sentence and that therefore cancer patients must be shielded from their diagnosis. It was also customary for a family to conceal the diagnosis from the public for, like tuberculosis, cancer was considered to be somehow a stain on a family's reputation. It might be contagious, it was felt, so family members would be stigmatized and become social outcasts.

Gradually, through public education, such Old World attitudes were dispelled as it was learned that cancer was not uniformly fatal and, certainly not contagious. What is more, as awareness of its ever-presence increased and as it was more openly discussed in the media and elsewhere, the word "cancer" was used, rather than euphemisms or white lies.

With the removal of most of the subterfuge and secrecy that had been so carefully maintained by relatives (and physicians), patients were able to understand and participate in the management of their disease. Such openness was particularly necessary so that those who had to undergo extensive surgery and/or radiation and chemotherapy would know why these were necessary. It was an age when hope replaced despair, when no longer was it a question of *whether* cancer would be cured, but *when*.

Because surgical excision was still considered the most reliable method to cure most cancers, with new confidence born of advances in anesthesia, antibiotics, blood banks, and so on, previous limits of operability were being extended to include cancers heretofore considered inoperable and referred to radiation therapy for palliation.

Radiation therapy, nevertheless, still played both a therapeutic as well as a palliative role, and its effectiveness was enhanced by more powerful machines and more sophisticated techniques. As a result of these, penetrating beams could be delivered more effectively at the level of the cancer within the body with less damaging effect on tissues in the pathway of the beam. Radioactive isotopes, by-products by the atomic bomb research, provided new diagnostic and therapeutic methods.

Chemotherapy, the newest modality, held great promise and attracted a group of specialists who became known as oncologists.

Electronic microscopes unveiled submicroscopic details of morphology—cellular structure—and enabled researchers to study the cells' genetic makeup. Such studies would eventually lead to an understanding of why cells become malignant, so that one day it might be possible that by altering their genes, we could induce cancer cells to revert to a nonmalignant state.

Intracellular chemistry revealed that different cancers had different chemical ingredients, and this, too, added to our expanding knowledge about the subtle mechanisms of cancer formation.

Most important of all, cancer prevention was assuming a major role as more and more carcinogens were identified or detected in our environment. As these advances made headlines and the public became aware of the rising incidence of cancer, seemingly touching everyone's life, there was a surging enthusiasm for a cancer-prevention crusade.

I will always believe that instead of calling the latter half of the twentieth century the Atomic Age, we might well call it the Age of Prevention, for not only did a variety of diseases (such as smallpox, tetanus, typhoid, poliomyelitis, and certain childhood diseases) come to be prevented by vaccines, but also this was a time when the public became aware of man-made pollutants and their hazards.

The omnipresence of cancer influenced those responsible for funding; governmental and private sources loosened their purse strings for research.

These innovations and attitudes flourished and were being vigorously pursued at Memorial under the leadership of Dr. Cornelius P. "Dusty" Rhoads, then in his forties. Dusty was a vibrant personality and an energetic, enthusiastic, and knowledgeable scientist. Dusty was about six feet tall, with cropped, sand-colored hair and rugged good looks; he rapidly delivered his stream of ideas in an authoritative baritone. One could not help but be fascinated and impressed by his dynamic personality and by the way he was able to gesticulate, holding a cigarette between his second and fourth fingers (his middle finger had been amputated because of an uncontrolled infection).

Dusty had been Memorial's director for three years and in World War II became a colonel in the Chemical Warfare Service. During his military tenure, an event occurred that some consider to have had a decided impact on the future of chemotherapy. In 1944–45, our troops had moved up the boot of Italy's east coast. In the port of Bari, Americans had anchored several ships containing mustard gas for retaliation should the Germans resort to this tactic. A lone German bomber flew over Bari and jettisoned its bombs, one of which hit a gas-laden ship that then spewed mustard gas over the surface of the harbor. As the sailors who survived the initial explosion swam ashore, they absorbed some of it. Some died from injuries, others from the rapid, irreversible drop in their blood counts—particularly the white blood corpuscles—secondary to bone marrow depression. This phenomenon had been previously observed during World War I when mustard gas had been used as an offensive weapon. However, nothing was made of it at the time. After the Bari episode, specimens of the bone marrow of these sailors taken at autopsy were sent to Dr. Rhoads. He speculated: Perhaps, given the depression of the white blood corpuscles, mustard gas might be valuable in treating leukemia, in which there is a drastic increase in these blood elements.

A solution of mustard gas called nitrogen mustard was developed. The first clinical trials with nitrogen mustard took place at Yale, where definite, although transient, benefit was found—not, as expected for leukemia, but for cancers of the lymphoid system such as lymphosarcoma. Shortly thereafter, nitrogen mustard was tried at Memorial for a variety of cancers.★ In most of these, it had little or no effect. However, it worked dramatically, although briefly, on one type of lung cancer, small (oat) cell carcinoma, by shrinking the shadow in the lung X ray and any lymph-node metastases that could be observed in the neck.

This was an exciting concept for, up to then, the only chemicals used for cancer therapy were male and female hormones for treating breast cancers. To use an injectable, synthetic chemical was revolutionary. Nitrogen mustard in a modified form is still used, usually in combination with other drugs.

In the late forties and fifties I had my first glimpse of the future: Before my incredulous eyes, metastases melted and disappeared, treated solely by hormones and chemicals. These early, dramatic experiences occurred in individuals whose large lymph nodes and lung shadows, secondary to prostate cancer and a type of lung cancer (small cell), shrank and disappeared, often within a few days or a few weeks after treatment.

Up to then, treating advanced cancer had relied on radiation therapy and surgery, so that it was astonishing to realize that these

★ Its pharmacology—the dose and frequency of administration—was evolved by Memorial's Dr. Fred Phillips.

effects could be produced. Unfortunately, the benefits were short-lived, and recurrences resistant to chemotherapy soon appeared. Nonetheless, it was inspirational to see that even so transient an effect could be produced.

The question that has haunted oncologists for all this time is: If such a dramatic impact can be made on certain cancers, why are they not equally effective in others? Also, why didn't these cancers remain obliterated?

The current answer has it that we are not going to get a single, longed-for "magic bullet," but that in all probability, each of the 110 or so cancers will require its own therapeutic regimen. However, recent discoveries hold out promise that such elements as monoclonal antibodies, tumor necrosis factors, tumor-suppressive genes, and genetic engineering may open all doors at once.

Shortly after the war, by the sheer force of Dusty's personality and by the dangling of the bright promise of a cancer cure before his eyes, the then president of General Motors, Alfred P. Sloan, Jr., was persuaded to donate six million dollars to cancer research. Sloan, in turn, persuaded GM's head of laboratory research, Charles F. Kettering, to give matching funds toward building the institute that now bears their names.

Dusty found two kindred spirits in these philanthropists, whom he convinced that significant advances could be made by applying to cancer research the same sound principles that had been so effective in making better automobiles. Kettering, the inventor of the self-starter and no-knock gasoline, was a great advocate of "bench-level" research, the equivalent or analogue of science's basic research, to which the Sloan-Kettering Institute was devoted.

Each year thereafter, Dusty celebrated Mr. Sloan's birthday with a staff party. We would dutifully convene in the Rhoadses' penthouse apartment atop the Sloan-Kettering Institute. Some of us were designated to tell Mr. Sloan about our recent research. As he was very deaf, we had to speak in high decibels.

I had been doing research into some of the finer points linking cigarettes and lung cancer, so when Dusty asked me to describe my preliminary findings to Mr. Sloan, I spoke as loudly as I could. When I noticed that my colleagues clustered around the canapé table had fallen silent, some with lighted cigarettes held in mid-air, I realized that probably they were hearing this for the first time.

When I finished, Mr. Sloan remained silent, looked thoughtful for a few moments, then said: "You know, Bill, I'm in the automobile business"—this was like God saying he was in the religion business—"and before we started to use ethyl gasoline, I insisted that laboratory studies be done on animals to see if any ill effects resulted from its vapors. Those tobacco fellows should be doing the same."

(I was deeply touched when I saw he had tears in his eyes. Later, I learned that Sloan was easily moved to tears, and shed them at all sorts of occasions, even at GM's board meetings when a large profit was announced.)

Dusty's dream was to combine both clinical and research facilities under one roof to further an interchange of ideas between laboratory researchers and those dealing with cancer patients. If Dusty Rhoads had a major fault, it was that he was overly optimistic, a classic example of how a man's dreams and visions far outdistance immediately achievable reality. In a *Time* magazine cover story that fairly exploded with optimism, he was quoted as saying, "The cure for cancer is just around the corner." His was a forgivable sin, for his optimism was contagious and pervaded the institution, inspiring and stimulating all of us.

By the time Dusty died in 1959, at the age of sixty-one, of a heart attack—he had been a heavy smoker—several significant gains had been made. Although these fell far short of his ultimate goal of a cure for all cancers, his vision spawned many ideas that undoubtedly changed the direction of cancer research.

My father used to take me to the Polo Grounds (Yankee Stadium had yet to be built) in the 1920s, not so much to see the Yankees play as to see Babe Ruth in action. Each time the Babe got up to bat, I longed for him to hit the home run my father had promised me. As do all kids, I used to fantasize that the ball would land in the stands where we were seated. Time after time we returned and, each time he came to bat, I prayed for that golden moment. One day the Bambino did hit that homer, and he trotted around the bases on those improbably thin legs. After that, we never went back: Nothing could ever top that ecstatic moment.

As part of Memorial's three-year residency program, residents spent three months on surgical and nonsurgical services. While assigned to radiation therapy in 1947, I met my boyhood hero. The Babe was a patient of Dr. Hayes Martin and was receiving radiation therapy for a large, inoperable cancer at the back of his throat that was clearly the result of prolonged use of chewing tobacco, snuff, cigars, and alcohol. When the man came into the treatment room, dressed in a silk bathrobe, pajamas, and slippers, I could see that he was somewhat hunched over and that his beloved, round face had begun to show signs of wasting. When he saw my obviously awestruck look, he smiled and, as we shook hands, said, "Hello, Doc," in a hoarse whisper; the radiation treatments had begun to inflame his vocal cords.

Each time Dr. Martin or another one of us positioned Ruth on the radiation-therapy table, he would look up and smile gamely as we brought a hollow metal tube attached to the radiation-therapy machine to the side of his neck over a tattoo used to center it over the cancer. Then a technician and I would retreat behind the safety of a lead-lined booth to observe him through a window to be sure he did not move during the three minutes of treatment.

As I watched him on the table, I felt a sense of disbelief. There before me lay an idol of mine, now looking so vulnerable, like a big, bouncing baby boy about to cry. I was struck most forcibly by the sight of his ankles and legs protruding below his pajama trousers; they had always seemed such dainty supports for someone with such bulk. I kept recalling how the Babe, with characteristic little quick steps, scurried around the bases on that unforgettable day at the Polo Grounds when he hit one for my father and me.

About two-thirds of the way through the Babe's planned four-week course of radiation therapy, his wife, yielding to the influence of well-intentioned friends, decided to remove him from Memorial and put him under the care of a Dr. Gerson, who espoused a much-publicized anticancer diet. Mrs. Ruth was influenced by the praise for Gerson in John Gunther's book *Death Be Not Proud,* in which Gunther incorrectly attributed transient improvement of his son's brain tumor to Gerson's diet.

The Babe was such a famous figure that there was bound to be a great deal of publicity surrounding the fracas that ensued. Physicians at Memorial felt that the Babe was being taken from established methods of treatment to what was clearly a quack remedy. The Gerson diet was a strict one, eliminating certain foods and stressing coffee enemas several times a day. It had no proven scientific value. Gerson woefully misrepresented its virtues and cynically took advantage of those with hopeless cancer, who clutch at any straw. (Years later, after a peer review by the New

York County Medical Society, Gerson was forbidden to practice medicine.)

Under those circumstances, Hayes Martin refused to continue his care of Ruth. He felt that should there be any improvement from the radiation therapy that the Babe had already received, it would enhance Gerson's reputation. Eventually, Mrs. Ruth was dissuaded from keeping her husband under Gerson's care. However, because of the conflict with Hayes Martin, who was not the most diplomatic of men, the Babe finished his radiation therapy elsewhere and, some months later, died at age fifty-two.

I was spending every spare moment on the neck-dissection paper that was begun before the war, readying it for publication. Getting down to its final draft, I looked for other research projects. Haunted by my friend Morton's fatal and, I thought, preventable experience, I was sensitive to, and on the lookout for, any ill effects that might result from radiation, particularly that used for medical purposes.

In 1947, while I was a resident on the bone service, I chanced upon an idea. I brought it to the attention of the service's chief, Dr. Bradley Coley, my ally in the investigation at Sheppard Field during the war. Dr. Coley, son of Dr. William Coley, the founder of Memorial's bone service, was an amiable aristocrat who had pioneered several operations for bone cancer, particularly cancer arising in the pelvis. He had a genuine affection for his patients; they, in turn, adored him.

Dr. Coley was very receptive to the idea, one that had suggested itself when I saw a thirty-eight-year-old woman, a clinic patient, who was scheduled to have a forearm amputation for a bone sarcoma of the wrist. I noticed that the skin overlying the sarcoma was dry, depigmented, and scaly: changes typical of those following heavy radiation treatments. When she told me that in her late teens she had had X-ray therapy at that site for a benign bone tumor (a giant cell tumor), I wondered whether irradiation might have caused the wrist bone to become malignant. I remembered Henry S. Martland's famous report in which he described how women who painted tiny numbers on watch faces to make them glow in the dark would dip their brushes in radium paint and point them to a fine tip with their lips. Ten to twenty-five years later, many developed bone sarcomas, from which they died. Martland correctly deduced that each time they tipped their brushes, they ingested small amounts of radium, which were deposited in their bones and by continuously emitting radiation eventually caused sarcomas.

Although the patient's wrist bone had been exposed to *external* radiation, rather than radioactivity from within, the biological effects of the two on bone was probably the same. Like those of the dial painters, this patient's sarcoma had appeared years after exposure.

I reviewed the records of all patients at Memorial who had bone sarcomas and found that ten others had benign bone conditions treated by radiation therapy years before. After assembling the data from their charts, I was surprised to learn what broadly varying amounts of radiation they had received and what relatively low doses of radiation produced malignant changes. In the article I was preparing describing these findings, "before" and "after" X rays were included that showed how initially benign-looking bone lesions had undergone malignant transformation.

In 1948, I had just completed my last draft and the article was about to be submitted for publication, when suddenly, while operating, I felt a sharp pain in the region of my left kidney. I finished the operation, took an aspirin, and managed to get through the day. I attributed the pain to a blow in that region I had received the day before during a touch football game in Central Park.

The next few days, the pain was made tolerable by taking hot showers and more aspirin; it slowly subsided.

Then one night, while I was lying down, the pain returned, this time in my left upper abdomen. It was more severe than ever. When I probed that area, to my horror I discovered a tender mass! My imagination ran wild. An occupational hazard among those working in cancer is that any abnormal swellings they have must be malignant. Shakespeare's line from *Julius Caesar* can be paraphrased: "Cowards, [and physicians] die many times before their deaths."

I passed a sleepless night, during which I all but convinced myself that I had kidney cancer and went through the typical reactions cancer patients have when told their diagnosis: "Why me?" "There's so much left undone." "How will I ever allay my parents' grief?" Et cetera.

The next day, an intravenous pyelogram (kidney X ray) and a cystoscopy revealed that my left kidney was enlarged because the urine outflow was dammed up by a blood clot (probably from the touch football injury) that had lodged in a congenitally narrowed section of my ureter (the tube that leads from the kidney to the bladder). I was told that to save the kidney, I must be operated on without delay.

On the day of my operation, a lovely movie actress, Elissa Landi, was also having surgery. We lay on adjacent stretchers, waiting to be wheeled into operating rooms. Probably because my guard was down from preoperative medications, I told her at length of my infatuation with her. Later, as we were wheeled through the O.R. doors, we waved to each other and I wished her good luck. That ended the romance.

Fortunately, the surgeons were able to repair the narrowed area in my ureter and save my kidney. And I heard later that Elissa's cancer was successfully removed.

Postoperatively, a strange thing happened: I could not shake the morbid fear that I really did have cancer, that the truth was being concealed from me. After all, I had camouflaged the truth for patients; why shouldn't my doctors be lying to me? I was also haunted by an episode that had occurred a few weeks before: One of our younger residents had had a sudden abdominal pain, which was interpreted as a ruptured peptic ulcer. Dr. George Pack operated on him at two A.M. while a group of us stood around the edges of the operating room. To our horror, as his abdomen was opened, it was found to be loaded with pancreatic cancer. Dr. Pack, with all of us accompanying him, told the resident's young wife the grim news and suggested that it would be humane never to let him regain full consciousness. When she agreed, he was kept heavily sedated, and he died three weeks later.

Although this episode may have triggered my morbid anxiety, the feeling quickly disappeared when Demerol, instead of morphine, was used to relieve my pain.

My fright was a false alarm, but it gave me an inkling of what it must be like to have cancer. For a physician, particularly a cancer specialist, to develop cancer adds an extra, poignant dimension to the usual shock of realization. If the cancer is incurable, a doctor recognizes the all-too-familiar, ominous signs and symptoms of his own impending death. Sadly, a fair number of our staff members have died of cancer.

It has been said many times that surgeons should undergo at least one major operation to know how it feels to be a patient, to know at first hand what it is like to wait to be called for an operation, when minutes seem like hours. The experience would also give them insight into the many tedious preoperative details patients undergo, such as being shaved in the area to be operated on; antiseptic showers; enemas; sedatives; laxatives; taking nothing by mouth. Finally, they would get to know, as they are being wheeled on a stretcher to the operating room, how it feels to watch the ceiling lights go by and to wish that one were among the healthy orderlies escorting one.

My experience never left me. And I can say, with feeling, to patients who are about to undergo surgery: "I know how you must feel—for I, too, have been through fear, pain, and extreme self-concern. Like you, and countless others, I have endured boring hospital routines, postoperative pain, and sleepless nights inhabited by those unwelcome visitors, doubt and self-concern, while waiting endlessly for daybreak." Most of all, I learned the power of reassurance both before and after surgery and, in particular, what it means to lie on the operating table and have one's surgeon say a few warm words of encouragement.

During my first postoperative days, while I was still groggy from Demerol, one of my co-authors, Helen Woodard, a specialist in bone chemistry, read me the proofs of the bone sarcoma paper. She said that the first issue of the journal *Cancer* was being held up, as ours was to be the lead article. Dr. Fred Stewart, Memorial's chief pathologist, the editor of the journal and also a co-author of the article, hesitated to impose an extra burden on me at that time. However, Dr. Woodard told him that I would probably welcome getting this finished as I thought I was going to die anyhow.*

The article immediately became the subject of controversy. Clearly we had made few friends and influenced few people. Radiation therapists, in particular, felt threatened and were outraged enough to condemn the piece publicly, saying at one medical meeting I attended that "just instances" were not enough reason to curtail using "such a long-established and effective method for treating bone conditions."

In time, as more and more patients developed radiation-caused bone sarcomas, all skepticism and resistance melted away. Radiation therapy is no longer used to treat either benign bone tumors or other non-malignant conditions, such as acne, adenoids, bur-

---

* Besides Helen Woodard and Fred Stewart, my co-authors were Bradley Coley and Norman Higinbotham.

sitis, sterility in the female, enlarged adenoids in children, corns, warts, or women's facial hirsutism.

Because I was unable to carry out my resident's duties immediately following the operation, and because Memorial encouraged residents to spend two months of their residency visiting other institutions to observe techniques and attitudes about cancer, I decided to go to Philadelphia and Boston, the sites of some of the best thoracic surgery in the world. While there, I kept detailed notes and mailed them each week to my mentors at Memorial.

As chief cardiologist at Hahnemann Hospital, my overseas friend Billy Likoff worked closely with cardiac surgeon Charles Bailey. Bailey pioneered an intracardiac operation called commissurotomy, which was designed to free up scarred heart valves that had been narrowed by infection (rheumatic fever or subacute bacterial endocarditis). In those days, his operation had to be done with great rapidity, for it involved making an incision in the heart chamber, inserting a forefinger covered with a surgical glove to which a knife blade had been attached, and, within seconds, cutting the valve in the heart and closing the incision. These days, thanks to the heart-lung machine, which was devised in Philadelphia, the operation can be done more deliberately, at a leisurely pace and with fewer fatalities.

At Jefferson Hospital, the prototype of the heart-lung machine was being tested and refined. The machine would eventually revolutionize cardiac surgery by allowing the heart to be at rest while extracorporeal circulation kept the patient oxygenated.

During my stay in Boston, I revisited the Peter Bent Brigham Hospital, where I had seen my first operation thirteen years before. I also couldn't resist visiting my old haunts at Harvard and walking around Cambridge.

While there, I ran into my former music professor, Walter Piston, who had become a well-known composer. I told him that his teaching had not been in vain. During my time with "Winged Victory" Sergeant Zeke Manners★ and I had written such master-

---

★ Zeke Manners, who used to call himself the Jewish Hillbilly, had a successful radio program for years before World War II. He wrote the hit song "The Pennsylvania Polka," which was made famous by the Andrews Sisters' recording. Zeke played both the piano and sang the lyrics for the recording of "Fat Man Blues" for Victor Records. It begins with a Bach fugue–like string section, then the vocal part is sung in boogie-woogie rhythm.

pieces as "A Teardrop Fell Upon My Purple Heart"—a parody of sentimental war songs—and "Fatman Blues"—advice about how to lose weight. Amused, Piston asked me to sing the lyrics then and there, but I could not bring myself to put him through such an experience. This is what I spared him:

FAT MAN BLUES

Fat man, fat man, don't get the fat man blues
Fat man, fat man, don't get the fat man blues
All this eatin' is defeatin' your chance
Of ever gettin' any good romance, oh you,
You better lose or get the fat man blues.

Before you get bigger, and bigger, and bigger
Here's a menu that will send you
Here's a diet, better try it
On your figger.

Cut out potatoes and ya cut out the bread
Cut out the butter, eat the salad instead
Cut out the sugar
And ya cut out the cream
Cheatin' on your eatin'
Puts ya off the beam.

No more thisa and no more of that
You can't feed your choppers when
It puts on fat
Delete meat, shun that bun,
Them ice cream sodas *were*
A lot of fun.

Fat man, fat man, don't get the fat man blues
Fat man, fat man, don't get the fat man blues
I'm talkin' to you entre nous
Boy, when you get up
There's room enough for two, oh
You better lose or get the fat man blues.

Returning to Memorial, I was assigned to the breast service, headed by Dr. Frank Adair. Dr. Adair was tall, white-haired, handsome, robust, and genial. We residents called him the Great White Father. He had a huge practice and it was not unusual for him to schedule eight to ten breast operations a day, two or three days a week. Some of the growths were malignant, so three or four radical mastectomies might be done in a day, a number that most general hospitals might have had in a month. (Modified radical mastectomies and lumpectomies for cancer were not done then.) Adair's large patient load made it possible for us, his assistants, to learn a great deal about breast cancer and breast surgery. In order to complete his heavy schedule, Dr. Adair would move from operating room to operating room, greeting each new arrival and remaining at her side while she was anesthetized. Then, although he would usually begin the skin incision, he might leave the rest for us to complete if he felt we were capable of doing so.

On one occasion, while Dr. Adair was removing a benign breast tumor in a full-breasted woman, he broke a needle deep within the tissue. In the frantic search that followed, I learned what it was like to look for a needle in a haystack. In addition to our concern for the patient, and although the very litigious atmosphere of malpractice suits was years away, surgeons were sued for accidents of this type. I'm sure Dr. Adair could visualize a jury's reaction as they saw an X ray of a breast in which there was a clearly defined needle fragment. Desperately we searched for the needle. For a brief second, I spied its glistening tip, and with a forceps clamp grabbed and carefully extracted it.

I always felt that Dr. Adair's gratitude for this search and seizure played a part in his asking me to join the breast service when I finished my residency. He also asked if I would assist him in his office practice, a highly attractive and lucrative offer.

My next three-month stint was on the newly formed thoracic surgical service. Thoracic surgery encompasses the preoperative evaluation, operative management, and postoperative care of patients with pathological conditions of the chest. Specifically, at Memorial, it included the diagnosis and treatment of benign and malignant tumors of the lung, esophagus, mediastinum (the "middle place"—between the lungs), chest wall, and diaphragm.

Before 1946, thoracic surgery was done only occasionally at Memorial and was considered ancillary to the hospital's well-established services. The paucity of patients undergoing thoracic surgery reflected hesitancy by other physicians to recommend a modality that they felt was still very risky. For the occasional patient who needed such an operation, thoracic surgeons from other institutions were called in.

The service's first chief was Dr. William L. Watson. Dr. John Pool, a general surgeon, was the other staff member. Watson and Pool had just returned from active war duty and, although they had relatively little formal training in thoracic surgery, they quickly became experts. As thoracic surgery became safer and the incidence of lung cancer increased precipitously, physicians referred more and more patients for surgery, rather than for radiation therapy as they had done previously.

Up to then, as a medical student and as an assistant resident, I had had only a brief experience with lung surgery. Therefore, the three months spent on the thoracic service was a new, exciting adventure. Under strict supervision, I performed many of the standard major operations for cancer of the lung and esophagus, as well as for a variety of other chest tumors. Great demands were made on one's energy and time to ensure these patients' survival. In those days, there was no recovery room or intensive-care unit, so that following long and delicate procedures, even patients in critical condition were returned directly to their rooms. Special nurses were assigned to them for at least the first forty-eight hours, a critical period requiring the most vigilance.

Near the end of my three months' training, Drs. Watson and Pool asked me to join the thoracic service when I finished my residency. I accepted their offer instead of Dr. Adair's, feeling that although it was far less financially rewarding, thoracic surgery represented much more of a challenge. Already, I was filled with ideas on how to refine standard thoracic surgical procedures and was anxious to start on a variety of research problems that had suggested themselves.

Not everything at Memorial was unrelentingly serious or morbid. All august attendings can always use a dose of humor and humility. With this in mind, another resident, Lem Bowden, and I founded the Ibex Society. We chose the ibex, a species of mountain goat, as our mascot because "Although sure-footed as he climbs the highest peaks, the ibex occasionally slips and falls into the deepest ravines." We knew this to be true not just for them but for us and for our mentors as well. Members were elected not because they chose to be, but because they qualified by having made genuine blunders. There was one other proviso: The patients involved must have recovered, none the worse for wear.

The society met once a year, at which time each novitiate (and ultimately this included all the heads of the services) stood, wearing a Norseman's helmet with a set of protruding horns, and recited his or her transgression. Lem and I each qualified easily. But our stories were less interesting than others'. For example, one surgeon was operating on a patient with colon cancer who had been given a spinal anesthetic, so that he was awake during the procedure. The surgeon was of the school that believed that if any cancer cells were spilled accidentally while the cancerous section of the colon was removed, the cells would be killed by pouring ether into the open abdomen. He had done this many times before. But on this occasion, after pouring in the ether, he noticed that the patient's appendix was there for the taking. Thinking that it would be to the patient's advantage to remove it, thus avoiding appendicitis in the future, he did so. One of the conventional methods at the time was to seal the remaining "stump" of the appendix using a red-hot electric cautery. Suddenly the abdomen became a crater of flame as the ether was ignited by the cautery. In an instant, flaming sponges were being removed and frantically thrown every which way; it looked as if a fireworks barge had exploded. Instruments clattered to the floor as the water-filled basin in which they had been discarded was used by the frenzied nurse to throw water in the wound to douse the flames.

Meanwhile, on the other side of the screen that shielded the patient's head from the area being operated on, the patient could be heard sniffing. Then he said to the anesthetist, who was standing there wild-eyed, "I smell something burning."

To the eternal credit of the anesthetist, she did not respond, "That's not something, that's *you*."

Finale: Other than the singed eyelashes, eyebrows, and reputations of the surgeons, the patient never turned a hair and was not injured—and P.S., the cancer never returned.

In the late forties, Pamela and I were filled with liberal zeal. We had a number of black friends, including physicians. With Dr. Aubre Maynard, a prominent black surgeon, we organized a group called Democracy in Action that devoted itself to improving interracial relations and particularly the lot of black physicians, who, we felt, were being discriminated against by the medical establishment. As a group, we wrote and spoke to heads of various hospitals and also suggested that this sensitive subject be brought up at medical society conventions.

We met regularly, at first in small groups at our various homes, then, as new members joined, in hired halls in Harlem.

Although the impact of this group was small, nevertheless, as one of the several pioneering interracial projects at that time, it illustrated that when different ethnic groups communicate and act constructively together, walls come tumbling down. Several years later, Democracy in Action was dissolved when Aubre became chief of surgery at Harlem Hospital and my duties were too burdensome to allow me to take his place.

In the early fifties, it was gratifying to see that Memorial was one of the first hospitals to accept nurses and house-staff members from a variety of minority groups. One of the first blacks, a nurse, sat in one corner of the cafeteria by herself. However, one nurse after another took her under their wings, and soon she was an integral and equal member of the staff. Later, she would reassure new black interns that Memorial was a prejudice-free institution.

Frank Perry, a talented, handsome, dedicated surgeon, was one of the first blacks to enter Memorial for a surgical residency. Frank came from Tennessee, where there were still vestiges of racial discrimination. Young black graduates of "black" medical schools could obtain internships only at black hospitals. When Frank heard from friends that in 1949 we had taken our first black resident, Jack White, he applied. He admitted to me that he and his family were apprehensive about coming north, particularly to such a prestigious institution. His father, also a physician, advised him to keep a low profile while here. However, in no time at all, he found himself in such a warm, friendly, unrestricted environment that he could be himself. Because his "faith in democracy" was restored, after finishing at Memorial he wrote an article for the *Saturday Evening Post* called "I Rejoined the Human Race."

As other black residents joined the house staff, I made an effort to alleviate any shyness or self-consciousness that they might feel and to smooth out any awkward reactions that some white patients might have. However, what at first seemed revolutionary soon became routine. There were no awkward incidents and no one gave further thought about color or the backgrounds of our staff. Rather, the crusade against cancer was the dominant consideration.

During our three-year residency, as we proceeded from one service to another, we came in close contact (naturally) with each chief of service as well as with other attending staff surgeons. An attending physician or surgeon is an appointed member of a hospital staff who has privileges to admit patients to the hospital and supervise their care. Attending surgeons also supervise the training of the house staff, residents (or fellows) and interns who are at the hospital to be trained for their future in medicine. When house-staff members finish their training and start practice, many will want to become attendings at some hospital. One learned to deal with attendings' different and sometimes conflicting points of view. It was left to us to sort out and select those opinions that we considered the best.

Most chiefs had not only founded but headed their own special surgical services and were strong, dedicated, colorful, and, like other surgeons of that era, often autocratic. Each felt secure in his own domain, in which he wielded almost unassailable power and influence. By limiting themselves solely to the diagnosis and treatment of tumors of one anatomic region, they gained the advantage of honing their diagnostic and technical skills beyond those of general surgeons.

Unquestioned authority can breed arrogance and indifference, but most attendings were devoted to teaching and to their patients, whom they visited religiously every day. The house staff and students would meet them for rounds, and proceed floor by floor until the last patient had been seen. The procession had the chief at its head, with the chief resident at his elbow. Then, in order of rank, there followed the assistant residents, the medical students, and the head nurse of each floor, who held a book open, ready to take orders. We were included in any discussion and felt free to ask questions. We were also allowed to examine patients whose tumors were accessible.

In my third year, as chief resident, I was given increased responsibility both inside and outside the operating room. One of the benefits was to be the first assistant of the attending surgeons while they operated. Thus, in the tradition of surgical preceptorship, we learned at first hand many of the techniques that made their operations successful.

In the 1950s and 1960s, many chiefs had become preeminent in their special fields; some were world-famous. Dr. George T. Pack, chief of the gastric service, was one of these.

When I met Dr. Pack for the first time, he was in his fifties.

Bald, of medium height, he dressed as impeccably as he did surgery. He scurried, not walked, to see patients, in several hospitals. Pack gave off an aura of being a highly efficient perfectionist and although outwardly cool, he was not detached; he was friendly, but abstracted enough to discourage intimacy, yet always willing to teach younger physicians.

Pack had been a pathologist. In his late thirties he decided to become a surgeon and with only elementary training applied himself to refining his technique. All through my surgical life, I tried to emulate his meticulous attention to detail and exquisite craftsmanship. Although Pack's main interest was in gastric surgery, he operated on almost all areas of the body with equal facility and great style. Pack had an encyclopedic knowledge of cancer and had written the bible on the subject, so that each time I brought what I thought was an unusual case to his attention, he would say quietly, "That *is* interesting, Bill. If you look on page such-and-such of my book [*Treatment of Cancer*], you'll find that I listed ten of those in there."

As his reputation increased, many American and foreign surgeons visited his operating room to observe him at work. He attracted patients of prominence from America and foreign countries, particularly from South America.

As a consequence, in 1952, when Evita Perón was found to have advanced cancer of the cervix, Argentinian surgeons felt that they should get Dr. Pack's opinion, and that he should perform the operation. However, Evita Perón's dislike and distrust of America and Americans was profound, and her chauvinism extended to physicians. Wanting the best for Mrs. Perón, and insecure about their own ability to perform very radical surgery should it be needed, her surgeons consulted with her husband, Juan Perón, and devised a plan.

She was anesthetized on the operating table when Pack's plane landed in Buenos Aires. He was rushed to the hospital, performed an exploratory operation, found her cancer too extensive to be removed, and, leaving the abdominal-wound closure to others, flew off before Evita came out of anesthesia. She never knew that he had been there.

The fact that her cervical cancer had progressed to such a far advanced stage was probably the result of her own negligence. However, one wonders whether her physicians were in such awe of her that they had temporized rather than act forthrightly in its —her—treatment.

Shortly after Evita died, Juan Perón showed his gratitude to Pack by giving him a medal, six fine specimens of Argentinian cattle to add to his herd in New Jersey, and a superb automobile, a Maserati.

Pack had another experience with a bovine ending. He decided that the cows in his herd needed the services of a fine Scottish bull. At great expense, one was flown over. Shortly afterward, Pack's veterinarian reported that the bull had begun to lose weight because it had developed a tumor (adamantinoma) of its jaw and was unable to chew. The veterinarian felt that nothing could be done and the animal would have to be sacrificed. George refused to accept this. "After all," he said, "I *am* a tumor surgeon!" So he decided to operate on the bull himself. To do so, he would use the New York town house occupied by the Pack Medical Group. He transformed its large ground-floor sitting-waiting room into an operating room for the bull.

Early one Sunday morning, he assembled surgical assistants, nurses, an anesthetist, and a dental surgeon—who, after the tumor had been removed, would construct a prosthesis to insert into the bull's jaw to enable it to chew.

The bull was brought into the city by truck and led across the sidewalk into the waiting room, where all was in readiness. The anesthetist injected an intravenous anesthetic; the bull's eyes closed, its legs buckled, and it fell to the floor, presumably asleep. However, it was soon apparent that the bull was not just asleep, but dead.

Naturally, George was hopping mad; here lay not only his huge investment, but also a chance to make veterinary history. Now, instead, he had a major problem. It was one thing to lead a two-thousand-pound bull into a town house under its own power, quite another to get a dead bull out again.

This feat was accomplished by bringing in—what else?—a bull-dozer. The strategy devised was to tie a cable to the bull's tail (à la bullfight losers), pull it out of the building across the sidewalk, and lift it into a truck.

This was accomplished early one Sunday morning. You can only wonder what any passing churchgoers—or drunks—must have thought as they witnessed this unexpected example of throwing the bull.

One day, Dorothy Rodgers, wife of the composer Richard Rodgers, called to say that Dick was about to have surgery.

My wife Pamela had introduced me to Rodgers, who was a co-producer of *John Loves Mary,* the play in which she was appearing. Would I stop by and say hello to him?

Rodgers had "smoked himself" (two to two and a half packs a day) into a large cancer in the floor of the mouth and jawbone. (At the time, he was working on a new musical.) To remove the cancer, Dr. Hayes Martin performed a "commando," oncospeak for the *com*bined removal of a portion of a *man*dible (jawbone) together with a part of the floor of the mouth and lymph nodes in the neck that drain the cancerous area. Rodgers gallantly adapted to the resulting deformity. When I visited him afterward in his room, I found him putting the finishing touches on the score of *Me and Juliet.*

Years later, Rodgers developed a new primary cancer of the vocal cords, also smoking-related. He bore this handicap gracefully, learning to talk with an "esophageal voice"—that is, producing reasonably audible speech by swallowing air and burping it forth, forming words.

In keeping with Memorial's plan to explore the value of more radical cancer surgery, Dr. Alexander Brunschwig was invited to head Memorial's gynecology department in 1947. Dr. Brunschwig had built a reputation in Chicago by operating on cancer patients other surgeons deemed to be inoperable. Most surgeons considered Brunschwig to be "super radical," even foolhardy and reckless. Yet, to their astonishment, there were long-term survivors following some of these extensive operations on those who would otherwise have died.

Brunschwig was in his mid-fifties when I first saw him. He was obese, bespectacled, broad-featured, of medium height. What distinguished him, among other things, was the preoccupied, bemused air with which he made rounds; it made him seem unaware of us trailing behind him. However, when he talked with patients, he became theirs alone, speaking in a gentle, quiet voice that was a balm to their worries. We hung on his words, for they often contained distilled droplets of wisdom. One of his phrases that residents especially cherished usually occurred while we were operating with him. If one of us made a move that he did not like, he would stop operating, lay his hands gently on top of ours, look us firmly in the eyes, sigh and say, almost in a whisper: "Poor—and *zero.*" No more telling rebuke existed.

Brunschwig was symbolic of a new era in cancer surgery. Certain cancers that up to then had been "inoperable" were now viewed with the idea that modern advances in parasurgical techniques and support systems might make them candidates for surgery: Improved monitoring of patients under anesthesia; broad-spectrum antibiotics; multiple transfusions; refined preoperative and postoperative care; and many other innovations encouraged surgeons to undertake more extensive and riskier operations. With new confidence, surgeons removed cancer involving the pelvic bones; portions of the tongue and jaw; the ribs and vertebrae; and sections of the liver.

Memorial's staff selection committee believed that Brunschwig's aggressiveness and expertise might resolve a serious gynecologic problem of the day: uncontrolled, extensive cancers of the uterus that were either far advanced when first seen, or had recurred locally following surgery and radiation therapy. Although it was understood that, in all probability, the majority of these cancers would eventually kill the patient by metastasizing to distant organs, nevertheless, for an as yet undetermined reason, some did so slowly. As a result, these cancers remained localized at the site of origin and eventually broke through the skin to become bloody, bulky, painful and putrescent. Such situations were considered hopeless, yet some patients lingered on in an agonizing state for many months. Brunschwig felt obligated to explore methods to palliate them. On their part, these hapless patients welcomed any method, even distorting, risk-laden surgery, if it rid them of their awful burden.

When such bulky cancers occur in the pelvic area, they often invade the nearby urinary bladder and colon, so that all or sections of these organs had to be removed in order to maintain a safe margin of noncancerous tissues around the cancer. As a consequence, operations had to be devised that were more radical than any previous ones. Surgery of this magnitude that removed pelvic organs could take many hours to complete, and taxed the surgeon's ingenuity to reconstruct the "plumbing" essential for survival.

To young, eager surgeons, participating in new, uncharted, and often unorthodox surgical adventures made any fatigue or strain we felt seem inconsequential. As never before, we had to draw upon all our training and improvisational skills to help bring these patients back alive.

At first, not unexpectedly, these operations had high mortality and morbidity (complication) rates. But as modifications were made, these rates diminished and, given the magnitude of the procedures, were considered to be "acceptable."

The majority of those who survived these operations lived for months; a few, for years. When requested to do so, those who had good results would be asked by Dr. Brunschwig to make personal appearances at medical meetings, usually peopled by skeptical surgeons, and to describe the dramatic improvement surgery had made in the quality of their lives.

Brunschwig's surgical techniques often bordered on the outrageous and sometimes made even the most sophisticated observers' hair stand on end. Nevertheless, his philosophy of surgery, particularly his courage, stood me in good stead later when I, too, was to initiate new ideas. One must expect to bear the pain of the pioneer and persist in the face of nay-sayers, to weather skepticism, if one believes in what one is doing.

I learned, too, that compassion has many faces. It is more readily accepted and understood when, for example, an Albert Schweitzer devotes himself to the care of lepers or a Mother Teresa helps starving, homeless Asians. However, it is less appreciated when a surgeon performs a deforming surgery to relieve suffering, hoping to at least palliate, if not extend, life.

Although initially strongly condemned for his "exercises in futility," Brunschwig remained unruffled and eventually convinced many skeptics who had serious reservations that, in selected cases, such measures had value. In time, even conservative surgeons adopted certain of his techniques, thus fulfilling the aphorism that today's radical surgery is tomorrow's standard procedure.

As a result of earlier diagnosis and better treatment, horrendous cancers have become uncommon, so that such very extensive surgery is rarely needed. Reliance is placed more on chemotherapy, radioactive seeds, and cryosurgery, plus antibiotics. In time, the need for such radical surgery will vanish and a dramatic era in the history of surgery will pass.

❖

CHAPTER VIII

Private Practices

Near the end of my residency, I made preparations for entering private practice. Because of the extensive training provided by war as well as by Memorial, I was not apprehensive but was eager to apply all that I had learned to patients of my own. Customarily on such occasions, a physician has hundreds of cards printed with his name, address, telephone number, and specialty. These are sent to friends, relatives, colleagues, mentors, *anyone* who could possibly provide a referral. In those days, that was almost the only form of self-advertising not frowned upon—a marked difference from today, when some physicians advertise their specialties on radio and television, in classified telephone directories, and in newspapers. One other form of advertising was allowed: At a party, my father presented me with a brass shingle on which was engraved WILLIAM G. CAHAN, M.D.

Pamela and I rented the top two floors of a hospital-owned brownstone at 226 East Sixty-ninth Street for seventy-five dollars a month. The lower two floors were occupied by Dr. and Mrs. Allen O. Whipple. Dr. Whipple, my former professor of surgery, had become director of surgery at Memorial in 1947, following his retirement from Columbia-Presbyterian Hospital. It was Dr. Whipple who was assigned to observe and evaluate me while I performed a radical mastectomy as part of my qualifying examination to become a diplomate of the American Board of Surgery.* These on-the-scene examinations were used to grade a candidate's technical ability; they are no longer required for board certification.

Dr. Whipple was a blade-thin, handsome man with steel-blue eyes and bushy white eyebrows. During the two-hour procedure, he stood silently by—an éminence grise—as I worked away. To have as an observer my former professor of surgery—and one of the most prestigious surgeons of our time—could have served as a distraction but, as soon as I began, I was no longer conscious of his presence. I had no idea whether my work was satisfactory.

Apparently Dr. Whipple must have approved for, after having taken written and oral examinations, I was notified that I had passed.

Red-letter day! On January 2, 1949, nine and a half years after earning my medical degree, I began my practice. Memorial provided a cubbyhole of an office, which I shared with my friend Henry Diamond and our mutual secretary. It consisted of a tiny consultation room, an examining room, and a secretary's cubicle. This was Memorial's first in-hospital office set aside for private practice.

Although I had been appointed to the staff of two other hospitals—Manhattan Eye and Ear, and St. Barnabas in the Bronx—I rarely used them for my patients, content instead to confine myself to Memorial. By conserving time and energy this way, I would be able to teach and do research as well as practice.

Henry Diamond was one of those precious individuals whom Nature meant to be a physician. He was an internist who specialized in lymphomas—cancers of the lymph and blood-forming systems, such as lymphosarcoma, Hodgkins's disease, leukemia, and so on. Henry had first come to Memorial in 1945, while he was a medical officer in the navy, where it was discovered that he had Hodgkin's disease. In those days, H.D. (in a grim coincidence, his initials) was treated solely by radiation therapy directed at the Hodgkin's disease–containing lymph nodes in the neck and chest. Henry had an unusually excellent response: All of his enlarged lymph nodes disappeared. However, he was well aware

---

* Each specialty has its own board: surgery, internal medicine, gynecology, etc. Candidates must receive a minimum amount of postgraduate training in the specialty, following which they must pass rigorous written and oral examinations. In my case, it was six and a half years plus the three years in the air corps.

that, although one may be in remission, Hodgkin's disease, like a bomb, can explode at any time, even years after seemingly successful treatment.

Henry received a medical discharge from the navy because of his disease. Dr. Lloyd Craver, who had treated Henry, asked him to join the lymphoma service as an attending physician. In time, both Dr. Craver and Henry became world-class authorities on lymphoma and wrote classic papers on the subject.

Like that of most young surgeons entering practice, mine was slow in starting. I was most grateful when my elders threw me a bone—that is, referred an easy case. Other referrals came through friends and relatives or from patients who applied on their own to the hospital for care and were assigned to a staff physician by rotation. As these were few and far between, to ease my financial burden I operated on an occasional breast cancer patient.

My first months were lean times, my monthly income averaging $350, from which I paid $50 a week to our secretary. Fortunately, Memorial also provided its new staff members with a modest stipend to encourage them to do research and to teach. Gradually, all too slowly, my practice increased as the reputation of the thoracic service grew, and the incidence of lung cancer increased. I became better known through medical writings and lectures, and patients also referred others to me.

I was soon faced with a major challenge: to devise a method to remove a two-by-four-inch cancer from the lower end of a nineteen-year-old man's trachea. The cancer lay just above the carina, the area where, like an inverted "Y," the trachea divides into the right and left main bronchi. It had begun to obstruct his breathing and cause copious amounts of blood-tinged sputum.

This was both a rare location and a rare type of cancer. I studied reports by surgeons who had dealt with somewhat similar situations. The methods they employed seemed risk-laden and primitive, so I developed my own approach.

With the patient anesthetized, a longer than usual endotracheal anesthesia tube, with an inflatable balloon near its end, was passed into his windpipe. The patient was turned right side up and a long skin incision was made, beginning at his vertebrae and extending below his wingbone (scapula) to his breastbone. I removed a sheet of fascia—tissue enclosing the chest muscles—that would be used in repairing the defect in his trachea once the cancer had been excised. The fascia was flattened out and attached to a three-by-four-inch fly screen–like piece of stainless (tantalum) steel mesh that would act as a support for the pliable fascia, preventing it from collapsing into the trachea and narrowing the passage.

As the chest cavity was entered, the anesthetist deflated the right lung so that the tracheal cancer could be seen. Leaving a margin of a few millimeters for safety, an incision was made beginning just above the cancer and continuing around it until it was removed. This left a gaping hole in the trachea, through which the tip of the anesthesia tube could be seen. The anesthetist deflated the balloon so that I could guide the tube into the opposite —left—main bronchus. Once there, the balloon was reinflated, making the left lung the sole source of the patient's oxygenation. As I began to sew the graft over the tracheal defect, oxygen leaked around its edges: The balloon in the opposite bronchus was not a perfect seal. The patient was not getting his full supply of oxygen. To remedy this, I covered the hole in the trachea with my finger while the anesthetist squeezed the anesthesia bag to give the patient a few quick respirations. Then, for a few seconds, I took my finger away and rapidly placed a few stitches. The anesthetist and I developed a rhythm: I said, "One breath for you [finger in place]; one stitch for me [finger removed]" until the patch was neatly sewed.

To test the airtightness of the closure, saline solution was poured into the chest cavity, enough to cover the graft. When the anesthetist squeezed the anesthesia bag, and no bubbles appeared, the closure was considered secure.

When the patient returned to his room, I virtually lived at his bedside for hours. Only when he stabilized did I feel secure enough to go home. But each time the phone rang, I was sure the resident was calling to say that something had gone wrong. However, the patient did well and left the hospital on his tenth postoperative day.

Two years later, in 1952, I submitted an article to the *Journal of Thoracic Surgery* describing and illustrating the operative technique. Dr. Evarts Graham, renowned for having done the first successful removal of a lung for cancer, was the editor of the journal. Therefore, I was particularly pleased that it was he who wrote the letter accepting my paper for publication.

The patient later married, had a daughter, and became my stockbroker. Forty-two years later, he is still cancer-free.

Had today's techniques been available, the risk and the drama of this operation would have been markedly reduced. The heart-lung machine (the embryonic form of which I had seen in Phila-delphia in 1948) would have allowed a leisurely repair of the tracheal defect. Also, instead of a metal mesh, rigid plastic material called Marlex would have been used to support the graft.

Soon afterward, an eighty-year-old woman was referred to me whose thyroid cancer had invaded a segment of the trachea in her neck. Ordinarily, because of the cancer's location, it would have been necessary to remove her larynx. Considering her age and infirmity, it would have been difficult for her to learn to speak by swallowing air and bringing it forth in order to produce audible words. Because she had severe deforming arthritis of her hands, she could not use the alternative, a battery-operated buzzer that, when held just beneath the jawbone, made sound that was trans-mitted into the oral cavity and could be used to form words with the mouth and tongue.

As the cancer had invaded one side of the tracheal wall, I used a technique similar to the one devised for my other patient to repair the defect once the cancer was removed. Almost immediately after the operation she was able to talk.

News of these patients crossed what was tacitly acknowledged to be an invisible barrier between Memorial and the Gothic cathe-dral–style façade of New York Hospital. Just why these two in-stitutions, barely a hundred yards apart across York Avenue, stayed detached from one another was unclear, but from the time Memorial moved to its new quarters on Sixty-eighth Street, New York Hospital's staff and administration seemed to distance them-selves. This was particularly odd because Memorial's staff mem-bers were listed as faculty members of Cornell University Medical College, an integral part of New York Hospital. It was, therefore, a pleasant surprise when I was asked to give a lecture at the med-ical college on the diagnosis and management of tracheal cancers.

For some reason, I had assumed that my talk would be held at a small conference of thoracic specialists, and would be followed by an informal discussion. However, meeting with my host one Saturday morning, I was ushered into the huge Uris Auditorium, with tiers of seats packed with faculty and students, and led to a seat in the first row. The program was already in progress. I remember thinking as I awaited my turn: *This must be a bad dream from which I'll awaken,* for it was clear that the audience was ex-pecting a formal presentation! What *was* I going to say?

Soon I was introduced and, as I stood looking up at a sea of faces, I improvised by defining the anatomical limits of the trachea, beginning at the voice box. Meanwhile, hoping my own vocal cords would not fail, I moved to safer ground and talked about the pathology of tracheal tumors and the techniques used to remove them. Even today I can relive the anxiety of that moment, which for me could be compared to a nightmare in which I was being presented at Buckingham Palace, somehow having forgotten my trousers.

When I finished and had answered several questions, the conference ended. Mingling with the medical students in the hallway, I thought: *Whatever value my lecture may have had, it demonstrated undeniably that ideas cannot be restrained behind walls*—or, in this case, by a stoplight on one side of York Avenue. It seemed to be a decided flaw in Cornell's medical-school curriculum to deprive students of the wealth of teaching material that MSK could provide.

I did two things. Remembering my Memorial experience as a student, I inaugurated an annual Cancer Teaching Day, during which third- and fourth-year medical students would hear selected subjects discussed in depth by MSK's staff.★ I used my research funds to pay for the day's activities, including lunch.

After several teaching sessions, Dr. Laird Myers and I met with Ted Cooper, the dean of the medical school, to explore the feasibility of weaving Memorial's treasure trove of teaching material into Cornell's curriculum, and this was inaugurated. (At the time, I did not foresee one of the advantages of such an arrangement: Years later, my son would spend time in his third and fourth year at MSK.)

Several months into practice, I operated on my first private lung-cancer patient. The day after his left lung was removed, just as I entered his L-shaped room, I stopped and did a massive double take: There, sitting in a chair, dressed in a business suit and reading a newspaper, was my patient!

Back then (although today we get patients out of bed as soon as possible after surgery) this was clearly extraordinary, for he should have been in bed, attached to tubes. Taking a few more steps, I glanced in consternation around the edge of the wall and saw to my relief my patient, lying in bed.

★ Dr. Laird Myers, an assistant dean at Cornell Medical College and a staff member of MSK, helped organize these sessions.

I had forgotten that he was a twin. No more uncanny resemblance ever existed. Like their friends, I had mistaken one for the other, although "my" twin's wife assured me that she could always tell which one was hers. I never asked just how.

Identical twins are of great interest in cancer research. Theoretically, by sharing a similar genetic makeup, they are both predisposed to developing identical cancers, perhaps in mirror-image locations. However, in this situation, only one twin developed lung cancer. I noted that he smoked; his brother did not. Unfortunately, a few years after surgery, the patient's cancer spread to his brain and he died. Through the years, we maintained constant vigilance on his twin, warning him to avoid chemical inhalants and, of course, not to smoke. He was also told to have annual chest X rays. More than forty years later, he has not developed cancer.

The spread of the twin's lung cancer to his brain was not unusual. Up to the late 1940s, most brain metastases were considered to be untreatable. On occasion, if only a single metastasis was present, and if it was on the surface of the brain, an enterprising neurosurgeon might remove it. At the time radiation therapy to the entire brain had just begun, but although my patient was treated, his cancer failed to respond.

The fact that he received radiation therapy to his brain went back to an earlier experience I had in 1949 with a fifty-six-year-old insurance executive whose lung cancer had been successfully removed by surgery. A year later he began having difficulty adding and subtracting numbers. What is more, an avid crossword puzzle fan, he could no longer insert the letters accurately in their boxes. Soon these symptoms were followed by headache, slurred speech, and some difficulty in walking. Those around him noticed that his personality changed from outgoing and cheerful to taciturn and moody. He became bedridden and had to be admitted to the hospital on a stretcher. Neurological examination and electroencephalogram (there were no CAT scans then), confirmed that he had multiple brain metastases. As there was no evidence that his cancer had spread elsewhere in his body, and he had deteriorated to incontinence, I felt that nothing could be lost by irradiating his brain. Perhaps his cancer might be radiation-sensitive; besides, there was nothing else to offer. (This was before chemotherapy, too.)

Because the man was not mentally responsible for making such decisions, I obtained his wife's permission. After two treatments, his neurological symptoms worsened and he became comatose. Nevertheless, we continued treatments, for the initial effect of large doses of irradiation, I knew, is to make cancers swell— which exaggerated his symptoms. After the fourth treatment, he regained consciousness. On treatment days five and six, he began to eat and move about. Soon control of his natural functions and unslurred speech returned, and ten days after the treatments began, he walked.

As his personality and cerebration returned, one of the first things he asked for was a crossword puzzle. This became a graphic measure of his improvement, for he was eventually able to solve the clues as well as make the fine motions necessary to insert the answers neatly. Watching his recovery was like watching evolution on a speeded-up film. It seemed miraculous to see someone who had been incoherent, immobile, a "vegetable," return to normal memory, speech, and intellect. Although he lost his hair as a result of brain irradiation, most of it returned months later, at first as a kind of benevolent peach fuzz.

He left the hospital under his own power and, a few weeks later, returned to his job.

This startling success did not last; eleven months later, the cancer spread to his liver and he died. Still, this patient's dramatic response to brain radiation made me wonder if it could be used to treat brain metastases from organs other than the lung. (I was unaware that *total* brain radiation had been reported in an obscure European journal.) Anxious for the idea to be given a broader application, I presented my patient's history at an in-hospital radiation-therapy conference. Following that, brain metastases from a variety of sites were treated and a fair number of patients benefited, some dramatically. When the radiation therapy department reported their results, whole-brain radiation for brain metastases became accepted practice.

As experiences with it accumulated, two problems remained: First, in spite of the heavy doses of radiation, not all brain metastases responded; second, those patients whose metastases did respond and who were fortunate enough to live for four or five years recurrence-free developed varying degrees of intellectual deficits. As a result of this belated aftereffect, the initially high radiation doses were reduced without interfering with the treatment's effectiveness and with fewer subsequent neurological difficulties.

One other refinement has since been made: to prevent the exaggeration of symptoms that initially occurred with my patient and with many others receiving their first brain-radiation treatments, large doses of cortisone are given a day or two before. Often cortisone is so effective in shrinking the cancer that the patient's neurological symptoms dramatically lessen and even disappear almost overnight. However, such an effect is only transient and must be supplemented by more radiation therapy.

During my residency, an idea had occurred to me that was a natural outgrowth of my training. I was taught that it is an established principle that when a cancerous organ is removed, accessible lymph nodes draining that organ should also be removed. Lymph nodes, present throughout the body, are oval or round fleshy filters that are connected to each other and to nearby major organs by lymph channels. Lymph nodes function as "pillboxes" of defense against infection, to which they react by becoming swollen and tender; almost everyone has experienced "swollen glands" in the neck secondary to a sore throat or tonsillitis. Lymph nodes are also likely to be the sites of secondary deposits of cancer from a nearby cancerous organ. Cancer surgery takes this possibility into consideration; for example, when a breast cancer is removed, lymph nodes in the armpit are also included. The same principle applies in colon, stomach, and uterine cancer, among others. However, up to 1949, lymph nodes present in the mediastinum (the middle place between the two lungs) were not included with a removal of lung cancer by pneumonectomy (removal of the lung).

All the pathology textbooks I consulted said that when lung cancer spread locally beyond the confines of the lung, it most often did so to lymph nodes in the mediastinum. I went next to consult anatomy textbooks to see if it were feasible to extract these nodes without threatening nearby vital structures. I performed "dry runs" of an operation I was devising, on cadavers at nearby Cornell's anatomy lab.

Confident that the rationale and feasibility of this new technique warranted a trial, I added this more extensive lymph-node removal to the standard lung-cancer operation. At first I moved slowly and gingerly, but as I became more expert, I found the extra lymph-node dissection took approximately thirty minutes' more operating time to complete. Happily, no complications or operative deaths attributable to this new procedure occurred.

I named the operation radical pneumonectomy, using the adjective "radical" to modify "pneumonectomy" because it is onco-speak for the surgical removal of a cancerous organ with its regional lymph nodes. For example, a radical mastectomy—modified or classical—means the removal of a breast together with lymph nodes on that same side; a radical hysterectomy, the removal of the cancerous uterus and the lymph nodes in nearby tissues. Within a year or so, thirty-nine radical pneumonectomies had been performed.

When these lung-cancer specimens were analyzed, one in three had metastases in the mediastinal lymph nodes. Such a finding is an index of the aggressiveness of the original cancer and carries a poorer prognosis than if the lymph nodes were found to be cancer-free. In addition, a finding of "positive" lymph nodes can mean that the cancer has spread elsewhere in the body, thus signaling the need for adjuvant (subsequent) radiation and/or, in later years, postoperative chemotherapy.

In time, I felt that the operation was worth reporting. In preparing an article, I summarized each patient's clinical details: his or her age and sex; the size, location, and pathological type of the lung cancer (there are several varieties); and, in particular, whether the mediastinal lymph nodes contained metastases. Although it was premature to list results from the procedure, some patients with positive lymph nodes had survived, without recurrence, for up to a year.

One of the rewards of research is the pride and satisfaction a scientist feels in making a contribution. Besides, as a novice, I was eager to make a name for myself in the scientific community. Reporting on thoughtful, original research was the time-honored way of doing so. As this operation was a novel approach that might have curative as well as prognostic value, and had not been associated with any ill effects, I was excited to think it might be an important contribution.

But, I asked, was my idea truly original? After all, what seemed so obvious to me might already have occurred to others, particularly as most thoracic surgeons had been doing chest surgery much longer than I. Did I have a clear claim for priority?

Somewhat apprehensively, I searched the medical literature under the heading "Cancer, Lung, Operations for" but could not find any references to the term "radical pneumonectomy" nor did I find in the many articles on lung-cancer surgery a procedure similar to the one that I had devised.

It is one thing for a physician to do research, another to describe the results clearly in writing. Many doctors find it difficult to convey their ideas and findings in the formal, terse language required by medical journals. I was no exception. However, the possibility that this could be a significant contribution made me labor long and hard until I finished the article. As the step-by-step operative technique was a major part of the article, I not only described it in words, but also commissioned an artist to illustrate each step. In this way, those who wished to perform a radical pneumonectomy could do so by following both the written and graphic instructions.

Before submitting the paper, I thought it respectful, practical, and polite to show it to Dr. William Watson, chief of the thoracic service, for any suggestions and criticisms. He was a member of the society before which I hoped to present my data. As a non-member, I needed an invitation by a sponsor to do so.

Dr. Watson read and approved the paper. He then made two requests that I thought were curious (and unreasonable): First, he wanted *himself* to be listed as the senior author. (When there are multiple authors on a paper, the name listed first is usually that of the individual who originated the idea and did the basic research and most of the work that made it possible.) Watson also insisted that both he and Dr. John Pool be listed as co-authors for "we always publish articles together as a service."

As diplomatically as possible, I resisted. Reluctantly, I compromised by agreeing to add their names as co-authors—but to follow, not precede, my own.

Customarily, a short summary of one's findings in article form is submitted to the program committee of a society months before its annual meeting so that they can judge its merits and decide whether it will interest the members. I prepared a summary and sent it off to the prestigious American Association for Thoracic Surgery. For weeks, I watched the mails anxiously. A few months later, a letter came in:

> We are pleased to inform you that your paper, "Radical Pneumonectomy," has been accepted and will be presented at our annual meeting in Atlantic City, New Jersey, on April 17, 1951. Your completed manuscript, ready for publication, must be handed to the Program Chairman just prior to your presentation.

The three of us, Watson, Pool, and I, went to Atlantic City. As senior author, I would present the paper.

National meetings are usually attended by as many as a thousand physicians or more. This one had that many and included the dean of lung-cancer surgeons, Dr. Evarts Graham. The ground rules stated that each presentation must be limited to ten minutes. To be sure that this time limit is strictly adhered to, a yellow warning light goes on at the podium nine minutes into the presentation. Then, a minute later, a red light flashes and a loud buzzer goes off. The speaker must stop immediately no matter what is left unsaid.

To cut out precious data, the result not only of extensive research, but also of a tedious assembling of facts, to fit the rigidly enforced time allowance is painful self-surgery. I rewrote the talk over twenty times and reluctantly removed deathless, or perhaps deadly, phrases. This was particularly difficult, as radical pneumonectomy was a new concept. With a stop watch, I rehearsed my speech repeatedly before a mirror until, by allowing no more than twenty seconds for each of eight slides, I squeezed in under the ten-minute limit, leaving a half-minute to spare for unforeseen errors or delays.

Finally, my big moment came: "The next paper is 'Radical Pneumonectomy' by Drs. Cahan, Watson, and Pool. Dr. Cahan will present it." I walked up the stairs to the stage and, as ordained, handed the completed manuscript to the chairman. All went well until I called for the first slide from those I'd carefully arranged in sequence and given to the projectionist. It appeared promptly enough on the huge screen—upside down.

We wasted seconds while the projectionist corrected the slide. When the next slide came on, it was in reverse, left to right.

I kept on talking gamely as it, too, was corrected. The rest of the slides were shown and I finished the paper just as the buzzer went off. (Later, I found out that the chairman, seeing my predicament, had stretched the time limit.)

During the intermission, my co-authors praised the presentation—as one might expect they would, good or bad. One of the deans of cardiothoracic surgery from a Southern medical school also came over to compliment me and added a recommendation for another removal: "Doc, if Ah were you, Ah would have taken a shotgun to that slide guy."

About a year later, the paper appeared in the *Journal of Thoracic Surgery*. In the days before photocopiers, authors gauged interest in their articles by the number of written requests for reprints.

They estimate the number and order the reprints beforehand. There were so many requests for the article, we had to order five hundred more than the original two hundred. For years, requests continued to come in from Russia, mainland China, India, and Japan. I also had letters suggesting that radical pneumonectomy had not originated with me.

Once Peter Medawar wrote: "Premonitions and foreshadowings in pretty well every scientific discovery can be found by people intent on seeking them out." This was borne out, for a few physicians wrote me claiming that they had written a paragraph here, a short statement there, that supposedly established their or someone else's priority. A few insisted that they had been doing radical pneumonectomies for some time but had "just not gotten around to reporting it." I took heart because I remembered how Dr. Evarts Graham, who performed the first successful pneumonectomy for lung cancer, had doubt cast on his priority. However, one criticism I took seriously drew my attention to a paragraph that Sir Russell Brock, King George VI's surgeon, had included in an article on the general subject of lung cancer. It had a brief description of an operation somewhat similar to mine. I wrote, apologizing for having omitted a reference to his book, explaining that I had missed it because the paragraph was tucked away in a much longer article. Sir Russell answered graciously, and in effect credited me for having so carefully described the indications for and the step-by-step technique of a radical pneumonectomy.

I was fully aware that certain scientists reach conclusions first and never change their minds even if the preponderance of evidence is to the contrary, so I was prepared for the barrage of skepticism that followed. Skeptics felt that if mediastinal lymph nodes were involved by cancer, it was pointless to remove them as the patient was incurable. Some pointed out that lung cancer frequently spreads via the bloodstream; thus, removing these nodes would not affect the final outcome. However, as time went by some of those who had positive mediastinal lymph nodes removed survived five or more years; this suggested that the extra effort might be worthwhile. What was becoming evident was that removing the nodes established more reliable guidelines for prognosis and the need for radiation and/or chemotherapy.

For years, pneumonectomy continued to be the standard operation for lung cancer. Yet within a relatively short span of twenty to twenty-five years, a change occurred in the location and type of lung cancer. Cancers of the lung are divided into several different microscopic types, and up until the 1950s and 1960s, epidermoid (squamous) cancers accounted for three out of four cases. However, within the short space of time, more adenocarcinomas are being seen. In addition, instead of lung cancers arising centrally in a main bronchus of the lungs, as they had for many years, now they arose more peripherally in the lung substance. As a result, it has become possible to remove cancers using a lobectomy (removal of a section of the lung) rather than a pneumonectomy (removal of the entire lung). Lobectomy is an attractive alternative, because it carries much lower operative mortality and leaves the patient with more lung tissue to breathe with. I adapted the mediastinal dissection to this lesser procedure, calling it a radical lobectomy.

Forty years later, support for my concept appeared in the *Bulletin of the American College of Surgeons* for January 1989.

> A retrospective study by the lung cancer study group reiterated the importance of mediastinal lymph node analysis accompanying pulmonary resection to establish prognosis and to allow for standardization and study of adjuvant treatment interventions.
>
> There is agreement that a pulmonary resection for primary carcinoma of the lung cannot be considered complete without, at the very least, some systematic sampling of mediastinal lymph nodes. Some would argue for complete mediastinal lymph node dissection.

Medical historians can decide the question of priority, and only time will tell whether the operation has value in prolonging life.

Shortly after my paper was presented, while I was teaching a resident to perform a radical pneumonectomy, a visitor entered the operating room's viewing balcony. Like all observers, he was masked, hatted, and gowned. He introduced himself, but mumbled his name behind his mask so that I could not catch it. Anxious to show off this new technique, I asked the resident to pause from time to time and step aside so that the visitor could have a better view. After several such requests, the resident, to my dismay, said in an audible whisper, "Let's quit showing him technique. That old fogey probably doesn't understand what we are doing anyway."

I was furious and whispered, less audibly, that if demonstrating seemed to be too much for him, I'd gladly take over and finish the operation. He shut up. Later, privately, I reprimanded him once more for his manners.

About a month later, I received a letter. "Dear Dr. Cahan," it said, "Thank you for the courtesy of showing me the steps of your new procedure. I was the 'old fogey' in the balcony." The letter was signed "Emil Holman, M.D., Professor of Surgery, Stanford University." He was one of the most renowned surgeons in America.

In 1958, the American Cancer Society asked me to produce a documentary film to commemorate the twenty-fifth anniversary of the first successful pneumonectomy. In a series of short takes, fictionalized characters were shown in episodes leading up to the surgery. In the last sequences of the film, real-life Dr. Evarts Graham, the surgeon, and Dr. James Gilmore, his patient, were interviewed on camera. I asked Gilmore how he felt when he learned he would undergo an operation that had never been performed before. He said, "I did two things: One was an act of confidence—I had my teeth cleaned. The other was not quite—I bought a cemetery plot."

Ironically, Dr. Gilmore outlived Dr. Graham who, having been a heavy smoker, died of lung cancer.

Without question, the most revolutionary, far-reaching discovery in cancer diagnosis in the past forty years has been the Pap test, or Pap smear. It was named for its discoverer, Dr. George N. Papanicolaou, or as we came to call him, Dr. Pap.

In 1928 Dr. Pap found that a reliable cancer diagnosis could be made from a few cells cast off by the cancer or scraped from suspicious areas and examined under the microscope. Such a study is called cytology.

When Dr. Pap first presented his findings, he was strongly criticized, particularly by pathologists, who felt that reliable cancer diagnosis could be made only by examining a biopsy—a fragment or piece of tissue taken from a suspected tumor. However, Pap doggedly persisted in his belief, and by painstakingly reviewing thousands of cell specimens and comparing them with their parent cancers, he demonstrated beyond doubt that even a *single* cancer cell, properly stained and viewed by an expert cytologist, could provide a reliable cancer diagnosis.

Initially, Dr. Pap tried this concept on cervical cancer, largely

Dr. George N. Papanicolaou of Pap test fame

because of the cervix's ready accessibility. When he had made his point irrefutably using that anatomic area, he began to investigate the test's value for lung-cancer diagnosis. Heretofore, to make the all-important preoperative pathological diagnosis for lung cancer, a biopsy had to be taken from a suspected area during bronchoscopy. To take a biopsy, the cancer had to be visible to the bronchoscopist, which it often was not. Using Pap's technique, a suspicious area not visible by bronchoscopy because it originated in the periphery of the lung was first irrigated with saline solution. Then the washings were collected and, using Pap's technique, examined for cancer cells.

Not only could cancer cells be found in these washings, but Dr. Pap also found that cancer cells could be found in sputum raised after a deep cough; many lung-cancer diagnoses were established by using this method.

In the earliest phases of this study, Dr. Pap tapped Memorial's large population of lung cancers. As the youngest member of the thoracic service, I was delegated to carry sputum and bronchial-washing specimens across York Avenue to Pap's laboratory in a building adjacent to New York Hospital. There I was always warmly greeted by this genial, broad-featured, slightly balding, clearly warmhearted man who, in his Greco-American accent, urged me to peer through his microscope at the cells he had stained. This was an exhilarating experience, and I considered myself fortunate to have the smallest walk-on role in his epoch-making discovery.

One of Pap's diagnostic triumphs, and an affirmation of the value of his method, occurred when I brought a sputum specimen from a patient whose symptoms strongly suggested that he had lung cancer, but whose chest X ray was negative. After staining and studying the specimen, Dr. Pap turned to me and said, "This patient has cancer; go find it and get rid of it."

He was correct, for in this patient and in others who followed, bronchoscopy revealed a tiny cancer at one edge of a bronchus; the cancer was too small to cast an X-ray shadow. Removing it at such an early stage distinctly improved a patient's chance of survival and emphasized the value of properly raised sputum in making a lung-cancer diagnosis.

Later, Dr. Pap's diagnostic method was used to detect cancers of the bladder, esophagus, oral cavity, kidney, and spinal cord.

He was not without the eccentricities that sometimes go with genius. Dr. Pap appeared one day with a very evident shiner. When we kidded him, suggesting that Mrs. Pap had given him the black eye (a gentler woman did not exist), he sheepishly explained that it had happened in his lab the night before. Apparently, this dedicated but sleepy scientist had worked into the early morning hours, as usual, and had dozed off, banging himself on the eyepiece of his microscope.

Dr. Papanicolaou died in 1962 at the age of seventy-eight, never having received the Nobel Prize he so richly deserved.

CHAPTER IX

Private Lives

Although my practice was growing, Pamela's and my marriage continued to weaken. My preoccupation with work was a contributing factor. Certainly my affair with Inga had not helped. The mortal blow came in 1947 when Pam, who had always longed to be an actress, auditioned and got a part as a Cockney maid in a Broadway comedy produced by Rodgers and Hammerstein and directed by Joshua Logan. *John Loves Mary,* a comedy written by Norman Krasna, starred Tom Ewell, Nina Foch, and William Prince. It was a huge success and played to S.R.O. houses for over a year. Gertrude Lawrence, still performing in *Lady in the Dark,* went to an Actors Equity benefit performance of *John Loves Mary.* Just as Pam had on Gee's opening night in *Lady in the Dark,* she yelled "Bravo!" as Pam took a curtain call.

What the play's success meant for our marriage was that I returned home after a hectic day at the hospital just as Pam left for the theater. When she returned, after eleven P.M., I was usually fast asleep. Then, at six A.M., I would leave for the hospital while she slept. We lived more like ships that pass in the night than like man and wife. While there was no animosity between us, clearly we had lost, along the way, the essential ingredients of a successful marriage.

When news reached Gee about our impending separation, she wrote:

Oldtown Lane, Dennis, Massachusetts
July 3, 1950

Dear Doctor Bill,

I cannot imagine why you did not return my telephone call or why you have not written me a line.

All this business between you and Pamela is most distressing, and even though *you* both feel you have made the right decision, it would seem to me that you would consider it only just to give me some explanation and expression of your feelings in the matter.

This is not a rebuke, Bill, people lead their own lives and make their own decisions in the long run; but where there are other interested and close ties, those other feelings have to be taken into consideration.

Pamela wrote me, and I have spoken to her. Although this break between you has apparently been in the offing for some time, I cannot believe that it is more than temporary. Even so, you must be very lonely and sad about the whole affair and in spite of what you both may call a "sensible attitude," I pray that this separation will, in the long run, bring you back closer together.

Richard and I are so fond of you, Bill, and come what may we hope that you will remain our friend and that you will not in any way become a stranger to the Aldriches, including Pamela.

I'm sure you need each other, each in your own way, and it seems such a shame that nine years has not proved to you both that Pamela was happy and doing her best to be a good, faithful and industrious wife, and that you are still the man she loved so deeply from the very first moment of your meeting. Do write me and be patient with my girl.

> Fondly,
> Gertrude

But the reconciliation that Gee hoped would occur seemed impossible. As we were childless, and our lives and interests had diverged more and more, we separated and, in 1950, were amicably divorced.

A few years after I began practice, a remarkable offer came my way. Murray Herman, a grateful patient, asked if he could make a donation to help my research. After the proposal was cleared with the hospital, a fund was established. Initially it was named for Albert Schweitzer, the Nobel prize–winning physician who had worked with leprosy victims in Africa, an idol of the donor.

As other patients made contributions over the years, the fund was, for administrative convenience, given my name.

I did not have the personal means to support research but the fund made me a kind of philanthropist by making many projects possible. Customarily, those seeking funds for research must fill out formal applications to various agencies, describing the aims of their project and its cost. Then, they usually wait for an extended length of time as their application is reviewed and, perhaps, approved. By controlling my fund, I avoided the often frustrating wrapping of grants in red tape. Left to my discretion, I used the grants carefully to provide seed money for research and, in the course of the years, the fund has helped speed projects that needed immediate solutions. For example, the research into cryosurgery —the use of extreme cold in therapeutics—which involved experiments on animals; new instruments, and the assembling of research data for publication, cost just $21,000. Surgical instruments of unquestioned need were purchased without having to wait for a long chain of bureaucratic approval. Other projects included research into Reglan, an antinauseant for those receiving chemotherapy; a study of the role of diet in cancer; antismoking campaigns; arranging for world-famous scientists to lecture at MSK; the annual Cancer Teaching Day for Cornell Medical College students; and the amassing of research data and publication of articles on the diagnosis and treatment of lung cancer.

With my growing reputation for raising funds (about $8 million by 1992), other staff doctors would ask how I did so. They confessed that they felt shy and somewhat embarrassed about approaching patients, or patients' relatives, for this purpose. Perhaps their hesitancy stemmed in part from a subconscious guilt when the subject of money was raised, I said. And I added: "You can overcome your hesitancy by concentrating on the serious purpose of your request: You're not asking for money for yourself, but for others. Those to whom you talk should be told that funds for research could benefit not only them, but humanity as well." They would be pleasantly surprised at how many people are willing and even anxious to be charitable.

In 1952, Gertrude Lawrence had been starring with Yul Brynner on Broadway in the smash hit *The King and I* for over a year when she became ill. She was admitted to New York Hospital. Her doctors were puzzled by what was described in the press as "a liver problem," and suspected that she might have cancer.

Hearing this, and without Gertrude's knowledge, her husband consulted me. Not wanting to alarm her by appearing in person (she knew, of course, that by now I was a cancer specialist), I sent some of my colleagues as consultants. They, too, were puzzled, and ordered an exploratory laparotomy (abdominal operation).

At dawn of the day the operation was to take place, Dick Aldrich called: Gertrude had become comatose; would I please come to the hospital at once? I found her surrounded by interns frantically pumping intravenous fluids and stimulants into her. As I bent over her, she opened her eyes for a second or two, looked up at me, and made a face as if to say, "What are *you* doing here?"

A few minutes later, she died.

Concerned and curious about what had caused her death, I was present at her autopsy. This showed that she had widespread liver and abdominal cancer, the source of which was never clarified. But there, immobile, eyes dulled by death, lay all the glorious talent, the nervous energy, the glamour that had lit up the stage and fascinated those around her. All the resentment I had often felt for her neglect of Pam vanished as I realized the role she had played in my life for I, too, had been elevated, even enriched, by our relationship.

The last time I saw Pamela was at her mother's funeral at St. Thomas Church on Fifth Avenue, a few hundred yards from where Gertrude and I had first met thirteen years before.

❖

CHAPTER X

Whispers of Nature

During my residency, I witnessed a rare and remarkable natural event: the spontaneous disappearance of cancer. To give some idea of how unusual this is: Out of the many millions of cancer patients, there have been only about three hundred recorded, scientifically sound, unequivocal examples of this phenomenon.*

For a case to qualify as a spontaneous disappearance, first, the diagnosis of cancer must be established by biopsy; second, far advanced, usually widespread and untreatable metastases must be present; third, all evidences of cancer must disappear either without any treatment, or following therapeutic measures that were clearly inadequate to have produced such a remarkable effect.

Some of these cases are the stuff of miracles and have often been attributed to the persuasive powers of prayer. Scientists look for inklings, subtle messages, whispers of nature, which they would like to seize and convert into shouts.

A young woman, seven months pregnant, had widespread melanoma ("black spot") metastases that appeared as dark nodules on and beneath her skin as well as in many of the lymph nodes in her neck and armpits. Questions were raised about ways to help her, questions complicated by her pregnancy. Should she be aborted? It was feared that pregnancy was accelerating her melanoma. Also, she might transmit the melanoma through the pla-

---

* Recently, I asked older MSK staff members if they had *ever* seen a spontaneous remission. None had.

centa to her unborn child. The patient and her husband decided against abortion.

As her melanoma was too far advanced for any form of therapy that medicine in that day could offer—this was the age before chemotherapy or vaccines—she was sent home to Florida to die.

Months passed. Because her physician at Memorial had not heard the expected somber news of her death, he decided to call her home. Her mother answered the phone and the doctor asked tentatively how "things" were.

The mother said, "Just fine. Alice is in the backyard hanging up the baby's diapers."

"What happened to the black spots and the enlarged glands she had?"

"Oh," her mother said. "Why, all those disappeared a few weeks after the baby was born. There are just white patches now where the dark patches were on her skin. The bumps she had on her neck and armpits are also gone."

"How's the baby?" my colleague asked, not believing his ears.

"He's fine, too. No, there are no spots on him."

This was startling news. Immediately, efforts were made at Memorial to act on it. Her local physician was contacted. He was dumbfounded, having been convinced by Alice's silence that she had long since died.

After he examined her and confirmed what her mother described, at our urging he convinced the patient to donate blood to be analyzed at the Sloan-Kettering Institute. Plasma from her blood sample was injected into patients who, like her, had widespread melanoma metastases. Unfortunately, the blood samples apparently had nothing in them that benefited the several patients who received injections.

Years later, another colleague's patient went through his own miracle: the spontaneous disappearance of widespread colon cancer. During his physician's search for anything in the patient's past that could have produced this, he discovered that, some months before, the patient had been bitten by a stray dog that could have been rabid. To protect him, he had been given antirabies vaccine. Hearing this, his physician immediately contacted the vaccine's manufacturer and asked for samples.

When the pharmaceutical company consulted their records, they discovered that the particular lot number that was used on this patient had later been found to be of "questionable purity," and had been discarded.

Could one cure for a cancer have gone down the drain just beyond our eager reach?

Despite efforts to reproduce the effect by giving antirabies inoculations to others, a similar result could never be reproduced, nor the "impurities" recaptured.

Undoubtedly an important secret lies tucked away in these two individuals and in all those who have had spontaneous disappearance of their cancers. Naturally, these phenomena tantalize and frustrate researchers. Although scientists are as yet unable to solve the basic riddles of such mysteries, the cases provide insight into the presence of unique mechanisms resident in very few individuals and not in others.* If nothing else, remarkable incidents like these provide a clue, an encouragement: Cancer-destroying forces exist in nature and, though currently out of reach, will one day be understood and imitated.

One theory has it that certain individuals harbor a unique immunologic response to their cancers that overcomes their disease once it has been spawned. Frequently, a parallel is drawn with antibodies that are normally formed in the body when an alien substance, such as bacteria or a foreign protein (such as pollen), enters it.

However, such an immune response seems unlikely, since cancer cells, however different in appearance from normal ones, still originate from a patient's own tissue. But perhaps, for mysterious reasons, they undergo a radical change in character, thus becoming like other foreign substances that the body neutralizes and renders harmless.

A somewhat similar idea is being explored, using genetic engineering, which has, at a laboratory level converted malignant cells to normal ones. Could this have happened spontaneously in the young pregnant woman when her black melanomatous spots became white patches? In addition to genetic engineering, other assaults on cancer cells take different forms. "Killer" cells—white

* Theories as to why cancers disappear: a) An unusual change in the endocrine gland system—for cancers of the ovary, testis, skin, breast, thyroid; b) high fever and infection; c) allergy or immunity—melanoma and kidney cancer; d) interference with nutrition of cancer (blood supply) and body metabolism; e) removal of carcinogen—bladder; f) unusual sensitivity to standard treatment.

blood corpuscles, or macrophages—are being "trained" to enter cancer cells and destroy them. Monoclonal antibodies are laboratory-devised substances that can home in on cancer cells; if they carry radioactivity or cancer-destructor chemicals "piggy-back," they could destroy the cancer without damaging surrounding, normal cells.

Yet another example of cancer's enigmatic behavior, and just as difficult to comprehend, is the reappearance of cancer as much as fifteen to twenty-five years after its first appearance and at its original site. When confronted with these exceptions, we ask ourselves: *Where* have the cancer cells been smoldering or "hibernating" all this time? What mechanisms in the patient's internal environment kept them inactive—and then changed, so that they became activated after all these years? Such experiences are not only rare, they raise the question as to whether some cancers are *ever* cured.

Although the majority of cancers obey fairly predictable patterns, some behave capriciously. Knowing this, physicians should avoid making flat-footed predictions or pronouncements about a patient's future. As tempting as it is to use terms such as "obvious" or "always" or "never" or, worst of all, "six months to live," it is far more prudent—and accurate—to couch such prophecies in guarded terms. Very often, incautious rosy forecasts may not turn out to be correct; at other times, the doomsayers are surprised at how long "obviously" hopeless patients survive.

In the meantime, scientists must continue to search for a way to amplify these "whispers of nature." All too slowly, the gap is narrowing between mystery and discovery, between enigma and solution.

❖

CHAPTER XI

The Flora Sign

In 1950, Mary Arnold Sykes, a beautiful woman known as "Sisi," and I had been introduced. Sisi was working at the *Saturday Review of Literature* as Norman Cousins's secretary. She was a highly intelligent and vivacious blonde with a keen since of humor. Her father was a naval attaché in Italy before World War II, and Sisi had learned to speak fluent Italian. We were steady companions for about eighteen months and were married in 1952. Her father, clad for the occasion in the full dress uniform of a rear admiral (ret.) of the U.S. Navy, complete with many rows of battle decorations and special honors, gave the bride away. When he and I first met, a week before the wedding, we shook hands as he said in a deep baritone, *"Welcome aboard!"* I didn't know whether I was getting married or had enlisted.

Our first son, Chris, was born in 1953. He was just three days old, and I was busy proudly rejoicing at home, when his pediatrician called: His anterior fontanelle seemed to be bulging. The anterior fontanelle is one of two spaces on a baby's skull that Nature leaves unsealed to allow for the brain to expand. The bulging described by the pediatrician suggested an increase of intracranial pressure from improperly drained cerebrospinal fluid. I knew that this could mean Chris would have hydrocephalus, a deformity of the skull and brain.

Horrified, I called a neurologist, who examined Chris and reviewed his X rays. They showed nothing abnormal. However, the neurologist said that this did not necessarily mean Chris was out of danger. He traced the diamond-shaped fontanelle on transparent paper and, using this outline, told me to check each day to see if the space between the cranial bones widened. I told no one about this, not even Sisi. Each time I measured the space, my heart was in my throat. After two weeks, the fontanelle's diameter began to decrease: Our son was going to be all right.

When Chris was nine months old, we bought a brownstone on East Sixty-second Street in Manhattan. By today's standards, the price we paid for the house seems ridiculously low. However, as with all such success stories, you have to remember the time and place. The Third Avenue El trains were still running fifty yards away and the boom in real estate had not begun. In any event, to me $46,000 was a lot of money. By using our savings, a veteran's mortgage loan of $25,000, and money from Sisi's father and my parents, we just managed to meet the sales price.

Eleven months later, our second son, Anthony, was born.

When our boys were five and seven years old, Sisi became pregnant once more. One afternoon while I was having office hours, Sisi, seven months into her term, called to say that she was having labor pains. I rushed home and took her to the hospital.

After Sisi had had a stillborn daughter, I returned home to find Christopher and Anthony waiting at the door expecting to see the new arrival. When I told them what had happened, they burst into tears and were inconsolable for days. Sisi returned a few days later and managed to submerge her own disappointment in order to comfort her sons.

Our home life soon resumed its frenetic pace. Sisi used to say that her father, the admiral, was admired by his shipmates for running a tight ship—or was it "taut"? At times, one felt that Sisi had her father in mind when she expected her orders to be obeyed immediately. She recognized these tendencies and with self-deprecating humor called herself the Dragon. She felt that I was such a marshmallow, *someone* had to maintain discipline to bring order out of the chaos that two rambunctious, highly inventive young men could create.

Sisi's mother had the warmth and charm of a Texas-born Southern belle. She and her husband lived on a hilly and many-laked eight-hundred-acre estate just outside of a tiny Texas town called Willis. The house had been designed and built by Sisi's father and was an architectural symbol of their past lives. Its sophisticated, marble-floored, Italianate design led directly into a log cabin with a shiplike interior—including a typical ship's bunk, in which the admiral slept.

Jimmy Sykes, my father-in-law, was a Naval Academy graduate (class of 1919) and had rowed on the varsity crew. He had the unique distinction of being both a submarine commander and a pilot. During World War II, he had commanded the U.S.S. *Card*, first, a "baby flattop" or *Essex*-class carrier, and then the huge aircraft carrier U.S.S. *Bennington*, which served in the Pacific. As many naval officers do, when he retired, he did so far from the sea.

The Sykeses would visit us in New York at Christmas. We would join them in Texas at Thanksgiving. My parents lived a short distance away and were able to see our children frequently. They felt so strongly about these late-in-life grandchildren that they had to be restrained (for the most part unsuccessfully) from spoiling them.

The backgrounds of our children's grandparents could not be more dissimilar: The Sykeses were descendants of New England pioneers and early Texas settlers. One of Margaret Sykes's ancestors had been in the second graduating class at Harvard in the seventeenth century. In the 1860s, another became a well-known riverboat gambler. In sharp contrast, my parents' forebears were Russian, English, Dutch, and Polish, and comparatively recent arrivals on these shores.

Although the grandparents assembled only at holiday time, they became genuinely fond of each other, bonded by delight in their grandsons.

Life was good: My practice was prospering; we had an outsized French poodle named Sabot, a waterfront property on Long Island, and interesting friends. With a live-in housekeeper-cook-childsitter we were able to lead a busy social life. The parties we went to at night I have forgotten, but what I do remember is the hurt looks on my sons's faces when they asked, "Are you going to be home tonight?" and I had to say no, over and over again.

However, we did not neglect them. Every weekday morning I drove both sons to the Dalton School. As a family, we fished, sailed, went to drive-in movies, worked on jigsaw puzzles, listened ad nauseam to the Beatles, and traveled in the United States and abroad. Sisi and I leaned over backward to distribute affection equally and tried to overcome the sibling rivalry that inevitably occurs in those who are born close together.

From the beginning, the boys had distinct personalities. Chris was more quick-tempered and kept his genuinely sensitive, warm nature hidden to keep from being traumatized by real or imagined hurts. Like many of his contemporaries, he was suspicious and resentful of authority, whether imposed by parents or teachers. To kids of that age, anyone over the age of thirty was not only someone you couldn't trust, but someone you had trouble living with, who was suitable only for scorn or satire. Despite Chris's best efforts to conceal his sentimental side, it often surfaced in acts of kindness for the downtrodden and in concern for animals.

For example, little Chris was an avid fisherman—until the day he refused to go fishing anymore because he felt sorry for the fish. Perhaps his concern stemmed from having seen a Disney cartoon character, Willie the Whale, who was routed from his briny home: Each time the cartoon was shown, Chris would burst into tears. He used to sit alone for hours, staring at and enraptured by our Christmas tree. He adored pets of all shapes and sizes, and felt strongly about helping the poor, the underprivileged, and all minorities.

Unquestionably, as he grew, Chris was traumatized and pummeled by a variety of personal setbacks—unrequited puppy love, parents with strong personalities, and, late in his adolescence, a stormy household.

He had a flair for theatricals and would stage amateur shows in our cellar with a cast of neighborhood kids. The audience was made up of dragooned but doting parents and grandparents, who felt that the ten-cent admission was worth every penny. These shows may have foreshadowed his career.

As they grew, the boys used our city backyard as a miniature baseball and football field and swam in a plastic pool that I had installed there. The yard also served as a hiding place for Easter eggs and a site for a lighted tree at Christmas. It was the burial ground of canaries, turtles, goldfish, and gerbils.

As boys, Chris and Anthony often overheard me expound my growing concerns about the evils of tobacco. On occasion, playing on the sidewalk in front of our brownstone, they would see a stranger walking along smoking. Both would stop, point their fingers at the stranger, and say: "Better quit or you'll die!"

There is no record of how these strangers reacted, but my guess is that, upon hearing such words out of the mouths of babes, some of them nervously tossed their cigarettes into the gutter. Maybe some even quit.

No one would have described our home as "all medicine." I

rarely brought patients' problems home with me or discussed my research over dinner. In fact, it was unusual for us to entertain colleagues at home, for few of them were close friends.

On rare occasions, I did take Chris and Anthony along to the hospital when I made Sunday rounds. They both came, I suspect, less from curiosity than to use the patients' pool table. Once there, Chris soon became restless and anxious to leave. I attributed this to his recently having witnessed the progressive stages of leukemia in a young friend. Anthony, on the other hand, seemed particularly interested when I or one of the nurses showed him patients' X rays or surgical instruments. Years later, Anthony told me how impressed he was when I picked them up at the end of rounds, and residents would crowd around and besiege me with questions. Perhaps even then, he longed to be one of those white-coated disciples.

One Sunday, the boys and I were driving along Long Island's Montauk Highway on the way to our usual after-dinner ice cream cones. It was just after dusk, and headlights had been turned on. A few minutes from the Carvel shop, we were stopped in a line of backed-up traffic. Up ahead, I could see the rotating lights of a police car. There must have been an accident. I asked a policeman if a doctor was needed. He looked at my M.D. plates and motioned to me to get out of line and drive closer to the scene.

There, illuminated in the headlights of the police car, I saw a man face down on the road. I told the boys to stay put, got out, and ran to the man's side. He was unconscious and lay a few yards away from a car that had a shattered windshield and caved-in front section. Apparently, he had had a head-on collision with a pickup truck, which was stalled several yards away. The truck's windshield was splintered, but had not broken. I could see a man and a woman behind it, looking pale but apparently in no acute physical distress.

I identified myself to a state trooper, who told me he had sent for an ambulance and added: "This guy's in real trouble, Doc. The couple in the pickup look shaken up, but not too bad."

As I leaned over the prostrate man, I glanced up and saw Christopher and Anthony watching intently from the car. Instinctively, I backed around so as to screen them from what was a gruesome sight.

The unconscious man's face was blue-tinged and he was bleeding profusely from his scalp, which had almost been torn off.

His arm was curled around his head and his blood had pooled within this enclosure, covering his nose and mouth so that he was drowning in it. With one hand, I gingerly raised his head above the blood and, with the other, moved his arm so that the blood could run free. He began breathing immediately and "pinked up." I returned his head to the pavement, pulled his scalp back over his skull and put manual pressure on it to control the bleeding.

A few minutes later, as the bleeding had slowed; I told the trooper to keep pressure on the scalp while I examined the other victims. In the distance, I heard a siren.

In the front seat of the truck, the man and woman sat looking dazed, but conscious. The woman had a bump on her forehead, and both told me that the backs of their necks hurt right after the collision. They could move their arms and legs and did not seem to be in any acute difficulty. I was somewhat reassured but, nevertheless, I told the trooper to send for a second ambulance.

When the first ambulance arrived, I helped the paramedics lift the injured man onto the stretcher, cautioning them to keep him prone with his head extended. Although by this time the bleeding had almost stopped, I instructed the ambulance attendant to maintain pressure on the scalp and to keep an adequate airway.

Once the second ambulance had left with the injured couple, I got back into our car. My sneakers and shorts and shirt were bloody. After my kids asked a few excited questions—"What happened?" "Is he dead?"—I drove us to Carvel. We got our cones and drove home in silence.

After I showered, I made a point of sitting for a time on the boy's beds, talking about the accident, before kissing them good night. I told them I thought that the injured man would be O.K. I was, naturally, curious as to their reactions. They were strikingly different: Chris confessed that he had felt somewhat squeamish; Anthony, on the other hand, said he would have given anything to be out there with me, being part of it. Both complained about my having obstructed their view.

The next morning, Chris searched the newspapers for an account of the accident. Anthony seemed unusually quiet. When asked why, he said he was wondering how the patients were doing. I was touched by his concern and called the hospital. Other than a bruised forehead and a whiplash injury the couple was fine —able to be discharged. The man, who had been driving drunk, had regained consciousness. Plastic surgery had closed his scalp wound and he was out of danger.

When I told this to my sons, they seemed relieved and told me how proud they were of the role I had played.

Thinking back, I can't help but feel that Chris was showing signs of the news-gathering career he has since chosen, and that the incident had ignited something in Anthony as my grandmother's death had in me.

On the housekeeper's nights off, my parents frequently acted as baby-sitters, which brought them closer to the boys. My father would make up Chris as Charlie Chaplin or some other comedian, and together they would act out comic scenes. He also gave drawing lessons to Anthony. My mother told them bedtime stories.

Although the boys saw little of Sisi's parents, when they did, they were warmly treated. Sisi's father, nicknamed "Grandpowder" by Chris, regaled them with war stories, took them fishing, and taught Anthony carpentry and Chris how to drive a jeep. Sisi's mother covered them with affection and filled them with wonderful Southern cooking. Ours seemed to be a fine example of an ideal family, from grandparents on down.

Somehow, into that contentment bickering and dissension intruded and became more insistent. Probably it was inevitable in light of the abrasive aspect of Sisi's and my strong personalities. One major source of contention continued to be how to bring up the boys. I was probably too soft and indulgent, whereas Sisi was more the disciplinarian and felt the kids needed to be "kept in line."

In 1953, my father painted Sisi's portrait as a gift to her parents, who admired it enough to hang it over the mantelpiece of their Texas home. A few years later, at my behest, my father worked to paint my portrait as a birthday surprise for Sisi. On several Saturday mornings, I posed in my office examining room, dressed in operating-room greens and a white surgical mask undone at the top, falling across my chest like a bib.

On the morning of her birthday, I had Sisi close her eyes while I brought the draped painting into our bedroom. When I removed the drape and told her to look, I stood back expectantly, awaiting her delighted reaction. Instead, she burst into tears, not of affection or appreciation but of anger. Sisi said how deeply disappointed she was. The painting was too literal for her taste. Besides, she added, "You know I don't like your father's painting anyhow."

Although it had been a labor of love, the painting was, in fact, not my father's best effort. He had painted the background, my examining table, the instrument cabinet, and the operating-room garb in true impressionist style, but lost this feeling in trying to get too good a likeness of me. Undoubtedly my father was too close to his subject, and being emotionally involved and overanxious to please Sisi blurred his artistic vision. In a way, my father's performance reminded me: Surgeons should not operate on close members of their families.

An episode with my mother began in 1958 while Sisi, our children, and I were having lunch with my parents. As we ate, my mother, whom I had not seen for some time, made a distinctly audible sound each time she swallowed. When questioned, she said she had noticed this herself only recently but it had not really bothered her and she had not wanted to trouble me with it. I did not recall ever having read or heard about such a symptom, but was immediately suspicious.

The next morning, looking over Dr. Leo Schwartz's shoulder at a larynx mirror that he held at the back of my mother's throat, I was shocked to see a large fungating★ tumor behind her tongue, just above her vocal cords. A biopsy showed it was cancer.

I consulted with several MSK staff members, some of whom thought that my mother's larynx should be removed; others opted for radiation therapy. As the final decision was left up to me, I decided on radiation therapy as the first line of defense. The bulk of the cancer seemed to emerge from the surface of her throat, rather than being rigidly fixed by having invaded into underlying tissue. Experience had taught me that cancers growing this way were usually radiation-sensitive. Besides, there were no enlarged lymph nodes in her neck to suggest that the cancer had spread. If radiation therapy were successful, my mother would keep her larynx and be able to talk in a reasonably normal manner; if not, surgery could then be instituted.

That afternoon, she began treatments. In six weeks, the tumor had melted away.

I was curious as to whether such a symptom, the exaggerated sound of swallowing, had ever been described in the medical literature, but found no reference to it. Therefore, I named it for my mother, calling it the Flora sign.

★ To fungate is to grow in funguslike masses.

❖

CHAPTER XII

Can't See It, Can't Smell It— Must Be Harmless

Without question, the excellent result that radiation therapy had produced in my mother was just one of many cures produced by this valuable therapeutic period. The control of my mother's cancers by radiation therapy was yet another example of the enormous value this technology has and of its mixed qualities as cure, danger, palliation, and paradox. It has diagnostic and curative powers and yet it is a carcinogen, a true two-edged sword.

Nevertheless, with Morton Kanner in mind, the hazards of irradiation were never far from my thoughts, and I kept searching for areas in medicine where it might be more harmful than helpful. Could, for example, using fluoroscopy to screen lungs be ill-advised?

In my generation, a physician starting practice purchased a fluoroscope as standard equipment. A fluoroscope is a device that uses X rays and a fluoroescent screen to examine the body beneath the skin. In a darkened room, the mobile screen is moved by hand from one anatomic area to another. The ease with which this is done and the fact that a physician was enabled to see through the skin made fluoroscopy seem to add an extra, harmless, more accurate dimension to the diagnosis of heart and lung conditions than that provided by a stethoscope. Beside being easy to perform, fluoroscopy was painless. In addition, patients often insisted upon being fluoroscoped as part of their routine medical checkup, believing that it gave them extra security.

On several occasions a few patients who had grossly visible

lung cancers on their X rays told me that they had been fluoroscoped several months before by their physicians as part of a routine checkup and been told that their lungs were "negative." From the size of the shadow I saw in their chest X rays, it seemed likely that the cancers had been present for some time and had probably been missed.

When I discussed this with Dr. Robert Sherman, then Memorial's chief of diagnostic radiology, he told me that it was virtually impossible to see lung shadows of one centimeter or less by fluoroscopy and that in inexperienced or inexpert hands even larger shadows could be missed. Consequently, not only early lung cancer, but tuberculosis and other pathologic lung conditions could go undetected while still asymptomatic (and curable); the patient would receive no treatment until symptoms became full-blown and a chest X ray was taken.

I became further concerned when I learned that radiologists themselves, who frequently used fluoroscopy, had a higher incidence of leukemia than other physicians. This meant that in spite of the protection of lead-lined gloves and lead aprons, radiation had leaked around these safeguards and, over a period of years, damaged their (blood-forming) bone marrow.

This unforeseen hazard was reminiscent of the early days of fluoroscopy, when physicians assumed it to be harmless because it was painless, odorless, and invisible. Consequently they used their bare hands to guide the fluoroscopic screen. Only after many of them developed multiple skin cancers, some of which were extensive enough to require amputations and even cause death, were protective lead gloves and lead aprons used.★

In 1958, in an article entitled "Isolated Fluoroscopy," published in the *New England Journal of Medicine,* Dr. Sherman and I called attention to the hazards of fluoroscopy when used to screen lungs. We emphasized that this method might give a false sense of security by judging lungs to be negative when in fact, a small shadow might be present. What is more, on average a fluoroscoped patient

★ Radiation seemed to be all too prevalent outside as well as inside medicine. Children were fitted into shoes by observing their feet by fluoroscopy; a "stimulating dose" of radiation was given to the ovaries, supposedly activating them, in those who were having difficulty conceiving. Dermatologists freely used radiation to treat acne, hirsutism, warts, and corns. Some ear, nose, and throat specialists used it on enlarged adenoids and to irradiate inflamed or tuberculous lymph nodes in the neck.

received at least ten times as much radiation as that delivered by taking a chest X ray. Unquestionably, a chest X ray—unlike fluoroscopy, which in a busy office practice may be done hurriedly— was a far more reliable diagnostic screening method. For one thing, physicians could take time to study the X ray at leisure. Besides, an X ray is a permanent record, which can be studied by others, and not the transient image seen with fluoroscopy. Finally, an X ray serves as a baseline study with which future X rays can be compared.

Although condemning the use of fluoroscopy for screening, we wrote that it is a valuable diagnostic tool when used to observe organ *function*. For example, watching the course of swallowed barium as it passes through the esophagus into the stomach can reveal a spasm or deformity in that organ. Or a barium enema can be used to see spasm or any other abnormal motility of the colon.

The *New England Journal* article opened up a sensitive subject. Thousands of fluoroscopes were in place in doctors' offices around the country. After all, it was heatedly argued, owning a fluoroscope represented a large investment for a physician. Besides, manufacturers were tooled up to make many more. Understandably, both groups were reluctant to change. However, shortly after the article's publication, unexpected support came from a *Newsweek* piece that summarized our findings. This caught the public's attention and, rather than insisting on fluoroscopy, patients began to object when a physician suggested using it to take a look at their hearts and lungs. As a result of public and professional enlightenment, fluoroscopy used for screening purposes has largely been discontinued.

At about this time, I became alarmed by yet another radiation threat: the testing of atom bombs in the atmosphere, which was taking place in America as well as in other countries. These tests were repeated at fairly regular intervals and there were plans to continue many more in the future. I knew from my experience with radiation-induced sarcomas how slowly and insidiously radiation can work until it produces a malignancy. I thought back on the radium-dial painters when I learned that one of the byproducts of radioactive fallout, strontium 90, has a great affinity for bone. Once deposited there, it has a half life of 28.8 years, which means that during that time, radioactivity in the form of dangerous gamma rays would be given off *continuously*.

In answer to the public's rising concerns about these explosions,

Atomic Energy Commission officials insisted that such tests were harmless, and that the amount of fallout was "negligible and posed no threat." I thought of how my friend Morton, as well as physicians who had used radiation in one form or another in the past, had been similarly lulled into a false sense of security. Using radiation in medicine should always be thought of in terms of its risks versus its benefits. No one knew for a fact the lowest dose that could be "safe."

But the less radiation to which an individual is exposed— whether to make a diagnosis or from other sources—the better. Therefore, before exposing populations to "safe levels," the lowest limits of safety had to be established by careful research. As there is usually a long delay before radiation's insidious effects appear, the amount released into the environment at the time could not possibly be categorically described by some commission members as being "too ridiculously low as to be harmless."

Such pronouncements were a source of considerable anxiety to those of us concerned about radiation's long-range effects, for we knew that not even the Atomic Energy Commission's prestigious chairman, Admiral Lewis Straus, or his commission members, knew precisely what was meant by "a harmless dose of radiation." In particular, they did not recognize the fact that radioactivity in its passage through nature can *increase exponentially*. For example, if tiny amounts of strontium 90 or radioactive iodine were repeatedly deposited on crops of grass consumed by cows, in time the radioactive elements would accumulate in the animals' bones and eventually kill them. And, of greater concern, the radioactive elements might pass into their milk and be consumed by both children and adults. In time, what with strontium 90's notorious affinity for bones, and iodine's for the thyroid, they might not only lead to the development of bone and thyroid cancers, but induce genetic abnormalities in reproductive organs as well. As it takes years for such insidious pathological changes to become evident, if and when they do, it would be too late to turn the clock back.

I felt strongly enough about this to write a letter to *The New York Times* on October 22, 1956. In it, I gave an example of how "harmless amounts" of radioactivity had been dumped into the river running beside the Oak Ridge, Tennessee, atomic plant. By chance, a muskrat had wandered onto the facility's grounds and was easily captured because it limped badly on a swollen right

hind leg. After it was put out of its misery, it was autopsied, and
the swelling was found to be a bone sarcoma. Fortunately, some
scientists stationed there were familiar with radiation's effect on
bone, so they placed the muskrat's affected leg against an unex-
posed X-ray film. The leg gave off enough radioactivity to expose
the film.

It was not difficult to reconstruct the sequence of events that
resulted in a bone sarcoma. A published report showed that the
radioactivity that had been emptied into the river had undergone
an exponential increase as it was absorbed and concentrated in the
water plants along the river banks; the plants contained *fifteen times*
as much radioactivity as the water did. The muskrat having eaten
these plants, the scientists then found radiation *150 times* that
which was in the water.

The letter set off widespread reaction and was one of the examples used by the Radiation Committee of the United Nations
in its campaign to warn countries to stop atmospheric testing.
Senator Richard Russell of Georgia believed the subject of such
testing important enough to read it into the *Congressional Record*
of January 9, 1957, calling it "one of the most important matters
confronting the people of the earth today."

In spite of these reports, Washington and the Atomic Energy
Commission refused to acknowledge them in public and went
ahead with plans for more tests.

Concerned by what I considered to be the AEC's head-in-the-
sand attitude, I asked Dusty Rhoads to talk to Admiral Straus,
who was a member of Memorial Hospital's board of managers.
He told me that Strauss dismissed such concerns as alarmist and
that the admiral's own scientists believed that any fallout from the
tests would be so low as to pose no threat.

Later that year, during the Eisenhower-Stevenson presidential
campaign, atmospheric testing became a politically sensitive issue.
Eisenhower stood behind his commission, arguing that tests were
necessary for national defense; Adlai Stevenson demurred, maintaining that they should be curtailed for health reasons. Although
Eisenhower was elected, the public's reaction against atmospheric
testing eventually became strong enough so that, a few years later,
the United States and other countries abandoned atmospheric
testing and exploded atomic devices below ground.

In the decades that followed, the radiation levels initially considered "safe" have been repeatedly revised downward as evi-

dence of delayed hazardous effects came to light. By the time of
the frightening episode at the atomic plant at Three Mile Island,
and, in particular, the terrible explosion at Chernobyl in what was
then the U.S.S.R., the public knew that apart from the initial
acute effects, long-range and far-reaching aspects of contamina-
tion would not be immediately evident. It could take years to
determine all the ill effects such accidents had produced.

As a corollary of this increased sensitivity to radiation's potential hazards, studies are being done on the effects of chronic exposure to microwave ovens, TV and computer monitors, and
electromagnetic fields from overhead or nearby wires and from
the electrical appliances that rouse people from sleep, heat the
morning shower, brew coffee, curl and dry hair, defrost meals,
cool or heat living spaces.

The journal *Science*: "An undeniable shift in attitude [about effects of irradiation] has occurred over time, transforming studies
from 'absurd notions' to examination as 'a legitimate open question.' Nevertheless," warned *Science,* "more research is needed to
validate and explore data. Experience has shown that seemingly
such innocuous objects as electric blankets increase the risk of
childhood cancers, leukemia or brain cancer in children and
adults. What is needed is a reliable system to correlate data on
various exposures on disease. . . ."

Moral: As with "always" or "never" or "impossible," be wary
of those who use the word "insignificant" or "harmless" where
radiation is involved.*

Osborn Elliott, then managing editor of *Newsweek,* had heard
me talk so much about the precipitous rise in lung-cancer deaths
that, in 1959, he decided to do a cover story on its diagnosis and
treatment. He asked if Calvin (Tad) Tomkins and Gordon Manning, the team assigned to this story, could be present at a lung-
cancer operation in order to give an eyewitness account. I obtained permission from both the patient and hospital officials.

---

* Many women are concerned about the exposure they receive from repeated
mammograms. In her lifetime, a woman of forty will probably have twenty to
forty of these, and although they could theoretically prove to be harmful in later
life, the good they do far outweighs this improbability. With new technical
advances mammogram machines now deliver less radiation than when they were
first used, currently 150 millirads, far less than for a chest X ray.

From previous experience, I knew that otherwise stalwart laymen, curious to observe an operation, can be distressed or even faint while watching, so I decided to break the reporters in as gently as possible. I invited them to my home, where I described in detail what they could expect to see in the operating room. I demonstrated how surgical knots are tied, using the tried and true tiny tufts in a Turkish towel to simulate blood vessels. First I gripped a single tuft with a hemostat clamp, then passed a loop of black silk thread about the clamp and slid the thread down to the clamp's tip and onto the tuft. After I had tied three knots, I released the clamp and cut the thread with a scissors just above the knot. On the day of the operation, I took the perspiring reporters to the O.R. dressed in scrub suits, caps, and masks. I watched them carefully during the operation but happily, they showed no visible ill effects.

Later, Tad Tomkins was asked whether he had felt queasy during the operation. "Queasy?" he said. "I almost fainted when Bill tied the knots on the towel."

Oz Elliott sent me the original drawing of the cover, signed by him, Tad Tomkins, and Gordon Manning, with the caption: FROM THE O.R. AT NEWSWEEK. The cover story they wrote was first-rate:

CASE NO. 248301

In an air-conditioned, green-tiled operating room on the twelfth floor of Memorial Hospital, a middle-aged man with thinning gray hair lies quietly waiting. He is groggy from medication, but still awake enough to notice the cloth-draped instrument tables, the hushed comings and goings of nurses, the compressed silence of the strangely cluttered room. His is 58 years old, an automobile salesman in a large Eastern city, married and twice a father, once a grandfather. He is listed impersonally on the records of this renowned hospital as Case No. 248301, and he is about to undergo massive surgery. The reason is visible on the wall: Two large, illuminated chest X rays, which show an irregular shadow on his left lung. The shadow is unexplained, but everyone in the operating room, including the patient, has a pretty good idea of what it probably is—cancer of the lung.

At precisely 8:10 a.m., fifteen minutes after the patient has been wheeled in, the operating surgeon enters briskly. A white face mask and green cotton cap frame his alert brown eyes. In these eyes, there is a hint of the "aggressive optimism" this surgeon brings to his austere and complex profession, a hint of eagerness to get on with the job and come to grips, once more, with the forces of life and death. It is like a tremendous game, the surgeon thinks, and he is "up" for it. He has performed hundreds of operations. This morning, as usual, he is well rested from a good night's sleep.

Casually, the surgeon greets the patient, and the men and women whose skill he will need almost as much as his own in the hours that stretch before him: The resident and assistant surgeons, fully qualified young doctors who have volunteered for Memorial's two-year program of specialized cancer training; the anesthesiologist, also an M.D., a darkly pretty girl from the Philippines (Memorial's staff has dozens of foreign-born doctors who have come to learn the new techniques of cancer warfare); the "sterile" nurse who handles the glittering array of several hundred instruments and the "unsterile" nurse who helps her but who need not be sterile, because her hands never touch an instrument (if she is called on to procure a special instrument from a cabinet, she uses tongs).

The anesthesiologist gives the patient an injection of Sodium Pentothal, and asks him to begin counting aloud. "One . . . two . . . three . . . four . . ." The patient's voice thickens—"five . . . six"—and then breaks off as the drug takes rapid effect. Two more injections follow: A local anesthetic below the Adam's apple to deaden the vocal cords and prevent coughing, and a paralytic (derived from curare, a South American Indian arrow poison) to prevent muscle spasms. Suddenly this man, who but a moment before was counting aloud, seems hardly a man at all.

He must be made to breathe, and to keep breathing during the long hours ahead. And so the professionals deftly insert a hard rubber tube down his windpipe, through which the anesthesiologist will pump a mixture of oxygen, ether, and other gases throughout the operation. (Without this tube, the patient's lungs would collapse the moment his chest was opened and the body's delicate pressure balance was upset.) He must be turned on his right side, and firmly secured with broad strips of adhesive tape; they put him into position. His left side must be painted with an orange-tinted antiseptic. And then he must be draped with sterile green sheets and towels, until only the operative area, about a foot square is still exposed. Even his head is curtained off from the operating area.

To an onlooker, the patient has lost all his identity. But not to the three surgeons who now go into the next room to scrub their hands and arms for five full minutes (sandglass timers over each deep sink mark the time). As they scrub, the doctors review the details of the case. The time is 8:40.

Three months ago, Case No. 248301 became aware of a dull pain in his chest. At first he blamed it on a fall from a stepladder a few days before, while he was painting a living-room ceiling. "That's what's so insidious," the surgeon observes, still scrubbing. "The pain masquerades as something else—a bruise, a touch of neuralgia —and they think nothing of it." When the chest pain persisted, the patient went to see his home-town doctor. He had no other symptoms, such as bloody sputum, weight loss, or night sweats. But the doctor advised chest X rays. These showed a shadow on the upper lobe of the left lung. Admitted to Memorial two days later on the advice of his family physician, he underwent sputum tests and bronchial examination. The results were suspicious enough to warrant an exploratory thoracotomy—the operation he now faces.

The surgeons return to the operating room. They are helped into rubber gloves so thin that the hair of their hands shows through, and into green operating robes by the sterile nurse (green is easier on the eyes than white). The anesthesiologist sits by the patient's head, where she will keep a running record of his pulse and blood pressure. It is now 8:55.

"All right," the surgeon says. The sterile nurse hands him the razor-keen, 4-inch-long scalpel. "Ready?"

The scalpel moves in a swift, unhesitating arc from mid-chest all the way around to a point near the spine, slicing through the thin envelope of skin and exposing fat and muscle. A spot of blood appears, and the resident quickly pinches off the blood vessel with a blunt, scissorlike clamp, which the nurse slaps smartly into his outstretched hand. Another spot of blood, another clamp, and still another and another. All three men then collaborate on tying off the clamped blood vessels with silk thread. The assistant sponges away what little blood has escaped.

Twice more the basic surgical cycle of cut-clamp-tie is repeated as the incision deepens. The surgeon is cutting "through the Lats," as they used to say when he was at Columbia College of Physicians and Surgeons—through the large muscles known as Latissimus Dorsi. A good surgeon, the old saying goes, must have "an eagle's eye, a lion's heart, and a woman's hand."

The ribs are visible now under their tough coating (perisoteum). The surgeon counts them with his fingers, locates the fifth, and scrapes away the periosteum with a Baily scraper. With a pair of powerful Bethune rib cutters he severs the curved bone at either end, and hands it across to the nurse. Ordinarily, the rib would go to the bone bank for possible use in plastic surgery (particularly useful in nose grafts). The surgeon says: "I wouldn't save this one. I think this fellow has cancer." Just beneath the rib cage, the lung can be seen through its translucent coating.

"Can we have a sponge count?" the surgeon asks quietly. "We're going into the chest." The "unsterile" nurse gathers up all the gauze pads (sponges) used so far and checks them against the inventory taken before the operation. From now on, to be sure that no small pads get mislaid inside the patient, only large sponges with heavy metal rings attached will be used in the chest. "Your count is correct," the "unsterile" nurse says. It is now 9:35; it has taken 1 hour and 25 minutes to reach this vital stage of the operation.

The pleura, a delicate membrane encasing the lungs, is severed easily. Heavy metal rib spreaders that operate like a vise in reverse force back the ribs on either side of the missing fifth, leaving an area some 5 inches across in which the surgeon can now maneuver. Suddenly the whole interior of the chest is laid open. It is nearly filled by the enormous, shiny, soft expanse of the lungs, purple and dark-mottled from years of (normal) carbon deposits, swelling and contracting as the anesthesiologist rhythmically squeezes a pressure bag to make the patient breathe.

"How's he doing?" the surgeon asks.

"He's doing fine," the anesthesiologist replies. (She had started a blood transfusion some time ago.) The surgery of the chest, heart, and lungs is a twentieth-century miracle, made possible by improved techniques in blood transfusion, anesthesia, and the antibiotic germkillers. Thirty years ago, this operation would have been unthinkable; today, less than 2 percent of patients fail to survive chest surgery. But the statistics of lung-cancer survival are grimmer. In about 55 percent of its victims, surgery is impossible because the cancer has already spread too far; when surgery is performed, only about 25 percent are alive five years later.

The surgeon has now begun his careful, thorough exploration of the chest cavity. He massages the lung, feeling over the entire surface and probing between the lobes (two for the left lung, three for the right). On the left upper lobe he has located the hard, grayish cellular lump that corresponds to the X-ray shadow. The resident and assistant both feel it, in turn. The surgeon then shaves off a small piece with a scalpel and hands it to a nurse, who quickly wraps it in waxed paper and sends it by pneumatic tube to the pathology lab ten floors below for a "frozen section," or quick microscopic analysis. It is 10:10.

With the lungs partially collapsed, the surgeon then reaches behind them to examine the heart and its major artery, the aorta. Adhering to the aorta, which is the size of a garden hose, is a suspicious growth.

While the assistant holds the lungs back with his hand, the surgeon reaches deep into the chest with long-handled scissors. Very slowly, he pushes the blunt tips between the aorta and the suspicious layer, snipping it up and away. A slip could mean disaster. Blood flows through the aorta under such pressure that a puncture could make it "hit the ceiling."

Ten minutes later, he has freed the growth and handed the nurse another piece of tissue for frozen section.

In the pathology lab, the first frozen section has been under the microscope, and the mosaiclike characteristics of the malignant cells are clearly visible. The pathologist telephones the surgical floor and, in a moment, a nurse pushes open the swinging door to announce in careful diction: "Doctor, Frozen Section No. 1 shows carcinoma." Minutes later she returns with the report on Section No. 2; it, too, shows cancer. The surgeon and his resident look at each other, over their masks.

"Radical pneumonectomy?"

"I'm afraid not," the surgeon replies. "The patient can't live on one lung."

Removal of the entire lung, or radical pneumonectomy, would perhaps give a better chance of catching all the cancer in this man. But preoperative tests which included having him run up a flight of stairs, proved that his respiratory system was too weak; with one lung gone, he would be a "respiratory cripple," unable to stand the least exertion. The surgeon has therefore decided to perform a radical lobectomy—removal of the diseased upper lobe and its regional lymph nodes—glands in which the cancer cells may be entrapped.

With the decision made, the tempo changes, quickens. The surgeons locate the main arterial branches leading to the upper lobe, tie them off, cut between the ties. They do the same with the corresponding pulmonary veins. Only a spur of the bronchus—the organ that brings air to the lungs—now joins the upper and lower lobes. The surgeon severs this with a right-angle scalpel. The assistant lifts out the soft, spongy lobe and passes it to the nurse. She wraps it, also, in waxed paper, labels it, and sends it to the lab for a thorough painstaking analysis.

The severed bronchus is sutured, then sealed with a flap of pleural tissue. Sewing deep within the chest is a delicate art; as a younger man, the surgeon used to practice by tying knots inside an empty tennis-ball can. Two bowlfuls of water are poured into the chest, to test for air leaks. There are no bubbles—the bronchus seal is tight. The resident injects a local anesthetic into exposed nerve endings, to deaden postoperative pain (its effects last five days). Now the doctors begin closing the chest.

Steel rib "approximators" pull the ribs back together. The patient will not miss his rib for long. In a year he will have grown a new one. Layer by layer, the chest wall, muscle, and skin tissue are sutured with curved needles. Muscles grow back better than before. "I've taken more slices out of golfers' drives," says the surgeon, "by removing lungs." Some 250–350 knots of black silk thread or catgut will be left inside the patient, harmless and permanent. Working at top speed, the sterile nurse keeps both surgeon and resident supplied with threaded needles; the assistant ties the knots.

At 12:20 the incision is closed. The whole operation has taken four and a half hours. The patient, who is already beginning to emerge from deep anesthesia, goes now to a recovery room where special nurses ease his post-operative hours. He will be uncomfortable for a while, but in no real pain. About ten days from now he will leave the hospital. But only time can tell whether the operation has been successful, or whether microscopic cancer cells have spread to other organs where they will continue their aggressive, deadly growth. If he is free of cancer five years from now, he will be one of the fortunate few—about ten out of every hundred lung-cancer victims—who can consider himself cured.

Pending a major breakthrough in cancer research, the doctors look to earlier diagnoses (i.e., regular X-ray checkups) as the best means of altering this grim average. X-ray therapy, the use of radioactive isotopes, and the experimental chemicals (such as nitrogen mustards) sometimes give spectacular relief of symptoms, and may eventually produce the long-sought cure. Surgery alone can do no more.

CHAPTER XIII

A Double Tragedy

The sixties began on a horrifying sorrowful note. The first Sunday night of the new year, I received a frantic call from my friend and colleague Dr. Henry Diamond, who was at Idlewild (now John F. Kennedy) airport. He and his wife, Rhoda, and their seven-year-old daughter, Judy, my goddaughter, had just returned from a tenth wedding anniversary vacation in California.

When Rhoda married Henry she had done so with the knowledge that the sword of Damocles dangled over their heads. Henry's Hodgkin's disease.

But the news this night was not about Henry. His voice on the phone said, *"My God, Bill, I'm out here at Idlewild and Rhoda just died!"* and he was sobbing. I said I'd drive out immediately.

I found him distraught and dazed, his hands and clothes bloodstained. On the way back to the city, Henry told the terrible story.

Right after they had arrived, he had gone to a telephone booth to call Rhoda's mother to tell her that they were safely back. Judy was in the booth with Henry when Rhoda, who was standing outside, suddenly collapsed. Henry dropped the phone and rushed to Rhoda and bent over her.

She had stopped breathing, was pulseless, and was rapidly become cyanotic (blue-tinged). Little Judy was taken away by cousins who had met them.

Henry used artificial respiration (cardiopulmonary resuscitation was unknown then). When Rhoda did not respond, Henry had only one recourse: He took out a penknife, opened Rhoda's chest, and massaged her heart. It was to no avail.

When we returned to their apartment in Manhattan, I stayed in the living room while Henry took Rhoda's mother, who had been waiting for them, into a bedroom to tell her what had happened. I cringed as I heard the wail of a mother suddenly bereft.

At the autopsy, it was found that Rhoda had ruptured an aneurysm of a brain artery and had died from the hemorrhage; nothing could have been done under the circumstances to save her.

Henry never recovered psychologically. Eventually he resumed his practice, but within a year, he began reexperiencing all-too-familiar afternoon fevers and sweats. As a world-class authority on his own disease, he knew that these were early signs of its reactivation.

Shortly thereafter, confirming his fear, enlarged lymph nodes appeared in his neck and chest. This time they were resistant to radiation therapy and, as his Hodgkin's disease became generalized and uncontrollable, he was admitted to Memorial.

When an MSK staff member, like Henry, has incurable cancer and is an inpatient, I force myself to overcome my feelings of dismay and guilt at being well when visiting him. I make a point of walking slowly as I enter the rooms to avoid emphasizing the contrast between his incapacity and my well-being. Like other visitors, I try to recreate our long-held camaraderie and, for all I'm worth, fill our time together with hospital gossip and funny stories. I avoid dispensing the usual encouragement that both of us have given many times to patients in this predicament, knowing how hollow it will sound to one who knows the score as well as I do.

Usually, they are the ones to bring up their problem and seem relieved to be able to discuss their situation in professional terms. Sometimes, they mention the irony of a cancer specialist being felled by his own specialty. When it is time to leave, I do so as if reluctantly, knowing full well that it could be our last meeting.

After doctors die, some widows serve as volunteers; working at the hospital makes them feel close to their departed spouses. Perhaps they feel dedicated to carry out some of the doctor's intentions to help those with cancer. Throughout all of this, of course, one cannot help but feel, "there but for the grace of God . . ."

When laymen learn that a cancer specialist has cancer, someone usually asks whether that individual caught it from his patients. When asked about such a possibility, I answer with an emphatic "No, it's not contagious," adding: "I hope not; I've been at Memorial for forty-six years."

Two years after his wife's death, Henry was dead. Judy was raised by her grandmother. Once again I had lost another close friend to cancer. It was no wonder, therefore, that given my daily contact with so much heartbreak, cancer was becoming not just a specialty, but an obsession.

When Henry's disease, dormant for over twenty-five years, returned, it raised an old question: Can an acute episode of enormous stress—such as the death of a loved one, a divorce, a business failure—make such major demands on mental and physical resources that these are depleted, body harmony disrupted, and natural defenses weakened? Could such marked discord so damage the body's immune system that dormant cancers are activated? In other words, was Henry's disease reignited by the shock of Rhoda's death?

As a scientist, one must be careful not to suspend caution and give rein to speculation. Nonetheless, there is ample evidence that certain diseases (peptic ulcers, spastic colitis, and certain skin conditions, among others) can have psychosomatic origins. But whether acute or chronic distress can encourage carcinogenesis is more difficult to answer. At present most scientists consider the connection to be unlikely. In anyone's lifetime wide variations in individual stress inevitably occur. At some time or other, everyone undergoes stress, the intensity and duration of which vary strikingly from individual to individual. No instrument has been devised that can measure every emotional peak and valley or its effects. And to complicate matters, those under stress and tension are prone to use such established carcinogens as tobacco and alcohol for relief. To sort out what role is played by these and what effect is added by stress is just one of dozens of problems facing serious investigators.

In one attempt at an objective study of the effects of stress, two groups of postoperative breast-cancer patients were analyzed. One group was deemed to be upbeat and optimistic; the other, depressed and pessimistic. According to the study, the former group seemed to develop fewer metastases and to live longer. However, you have to be skeptical about drawing conclusions, as the study was based upon a small number of patients—175—in each group. And it is difficult to sort out and evaluate the several variables that influence breast-cancer survival rates.

Somewhat similarly, it is often debated in and out of law courts whether a single blow injury can initiate a cancer. Some examples: When a child develops bone sarcoma, its patients often recall the child having an injury in that area shortly before. A patient of mine, a freight hauler, developed a skin cancer at the exact site on his scalp that had been struck by a loading hook several months before. The question of workmen's compensation was decided in his favor. Lawsuits have been brought by women whose breasts were bruised in car accidents and who later developed cancer at the site of the bruise.

Beyond the scientific question of whether acute trauma can be carcinogenic, in compensation or insurance claims the pivotal question is whether the cancer was initiated by, or was secondary to, that specific trauma, as lawyers for the plaintiff try to establish. Coincidence can have been a factor, for an undetected cancer may have been present at the time of the accident. The point can be made that a small, undetected cancer could have its growth and spread accelerated following a severe blow.

A patient of mine bruised his chest in an automobile accident. As part of his emergency care, a chest X ray was taken. No rib fractures were found, but a "silent" (asymptomatic) lung shadow was discovered that later proved to be lung cancer. Had a chest X ray not been taken and the lung cancer been discovered months later, it might have been erroneously attributed to the accident.

Physicians who testify in such cases are sharply examined by lawyers. If the physician states that he does not believe that a single injury caused the cancer in question, the plaintiff's lawyers have been known to ask, "Doctor, how can you be so sure this injury did not cause cancer? If you are so certain you know what causes cancer, why haven't you won the Nobel Prize?"

The physician would do well not to react angrily or impatiently to the goading. Instead, he or she should quietly explain that the relationship of trauma to cancer formation is unclear and many questions remain unanswered. For example, why don't prize-fighters and other athletes who have frequent and severe physical contact get breast (or other related cancers) at the sites of injury? Children are constantly falling and getting hurt; why don't *many* more of them get bone sarcomas? All of us have been injured one way or another in our lifetimes, yet cancer rarely occurs at the site of the trauma.

At present, no convincing or conclusive proof exists of the relationship of stress and trauma to cancer. Psychiatrists and endocrinologist search for reliable, objective methods to measure these influences. In the meantime, one must remain both skeptical and open-minded on the subject of stress and cancer—the question that Henry's death had sadly and forcefully raised once again.

Of all diseases, cancer is the most feared; of all cancers in women, that of the breast is the most feared. Despite what seems an epidemic, within the last decade three remarkable advances have occurred in its treatment. The first is mammography, the method that can detect early breast cancer long before it can be palpated by a physician's fingertip examination. The second is the increase of cosmetically acceptable surgery, so that the classic radical mastectomy has been replaced by the modified radical mastectomy and by what is truly revolutionary, the lumpectomy—the breast-sparing local removal of small breast cancers, usually with the nearby lymph nodes.* Finally, chemotherapy, although presently in a state of flux, is constantly being refined. The chemicals used for this purpose, and the indications for and duration of their administration, are becoming better understood.

There are many unsolved mysteries in breast cancer. Why is

* In considering lumpectomy, which I advocate in specific settings, it must be kept in mind that when mastectomy specimens are studied, 30 to 50 percent show unsuspected multiple breast cancer foci at different sites.

Three years after the radical mastectomy that spawned her book *Illness as Metaphor,* Susan Sontag asked me whether, in light of the lumpectomy trend, a lesser procedure would have been just as curative in her case. I showed her the pathology report on her breast specimen. She read that in addition to the cancer that was palpable before surgery, two other unsuspected separate cancers were found. These would have been left in place had just a lumpectomy been done.

Although one day these sites may have been detected by mammograms and physical examination and removed without necessarily jeopardizing her chances of survival, still, the presence of such sites does express one of lumpectomy's weaknesses. Another is the increased chance of local recurrence because the surgeon doing a lumpectomy left too narrow a margin of normal tissue about the cancer.

One day, I suspect, that following the initial biopsy to establish the diagnosis, breast cancer will be treated by hormones and/or chemotherapy without further surgery.

there a rising incidence in America—from one woman in ten to one woman in nine in the last few years? At the moment, epidemiologists are trying to determine the cause of this, and can only say that the widespread use of mammography—with its early detection of cancers—may be one reason, but is not the full explanation.

Although breast cancer is being caught earlier and over 90 percent in the very early stage can be cured, because the disease strikes at the very identity of the woman, her concept of her appeal and sexuality is dealt a devastating blow. Fortunately, even when a breast has to be wholly removed, a reasonable facsimile, including the nipple, can be constructed. Some of this work is done immediately, at the time of the mastectomy; the rest is done later. There is a real question whether prostheses are hazardous; some even wonder if they are carcinogenic. This is yet to be resolved. The FDA has suspended judgment until further data are assembled. In the meantime, women can decide whether to go ahead, knowing of the risks involved.

Such measures were not available thirty years ago. Many women made the best of mastectomy and adapted to overcome what was a severe psychological blow, the impact of which hit their husbands or lovers, too. But for understanding men, loss of a breast causes no loss of love or allure.

I had known Mary Healy—Mrs. Peter Lind Hayes—since *Winged Victory,* when, with other wives of cast members (as well as my own), she appeared in crowd scenes. In later years, she and Peter had a very successful nightclub and stage career as well as a long-running radio show. Mary was gracious, charming, the essence of what is called pretty and feminine. She had been Miss New Orleans of 1935. As she matured, her beauty deepened, she sang beautifully, and the husband-and-wife team frequently appeared in such showcases as Atlantic City and Las Vegas.

In June 1960, when Mary was forty-one, she came to see me, knowing that I was not only a chest surgeon, but a breast surgeon as well. She had developed a black-and-blue mark over a longstanding lump in her breast. She thought the mark might have been caused by golfing. Although the bluish mark itself gradually disappeared, she continued to be sufficiently alarmed to seek attention.

Mary Hayes had a hard, skin-dimpling tumor. A biopsy was imperative. The biopsy was positive and a radical mastectomy was performed. Before the operation, she asked if a very close friend of hers, neurosurgeon Irving Cooper, could stand by throughout the procedure. I had no objections.

Mary's recovery was uneventful and she was discharged a week after surgery. Although she had cancer, a favorable element in her pathology report was that the cancer had not spread to her lymph nodes. Nevertheless, on her discharge summary I entered the word "guarded" after "Prognosis."

Following her radical mastectomy, Mary did an extraordinary thing for that time: She went public with her cancer and her operation.

This was a time when patients with cancer, particularly breast cancer, made every effort to keep that fact hidden. Long before Betty Ford, Happy Rockefeller, Jill Ireland, Nancy Brinker, Mary openly discussed her cancer and, as a beautiful woman and a popular performer, she demonstrated how life after cancer was not only possible, but compatible with being a wife and mother, a glamourous, productive, and athletic (she plays golf and tennis) individual.

Hearing and seeing Mary, many women took heart and were encouraged not to feel handicapped, despondent, or discarded, but to resume control of themselves and their destinies.

Though I felt we would win this war, not every case worked out so well. We took our losses, and with them came tears.

The day after our usual festive, F. A. O. Schwarzian overtoyed Christmas, we made our annual trip to Boca Grande, Florida, to visit Betty and Arthur Houghton. Arthur was a member of the Corning Glass Corporation and the president of Steuben Glass, its elegant Fifth Avenue store, from 1933 to 1973. After that, he was chairman of the board until his death in 1991. Traditionally, we spent New Year's Eve at the home of Jane and Charles Engelhardt. (Charlie, a mining tycoon, was, among other things, purportedly the model for Ian Fleming's character Goldfinger.)

After the midnight celebration, Jane Engelhardt quietly took me aside to say that she was worried about her sister-in-law, an unmarried sixty-year-old woman who had told Jane earlier that she had noticed a lump in her breast, but, out of shyness or fear, had not sought medical attention. Unobtrusively, Jane, her sister-in-law, and I left the gathering and went to a nearby bedroom. It was immediately evident that I was seeing an advanced breast cancer. As gently as possible, I urged Jane's sister-in-law to get medical attention right after the holidays, when she returned to New York. Jane sensed the seriousness of the situation and, when she and I had a moment alone, I told her of my concern. Jane persuaded her sister-in-law to go to New York's Presbyterian Hospital for treatment, but she died within a year.

Unofficial encounters do not all end tragically. In fact, most of mine have not. And I was increasingly encountering invitations to do diagnoses in all sorts of situations. A particularly droll example occurred when I was asked, during one of my periodic bouts of bachelorhood, to escort a handsome, well-known lady to the movie premiere of *Paint Your Wagon* (with lyrics by our friend Alan Jay Lerner). A dinner party followed in the grand ballroom of a large hotel. There were many celebrities present, and much TV coverage.

Somewhere between the entrée and the dessert, my companion whispered: "Bill, I'm worried sick about a lump I've been feeling in my left breast. I purposely wore this halter so you could feel it and tell me if it's malignant."

I was about to smile in disbelief, but saw that she was on the verge of tears.

"You want me to examine you *now*?"

She nodded. "I'm so worried."

Well! We were seated at a round table with eight others. The television crews were moving toward us, table by table, and when they arrived at ours would undoubtedly focus on my companion. As they were several tables away, I estimated that I still had time, so I said, "Move your chair back a little, lean forward, and put your elbows on the table." Keeping an eye on the approaching cameraman and using the access the halter provided, I was able to examine the worrisome area. Actually, the swelling was not in the breast but just below it, so I whispered that it was not serious.

When the cameras arrived a few minutes later, my date was seen soon on screens, all beaming smiles. Meanwhile, I wondered whether the unorthodox examination would make its way into medical history—or the next morning's newspaper.

I knew that I had been at a mechanical disadvantage, and although fairly certain of the diagnosis, insisted that she have a more thorough examination. Happily, it confirmed my table d'hôte opinion.

Sometime in the dim past, a rule of etiquette was laid down that one must never ask doctors, lawyers, or brokers professional questions in social situations. Some doctors resent being questioned on these occasions. To me, being a doctor is not just a nine-to-five job from Monday through Friday, so I see no reason why advice cannot be given outside one's office or hospital. Besides, how can any physician in good conscience ignore a plea for help? If someone asks for my opinion about some condition of concern, I am flattered. Another dinner companion, fortified by two martinis, asked about a breast lump, saying she had become panic-stricken when she found it just as she was getting ready to go to dinner. At my insistence, she, another person, and I went into a side room. The dazzling smile and look of relief on her face as she emerged might easily have been misinterpreted—except that it was her husband who was with us.

I am not above making house calls if needed. I've made them for my own flesh and blood. One winter, the city was buried under a huge snowstorm. Traffic was immobilized, so I walked to the hospital to make rounds. Just as I entered, I was paged on the public-address system. Answering, I was told to call home immediately. Sisi said that while Anthony, then six, and some friends were clearing snow from the steps of our brownstone, he had accidentally been struck on the head with the edge of a snow shovel and was bleeding from the laceration.

I told Sisi to use a towel to press firmly on the wound until I got there. Then, grabbing a sterile instrument set plus sutures, syringes, and Novocain, I ran the several blocks home through the snow-drifted streets. By the time I arrived, the bleeding had stopped, but Anthony had a gaping two-inch wound on the top of his head. We laid him down on our bed and, while Sisi held and reassured him, I trimmed the hair about the wound, injected Novocain into its edges, and stitched him up.

Anthony seemed relieved and grateful, and maybe admiring. Looking back now, was I beginning to see the glint of an idea in his eyes even then?

In fact, house calls—to *my* house—were becoming almost routine. My sons had the same facility for inspiring emergencies that I did at an early age.

That summer, with some friends, Sisi and I took Anthony and Chris for a day-long family outing on Fire Island. Late in the afternoon, when we docked our motorboat, Anthony looked somewhat droopy. I attributed it to his being overtired. When he refused dinner, I didn't press him but took him upstairs and put him to bed. I noticed that he felt warm to my touch, but I thought it was probably a slight sunburn.

We were downstairs chatting when suddenly I heard Anthony cry out in an unnatural way. I ran to his room and found him in convulsions. I yelled for Sisi to come immediately. Chris appeared too. Then, while convulsing, Anthony stopped breathing. He began to turn blue.

I quickly put him facedown on my thigh and, using it as a backboard, began artificial respiration. Try as I might, I could not get air to move in or out of his lungs; his larynx was closed in spasm. If it remained shut, I would have to perform a tracheotomy—cut an opening in Anthony's windpipe. I was just about to ask Sisi to get a sharp knife from the kitchen when he began to breathe on his own. Soon he "pinked up" and lapsed into a deep sleep. His temperature was 104 degrees.

In the urgency of those moments, I had forgotten the advice of my teacher of pediatrics: that when some young children get a high fever, they will convulse and stop breathing. Experienced pediatricians advised younger ones that when a frantic mother calls about her baby's convulsions, they should instruct her to keep the baby facedown until they arrive. Then the pediatrician should drive around the block several times—because, by the time he or she arrives, the convulsions will usually be over. This advice, semi-facetious and clearly dangerous, implies that, as frightening as convulsions are in children, most are self-limiting.

But at that time such advice was furthest from my thoughts and it took all my self-control not to panic. It was one thing to read or hear about such episodes, another to see your child not breathing, turning blue before your eyes.

With aspirin and liquids, his temperature came down and he recovered without further episodes of this type.

Christopher had heard his brother's terrifying cry and stood by witnessing the shouts and commotion that followed. I can still see him in his Yankees T-shirt, standing outside of Anthony's room, looking forlorn. When I emerged, visibly shaken, he asked plaintively: "What happened, Daddy?" Then: "Is Anthony going to be all right?"

"Yes," I said, and pulled him to me.

CHAPTER XIV

The Iceman Cometh

An incident in February 1962, may have marked the renaissance of interest in using extreme cold to alleviate, perhaps even cure, certain localized cancers.

The use of cold as a therapeutic agent goes back at least three thousand years; papyri describe its use by Egyptians who applied cool wet cloths to a variety of conditions, one of which, it is believed, was cancer. I remember my mother applying ice to my injuries and an ice collar to inflamed, swollen lymph nodes in my neck.

Irving Cooper, a friend of the Peter Hayeses and of mine, was an excellent neurosurgeon. It was he who had stood by during Mary Healy Hayes's surgery. Cooper had devised a technique to relieve the tremor of Parkinson's disease by applying the nerve-deadening effects of absolute alcohol to a tiny focus of tissue deep within the brain. However, the alcohol could not be kept localized; it leaked into and damaged adjacent brain tissues. In looking for a controlled method, Coop hit upon the tissue-destroying effect of extreme cold. By circulating liquid nitrogen (-196 degrees centigrade) through tiny steel probes inserted into the area responsible for the tremors, he was able to stop them dramatically.

When we met socially, Coop and I rarely talked medicine. We discussed music or art and played tennis. When I saw that he was scheduled to give a lecture before the New York Thoracic Surgical Society in Memorial's auditorium, I invited him to dinner beforehand.

Coop's lecture dealt largely with the neurosurgical relief of chest pain. Toward the end of his remarks, he paused and said, "As I'm in a cancer hospital, I would like to describe an experience I had." He then described his new technique of using liquid nitrogen to help patients with Parkinsonism, while operating on the brain. It had dawned on him that if extreme cold destroyed brain tissue, perhaps such profoundly low temperatures might also destroy cancer. "I thought it best to try it first on someone whose cancer was readily accessible and visible." The patient in question had advanced rectal cancer that extruded to the surface. Using his tiny probe, Coop froze a small area at the center of the cancer. At no time did the patient complain of pain. A few days later, Coop inspected the area he had frozen; instead of being pink and fleshy, it appeared gray, lifeless, necrotic. Having said that, he ended his discussion and, to polite applause, came and sat down beside me.

I could hardly contain myself. The profoundly low temperatures of liquid nitrogen, and the new instrumentation, might be a novel way of treating localized cancer. Certainly, cryosurgery,★ as we called it, should be fully investigated.

I waited until the last of the audience had left so that I could talk to Coop about the variety of applications extreme cold might have in cancer. My enthusiasm was infectious and we sat talking in the front row of Memorial's auditorium for hours. I sketched out a plan whereby Coop would provide the liquid nitrogen and instruments and continue to confine his research to the serene, orderly area called the brain, while I would explore its use in the underbrush, the jungle, that is the rest of the body—and start on animals other than humans.

Coop's hospital, St. Barnabas in the Bronx, was primarily devoted to the treatment of chronic diseases, particularly in the elderly. It had no animal-research facilities. However, at the Sloan-Kettering Institute, I found an ideal subject for our first experiment: a hamster into whose cheek pouch a human rectal cancer had been transplanted and was growing. As the hamster was no longer needed and would die, I carried it in its cage up to

★ The prefix cryo—or kryos—is from the Greek and means "cold" or "ice." Beginning with Coop's work, all instruments for this modality would be called cryoprobes, and the killing effect of cold on tissue would be called cryonecrosis. Cryogenics, a commonly used term, applies generally to the use of cold for a large variety of conditions.

St. Barnabas, where Coop and I set up an improvised animal operating table.

Anesthetizing the hamster, I exposed the cancer through a tiny incision. With Coop working the main controls of the cryosurgical instrument, I inserted the tip of the brain probe into the center of the cancer. The thermostat was set to produce a temperature of −196 degrees centigrade (−320 degrees Fahrenheit) at the probe's tip.

Within seconds the cancer became a tiny white snowball.

We had some sense that history was being made. Photographs were taken to record what promised to be the first step of a new frontier. When the ice ball thawed, I closed the incision and returned the hamster to the Sloan-Kettering animal facility. Each day I "made rounds" and visited it, fascinated and elated to observe that the cancer gradually became smaller and, within seven days, had disappeared!

Encouraged, I carried to St. Barnabas a procession of small animals, with transplanted tumors, that were no longer needed for experiments and would otherwise be sacrificed. Their tumors responded like that of the original hamster.

Eager to see what effect cryosurgery would have on spontaneous, rather than transplanted, cancers, I tested it on a group of mice that had been bred to form breast cancers. Tiny serial biopsies of the areas that had been frozen were taken daily and under the microscope, showed the cancer cells gradually losing their vivid color and distinct outlines to become pale ghosts of themselves. Eventually they lost any resemblance to their original morphology or appearance.

The next step was to study what effect profound freezing might have on organs such as the liver, bladder, kidney, lung, intestine, and prostate.

As long as small animals were used, we could work with Coop's tiny probe, but if we were to freeze bigger areas in larger animals, it could be like trying to kill an elephant with a fly swatter. I devised larger instruments of various shapes and sizes that could be adapted for use in different locations. One of these, the bullet-shaped "all-purpose probe" had a blunt-nosed three-inch-by-half-inch copper tip to freeze large tumors; another had a flat three-inch face for use on a cancer that had spread over a broad area; a third, angled like a hockey stick, could freeze tonsils and was insulated along its barrel to protect the tongue. Yet another was slightly curved (like a uterine probe) and would freeze the interior of the uterus.

As usual, space for experiments was at a premium at MSK, but I was able to usurp a cubbyhole that housed vents from lower floors. By using this crowded little space and the new instruments, I no longer had to travel to St. Barnabas. Luckily, my improvised lab was across the hall from Memorial's machine shop, so at my doorstep, I had the technical help of master mechanics Joe Thomas and Kurt Vogel.

As the experiments went on, my exhilaration grew and, like a monk, I yearned to retreat at every spare moment to my cell and work on the "micicles." With the whirring of the dust-covered ventilation ducts and the hissing vapor clouds of the liquid nitrogen as it gushed from storage tanks, I felt like a movie version of a mad scientist.

Primitive as these surroundings were, I was able to study the effects of freezing on a variety of organs and to evolve basic principles of cryosurgery from them. What unfolded was this:

1. With the exception of large arteries, all tissues exposed to profoundly low temperatures (-80 degrees centigrade or lower) and maintained that way for more than a minute were killed.

2. Rapid freezing followed by slow thawing was more effective than if thawing was hurried.

3. As the frozen area died, it was sharply demarcated from normal tissues immediately surrounding it. As a result, when healing began, a fine scar resulted. This was different from electrocautery in that, as the latter burned off the lesion, it also damaged several rows of cells in its immediate vicinity, producing a less cosmetically acceptable scar.

4. Two or more freeze-thaw cycles produced more tissue destruction than one. This principle was derived from the experience of MSK's tissue bank. It had been found that if cancerous tissue kept in a deep freeze waiting to be transplanted into animals was allowed to thaw, then refrozen and thawed again, it would not take; seemingly, it had lost viability. (Similarly, when frozen food thaws and is refrozen, it undergoes changes in taste and consistency.) Other than a mild stinging sensation, relatively little pain occurs during or following cryosurgery.

Because nerves are particularly susceptible to, and quickly desensitized by profound freezing, it can be used to relieve pain in localized areas. Athletic trainers use ultracold ethylene spray to ease the acute pain athletes have following a sharp blow or a muscle sprain.

In six months I had assembled enough basic data in small animals to move to larger ones. I called the New York Veterinary Society and the Animal Medical Center, and after describing the research, asked if they had any patients that had incurable surface cancers and would otherwise die.

I was besieged by droves of owners whose pets had a wide variety of cancers that I had never known existed in animals. They came in during office hours. As a result, my waiting room became an interesting mixture of people and animals, who often had the same disease. Between raised eyebrows and raised legs, it was a noisy, curious circus. One woman spelled out her cat's disease— "C-A-N-C-E-R"—when she referred to it, so that the cat wouldn't understand.

Although cryosurgery did not cure dogs or cats of their advanced cancer, it did reduce the bulk of their tumors and, in some cases, relieved pain. I had happy reports from owners whose animals had refused food earlier and now had begun to eat again. Those with tumors involving a limb walked on all fours rather than elevating the affected leg with each step. One benefit resulted from treating a condition called perianal papillomas, which, till then, vets had difficulty controlling. These benign, wartlike growths, probably of viral origin, can be very irritating and frequently bleed. In the past, vets had used cautery, or surgery, to remove them, but recurrences were frequent. However, after cryosurgery, these growths sloughed away and did not reappear.

Word got around about the experiments. The press became interested. They kept nagging us for interviews and bombarding us with questions. To my relief, reporters focused on Coop because of his well-known work with Parkinsonism, so I was able to duck them and avoid discussing research that was not yet ready for presentation. However, Coop, who had a flair for publicity, talked freely to the press without consulting me, emphasizing cryogenics' potential value in treating cancer.

Articles in several publications made glowing references to the work that Coop and I had been doing. When these appeared in *Look* and *Reader's Digest,* they brought national attention to the new "scalpel of ice."

As a result, I was called before a board composed of Memorial's publicity-shy elders, who were understandably sensitive to the slightest suggestion that a staff member of the hospital might be seeking publicity. Although I disclaimed an active role in the publicity, I was criticized for permitting my name to be used before the experiments were completed. I was also told that I must present my laboratory data to the board as they accumulated.

Each month, feeling like a naughty boy before his teachers, I described the results of my most recent experiments. I had faith in the project and in the fairness of the medical board and swallowed my pride. Cryosurgery, like any other revolutionary idea, was bound to breed skepticism and raise questions. I supplemented my findings with slides and live demonstrations.

After several appearances, these meetings were discontinued. Apparently the board was sufficiently impressed and now anxious for me to begin using the technique on selected patients. They thought it advisable to try freezing first on those whose advanced cancers had resisted all established methods of treatment and were visible on the body surface.

The first patient had a rectal cancer that had metastasized to his liver. Although he probably had a short time to live, his cancer had continued to grow at the original site, despite surgery and radiation therapy. It oozed and was painful and malodorous. What was equally disturbing was that the patient, in pain, was prevented from sitting. He was forced to stand as he ate his meals and could sleep only on his side. His physicians told him, "We have nothing else to offer. Why not try this new freezing method? It won't harm you and it might just help." We described the procedure in detail and he, desparate, agreed to try it.

Once he was anesthetized, I brought the tip of the large all-purpose probe into contact with the cancer. The cancer measured about four inches in diameter. As the liquid nitrogen circulated through the probe, a white, frozen area appeared about the instrument's tip. It enlarged in ever-widening circles. Within twenty minutes, the entire tumor had become a hard snowball. Freezing was discontinued and the cancer allowed to thaw spontaneously. While waiting for it to do so, I decided to sit down. However, I could not extricate the probe. It was rigidly held within the frozen tumor, like King Arthur's Excalibur. As a result, I had to stand, supporting it, for twenty minutes until thawing was complete, at which point a second freeze-thaw cycle was carried out.

A few hours after freezing, several changes occurred. The cancer no longer bled as the tiny capillary vessels that covered it clotted. More dramatically, the patient on awakening volunteered that he no longer felt pain. The next day, the cancer began to lose its pink, fleshy appearance; a few days later, it appeared gray and lifeless. Its odor also disappeared. About the fourth day following the operation, in the presence of residents and nurses, I asked the patient to sit squarely on a wooden chair. This simple act, which everyone takes for granted, he approached apprehensively. Then, very tentatively, he eased himself down onto the chair. One could not help but be moved by the evident delight that lit up his face. He told us that this was the first time in many months he had been able to sit without pain. In three weeks, the bulk of the cancer had sloughed away, leaving a clean, raw surface that eventually scarred over.

This experiment was repeated on other patients with similar conditions until it became clear that, if cryosurgery did not cure, at least offered, for some, a new method of palliation.

Following this experience, all manner of patients were referred to me with surface cancers that were otherwise untreatable. Although some would die months later from the cancers' spread, their cancers were debulked, and the pain, bleeding, and odor attending them were reduced. For the terminally ill, a measure of dignity and relief had been restored.

Remembering how long it took to remove the probe, I looked for a method to warm its tip so that the probe could be quickly withdrawn while we waited for the bulk of the cancer to thaw. Max Shula, a Sloan-Kettering researcher, devised an electric warmer so that the probe could be disengaged within seconds once freezing was completed.

Dr. John Lewis, an ear, nose, and throat specialist at Memorial, consulted me about a patient who had a benign nerve tumor (glomus jugularis) just inside the eardrum near the semicircular canals. The canals are sensitive structures, affecting hearing and equilibrium. With inflammation or pressure, as from an infection or a tumor, hearing diminishes, the patient hears a continuous ringing noise, and, in an advanced situation, deafness can result.

If a tumor is causing these symptoms, it must be removed surgically. At that time, the established, standard operation was both delicate and hazardous. Such tumors lie in close proximity, and can adhere to the jugular vein, which carries blood from the brain to the heart. The surgeon must operate through the very confined space of the ear canal and, after exposing the tumor by removing the eardrum, pluck fragments of the tumor away piecemeal. This can cause a brisk—and possibly fatal—hemorrhage from the nearby jugular vein.

Having heard that cryosurgery desensitizes nerves, Dr. Lewis wondered if his patient's tumor could be frozen and left in place to disintegrate, thereby avoiding the risk of hemorrhage.

We explained our plan to the patient. She gave us permission to proceed.

With the patient under general anesthesia, Dr. Lewis first removed her eardrum and exposed the pea-sized tumor. Through the narrow opening in her ear canal, I managed to see just enough to guide the tip of the smallest cryoprobe into contact with the tumor. Freezing began. Within minutes, the probe's tip was stuck fast to the tumor as it became a tiny snowball. Our plan was to complete two or three freeze-thaw cycles, then wait until the patient regained consciousness to see if her symptoms were improved. While I held the probe in place during the freezing part of the cycle, one of our residents accidentally brushed against my hand. Instead of being rigidly fixed, the probe was suddenly mobile. Both Dr. Lewis and I were immediately apprehensive, fearing that something had been torn loose. I expected to see a sudden gush of blood emerge from the torn jugular vein deep inside the ear. With some trepidation, I gently withdrew the probe. No hemorrhage followed—but, to our astonishment, the entire tumor, still frozen, was impaled on the probe's tip!

Instead of reprimanding the resident, I joined in the general relief and amusement. When the patient awakened, all of her symptoms had disappeared.

Dr. Lewis and I published a report on this operation in a 1967 medical journal that shows the still-frozen tumor on the tip of the probe. However, we did not give all the details.

I began to explore cryosurgery's value in other nonmalignant conditions and, using the probe I designed for the purpose, performed probably the first cryo-tonsillectomy (at Manhattan Eye and Ear Hospital). I had already performed several of these operations on dogs with good results. As I well remembered the pain and the hemorrhage I had had as a child, I was hoping that this method would do away with those problems. The operation was performed under general anesthesia and, as I had hoped, no pain or bleeding resulted. Since then, the procedure has been refined and some ENT specialists perform cryo-tonsillectomies as outpatient procedures.

I used cryosurgery to destroy papillomas, persistent, recurrent, wartlike growths of the vocal cords. Remembering cold's clotting effect on capillaries, I was able to reduce frequent, severe nasal hemorrhages associated with a rare congenital blood-vessel condition called Osler-Weber-Rendu syndrome. A gynecologist inserted the uterine probe to reduce profuse, benign uterine bleeding in a patient who was too great a risk to tolerate a hysterectomy. Before the advent of the Pill, Dr. Fred Martens and I used it to seal the intrauterine openings of the fallopian tubes to produce permanent birth control.

Physicians in other specialties adapted cryosurgery to special conditions. Eye surgeons used its remarkable adhesive property to extract cataracts and, because it produced such a fine scar, also used it to reattach detached retinas. (Later, both of these procedures would be replaced by newer methods such as the laser.)

Concurrent with the technique's widening use, a journal, *Cryosurgery*, began publication and annual, well-attended meetings were held at which experiments in new uses were described.

Cryosurgery seemed easy to do—or Coop and I *made* it seem so. As a result, some physicians with little experience in the treatment of benign and certain malignant conditions failed to get satisfactory results. Some expected too much from cryosurgery and, in trying to cure extensively invasive cancers, would freeze them too superficially, thereby missing the cancer's deeper extensions.

When several investigators prematurely published reports of questionable scientific value, cryosurgery's reputation began to decline. In the intervening years, it has gradually found its own level and, as instrumentation and techniques improved, has become a method with specific value for certain conditions. At present it is used at MSK and elsewhere to treat certain benign bone tumors and to relieve pain from metastases to bone. Some gynecologists use it to treat chronic inflammation of the cervix, and dermatologists frequently apply it to precancerous conditions of the skin and to superficial skin cancers. Utilizing its nerve-desensitizing effect, a neurologist is investigating its use to reduce postoperative pain after thoracic surgery. Other institutions are experimenting with using cold for hemorrhoids and to destroy isolated liver metastases.

As interest in the method increased, the Frigitronics Corporation, then the primary manufacturer of cryosurgical equipment, asked permission to name a cryosurgical instrument after me.

Although I appreciated the gesture, I have long felt that although such naming is done as a tribute, instruments named for a well-known physician (e.g., Halsted's forceps or Ochsner clamps) would better be given a name that indicates their function instead.

During a conference, an acolyte of mine called radical lobectomy for lung cancer the Cahan procedure. I thanked him, but said that I would be relieved if I never heard it called that again. If I am to be immortalized, I'd prefer being quoted to turning into a brand name: Ideas are more important than eponymity.

Many years later, a solar keratosis, a "sun spot," appeared on my left cheek, the emblem of my youth as a sun worshiper. A dermatologist in her thirties suggested spraying the souvenir with liquid nitrogen, patiently explaining that "cryosurgery, a technique using extreme cold," would get rid of it. As she began the procedure, she told me that after the second freeze-thaw, there would be a slight swelling, but that within a few days, the keratosis would begin to scale and then peel off, leaving a patch of clear skin.

When she was finished, I told her she had done a fine job, and remarked that I had something of a cryo-connection. The next day, I sent her a copy of *Cryogenics in Surgery,* a text that I wrote with Hans Von Leden and published in 1971, when she was probably a teenager soaking up the sun's rays on the beach, risking her own keratosis.

After the book was published, I set aside any more substantial research in cryosurgery to concentrate more and more on what had become a deep concern and, eventually, a passion and an obsession.

It had to do with tobacco.

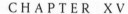

CHAPTER XV

The Hippocratic Tree

No one forgets where they were when they heard about the attack on Pearl Harbor, or where they were that day in 1963 when they first heard about the assassination of John F. Kennedy. For those of us alive then, they are our common locations in time. I was in the surgeons' dining room waiting for my next patient to be made ready when a resident rushed in and said that the President had been shot. All of us ran for the television set in the nearby lounge and stood there horrified as we watched the ghastly tragedy unfold.

When it was confirmed that Jack Kennedy was dead, although hardened to catastrophes and seemingly more stolid and successful at restraining emotion than others, some surgeons were misty-eyed. Stung and depressed, we went back to operate on our patients, thinking of the surgeons in Dallas and the loss of a life and a light.

That night, Sisi and I told our boys what had happened; together we watched the extraordinary event replayed on television and, a few days later, the stately, somber cadence of JFK's funeral procession.

That summer of 1963, Sisi and I took the boys to visit Italy, parts of Greece, Turkey, and the Black Sea ports of Russia. Arthur and Betty Houghton and their daughter, Holly, went with us. Arthur, a member of his family's Corning Glass corporation, was the president of Steuben Glass, Corning's flagship Fifth Avenue store.

One day in Istanbul—it happened to be July 4—we set out from the cruise ship, which was moored at a dock, in two cars to visit a mosque. Chris, Arthur, Holly, and I were in one car and the others were in a car ahead.

Chris and I were sitting up front with the Turkish driver. As we were riding over a sun-baked, cobblestoned street, Chris said: "Daddy, I feel sick."

Thinking he was probably carsick, I had the driver stop and got Chris out of the car in case he wanted to vomit. As we stood in the nearby field, he said, "Daddy, there's a black curtain coming down in front of my eyes," . . . and he collapsed, unconscious, and stopped breathing.

I knelt beside him and saw that he was turning blue. I put him facedown and, pressing his chest with my hands, managed to force air into his lungs. At the same time, as they recognized the seriousness of Chris's condition, Arthur and Holly immediately got out of the car. They could see I needed room to care for Chris on the way to the nearest hospital, wherever that was.

Chris began convulsing. To maintain an airway for him to breathe and to prevent him from biting his tongue, I put my forefinger in his mouth. In the frenzy of one seizure, he bit deeply into the finger (the scar is still there). I carried Chris, now breathing on his own, to the backseat, yelling to the driver: "Emergencia! Hospitale!"

Honking his horn furiously, the driver raced across the Galata Bridge, scattering mules and people. Just as we reached the other side, Chris stopped breathing again. Because I could not get a good purchase on his chest in the backseat, I signaled the driver to stop, carried Chris out of the car, put him facedown on the road, and started artificial respiration once more.

Immediately a crowd gathered. When Chris began breathing on his own, I carried him back into the car and was surprised to find that we had been joined by strangers: two men dressed in open shirts and baggy pants, who looked to be laborers. With hand gestures they indicated that they had joined us to be of help. Within a few minutes, we raced up a steep hill and stopped before an old ramshackle building with a faded red cross on its wall and a ceramic sign in Turkish that indicated it was a dispensary. The entrance led directly into a whitewashed room, where a number of people in tattered clothes sat on simple wooden benches waiting their turn. As I stood there with nine-year-old Chris in my arms, my two new Turkish friends gesticulated and excitedly talked to those waiting. Without a word, they got up and stood outside the dispensary in a huddle, talking amongst themselves.

This primitive dispensary was run by two nurses—one about twenty, the other in her mid-thirties. My new adopted friends described to them the "seriosa" situation they had just witnessed. Using hand gestures and a mixture of Italian and French phrases, I conveyed to the nurses that I was a physician. I carried Chris as the nurses took us down a short corridor to a room with two beds. I put my boy in one and described to the nurses in sign language what had happened; they quickly provided me with a hypodermic syringe and a vial of barbiturates to be used as an anticonvulsant should Chris have another seizure.

This became like a Kafkaesque nightmare. No one of our group knew where we were. I dared not risk taking Chris on the fifteen-minute trip back to the ship or leave him to go for help myself. I phoned the American embassy to ask for the name of a physician, but it was closed because of the American holiday. Chris remained unconscious, but was breathing on his own. Via our driver, I sent a note to Arthur Houghton, hoping he had managed to return to the ship. A few hours, or an eternity, later, Arthur appeared and told me that the others were still out sight-seeing and knew nothing of what had happened.

With Arthur there, and my son seemingly stabilized, I decided to chance taking Chris back to the ship. Before we left, Arthur tried to compensate the nurses, but they refused. Hurriedly, I took their names and addresses as well as those of the two volunteers who had materialized out of the crowd.

Betty and Sisi were walking toward the ship from their car just as I was carrying Chris up the gangplank. While we hurried Chris to the ship's dispensary, I told Sisi what had happened. Chris's temperature was 103 degrees. He remained in a deep sleep and I injected him with antibiotics. In a few hours, he seemed to be out of immediate danger.

I cabled Chris's pediatrician in New York, describing what had happened. She cabled back agreeing that antibiotics should be given and adding that as soon as Chris returned to New York, he must have an electroencephalogram to determine if there was an organic reason for his seizure.

He improved rapidly. Back in the United States, all his tests were negative, and he never had a recurrence.

In trying to reconstruct the cause of that episode, I remembered how Chris had spent hours in the ship's swimming pool, a lot of it swimming underwater. Perhaps the water was contaminated and, in some way, infected his sinuses, producing an acute encephalitis.

I wrote a letter to Turkey's President Inaou in which I described our experience. I gave him the names and addresses of the people who had helped us. He replied with a letter thanking me, saying that he had made contact with each individual I had mentioned and had personally commended them for their actions. As another gesture of gratitude, I sent packages of nylon stockings to the nurses and a year's subscription to American medical journals to the dispensary.

That fall, the boys returned to their school, Dalton, where each student received written reports instead of grades. Anthony had just entered the first grade. Chris's third-grade teacher let us know that Chris excused himself from class two or three times a day in order to visit his younger brother. When we questioned Chris about this, he answered that he wanted to make sure that Anthony was all right, to explain to him what to expect, and to tell him not to worry as he, Chris, was there if Anthony needed him.

Again, the big, caring brother.

Anthony showed an unusual degree of manual dexterity. Like many children, he liked to build things and was curious to find out, for example, what made clocks tick, radios play, and engines run. When he took them apart and figured out what made them tick, he put them back together again. In 1965, at ten, he wrote: *My life is a lonely life. But I have fun watching the dainty dove fly freely across the dark blue sky. I like the way roses sway back and forth, the grass making white streaks when the wind blows. I'll never be free so let the free be free.*

In Anthony's early teens, he took to bed books with mathematical problems instead of adventure stories or comics.

Chris was the more emotional of the two and, in his fierce independence, resisted the authority of parents and teachers. His intransigence often ended in shouting matches and tears as he butted his ego and convictions against the wall of his two strong-minded parents. We should have reacted with less anger and with more understanding of his inner turbulence.

When Chris was thirteen, he fell in love with Elizabeth Barrett (not Browning), whom he met at a party. It was an O. Henry–

like tale. Elizabeth was the granddaughter of Israel Baline, an old friend of my father's. Izzy was a singing waiter in a small restaurant in Chinatown in the first decade of this century. He used to ask my father to come to the restaurant at night after work at the nearby World Building to shill for him by tossing dimes on the floor of the restaurant when he finished singing. In this way, Izzy hoped to encourage other patrons to do the same. Eventually the two friends went their separate ways. One night, thirty-five years later, I invited my parents to a performance of *Winged Victory*. While waiting in the theater lobby during intermission, my father recognized Baline and greeted him by name, calling out loudly, "Izzy!" After some reminiscences, Izzy Baline, now Irving Berlin, said to my father, "You know, Sam, you're the only person I let call me Izzy." Twenty-plus years later, by an extraordinary coincidence, their grandchildren had met and became enamored of each other.

What with my growing practice and experience gained by operating with residents on many clinic patients, I felt more confident, and competent to embark on more extensive operations when I believed that these would be beneficial. In 1966, J.S., a social worker in his forties, consulted me. He was cheerful, husky, and muscular—and had smoked two packs of cigarettes a day for over twenty years. Chest X rays showed that his lung cancer extended beyond the confines of his right upper lobe and had invaded several nearby ribs. This meant they would have to be taken together with the cancer-containing lobe. When informed about our plan, without batting an eyelash he said, "When can I be admitted?"

In surgery, it was necessary to remove four ribs plus the affected lobe to be certain that a margin of safety around the cancer was obtained. The large chest-wall defect was repaired with a sheet of tantalum-steel mesh.

He did well and, within a few months not only returned to work but was back exercising vigorously. I decided to present him at one of our weekly surgical conferences. There, to the amazement of my colleagues, he demonstrated his prowess by doing twenty pushups in less than a minute! Now, over twenty-five years later, there is no recurrence and he, in his mid-sixties, is still doing pushups.

In the summer of 1965, once again we toured the Greek islands. I was able to afford this junket thanks to the royalties from a movie

I had written with Otis Guernsey, Jr., then the movie critic of the *New York Herald-Tribune,* called *One Hundred Frightened Girls.** I had been asked to give a lecture in Athens, and this fitted neatly into our plans.

I was particularly anxious to visit the island of Kos, where Hippocrates, the father of modern medicine, held forth around 400 B.C. Hippocrates is credited with establishing some of medicine's basic principles and, in particular, the ethics that have guided medical practice through the centuries. The Hippocratic oath stems from his teachings.

The ruins of Hippocrates' "hospital" stood on a hill and consisted of the remains of rough-hewn stone walls from which the roofs had long since disappeared. In one room, the height and dimensions of a stone table at its center suggested that it had been used as an operating room. In the center of the hospital, a seat had been carved into a rough low wall; this, we were told, was Hippocrates' chair. In true tourist fashion, my sons and I had snapshots taken as we took turns sitting in it.

Of great interest was a huge rambling tree beneath which Hippocrates purportedly—and the Greeks do have a way with legends—taught students and received new patients. This would have meant that the tree was more than two thousand years old, an impossibility as only redwoods and bristlecone pines are *that* ancient—but why spoil the fun?

I asked if I could have one of the small saplings beneath the tree. That night our guide brought me a terra-cotta flowerpot containing a spindly shoot about eighteen inches tall, which had two small leaves at its tip. For the rest of the cruise, I behaved like Captain Queeg in *Mister Roberts:* No one could touch my "baby" but me, and only I could water it and move it from port to starboard to catch the sun or avoid the wind.

In Athens, where I was scheduled to lecture and then return home the next day, I realized I had a problem: How was I going

* A fictionalized version of an experience Sisi had in her preteens when she accompanied her father to Italy; he was the naval attaché at our embassy in Rome. At her school, Marymount, some of her classmates were daughters of Mussolini's high-ranking admirals and generals. They would discuss their fathers' comings and goings. Sisi would recite these to her parents when she got home. Her father pricked up his ears: The information Sisi unwittingly gave contained valuable clues to Italian troop and naval movements. So Sisi was a teenage spy. In the movie, the enemy was Communist China instead of Italy, and the school was in England.

to get my sapling through customs? I explained my predicament to Dr. George Doxiades, chief surgeon of Evangelikos Hospital, who had invited me to lecture. He told me not to worry and to leave the tree with him. He would arrange everything.

Back home, weeks went by, until one day my secretary Phyllis Atkinson, announced with some excitement that a customs officer at the airport was on the phone.

"Doc," he said, "your tree is here."

Overjoyed, I said, "What has it got to say for itself?"

"It's got a note on it: 'Please give me a drink of water in the morning and another one at night.' "

Just like any anxious parent, I asked, "How does it look?"

"Okay, Doc, but you've got problems." He said that, because of Department of Agriculture regulations, the tree would have to be removed from its pot, the earth incinerated, and the shoot washed off and replanted in American soil.

Such an operation gave me visions of disaster. The customs officer listened to me patiently as I told him what I had in mind for my tree.

Three days later Phyllis rushed in and said, "The tree is here!"

And so it was. Its note was still attached and the tree was in its original pot: The Greek soil had not been changed.

When I called Dr. Henry Pratt, then director of New York Hospital–Cornell Medical Center, and told him my plan, he referred me to the hospital's gardener.

The gardener asked, "What species of tree is it?"

"I don't know."

"What sex is it?"

"Under what leaf do I look?"

(Later I learned that it was an Oriental plane tree and a female.)

We selected a spot alongside a walk leading to the Stanton Griffis Faculty Club where it would have plenty of sunlight and be shielded from north winds by nearby buildings. I suggested that, accustomed to a warm climate, it should be burlapped for the winter.

That winter was a severe one. Finally, on the first warm day of spring, I watched anxiously as the gardener unwrapped my "baby." There, to my delight, was a single bud on its tip.

Over the years, the tree grew rapidly until it was over thirty feet tall. It became known in that medical community as the Hippocratic Tree. My plan was to give a leaf from it to each graduating Cornell medical student after the Hippocratic oath was

The Hippocratic tree with a dedicatory plaque to
George M. Papanicolaou, M.D.

recited. And I was beginning to suspect Anthony might one day
be one of them.

In 1967, I operated on the actor Melvyn Douglas to remove a
melanoma from his foot. (He insisted that it had been named after
him—Mel['s] anoma.)

When well-known patients are scheduled for admission, particularly those in politics or the performing arts, we offer them
anonymity in the form of a pseudonym or *nom d'hôpital*. I suggested this to the handsome, outgoing Mel, but he would have
none of it: "After all, I've had top billing for years. Why stop
now?"

While we were operating, one of our staff surgeons, a woman
of, as we used to say delicately, a certain age, dressed in a scrub
suit, cap, and mask, came into the O.R. I was surprised to see her
because her surgical specialty, gynecology, seemed somewhat unrelated to the operation at hand. We greeted each other, and as I
went on operating, she stood quietly watching. After a few minutes, she said, "Bill, is that who I think it is?"

"Yes, it is."

Then—a long pause—she said, "May I ask you a favor?"

"Sure."

"May I kiss him? I've been in love with him for twenty years."

I looked at her over my mask. "Go ahead. But please keep sterile precautions."

So she went to the head of the table behind the sheet-draped wire loop (the "ether screen") that shields the anesthetist and the head of the patient from the operative area, dropped her mask, gave Mel a brief kiss, readjusted the mask, squared her narrow shoulders, and walked straight out of the room.

As they say in the theater, and amphitheater, there wasn't a dry eye in the house. Or a face without a smile.

I hesitated to tell this story to Mel for years, but one day I did. He frowned. "I may never forgive you."

Startled, I asked, "Why? It really wasn't risky. We kept everything sterile."

"*Why?* Sterile? For years you've deprived me of one of the greatest fan stories I've ever heard."

Mel introduced me to his beautiful wife, Helen Gahagan Douglas, of whom I had always been a fan. Helen had gone straight from Barnard College to a career as an opera singer and, later, an actress. It was in 1930, while she was in a play produced by David Belasco, that she met Mel. When they married, she gave up her acting career and began championing the rights of minorities. Helen was elected to Congress three times from her California district. In 1950 she was the Democratic candidate for the U.S. Senate, running against a newcomer named Richard Nixon. Nixon's campaign tactics ran to scurrilous attacks on Helen, emphasizing that her voting record was similar to that of an avowed Communist, New York's Vito Marcantonio. A whispering campaign was started about another crime: The rumor mongers implied that she was married to a Jew. Although she lost the election, Helen kept speaking out on issues, especially those which involved the shabby treatment of the poor and underprivileged.

Helen was appointed to national committees by several presidents and, serving with Eleanor Roosevelt, was an alternate representative to the United Nations.

Ultimately, I performed a radical mastectomy on Helen, then seventy. She took the diagnosis and the surgery with her usual calm gallantry. When she was scheduled for admission to the hospital, she behaved in a way typical of her, insisting that she not occupy a private room, for she did not believe in privilege. Throughout several medical sieges, she constantly kept her principles flying. As a staunch champion of the underdog, she would complain of how overworked the nurses were and bemoaned the shabbiness of the cleanup woman's shoes, wanting to know if she was being paid enough. Helen's charm, indeed the breadth of her nobility, was such that she was adored by every staff member who took care of her. She gave off such an aura of truth and beauty that intuitively those around her felt they were in the company of great goodness and enriched by her presence. Many, after their tour of duty, would come and sit at her bedside to listen to her.

Helen and I had many long talks about civil rights. One day, I asked her about her treatment by Nixon, but she would not open up on the subject. As her husband wrote in his autobiography,

Melvyn and Helen Gahagan Douglas. He, veteran actor, and she,
actress, activist, and political figure, were both patients of the author.
Both were widely admired; he was secretly kissed.

"If someone treated her badly, she disliked the action, not the man." Mel, on the other hand, could be quite vocal and furious, describing how during the senatorial campaign, leaflets claiming that Helen had strong Communist leanings had been dropped from airplanes.

During the awful days of Watergate, with the exposure of Nixon's skullduggery, I told Helen I had been thinking of her and wondering what she thought of him now. She looked at me, her lovely face and blue eyes a study in composure, and said quietly: "So what else is new?"

As Mel wrote, "She loved the light, never the shade."

To my horror, six years after her mastectomy, Helen complained of pain that turned out to be caused by the spread of cancer to her bones. To fail with one as heroic as Helen Douglas was somehow doubly distressing. Once more, all I could do was stand by helplessly while cancer took over and destroyed someone I admired and adored. As she lay in a coma in her hospital room, just a few hours before she died, I could not resist kissing her.

At the memorial service in a Unitarian church in New York, a eulogist appropriately paraphrased Shakespeare:

> When she shall die, take her
> And cut her out in little stars
> And she will make the face of heaven so fine
> That all the world will be in love with night
> And pay no worship to the garish sun.

In 1981, a year after Helen, Mel died of pneumonia. He had just finished his last movie, *Ghost Story,* with two other veteran troopers, Fred Astaire and Douglas Fairbanks, Jr. Offstage, the man seemed resigned, fightless; he said to me that "with Helen gone, there seems little point in living."

Both live on as cherished memories for me and for millions. Frequently, I see Mel looking debonair and handsome in reruns of movies he made with Garbo and think back—and understand —the irresistible urge of the kissing surgeon.

As medicine continued its up-and-down course, so did family life, the surprises causing emotions to go up and down like a yo-yo.

On February 13, 1969, I opened *The New York Times* and read the Quotation of the Day:

It may not be Lindbergh's crossing the Atlantic, but it's almost as important.
                              —Christopher Cahan,
                  whose brother Anthony built a ten-story yo-yo.

Flabbergasted, I read on:

It was the day of the giant yo-yo experiment at Dalton School yesterday.

Would the 15-inch, four-pound, plywood yo-yo emblazoned with orange and pink flowers and built by 13-year-old Anthony Cahan survive its descent from a 10th floor window and rise again?

Bets were taken. (The faculty bet no; the students bet yes.)

Cheers were chanted. ("Go, go, yo-yo.")

Pronouncements, in keeping with the occasion, were uttered:

"It may not be Lindbergh's crossing of the Atlantic, but it's almost as important," said Christopher Cahan, Anthony's older brother.

"It's kind of a heroic conception, the largest yo-yo in the world," said Donald Barr, the headmaster.

A group of boys and girls and some faculty members gathered in front of the school's brick facade at 108 East 89th Street at noon. They assumed yo-yo watching positions (head tilted, eyes and mouths wide open) and like a Times Square crowd on New Year's Eve, waited for the sphere to drop.

After a few successful trials from a lower floor, the psychedelic yo-yo was carefully lowered from a 10th floor library window by Anthony Cahan and Paul Sailer, a mathematics teacher who had thought up the project.

Down it spun, a swirling orange blur, as Anthony let out the nylon line. Then up it rose to the seventh floor. Then a downward dip to the fourth floor (the crowd gasped), then back to the tenth floor where it hit the window sill and began to spin wildly.

Hand over hand, Anthony and Mr. Sailer pulled on the string and finally hauled the whirling yo-yo back into the building.

As for Anthony's reasons for building the yo-yo, he said: "I like to build things, I guess, and I love flowered yo-yo's."

A photograph of Anthony and the yo-yo accompanied the story. Since Anthony had mentioned the project only in passing, I was astonished.

At the time, Sisi was traveling in Africa with Betty Houghton. When she boarded a plane there, she saw a fellow passenger read ing a copy of *The New York Times*. She asked him if, when he was through, she might borrow it to do the crossword puzzle. To *her* astonishment, she saw Chris's quote and the yo-yo story. She cabled Anthony: THRILLED. YO-YO TRIUMPH. FANTASTIC COINCIDENCE. SAW ONLY *TIMES* IN LAGOS. LOVE, MOTHER.

The yo-yo article was picked up by newspapers throughout the world and even became the subject of cartoon strips. For weeks we were deluged by congratulatory letters from friends and strangers. Wil Glickman, the playwright, wrote from California: "On the front page of the *San Francisco Chronicle,* yet! Why is that kid fooling around with yo-yos instead of smoking pot like a normal, average American boy!"

When I heard that CBS-TV had decided to do a feature on the flight of the yo-yo, I decided I'd better see Anthony and his yo-yo in action for myself. Without telling him that I'd be there, I joined the crowd of students and passersby in the streets outside Dalton and watched as he and a friend prepared to stage the re-enactment. As I looked up, I saw that his friend was smoking a cigarette—and to my dismay, he passed it to Anthony. From the practiced way Anthony inhaled, I knew it was by no means his first.

At that moment Anthony let the yo-yo go. It glided down and up again smoothly to the cheers of the spectators. I cheered, too, but was nagged by disappointment. Anthony knew how I felt about smoking. However, I made up my mind not to spoil his triumph.

Not long after—and this time at home—I discovered Anthony secretly smoking in our cellar. When he admitted that he smoked habitually, I blew my top.

In tears, Anthony issued a challenge. "All right, Dad, I'll quit smoking if *you* give up martinis."

I looked at him long and hard. "Okay," I said. "It's a deal."

We sealed the bargain with a hug and a kiss. I stopped drinking a before-dinner martini and Anthony never smoked again.

When Sisi returned from her trip, she was delighted by the praise Anthony was receiving. Still, in spite of so many things going for us, we had grown uneasy in each other's presence and could no longer rely on a sense of humor or of the ridiculous to rescue us from our conflicts. (I nicknamed our house the Bicker-age.) Although undoubtedly the conflict in our home had its origins in our personalities, my mother played a role—albeit unwittingly—in the difficulties. One flashpoint could be counted on to unleash a firestorm: the habit my mother had of dropping in to visit us, unannounced, or calling Sisi to chat at length, usually at the most inappropriate times. (My father never transgressed.)

Once in our house, my mother thought nothing of going to the refrigerator to look for something to eat. Sisi felt that this was an unpardonable invasion of her privacy and, although Sisi knew that I had asked my mother not to do so, this aspect of my mother's behavior invariably set off accusation and counteraccusation. Since life at home had begun to fester, when I was invited to give a series of lectures in Israel in the summer of 1969 I jumped at the opportunity. Chris, then sixteen, begged to accompany me. He wanted to break with a group of friends who he suggested, were not good influences.

In Israel, we stayed on the grounds of the Weizmann Institute, in a house made available to us by my colleague Dr. Mathilde Krim. Alfred Sabin, of polio-vaccine fame, headed the institute then.

Israel was at war, and each morning Chris listened to the fighter planes taking off. With a guide, we drove all over Israel, often giving lifts to soldiers, male and female, with guns slung over their shoulders. When we visited Israel's northern border, we saw numerous patrols of troops and tanks, towns that had air-raid shelters, and the grim remains of houses destroyed by war.

In the old city of Jerusalem, Chris and I visited the Wailing Wall, the sacred remnant of a temple built two centuries B.C. The Wall, constructed of huge blocks of sand-colored stone, stands perhaps sixty or seventy feet high. Jews from all over the world make pilgrimages to this site, where, it is said, God is forever present and all the pain of Jewish history is remembered in the stones. Bearded men in long black coats, wearing yarmulkes or broad-brimmed fedoras, were davening (crying out in prayer), separated by a small fence from a section in which women in black dresses, with scarves around their heads, were also praying. From time to time, small papers were inserted into cracks between the stones, papers that I later learned had prayers written on them. I had not been in a synagogue except for weddings or funerals since I was bar mitzvahed, and certainly had no special religious bent. Yet, as I laid my hands on the sun-warmed, irregular stones of the Wall, the sufferings of the millions of Jews who had died through the centuries because of their beliefs seemed to come into my fingers, and I found myself sobbing uncontrollably. Chris was stunned as he saw me cry for the first time.

Instead of accompanying me on the lecture tour, Chris decided that he wanted to spend time in a kibbutz. Jerusalem's mayor, Teddy Kollek, whom I met through friends in New York, arranged for Chris to enter the En Gev, one that Kollek had attended, on the eastern shore of the Sea of Galilee. Chris's duty there was to sail out early each morning on the Sea of Galilee, together with other members of the kibbutz, to catch "(Saint) Peter's fish." Later that day, their catch was served in the kibbutz-run restaurant on the shore of the lake.

After each of my lectures at the hospitals, my physician-hosts would take me on rounds and ask me to discuss the care of cancer patients. After I had seen a wide variety of cancers, I remarked on the surprising scarcity of patients with cancer of the cervix. The physicians understood my point, for cancers of the cervix, as distinguished from those of the main part of the uterus—its body or corpus—rarely occur in Jewish women. This finding has been variously interpreted. One theory has it that Jewish women usually marry Jewish men, who are circumcised. Uncircumcised males can have secretions, called smegma, beneath their foreskins; in laboratory experiments, smegma has been found to be carcinogenic.

The evidence for this cause and effect is still questionable. What is established, however, is that girls who begin heterosexual activity in their early teens and who go on to have multiple sex partners are predisposed to developing cervical cancer. As Jewish women of my generation were brought up in a tradition of moral restraints that strictly forbade premarital sex and encouraged monogamy, theoretically such circumspection reduced their chances of getting cervical cancer. A corollary of this deduction is that nuns rarely develop cancer at this site.

My guides were aware of this, of course, and told me that recently, they were seeing increased numbers of cervical cancers. In searching for an explanation, it was found that often these women were émigrés from North Africa (Algeria and Morocco).

When questioned about their past, more than a few reluctantly admitted that when they were young, Arab "recruiters" had abducted them and forced them into prostitution. After several years, a number were able to free themselves and emigrate to Israel.

Recently, herpeslike viruses have been found in patients with cervical cancer. However, their causative role is not yet established. The most recent possible contributory cause: cigarette smoking. As most patients with cervix cancer have been heavy smokers, thus risking lung and larynx cancer as well, it can be said, grimly, that they are burning their candles at both ends.

The trip to Israel gave me a chance to get to know one of my sons better. Chris, more than Anthony, seemed to have inherited the committed qualities of both families.

Therefore, I was not surprised that Chris returned from Israel full of idealistic zeal. Rather than hang out, he elected to finish his vacation time volunteering in an East Bronx storefront recreation center. These city-sponsored centers were scattered in underprivileged neighborhoods to help occupy kids through their summer recess. The storefront to which Chris reported had been refurbished as a club, and offered Ping-Pong, pool tables, arts and

HANS NAMUTH

The brothers Cahan, looking not a little like the ones called Karamazov. Anthony, right, was to follow in his father's footsteps until he began to make strides of his own; Christopher, took another direction, into California and television. Each has since had a haircut.

crafts, and other pastimes. The area it served was foreign turf to most whites. With Chris's overriding concern for those less fortunate than himself, he went there each day by subway and returned home exhilarated at night feeling I'm sure, as if he were in the East Bronx division of the Peace Corps. One of the unit's activities was to outline baseball fields in chalk on the local city streets and supply bats, balls, and gloves. Chris loved umpiring these games, and, from what we were told, kids adored him.

After Chris had been working there for several weeks, he asked Sisi and me to visit the storefront club. He introduced us to the counselors and to some of the children. We were impressed with the attractive way the store had been converted and by the dedication of its workers.

One day, a few weeks later, a unit leader abruptly approached Chris and told him he must leave immediately. His life was in danger. It seems that an older boy, with a record of violence, had launched into a vitriolic antiwhite tirade before one of the counselors. He singled out Chris by name and finished by stating, "I'm going to get that whitey."

So, reluctantly, Chris left. But by working in that dismal area, he learned, firsthand, about the plight of lower socioeconomic groups of our city. I admired his spunk in sticking it out as long as he did, but have to say I was relieved when he left. I did not want him maimed or murdered for his principles.

There is little question that Chris was pummelled by personal setbacks, as I've said, like unrequited puppy love and strongminded, bickering parents. Lots of tears, shouts, and door-slammings later, Chris left a domestic mess to enter Sarah Lawrence College.

♦

CHAPTER XVI

Man's Inhumanity to Man Makes Countless Thousands Mourn

For generations, they had been known as coffin nails (aka "coughin' nails") and were laughed at and dismissed as a joke. Parents, who usually smoked themselves, tried to keep their youngsters from smoking (it was not "nice" for girls to smoke), telling boys that smoking would "stunt your growth." Athletes knew they were bad for one's wind.

For years, medicine had known about Buerger's disease, in which some individuals, usually men of Russian-Jewish background, had arteries that seemed particularly sensitive to nicotine and would vigorously constrict each time one smoked. The more one smoked, the more irreparable damage was done to the arteries and, secondarily, to the tissues of the lower extremities. After a while, first the toes, then the feet, then the upper leg and thigh became gangrenous and had to be amputated. Even though patients were faced with the threat of progressively higher amputation, they continued to smoke because "I can't seem to stop." Buerger's disease was an early example of the strongly addictive nature of tobacco.

But the fact that smoking shortened lives and caused cancer was not fully realized until the early 1930s and was given impetus in the 1940s, when thoracic surgeons Alton Ochsner and Richard Overholt began describing at medical meetings the possible connection between cigarette smoking and lung cancer.

In 1948, a third-year medical student, Ernst Wynder, at George Washington University Medical School in St. Louis and Doctor

Evarts Graham began an experiment in which tar collected from cigarette smoke was repeatedly painted on the shaved backs of hamsters and mice. Within months, cancers developed at these sites, and the researchers speculated that repeated smoking caused lung cancer in much the same way. On a personal level, this was borne out for a patient of Dr. Graham's. The first patient to have a successful lung removal for cancer had been a smoker, as was Graham himself—who quit as soon as he saw the final results of his and Wynder's research.

In order to support the laboratory findings with clinical data, Wynder asked MSK if he could interview lung-cancer patients about their smoking.

I had heard only vaguely about Ochsner's and Overholt's theory, but when Wynder told me about his tar-painting experiments, I'm sure my eyes widened with amazement. All I could think of saying was "Of course!"

With Wynder's guidance, our staff revised the way we questioned patients about smoking. Previously, a smoking history in its entirety might be: "Do you smoke?" The answer was recorded as a monosyllabic yes or no. Clearly, more details were needed to understand the possible impact of cigarettes. We added: "How old were you when you started smoking?" "How many packs per day do you smoke?" "Do you inhale deeply?" "What brand do you smoke?" "Filtered or unfiltered?" Et cetera.

Once we started tapping the history of lung-cancer patients at Memorial, it did not take long to confirm that cigarette smoking was the common denominator in almost all. When, for the first time, I heard it said that there might be a smoking–lung cancer connection, I immediately recognized its validity: Like many a simple truth, it had been out there waiting to be found.

Graham's and Wynder's published findings caused consternation among the cigarette manufacturers, who realized that their up-to-then unassailable position would be seriously threatened. Advertising slogans and claims such as "More doctors smoke Camels than any other cigarette" began to sound hollow and ridiculous. The manufacturers counterattacked by trying to confuse the public, insisting that the laboratory studies in which cigarette tars had been painted on the backs of small animals were, "after all, not the way people smoke. People smoke cigarettes, they don't paint tar on their lungs." Even though their reasoning was completely at variance with accumulating scientific facts, the cigarette manufacturers maintained this line, as they do now, refusing to acknowledge the hazards of tobacco.

The tobacco companies' skepticism gained a certain amount of credence with the public, many of whom didn't want to believe. I began to search for a way that would provide still stronger proof. Perhaps, I thought, this could best be done by simulating human smoking in laboratory animals.

In January 1962, I submitted a protocol to the chief of thoracic surgery, outlining the aims, methods, and significance of an experiment with dogs. When it was approved, I performed tracheotomies on thirteen animals as a first step. Before I could get to the second phase, hospital authorities complained that space in the hospital's research kennels was at such a premium that housing these dogs for the long period that would be necessary was not possible. Consequently, I had either to move my experiment elsewhere or abandon it altogether.

At this juncture, I happened to meet a fellow physician in the corridor at Memorial. A pathologist at the Veterans Administration hospital in East Orange, New Jersey, he had done extraordinarily detailed research that helped to reinforce the smoking–lung cancer relationship. By painstakingly examining three hundred microscopic sections of the bronchial tree of each autopsy patient at his hospital, he could, without knowing their smoking histories, identify those who smoked by the microscopic changes in their mucous membranes.

We were about the same age, forty-nine, and had known each other for years. His dynamic personality was reflected in his rapid-fire conversational delivery and endless energy. We were bonded by our mutual interest in the smoking-cancer relationship, and always discussed some phase of it when we met. Therefore, when I ran into him that day, it seemed appropriate to tell him about the experiment and ask if he knew where I might possibly house the dogs until it was completed. He was enthusiastic and suggested that we could continue the experiment together by using space at his hospital's grounds in New Jersey.

He arranged to house the dogs in a special facility, and for about a year I journeyed there once a month. The trip back and forth occupied the better part of a day, time that I could ill afford what with my teaching, growing private practice, and other research. To ease the burden somewhat, I taught one of the V.A. hospital's residents how to perform tracheostomies. As part of the research group, David Kerman had been added. A veterinarian and a mechanically minded technician, Kerman devised a collar that held the tracheostomy tube in place that could be attached to a pump that would "smoke" cigarettes.

We applied to the American Cancer Society for additional funds to continue the experiment. The society granted us $41,000 to fund the experiment from March 1964 to March 1965. After a few months, mongrel dogs were felt to introduce too many variables, so two-year-old purebred male beagles were used instead. Their size, short hair, long necks, and good disposition made them excellent subjects. When I learned of this, I had a crisis of conscience because I had owned and adored Wiffals, a beagle of my own. But there were many lives, present and future, at stake.

The dogs were housed in a large, clean, well-ventilated facility, and were well fed and exercised regularly. Each day, they "smoked" five king-size Pall Mall cigarettes. One group of dogs served as controls; i.e., they had tracheostomies, but did not "smoke."

When the dogs first began to inhale smoke, they resembled teenagers having their first drag: Their eyes watered, they salivated, looked bilious, and coughed repeatedly. After a week or two, these acute reactions subsided, and soon the dogs eagerly jumped into position on the "smoking table," anxiously panting for their fix: They had become addicted. Once, when a power failure stopped the pumps for a day, the dogs became as anxious and restless as smokers on a holiday or a weekend who have run out of cigarettes and panic because all stores are closed.

Early in 1966, a news conference was held at the Roosevelt Hotel in New York City to report the findings of the smoking-dog experiment. It was well attended by the press and it made front-page news. The experiment had accomplished what I had hoped: it had delivered a new and telling blow to the tobacco industry's denial of smoking's ill effects.★

My name was not used at the news conference. This at least spared me the criticism from dog lovers and antivivisectionists, furious that these animals were "tortured in this way." However

---

★ In 1968, along with David Kerman (whose equipment and technique had made the experiment possible), I wrote a detailed description of the project, with illustrations. I carefully chronicled the events that led to the experiment. This article was published in the *Journal of Surgical Research.*

well intentioned the sentiment, the true torturers were in the tobacco industry. Were it not for their lethal products, such experiments would have been unnecessary.

In 1964, Surgeon General Luther B. Terry issued a report stating unequivocally that smoking caused lung cancer. In 1966, a
new law required warnings to be put on cigarette packages and in
advertisements: "Cigarette smoking may be hazardous to your
health." Four years later, this warning was modified: "The Surgeon General has determined that cigarette smoking is dangerous
to your health."

The battle was now joined between concerned physicians,
health organizations, and crusaders for the public, and their ad-
versaries, the tobacco interests. Although still refusing to admit
that smoking was hazardous, the tobacco people tacitly admitted
it and tried to allay the public's concern by adding filters and
vying with each other in ads about which brand contained the
lowest amounts of nicotine and tar.

Five years earlier, the great broadcast journalist Edward R.
Murrow had died of lung cancer. Famous for his war reports from
England and for his television interview show, *Person to Person,* as
host of which he interviewed notables in their homes. As he did
so, he would turn his swivel chair to face a large screen that
showed his guest. And with his back to the viewer, he always
held a lighted cigarette between his fingers. In the fifties, I had
remarked on this to Sam Goldwyn, Jr., a mutual friend. Sam tried
to get him to stop smoking his three-plus packs of Camels, without success. (Geoffrey C. Ward, in *American Heritage,* wrote that
Ed was uncomfortable with fame and never overcame the mike
fright that made his legs shake and sweat stream down his neck.
The unfiltered Camels on which he pulled with such ferocity—
up to ninety a day—helped steady him. They did more than that.)

A year or two later, when I met Ed, I said: "You're such a
beloved image, at least stop smoking on camera." He agreed to
try to quit, but added: "I must smoke on camera, because the
cigarette is like an orchestra leader's baton for me." Needless to
say, when he developed lung cancer, he quit immediately. By
then, it was too late. As Ward wrote, "He was wasted, unable to
stand, wearing a red stocking cap to hide the signs of surgery and
radiation, but he watched the television screen with something of
his old intensity."

(In a TV documentary about Nat King Cole shown on television in 1991, Cole was shown being interviewed by Ed Murrow on *Person to Person*. Both held lighted cigarettes as they talked; both died of lung cancer.)

At a Greenwich Village studio party, I spotted a very attractive, animated, fine-featured woman who was smoking even while she danced. I was fascinated by her looks and, when the music stopped, introduced myself to her with a flippant: "What's a beautiful dame like you doing killing yourself?" She smiled, admitted she was a chain-smoker, and shrugged off the question. As we danced, I refrained from giving my usual warnings. Later, I found out that she was Aline Bernstein Saarinen, widow of the famous architect Eero and herself an authority on art. She had written a best-selling book, *The Proud Possessors*. Whenever we met socially, she was puffing away. She would grin as soon as she spotted me, take a deep drag, and blow the smoke in my direction.

One day, in 1972, I was passing through Memorial's radiation therapy department, where I saw Aline waiting to be treated. She was barely recognizable in the turban she wore to cover the hair loss from radiation therapy for lung cancer that had metastasized to her brain. She had lost considerable weight and I sensed that her cancer was gaining the upper hand. I was deeply touched to see her in that sad condition and, as we sat and talked, I was careful not to allude to my previous scoldings. She was called to enter the radiation treatment room and I walked with her as far as the door. Just as she was about to enter, she looked at me wistfully and said softly, "I remember our first dance together." Within a few months, this brilliant, beautiful woman was gone.

Aline's story resembled that of another fifty-year-old woman who awakened one spring morning with a severe headache. Barely able to raise her head from the pillow, she finally managed to crawl out of bed to take an aspirin. She felt so strange that she refrained from smoking her usual "wake-up" cigarette. She saw a physician later that day, who ordered a CAT scan; it revealed a brain tumor that, like Aline's, was a metastasis from her lung cancer. Not infrequently, the first symptom of lung cancer will not be from the lung but from a metastasis to the brain, bone, or another organ. Because the brain is a favorite site for these, when neurologists see patients with brain tumors they automatically order a chest X ray. The woman was referred to me and, without being asked, said she had given up her two and a half packs a day. Sometimes a metastasis from a lung cancer to the brain can be solitary. However, I discovered a large, hard lymph node behind her collarbone—a signal that the cancer has probably spread to other organs.

She was another person who insisted upon knowing the facts of her case. After I finished outlining her treatment, she asked, bluntly, "How long do I have to live?" As noted the vagaries of the disease make such estimates untrustworthy. The only safe prediction is that invariably one guesses too short or too long. I explained that it was impossible to predict survival time. After she absorbed this information, she asked: "Can I make it at least until Christmas and New Year's Eve?"

These holidays were five months away, and I did not want to extinguish hope. I said, "Of course you will."

Secretly, I was glad she didn't ask me about surviving until the following Easter. She had her Christmas and New Year's holidays and she died three months later.

The more preventable tragedies I saw day after day, the more outspoken I became in alerting smokers to the hazards of their habit. I didn't go so far as to stop them on the streets as my boys had done, although I was tempted. But those who are a captive audience, such as fellow guests at a dinner party, probably hear from me sooner or later. If I've saved more lives at dinner tables than I have on operating tables, I hasten to add: I am *not* a bad surgeon.

Taxicab drivers are another favorite target. In New York City, it is now illegal to smoke in taxis, but before the law went into effect on 1980, I usually began with: "I see you smoke. Why don't you quit?"

After a pause, the cabby usually says something like "I've tried like hell, but I can't. With this job and all . . ."

"Do you know what I do for a living?"

"You an actor? A lawyer?"

"I'm a lung-cancer surgeon at the hospital you are taking me to. I call my operating room Marlboro Country." Then I add, "One out of three adult patients wouldn't be at Memorial if they hadn't smoked. You work too hard for a living. Why blow your hard-earned money on cigarettes and wind up in the hospital with cancer? Better quit. Stay out of Marlboro Country."

On one occasion, when I'd finished my sermon the cabby threw his cigarette pack out the window, saying, "That's my last one!" Most look thoughtful and promise that they will try to quit.

None resent my advice; all thank me. Even in New York City. Sometimes I will add to the five-minute lecture: "Think of it this way: The good Lord, or your guardian angel, sent me to tell you to quit."

Every morning at the corner of Sixty-second Street and Third Avenue, I hail a cab to go to the hospital. One morning, I gave my usual warning to the driver. A week later, as I got into a cab, the driver said, "I suppose you're going to give me an antismoking lecture again."

I asked how he was doing and he told me he was not having much luck fighting the addiction.

Three or four weeks later, just as I seated myself, the cabby said, "I give up! This is the *third* time you got me. God, or somebody, is trying to tell me something. I quit!"

At Memorial's entrance, he refused payment, we shook hands, and he drove away, glad to be rid of his habit—and/or of me.

I not only accost cabbies, and do examinations at dinner, I diagnose at both short and long range, making myself a really versatile nuisance. The first such diagnosis was, I suppose, the one of the sergeant in New Guinea. But the charge to do so came from an admirable physician and teacher, Dr. Robert F. Loeb.

Dr. Loeb gave a course in physical diagnosis in our second year of medical school, and it was he who taught us to sharpen our vision, to be constantly alert to the pathological conditions that can be seen everywhere. He told us to take a pad and pencil and record abnormalities that we saw in the streets, in the subways, in class, or wherever. In no time, we were startled to see a veritable museum of pathology on exhibit around us: the masklike faces and tremors of Parkinsonism; acne in the young; hunchbacks; port-wine stains; facial moles; people limping from hemiparesis; staggering alcoholics; the blind; conditions obvious and rare. The list could go on endlessly. As a result, it has become almost reflexive for me to notice physical abnormalities.

On one occasion (it would not be the last), I saw a suspicious skin tumor half a world away. After meeting with an official of Union Carbide in their building at Forty-seventh Street and Park Avenue to discuss a cryosurgical instrument, I noticed that photo portraits by Yousuf Karsh were being exhibited in the building's street-level gallery. I took a few minutes to stroll through the exhibition to admire Karsh's work. Many famous personalities—Winston Churchill; Nehru—were captured and enlarged to three to four times life-size. When I came face-to-face with Russia's premier, Aleksey Kosygin, I noticed a spot on his forehead, just above his eyebrow, that looked like a basal cell carcinoma. To be certain of the diagnosis before I took any action, I called John Dougherty, a dermatologist, and invited him to come to the show the next day with his magnifying glass. He was good enough to indulge me and we planned to rendezvous at the southwest corner of Forty-seventh and Park.

Although I had spoken to John on the phone many times and had referred patients to him, we had never met. As luck would have it, the Royal Canadian Mounted Police were staging a tattoo (an exhibition drill) on Park Avenue that day, and crowds had assembled on the sidewalks to watch it. It's difficult to tell a dermatologist from a stockbroker in a mass, so that I wandered from one likely candidate to another tentatively inquiring, "John? . . . John?" and getting the sort of welcome usually reserved for lepers. Finally a voice said, "You must be Bill." Together we entered the exhibition hall. John took out his magnifying glass, through which we scrutinized the already magnified head of the premier. After a few minutes of study, John said, "It looks like a basal cell carcinoma, all right, but it could also be a seborrheic granuloma [a benign skin tumor]. However, it certainly should be biopsied."

Llewellyn (Tommy) Thompson, a friend, was our ambassador to the Soviet Union. I wrote him about what John and I had found and suggested that the next time he met with Kosygin, he report our suspicions and suggest that the premier have the area attended to. This was at a time when the U.S.S.R. and America were not on good terms, so I hoped that the suggestion would be a friendly, hands-across-the-barbed-wire-fence gesture.

During the following months, I scrutinized photographs of Kosygin, hoping to get a good closeup that might show a scar or a depigmented area such as is seen following radiation therapy of skin cancers. However, no photo was clear enough for such definition.

In time, Thompson was relieved of his assignment and came back through New York. Eagerly, I asked if he had said anything to Kosygin. Tommy said, "I have to confess, I didn't have nerve enough to do so."

Some months later, at a dinner party at Barbara Walters's, I was introduced to Karsh and told him the story. He was amused, and proposed that, as a friend of Kosygin's, he call him right then and there on the telephone in Barbara's bedroom. Karsh tried to reach him but could not get through to Moscow. However, he promised that he would continue to try.

Years later, when I first met Henry Kissinger, I felt it would amuse him to hear this story.

He said, "We know that Kosygin had a cancer operation."

This was not the end of my attempts to do helpful diagnoses up close or at a distance—and one in the future would leave me with egg on my face, but undeterred.

CHAPTER XVII

Paradise Lost

In 1970, when he was sixteen, Anthony said: "You know, Dad, there's this one big talent you have that no one in the family has ever seen. Other kids get to see what their fathers do. Why can't I watch you operate?"

I hesitated for a moment, but it seemed to me he could handle it. I thought it best if, at first, Anthony saw another surgeon work while we watched together. So one day I took him to a glass-enclosed balcony overlooking an operating room at Memorial where a colleague performed a two-hour thyroidectomy. Watching Anthony's reactions, I remembered going to see my first operation and was concerned that, at his tender age, he might become sick. I needn't have worried; Anthony was no less absorbed than I had been thirty-five years before.

Encouraged by his eagerness to see more—and by his coolheadedness—I let him observe me in action. This time I brought him right onto the O.R. floor. He had to dress in a scrub suit, but was so thin and hipless that his pants had to be pinned to his shirt to keep them from falling down. But he never fell down— or even sat down. Instead, for six hours, he stood an arm's length away from me, silent, while I removed a stomach cancer. Now and then, I pointed out a particular anatomical structure. When the operation was completed and the dressing applied, Anthony helped lift the patient onto a stretcher. Then both of us went to change. In a new-with-him respectful tone, he thanked me quietly. We dressed in silence and, after I checked the patient in the recovery room and talked to his relatives, we went home.

I was eager to hear Anthony's reactions, but days passed without his making any reference to the operation. Then one night at dinner he said: "Dad, that was better than any LSD trip that guys talk about."

Even with my son watching, I had been totally absorbed in the work at hand. Although from time to time I was able to abstract myself to say a few words to him, my attention, like that of a concert pianist, was riveted on the performance.

This discipline has been tested several times. Once in 1970, while I was performing a lung operation, the O.R. rotating nurse, after asking permission, relayed a message from my secretary that my eighty-year-old mother had just been admitted to the emergency room at New York Hospital. I asked the nurse to get further details as a host of unpleasant possibilities rushed into my mind. I was one and a half hours into the operation and had about two and a half hours to go.

The nurse returned and reported that my mother had fallen while entering her bank, after being forcibly propelled out of the revolving door. She had suffered a laceration and contusion over her left eye, a fractured arm, and a possible fracture of one of her thinned-out, osteoporotic vertebrae. But she was in no immediate danger. Her arm was being put into a cast by the orthopedic resident, and a plastic surgeon had sewed up her wound.

As soon as the operation was completed and I had reassured the waiting relatives, I hurried across the street to New York Hospital's emergency room, where my gallant little mother lay in great pain. After consulting and thanking those who had attended her, I had her moved by ambulance to Memorial so that I could be near at hand.

Once the pain subsided, she did well. However, her four-foot-eleven-inch height had been reduced to about four feet eight inches by the collapsed vertebrae. All of those attending admired her fortitude. She told me that she could endure anything, just so long as she could stay alive to be with her "best beloveds"—a Kipling-esque name she had given to Chris, Anthony, and me.

Had my mother's accident occurred a generation earlier, she would have been confined to bed, and probably would have developed pneumonia and died. Such a series of events had resulted in the death of my father's mother, who, in her seventies, had fractured her hip and died from "the old folks' friend," pneumonia, because of enforced inactivity. Today, regardless of the patient's age, hip fractures in the elderly are often "nailed" or plated together soon after the accident and the patient is out of bed and walking soon afterward.

Although it was painful to do so, my mother was made to move immediately, and she gradually regained enough arm function to be sent home.

During a follow-up, I saw the seventy-year-old man on whom I had operated when Anthony was watching. He had already lived well beyond the five-year survival period that statisticians arbitrarily use to determine the value of a particular treatment. I reported this to Anthony, who by then had sufficient knowledge of pathology to realize that this man had survived against great odds, for his stomach-cancer specimen showed that he had multiple metastatic lymph nodes.

In each physician's experience, there are patients like this who have been given the gravest prognosis but who nevertheless survive. Each time this happens I wonder why this particular individual did so while those with almost identical pathological findings succumb. The message implicit in these phenomena is that physicians should not give up too soon; if any doubt exists, the patient must not hesitate to get a specialist's second opinion; again, most prognosis-making in cancer is, at best, a guesstimate.

Without question, statistics are valuable aids in making generalized forecasts, but they cannot, and often do not, take an individual's response into consideration. Nellie R. is just such an example.

Nellie first consulted me in 1971. She was a charming, intelligent teacher who had a cancer of the left lung that had metastasized to two lymph nodes on the right side of her neck. This is a very ominous sign, as it strongly suggests that the cancer has or will spread elsewhere in the body. In addition, Nellie R.'s lung cancer had invaded the nerve that innervates the left vocal cord, thereby paralyzing it and making her speak in a hoarse whisper. Without question, this combination of findings precluded surgery. Nellie knew from the first that her outlook was grim, but was willing, as were we, to try any reasonable alternative rather than sit by passively waiting for cancer to overwhelm her.

After four weeks of radiation therapy (chemotherapy was not yet available), to our surprise and delight the shadow in her lung disappeared, as did the large lymph nodes in her neck. Her vocal cord, however, remained paralyzed. During this time, knowing how grave her prognosis was (in spite of her cancer's dramatic response to radiation), Nellie said, "I no longer allow minor irritations and concerns to disturb me. I've distilled my appreciation of life and am grateful for each day I am alive."

Something to this effect was echoed by another patient who said, "It takes dying to know what is important in living."

A few months later, Nellie resumed her usual activities. She remained well until three years later when she developed numbness and pain in her legs, secondary to a cancer metastasis in her vertebra. Again, radiation therapy was directed at the affected area and, within a month, her symptoms cleared.

As if this were not remarkable enough, *five years* later—eight years after the initial treatment for her lung cancer—Nellie developed a metastasis beneath the skin of her groin. When this was removed and the specimen analyzed, it showed conclusively that it was a spread from the original lung cancer.

Over two decades have passed since then. Nellie, now a young eighty-eight, energetically walks a mile and a half every day. She is optimistic, busy, eager to continue living. Without question her story is unique. And she is one of a small group of patients whom I call Improbable Cures.

Few patients match Nellie's remarkable story, flying as it does in the face of probability. Mindful of such rare experiences, cancer specialists will often persist in treatment against what seem to be hopeless odds, hoping that the patient's unknown bodily forces might rally to prolong survival. A fine distinction must be made about the value of subjecting a patient to endless, debilitating side effects when there is only the remotest chance that the treatment may be beneficial. In Nellie, this was not a problem, as radiation therapy in local areas is usually well tolerated and poses little extra burden. Chemotherapy, on the other hand, notoriously has both physiologic and cosmetic side effects, and physicians are understandably loath to add this additional burden to someone already being ravaged by cancer. Nevertheless, there are enough graphic examples of cancer's unpredictability and the success of these treatments to justify their use in selected cases.

There are still other messages in Nellie's story in addition to "Do not give up trying." Although tempted to do otherwise, she stayed with our recommendations instead of turning in desperation to what the American Cancer Society euphemistically calls unproved methods of cancer treatment. However, many patients who feel that their physicians have given up on them try these "cures," which have been recommended to them by well-intentioned friends or which they have seen in newspaper headlines, especially those suggesting miraculous results. A man in his sixties who had been a heavy smoker and drinker developed a cancer just behind his larynx that was treated by radiation therapy. Although the cancer responded well and disappeared, months later a chest X ray showed multiple metastases in both lungs. For such widespread cancer, surgery and radiation therapy would be of no value, so he was declared incurable. However, he was offered chemotherapy that is known to be effective in 45 percent of cases either by maintaining the metastases at their present size for extended lengths of time or, in 2 percent, causing them to disappear.

The patient, however, was searching for medicines that "don't break down, but build up my immunity." He had read somewhere that chemotherapy lowers the body's immune forces. With this fixed in mind, he seriously considered trying some bizarre methods that he had heard about "somewhere." When he confessed that he still surreptitiously smoked, I told him that smoking also lowers immune reactions and, with his type of cancer, was like pouring gasoline on a fire.

His was a typical "last-straw syndrome." Quacks, mindful of this desperation, feed on these cancer victims and their families, promising all manner of benefits. They are attractive because all too often such patients feel abandoned by their own physicians, who frequently seem to wash their hands of the whole affair and suggest, in effect, that the patient go home and die. Good oncologists will not promise them the moon and the stars and will tell them that though no promises can be made, there may be some value in an established regimen of chemotherapy. I explained this to the patient and his family; I also had to say that in my lifetime, most so-called miracle cures that made headlines have subsequently proved to be worthless. I called them the Cancer Cure of the Month Club: Krebiozen, laetrile, egg whites, dehydrated umbilical cord, Gerson's diet, whole-milk injections, and so forth, after publicity galore, are no longer news. Usually, the opportunists who promise them amass quick fortunes until they are exposed, then rapidly fade into anonymity aboard their yachts or, with more justice, lose their license to practice.

The patient countered my skepticism by saying, "I've heard people swear by this method. They said it prolonged their lives."

I explained that, not infrequently, those making these enthusiastic claims fall into several categories, the largest being that of patients whose diagnosis of cancer was not established by biopsy. Assumed to be malignant by the physician, the tumor was actually benign. Other patients, persuaded that the treatments slowed their cancer's growth, are unmindful that some cancers are naturally slow-growing. And some of those touting cures are not above paying "plants" to hype the method.

If any virtue comes from the quacks' methods, spurious though they are, it is that they at least provide patients with a measure of hope. Some patients believe this to be preferable to the unfeeling dismissal they have received from their physicians.

Lest you think, as the quacks would like you to do, that the cancer "establishment" resists unorthodox suggestions because they would reflect upon orthodox doctors' own ineffectiveness and put them out of business, you must know that at MSK alone, thousands of leads have been tested. When a new drug appears, it is first given a variety of basic laboratory tests. Then, if this screening shows any promise, more detailed, sophisticated, and carefully controlled laboratory studies are done. If the drug survives these hurdles, committees will review the data before deciding whether to permit human trials. Finally, the results of these experiments are reviewed before a report is published or delivered at scientific meetings.

Such reports describe the treatment in detail so the results can be corroborated or contradicted by other investigators. In sharp contrast, those making spurious claims are easily spotted. They invariably follow similar patterns: They alone can get remarkable results by using a special formula, the ingredients of which are usually kept secret. Their "experimental proof," if published, appeared either in some obscure journal or in their own "in-house" medical releases. Somehow, their epoch-making, Nobel-winning results can never be corroborated by others. Many, however, thrive and gain sympathy by claiming they are being restricted or persecuted by the medical establishment.

In spite of my efforts, my desperate patient tried a Bahamian Ph.D.'s method ($5,000 for four weeks). "Then," he said, "if it fails, I'll try chemotherapy." But almost in the same breath he said: "Of course, there is a man in Bonn, Germany, who was recommended by a friend . . ."

Three months later he died, a victim of those who prey on those who clutch at any straw.

I received a letter from a patient who had advanced lung cancer who resisted grasping the "last straw":

> I've been giving serious thought to the idea of taking chemotherapy. From everything I've heard, chemo has not been successful in my type of lung cancer. I had decided some time ago that the quality of life was more important to me than quantity and I still feel that way. If the statistics for my type of cancer were more optimistic, perhaps I would reconsider, but as things now stand, I think I will remain with my doctors here and not consider chemo. I do hope you can understand my decision.

Four months later, she died.

Sisi and I eventually reached the point where any discussions we had were limited to the mundane details of running a house. We had not only lost that important ingredient of a happy married life, a sense of humor, but had grown suspicious of each other and attributed to an alien presence any prolonged lateness or absence, or a ringing telephone that when answered clicked dead.

For example: Pamela and Leland Hayward were friends of long standing. Leland was a highly acclaimed producer of plays and movies—*The Sound of Music,* for one. In 1970, he had a play in rehearsal, *The Trial of the Catonsville Nine.* It was scheduled to open, when suddenly Leland required emergency surgery to replace a narrowed neck artery that carried blood to his brain.

Bed-bound in New York Hospital, and convalescing, he asked if I would take Pamela to the opening night. *The Catonsville Nine* was an artistic and dramatic success and Pam and I returned to Leland's room that night to tell him so. He was elated.

However, what with the cumulative tensions between Sisi and me, the fact that I had escorted Pamela became another bone of contention, particularly as there had been some attendant gossip about us, all of which was untrue. Several days later, Leland developed complications and died.

Our squabbles became more intense, the intervals between them shorter, and the subsequent moody silences longer. As our discord seemed irreversible, by the following Easter, Sisi and I were separated. This move shocked our sons' sense of security and, naturally, altered their thoughts of home as a haven and the family as a unit, for better or worse. Undoubtedly, it tarnished remembered glories of a family life that, despite everything, had been filled with many more rewards than crises. However, as Anthony was sixteen and Chris eighteen and away at Sarah Lawrence, they were old enough to adapt to the situation.

I moved to temporary quarters in my office, where I slept on a cot, and ate most of my meals at Memorial's cafeteria. For the first post-separation Christmas, I was living in a room in an apartment at United Nations Plaza that was occupied by the Lasker Foundation. Mary Lasker had offered it to me when she learned I was sleeping in my office, a typical example of the infinite thoughtfulness of this great lady that came at a time when I needed a morale-booster. A great philanthropist, she was also an extraordinarily effective lobbyist in obtaining government funds for cancer, heart-disease, and stroke research. On Christmas Day, the endless view of the East River and beyond from the Lasker apartment was scant consolation for the treeless Christmas. Chris, Anthony, and my parents joined me briefly to exchange presents. I remembered the Christmas before, when Sisi and I had gamely tried to keep some of the illusions of previous holidays, but the friction between us showed through and the boys could not have failed to notice the perfunctory way Sisi and I received our token gifts. We attempted to jolly up the occasion by lavishing presents on our sons. That bittersweet memory and the nonevent in the Lasker apartment made for as poignant and sad a Christmas as the one I spent during the war, waiting to be shipped overseas.

As I had no plans for the rest of that day and dreaded being alone to wallow in self-pity, I did as I had done many years before, going to visit hospitalized patients and joining a group of staff members who went from floor to floor singing carols.

When separation legalities were concluded, Sisi moved to an apartment and I bought her share of our Sixty-second Street brownstone. Chris was still away at college and Anthony stayed there with me until he finished at Friends Seminary.

Through the last phases of my marriage, I had become romantically attached to a woman whom I will call Joan. I had known Joan for many years before our affair began. She was married to a friend of mine with whom she had had several children. The truism that you can't break up a happy home applied here, for we both sought and found an escape and a refuge from trying domestic situations. Since, after the separation, we were constantly in each other's company, it seemed likely that one day Joan and I would marry.

When Anthony finished Friends Seminary, he decided to take a year off. This was a constructive move for, during this time, he composed songs, read mathematics and physics, played ice hockey and his guitar, did some carpentry and sculpting in wood and, as he had promised himself, thought about his future.

He applied to Harvard, more out of respect for my wishes than for his own desires. Anthony's application was turned down. He was relieved, for he was eager to go to Hampshire College in Amherst, Massachusetts, where students were encouraged to design their own curricula and pursue their special interests without being restricted or confined by a rigid academic program. Hampshire's milieu resembled that of the ultra-liberal Dalton program of his younger schooldays, and it suited Anthony fine.

College was helping to channel some of Chris's energies. At Sarah Lawrence, he wrote short stories and steeped himself in the history of the Russian Revolution. He joined liberal groups and organized student political meetings and discussions that I would always attend when invited.

After graduation, he went to Florida with a girlfriend and landed a job as a reporter with the Orlando *Sentinel,* where he reviewed movies and acted as a weather and obituary editor, a nice combination. Despite long periods of telephone silence, blood again ran thicker than water, so that when advice or help was needed, medical or otherwise, he would call. I used to say that we had a WFB relationship: Weddings, Funerals, and Birthdays—to which Christmas should be added, for Chris was so enchanted by this holiday that, wherever he was, he never failed to appear.

After breaking up with his girl, he returned to New York and worked as a waiter at Tavern on the Green until he landed a job at NBC-TV as a reporter on NBC's magazine with David Brinkley. While he was there, he and Garrick Utley produced a documentary called *Rockets for Sale.* Through hard-driving investigative reporting, Garrick and Chris uncovered a German rocket maker who was selling rockets to Libya to be used for "testing the atmosphere." The fact that the rockets could carry a huge bomb and had a range of one thousand miles—enough to reach Israel—came out in the tape, which won an Emmy.

As part of his job, Chris began to travel to many countries, and the only way we kept track of him was because of his devotion to my mother, to whom he would send postcards from all over the world.

In his travels, he became enamored of Los Angeles and, in 1982, asked to be transferred to an NBC affiliate there. In a series of jumps, he went to CBS, then BBC, then finally started his own production company making in-house television commercials for Western Airlines. These won awards from national associations that specialized in promotional films.

Chris had several romances and engagements along the way. I was introduced to at least three fiancées, all of whom I greeted with a phrase borrowed from Sisi's father: "Welcome aboard." (I should have added, sotto voce, "Wear a life preserver at all times, in case you fall or are pushed overboard.") He became a director-producer for the Financial News Network and is now on the staff of Dr. David Viscott's popular call-in psychiatric advice sessions on radio and TV.

❖

CHAPTER XVIII

"Surprise Is What Scientists Live For"

Over coffee, following Saturday morning rounds with my residents, I often search for subjects to discuss. Occasionally we have seen a patient with a unique condition and/or an unusual response to treatment. I point out that although this is an "anecdotal case," it could have important implications.

An anecdotal case is one in which a single example of an unusual medical condition occurs. Although of great significance to patients and their concerned doctors, these are medical curiosities from which not too many conclusions can be drawn. Published reports of most anecdotal cases disappear into the vast reservoir of medical data, to be resurrected, perhaps, by a physician reporting a similar condition. If in time anecdotal cases describing the same condition multiply, a trend may become evident. Thus, when the first patients with AIDS developed Kaposi's sarcoma—a cancer in which purple nodules appear and increase in size over the entire body—it must have seemed unique until additional reports indicated that the association between Kaposi's sarcoma and AIDS was no longer merely anecdotal.

I felt this point worth emphasizing to my residents, adding that the history of science is filled with stories of how major breakthroughs were made when readied minds were suddenly struck by an insight that enabled them to recognize the important implications of unpredicted, often minuscule findings. Good scientists are really midwives to ideas waiting to be born.

My friend and colleague Lewis Thomas writes: "Surprise is

what scientists live for. And the ability to capitalize on moments of surprise, plus the gift amounting to something like good taste, of distinguishing an important surprise from a trivial one, are the marks of a good investigator. The very best ones revel in surprise, dance in the presence of astonishment.''

As an illustration of Lewis Thomas's wisdom, I remind them of Sir Alexander Fleming's observation when he saw that on a culture dish accidentally contaminated by a penicillium mold, certain bacteria failed to grow in the mold's immediate vicinity. He wondered: Did the mold kill the bacteria? And the saga of penicillin began.

I stress to young, eager faces that in future contacts with cancer, they must be constantly alert for the smallest clues, the subtlest hints, the unexpected phenomena, that could in some way lead to bigger ideas and solutions to some of cancer's enigmas.

Just such a single report in the early days of my residency gave rise to a new way of looking at a particular cancer problem.

In the early 1950s, Dr. Edward Churchill of Harvard Medical School reported having removed from a young woman, years before, a tumor that he had assumed was a lung cancer. However, when the tumor was analyzed, its microscopic appearance suggested that it had not originated in the lung but, instead, was a metastasis from a kidney cancer. When the kidney cancer was removed, the patient lived over fifteen years without a recurrence.

To appreciate how unique this phenomenon is, it must be understood that when the vast majority of cancers spread, they do so in large numbers and at many sites. This is to be expected as, when cancer cells are unleashed into the body's circulation from the primary source, it must be by the millions. Yet, in some individuals, for unknown reasons, one cell survives and propagates itself, and all the others disappear.

Churchill's and other reports that followed intrigued me, flying as they did in the face of probability and accepted practice. In 1947, they had provided an invaluable precedent when, as a resident on the thoracic service, I saw a clinic patient who had a solitary shadow on her lung X ray seven years after her leg had been amputated for a bone sarcoma. After a search showed that the sarcoma had not spread elsewhere, I could then say to my elders that it probably was a solitary metastasis and should be surgically removed. No other treatment would be effective.

It proved to be a metastasis from her bone sarcoma, and the

patient is still alive over forty years later without ever having developed any other cancer.

Intrigued and inspired by this experience, I asked my hospital colleagues to be on the lookout for solitary lung shadows in their cancer patients.

What began as a medical oddity became a common experience, for within a thirty-five-year period, over one thousand solitary lesions were analyzed and, although as expected some *were* solitary metastases—from breast, kidney, testicle, uterus, sarcoma, and melanoma—others proved to be either a new primary lung cancer or a benign tumor or an inflammatory condition.

The implications were clear: Never guess or presume to know the nature of a solitary lung shadow, for it is only two-dimensional. Insist upon having a microscopic diagnosis before instituting treatment.

In a lecture on this subject in Cairo, I illustrated the enigmatic nature of such shadows by showing a slide on which an outline drawing of the lungs and heart was portrayed. In one lung, I drew a circle to represent the X-ray shadow and, within it, a sketch of the sphinx, the symbol of mystery and enigma. For such a group, in such a city, it was an appropriate symbol.

Jay Weinberg was one who benefited from these findings.

"As malignant melanoma is one of the most lethal of cancers, it might appear at first that the excision of the lung metastases is an unjustified gamble." So began my article published in the *Annals of Surgery* in 1973.

Melanoma, commonly called "black spot cancer," is usually a darkly pigmented malignant tumor originating in the skin, oral, or anal mucous membranes or the retina and sclera (white section) of the eye. Melanomas most often arise in pre-existing moles subjected to chronic irritation, which accounts for their rise in incidence in the South and Southwest, a result of the carcinogenic effects of excessive sunlight on a mole. The sign that a mole may be malignant is that it enlarges, darkens, and/or bleeds. Those with melanoma of the retina get progressive blindness in that eye. The first symptom of anal melanoma can be bleeding. In the mouth, a bluish-black swelling could indicate a melanoma.

Melanoma is probably the most capricious and unpredictable of all cancers, and notoriously spreads to local lymph nodes as well as to the liver, lungs, and other sections of the body. Melanoma can be a highly lethal form of cancer, particularly if it has begun to metastasize widely. It also makes up a major group of cancers that spontaneously disappear.

In 1974, a colleague at MSK, Man E. Shiu, referred a remarkable personality to me. Five months before, Dr. Shiu had removed a melanoma from the skin of a fifty-six-year-old man's back, along with the lymph nodes in his armpit. One lymph node contained a metastasis, a finding of serious portent. Eight months later, a solitary shadow was found on a routine chest X ray. Its appearance in Jay Weinberg, Dr. Shiu's patient, so soon after the removal of its original site sounded ominous.

As soon as one meets Jay Weinberg,★ one is immediately drawn to him. He is five foot five, bald, with the world's widest ear-to-ear grin. He fairly bounces with enthusiasm and, along with his smile, his eyes constantly light up with merriment. They did so even as we discussed his grave X-ray findings. Jay knew the probable nature of his shadow and told me that other physicians had advised him against doing anything about it, as it would be an exercise in futility since undoubtedly, sooner or later, the melanoma would spread and appear elsewhere. Therefore, he had been told that his prognosis was hopeless. However, the fact that the lung shadow was *solitary* was unique; melanoma almost always spreads to the lung in multiples.

After a careful search of the rest of his body—liver, bones, lymph nodes, brain—revealed no other evidence of spread, I told Jay that I believed this single focus should be removed.

Entirely upbeat and without hesitation, Jay said, "Let's go, Doc. If you think so, let's get it out." And we did.

Jay seemed less concerned about the surgery than whether he would be in good enough physical condition three weeks later to go on a skiing trip he had planned months before. It was typical of Jay to devise a postoperative activity to make that plan possible. The hospital corridors were covered with eight-by-twelve-inch tiles. By counting the number of tiles he walked each day, he calculated that, a week after surgery, he was walking one and a half (corridor) miles a day. Three weeks later, he went skiing.

A year later at a follow-up examination, Jay said that he heard that I played tennis. "Why don't we have a game together?"

★ Jay's story is told in detail in the book *We The Victors* by Curtis Bill Pepper.

Now, it is one thing to have a tough adversary on the other side of the net, but if he happens to be a patient, half of whose lung you have removed, a doctor has mixed feelings. For example, you hesitate to use drop shots or lobs, for fear that it will tax his breathing or exhaust him. However, when I began losing at an alarming rate, I forgot all that and tried every trick I knew to beat him—without success then, or since.

It is now fifteen years since Jay's lung operation. In this time, Jay has started the Corporate Angel Network (CAN) with Mrs. Patricia Blum, who also had cancer. CAN is a clearinghouse for patients who need transportation to and/or from cancer centers in all parts of the country. CAN keeps a roster of over four hundred corporations whose planes ordinarily return empty after depositing executives at their destinations. Social Services workers in hospitals will call CAN and describe a patient's need for transportation. Since its inception, it has arranged transportation for over 2,400 patients, and that number is growing. In 1982, Jay and Mrs. Blum's CAN-do organization received a Presidential citation for its humane work.

Not content with that, Jay helped organize and became part of the Patient-to-Patient Program at MSK. This is a group composed of volunteers who make themselves available to talk to patients scheduled to undergo surgery similar to that they themselves had. Without question, someone who has been through a similar trial can be more reassuring than even the most caring physicians and nurses.

Jay's was a good life to save.

Each one is.

Nellie's, Jay's, and so many others' survival of cancer's unpredictable behavior kept nagging me. One day, I had a recurrent attack of the "why's." It happened while I was cleaning out weeds that grew here and there in my driveway. I wondered why some grew in one place and not in another. It must not be entirely by chance; more likely, I reasoned, some extra dampness, some nutrient, a sunlit patch, made that particular site hospitable, fertile.

It occurred to me that, like weeds, there is a reason why a cancer develops at one anatomic site and not at another; e.g., on the tip of President Reagan's nose and not on its bridge or elsewhere on his face. After all, these areas were exposed to equal amounts of sunlight.

Similarly, why does cancer usually develop in *one* breast, *one* lung, *one* kidney, or at *one* side of the larynx or tongue?

Now, after years of shrugging shoulders, there is at least a working hypothesis: *oncogenes.*

Oncogenes, as the prefix suggests (*onco-* means "tumor"), are normally present in cells and are believed to be cancer-potential. Theory has it that tumor suppressor genes hold oncogenes in check unless the suppressor genes are damaged, for example, by sunlight or irradiation, and lose their ability to suppress. Once these restraints are damaged or gone, oncogenes cause cells to become malignant.

But why here and not there?

Possibly, when an embryo is forming, suppressor genes and oncogenes are distributed seemingly at random throughout the body like freckles or moles. Perhaps the weaker ones are present only at certain sites, at some organs and not others. There they could remain dormant for a lifetime unless a specific carcinogen damages them. Working with this hypothesis, these unusually sensitive genes were present on the tip, but not on the bridge, of Reagan's nose, or his cheek or forehead: Sunlight did the rest.

This theory neatly, perhaps too neatly, explains why one tiny area in a nine-foot colon, or a single focus in one of two lungs, or in one of a pair of matched organs, becomes cancerous.

It also affords a possible, albeit simplistic, explanation of why some individuals who have been exposed to a lifetime of carcinogens—"my grandfather smoked all his life and died at ninety-four of a stroke"—did not develop cancer: The tumor-suppressor genes in Grandpa's lungs resisted being perturbed and activated by tobacco smoke.

Once an attack of the why's begins, it is not easily subdued. Usually, it starts in the middle of the night and occupies a good deal of the next few hours. Tossing and turning, I ask myself why some cancers spontaneously disappear; why some respond to chemo- or radiation therapy, while others of identical microscopic appearance do not; why some cancers metastasize only to bone, or liver, or brain, or lung; why some cancers follow genetic pathways; e.g., breast cancers in a grandmother, mother, and daughter; why some cancers following treatment remain dormant for fifteen to twenty or twenty-five years, only to reappear at their original or at another site—and where they have been "hibernating" and what incited them to reappear; what other carcinogens besides those we know—smoking, sunlight, asbestos, irradiation —are insidiously committing assault and battery on genes, changing them into cancer-forming influences; why children in their preteens get certain cancers—neuroblastomas, Wilms' tumor, acute leukemias—when they have not lived long enough to have the chronic exposure to carcinogens like adults.

Why, indeed.

CHAPTER XIX

Tommy

Invited to participate in the first world conference on the general subject of multiple primary cancers, I went to Perugia in 1974. Multiple primary cancers are not uncommon and can be found in one organ; e.g., colon or breast; or in related organ systems; e.g., larnyx and lung. They also occur in paired organs such as the kidneys, ovaries, and lungs.

When multiple cancers appear in paired organs or in related organ systems, they are probably caused by a common carcinogen; for example, skin cancers by chronic exposure to sunlight; oral cavity, larynx, and lung cancers by exposure to cigarette smoke. It is difficult to explain the origin of multiple cancers when they occur in *unrelated* organs, such as the stomach and lung, or the breast and colon. (My mother had separate cancers of the throat and the breast.)

Although a single cancer can be lethal, those with two or more cancers are not necessarily doubly or triply jeopardized, for the prognosis is not determined by the aggregate effect of multiple cancers, but by that of the most aggressive cancer of the group. For example, a patient with both skin and stomach cancer is far more threatened by the latter. Similarly, someone with both breast and lung cancer is more likely to die from lung cancer. Therefore, although multiple operations may be done, each cancer should be treated aggressively as if it existed alone.

After three days of presentation and discussion on the possible causes and management of multiple cancers, the conference ended with many questions. Why do some individuals have only one cancer while others have as many as six separate primaries? Assuming that paired organs such as the breasts, kidneys, and lungs are subjected to the same carcinogens, why does only one of the pair develop a primary cancer? Or why does first one, then the other develop, but years later, instead of simultaneously?

When the composer Samuel Barber, a friend and patient, learned that I would be in Italy, he persuaded me to attend Gian Carlo Menotti's "Festival of Two Worlds" in Spoleto, once the conference was over. There, Sam introduced me to Thomas Schippers, who was conducting the festival's symphony orchestra. Schippers was in his early forties and was a strikingly handsome, slender, dark-haired, dark-eyed man with an angular, aristocratic face. Later, as he conducted works by Debussy, it made for an unforgettable experience to hear such exquisite music beautifully played in a picturesque medieval Umbrian town.

A year later, after giving a lecture at a cancer symposium in Louisville, Kentucky, I drove to Cincinnati to visit friends. Schippers was the music director of the Cincinnati Symphony and, that night, conducted a sensitive performance of a work by Poulenc, one of my favorite composers. After the concert, when I congratulated him, he spoke enthusiastically of his plans to return to Spoleto the next summer.

Four years later, I was called by Tommy's physician in Cincinnati, Henry Heimlich of the Heimlich maneuver. I had known Heimlich since the mid-fifties, when he was a thoracic surgeon at a New York hospital. He said he was sending Tommy to consult with me about a "lung problem." At first, Tommy had been reluctant to come, but Sam Barber, Gian Carlo Menotti, and Tommy's friend Martha had persuaded him to do so.

When we met, he told me that he had smoked two packs a day for thirty years and believed that this had probably caused him to have increased shortness of breath and a dry, hacking cough. He said that his cough was now of such intensity that it took three or four hours just to recover from the exertion.

After a few days of tests, to our horror, we found that not only did he have lung cancer, but that it had affected both lungs.

He was not a candidate for surgery and was given two courses of chemotherapy without benefit. As he was anxious to fulfill several conducting commitments, radiation therapy was directed at the larger cancer, in the hope that it would give temporary relief so he could get through his performances.

Not yet totally incapacitated, Tommy valiantly made new recordings with both the Cincinnati and the New York Philharmonic orchestras. But his breathing became still more labored and finally forced him to abandon physical activity.

One evening, Martha called urging me to come to Tommy's apartment. His condition was deteriorating and he was in considerable distress. I arrived to find Tommy breathing rapidly in spite of the oxygen he was receiving.

As I sat beside him through most of the night, Tommy's shaggy white dog, who had a large black mark around one eye that looked painted on, frequently hopped up on his bed to lie down beside him. Tommy constantly tried to clear his throat of tenacious secretions. I had brought a small supply of morphine I had kept at home for emergencies, and used it to reduce his anxiety and chest pain, which worsened each time he coughed.

From time to time, while he was semi-stuporous, Tommy's long sensitive, bony fingers would suddenly make articulate gestures in the air—as if he were leading some celestial orchestra. At times he seemed to beckon unseen woodwinds and brasses to fortissimo; at others he calmed violins to pianissimo. These efforts taxed his breathing even with nasal oxygen flowing.

As he strained to breathe, he kept asking anxiously if he was getting *any* air into his lungs. To reassure him, I placed the earpiece of the stethoscope in his ears and its listening bell on his chest so he could hear his own respirations. Then he himself moved the bell down to his abdomen and heard, as he said, "kettle drums" (intestinal rumblings—borborygmi), and he smiled.

During that night's vigil, I recalled Tommy at the height of his career at Spoleto and Cincinnati. I looked around his bedroom at the bookcases filled with orchestral scores and art books. His desk was piled high with the scores he had been studying and several manila envelopes that, Martha said, were filled with unanswered messages and fan letters. Most touching was a diary that lay open on his desk; in it, bookings for future concerts were listed. All that sensitivity, art, and talent was being consumed by a voracious cancer, the tragic consequence of smoking.

As his fine face began to show traces of cyanosis—a sign of inadequate oxygen—he came to resemble a figure by El Greco. He looked around the room as if eager to absorb the things he adored, his eyes fearfully large in the thin face. No longer able to speak, he looked at me pleadingly, so I gave more sedation, for I did not want to let him hear the plaintive, hoarse whispers of his own farewell. Gradually, his shallow, rapid respirations came in groups of three or four, followed by long intervals during which he did not breathe. Clearly, the drawn-out process had gone on long enough; Tommy would have thought it was bad art, too long a codetta. So I kept him well sedated to ease him on his way.

CHAPTER XX

The Year of Grace

In 1971, at a well-attended cocktail party in Joanne and Nate Cummings's (Nathan Cummings, a philanthropist and collector of art, was the president of Consolidated Foods Corporation, which later became the Sara Lee Corporation) magnificent Waldorf Towers apartment, I met a woman named Grace Mirabella. Grace had just been made editor-in-chief of *Vogue* magazine, and the party was given in her honor. Ms. Mirabella had risen through the magazine's ranks for seventeen years and was succeeding that extraordinary personality under whom she had worked: Diana Vreeland.

I had known the redoubtable Diana for years and, like so many others, was fascinated by her standard-setting chic, her chalk-white makeup and tightly-drawn-back jet-black hair. And enchanted by her unpredictable and often outrageous pronouncements on any and all things. Diana once regaled me at length about how she could predict snowstorms because the day before one, she always fainted and had to take to her bed. Without doubt, she had a bravura aura that made her a legend in her own time. And she shaped her time. To many, her reputation and her unpredictable manner meant that she was unapproachable and forbidding—that is, until you knew her. No more charming or affectionate woman existed.

This Grace person, on the other hand, gave off an air of quiet elegance, and one instinctively felt her to be modest and generally approachable. I approached and was immediately struck by the beguiling, diffident way she accepted my congratulations on her new post. She was of medium height and had ash-blond hair, dark brown eyes, a ready toothy smile, and a splendid, slightly prominent nose that she called Roman.

What might have been a magical moment—our first meeting—was not. I was deeply involved with Joan. Although I was attracted by Grace's warm personality, all we did was chat; then each of us moved on to mix and mingle.

A year later, we met again. By that time, Joan and I had recognized that the intensity and momentum of our affair was waning, that time had stolen love away, leaving friendship in its place. (And a short time later, she married.) Still, once more, Grace and I, after a brief handshake, had only a perfunctory, light conversation.

That summer I rented a house in Bedford, New York. One rainy Saturday afternoon with time to kill, Anthony and I visited the Bedford Green Antique Shop owned by our friends, Jeannie (Mrs. Harcourt) Amory and Sandra (Mrs. Richard) Feigen. As we entered the shop, I saw Grace standing there; she had been visiting Sandra for the weekend. Somehow, that third meeting with Grace began something. It did for her, too. I often said afterward, Grace was in an antique shop looking for an antique and she found one!

During our first dinner together, Grace brought out a pack of cigarettes and began to light up. When she confessed to smoking two to two and a half packs a day, I dropped my bombs on her. The next time we dined, I noticed that she did not smoke. I asked her about this and, very quietly, she said: "I've given them up." Pleased, I somewhat archly asked: "Why?" Then out into the evening air floated her answer, which was like an irresistible lure to a trout: "Because it made you uncomfortable."

Wow! Hey! Anyone who would make such an enormous sacrifice was somebody I had better look into—and perhaps try to lock up.

Grace never smoked again. Nor did she gain an ounce after quitting. What is more, *Vogue* ran several antismoking articles that, because of their frequency and accuracy, caused antismoking groups to rate the magazine as one of the most aggressive in supporting their crusade.

It was a source of chronic embarrassment to Grace to endure the inconsistency of including articles describing smoking's hazards, while still carrying cigarette ads. Readers repeatedly pointed this out, and she raised the subject with her management. They explained that *Vogue* readers were "mature enough to make their own choices"—which, translated into English, means $10 million a year in advertising revenues. On occasion, Grace was asked to soft-pedal the tone and frequency of antismoking articles as tobacco companies threatened to withdraw their ads. Needless to say, she never did, nor did tobacco companies stop using this prestigious magazine to convey their lethal messages.

One evening Grace remarked that I looked unusually fatigued. I explained that I had just completed a seven-hour operation. She looked thoughtful for a moment.

"Do you know what I was doing while you were operating?" she said. "I was choosing between different shades of lipstick for the cover of the next issue."

What she implied, of course, was that our professional worlds were 180 degrees apart, that hers was frivolous, superficial, ornamental—and mine, no-nonsense, serious, essential, daunting. So I told her the following.

When making rounds with my residents I often stop at the bedside of a woman who, two or three days before, has had major surgery. Usually, I see a sign that I have seen many times before and, recognizing its teaching value and knowing that it will also amuse and delight the patient, I ask: "What's different about this patient?"

At first, my residents will look at her chart or feel her pulse. After a time, I interrupt: "Never mind all that. Just *look* at her. She has lipstick on. Once you see that, it is a sure sign that a woman feels better about herself. Making an effort, she is well on the road to recovery—can't help but get better." And then a second symptom: Three days later she will ask: "When can I wash my hair?" A day or two afterward, she goes home.

I call this the Lipstick sign. And I added, "So, dear Grace, your world, your feeling for fashion, is no less significant than mine. It's just forty-eight hours or so later."

Little did I know at the time what this conversation about the relationship between such matters as fashion, medicine, vanity, self-respect, and healing would lead to.

As our courtship continued, *Vogue* carried even more articles on cancer and the dangers of smoking. Some of our friends thought this indicated my influence, and they said so. One also remarked, "Say, by the way, what influence has Grace had on *you*?"

Before answering, I tried to look thoughtful.

"Now, when I make an incision, I cut more on the bias."

Women laugh when they hear this; men wonder why they do.

Like me, Grace is an only child. She was born in Beth Israel Hospital in Newark, New Jersey, where, years later, I became a member of the consultant staff. One day, a very regal lady asked Grace where she was born. Upon hearing her answer, the lady said, as if horrorstruck, "Just imagine: the editor-in-chief of *Vogue* . . . from *New Jersey!*"

During our courtship, Grace occasionally accompanied me when I went to make evening rounds. However, she had more than the average apprehension about hospitals and preferred to wait in the car rather than in the comfortable visitors' waiting room. Gradually, she overcame much of this phobia, so that when close friends were patients she drummed up enough courage to accompany me to visit them. This was fortunate, for by the time she herself became a patient at Memorial, years later, her hospital phobia was gone.

Overcoming this fear gave Grace the courage to ask to see at first hand the unusual, picturesque scene that I had once described to her. It centers around a queen.

In a long list of unforgettable patients, the Queen of the Gypsies stands out. Apparently, there are many kings and queens of gypsy tribes scattered throughout the world. This queen headed a group from, well—where else?—Queens. Although she did not smoke, she had probably inhaled the secondhand smoke of the many men around her who constantly did; and it is reasonable to speculate that as a gypsy, even if now in Queens, she had probably breathed in the smoke of many campfires.

Ethnic delicacies aside, MSK always braces itself when a gypsy becomes an inpatient. The visitors' waiting room or the lobby fills with members of the patient's tribe. This makes for a colorful panorama as the women, wrapped in bandanas and voluminous multicolored skirts, sit in a large circle with children of all ages moving among them. Many of the men are dressed colorful velveteen jackets; they gather in a separate grouping. Fortunately, there are no campfires. MSK has grown wise to gypsy ways and brings in a full-time guard when they are in residence, because cushions, ashtrays, floral decorations, even a life-sized white marble bust of one of MSK's founders have been known to migrate from their usual positions and are never seen again. As alert as the guards may be, on occasion other visitors' pockets have been picked, and a few objects have disappeared from the hospital's gift shop.

When I took Grace to the waiting room where the King of the Gypsies, my patient's husband, sat surrounded by his subjects, the king rose to his full six-feet-two-inch self—mustachioed, florid-faced, potbellied—and, like a Spanish galleon, sailed gracefully across the waiting room to greet us. He wore his beautifully brocaded vest, on which he sported a thick gold watch chain. After Grace and the king were introduced, he said, flashing a brilliant, gilt-toothed smile, "Why not have my wife read your palm upstairs?" Then his smile brightened even more: "Why not have your palm read in exchange for the doctor's fee?"

Afterward, I thought we should have taken the offer. My bill was somehow never paid.

The queen did well and was discharged. For a while, I heard nothing from them. Then I received a notice that Blue Shield had forwarded the check for my services to the king. I traced him to Arizona, where he had taken his followers, in a caravan of station wagons, to spend the winter. I called, explaining that the check did not belong to him.

"Doc," he said, "don't worry, I'm sending it to you. I'm no fly-by-night gypsy."

Despite his assurances he continued to fly by night . . . and by day.

Another Grace, this time a princess, came briefly, too briefly, into my life.

One summer, while Grace was in Paris for the haute couture collections, I waited for her, roughing it at Mary Lasker's glorious mansion in St.-Jean-Cap-Ferrat on the French Riviera. During this visit, I met Princess Grace of Monaco. She and I were godparents of Madeline (Mrs. Roswell) ★ Gilpatric's grandson.

She knew I was a specialist and remarked that Monaco had an unusually low death rate from leukemia. In fact, she thought, it was lower than anywhere in Europe. The possible reason for this,

★ Roswell Gilpatric was deputy secretary of defense under Robert MacNamara in the Kennedy administration.

she had been told, was that, for generations, the children of Monaco had received BCG (bacillus Calmette-Guérin) injections to immunize them against tuberculosis. Perhaps this also immunized them against leukemia.

Naturally, I was skeptical, but as a single observation could lead to a big idea, I promised to look into it and report back to her.

In August 1973, after having met with her public-health officer, I wrote Princess Grace to say that although the statistics she reported were accurate, they might be inadvertently misleading, for as soon as a diagnosis of leukemia was made, Monegasque patients went to Nice, Paris, or the United States for treatment. While being treated elsewhere, some of those patients died; hence Monaco's low mortality rate.

There the matter seemed to rest until seventeen years later, when an authoritative scientific report stated that BCG may protect against certain malignant diseases.

My apologies, Princess Grace, wherever you are.

CHAPTER XXI

"Why the Hell Didn't I Listen?"

The eighties. At the start of each decade, I ask myself the eternal question: Are we getting anywhere in cancer? Laymen want to hear that this most dreaded of diseases is soon to be controlled by some simple, direct measure, as were smallpox and polio. After all: "We put a man on the moon. Why can't we cure cancer?"

I have to tell them that cancer is not a single disease and that it's unlikely that we'll find a single key to unlock all 110 or so extremely complex locked doors. But there have been many advances in recent years in diagnosis, treatment, and basic research. Our understanding of carcinogens and cancer itself is progressing, sometimes by leaps, at other times by inches.

What must not be overlooked are the clearly visible gains being made in cancer *prevention*. In this generation, we have become aware of the natural and man-made hazards in our environment: excessive exposure to sunlight; smoking; asbestos; radioactivity; and certain diets are established causes of certain cancers. It has been said: "We swim in a sea of carcinogens," and I add: "in which the cigarette is the great white shark." Fully one-third of all adult cancers, as well as many cardiovascular diseases and much emphysema, result from this single self-destructive activity.

During the last decades, as a result of inspired campaigns by educators, by cancer, lung, and heart societies, and by public-spirited activists, what may be the greatest public-health measure in history has come to pass: Millions of Americans have stopped smoking. Former surgeon general C. Everett Koop's projection of a smoke-free America by the year 2000 does not seem too visionary or unattainable.

Each year, 3 percent of current smokers quit—and, sadly, many of those who don't will die by decade's end. What is more, a major effort is now being made to discourage children by teaching them to say no to lighting up, just as they are taught to say no to drugs. Smoking by children and teens is of particular importance, because studies show that young, growing membranes are even more vulnerable to carcinogens than are those of adults. Parents who smoke must be made to realize that the smoke from their cigarettes is not just irritating but can cause increased numbers of ear, nose, throat, and respiratory problems in their children and can permanently scar their lungs. Cigarette smoke could predispose their children to lung cancer in later life.

But some do not hear—or listen. And they are not just children. "Of all sad words of tongue or pen, the saddest are these: 'It might have been!' " Alas, the current emphasis on prevention came too late for many of my friends who were so addicted that although they could read, they could not heed. Too often I listened to a heartrending phrase from those I'd warned: "Why the hell didn't I listen to you?"

Yul Brynner was one who did not listen.

We met in 1951 when his first "Anna," my mother-in-law Gertrude Lawrence, introduced us. Backstage in his dressing room, I could hardly make out his trademark bald, shiny head in the clouds of smoke that shrouded him. He smoked four to five packs a day. I knew that he was on a collision course with some smoking-caused disease.

Afterward, whenever Yul and I met, I would plead with him to quit. For a fleeting moment, his super-macho "King" would smile mischievously, like a naughty boy and, drawing himself up so that he looked indestructible, would say something like "Don't worry, Bill. They'll never get me."

We met for the last time at MSK, thirty-six years after our first introduction. Yul was in a wheelchair, on his way to radiation therapy for painful lung-cancer metastases in his spine.

We chatted for a few minutes and, as he was being wheeled away, he looked back at me, shook his head, and said, "Why the hell didn't I listen to you?"

In spite of the agony of his last weeks, Yul stayed onstage in *The King and I*. One can only guess what his thoughts were in each performance of the last scene when he, as the Siamese monarch, lay dying.

Posthumously, Yul helped many people quit smoking because of his remarkable TV spot in which he says, looking directly at the viewer: "I would not be sick today had I not smoked. I am convinced of it. *Now that I am gone,* let me say: Don't smoke. *Please don't smoke.*"

Charles Lemaistre, past president of the American Cancer Society, said: "Smoking is one of the most grievous examples of destructive behavior in the history of mankind."

One of the eulogists at Yul's memorial service, held at New York's Shubert Theater, was Alan Jay Lerner, the stunningly accomplished lyricist of *My Fair Lady, Brigadoon, Gigi, Camelot,* and *Paint Your Wagon.*

Alan and I had been friends for years and as he smoked two, often three packs of cigarettes per day, I repeatedly warned him to quit. I also worried about his frequent visits to Dr. Max Jacobson—"Dr. Feelgood," as he was nicknamed. Dr. Jacobson's warm, avuncular style appealed to those whose work involved a great deal of strain and stress and who functioned at all times at peak intensity. As a result, he had many famous patients to whom he gave pickup injections. Only God knows what was in that syringe, but it was probably filled with hormones, "bennies," and vitamins that made patients emerge from his office bouncing and with sparkling eyes. Feeling super-vitalized, they all swore by him.

As members of Harvard's Overseers Committee (chaired by Gardner Cowles, publisher of *Look* magazine), Alan and I, along with Leonard Bernstein, composers Johnny Green and Leroy Anderson, and Kitty Carlisle Hart, would visit the Harvard Music School each year. The committee would sit in on classes and talk with students during the rest of the day. One of the classes we attended was headed by a woman who told us the class would sing, a cappella, a student's contest-winning chorale based on a musical theme.

When they finished, the professor somewhat slyly asked the committee whether any of us knew the theme. I began examining my fingernails and looking out at the spring leaves. In the meantime, Lenny was saying he thought it was a theme from Haydn's Thirty-second Symphony. After others made their guesses, the class turned and looked at Alan. The theme?

"Get Me to the Church on Time," from *My Fair Lady*.

As we flew back to New York, Lenny was chain-smoking. Alan, obviously jittery, was biting his fingernails and nervously fingering worry beads. He said to me, "I feel so guilty; I'm trying to give up the goddamn weed and every time I see you, I get into a panic, so I brought these beads." He was working the beads for all they were worth. In light of subsequent events, that was a fateful planeload.

In 1986, perhaps sensing something wrong and with an intuitive sense of impending disaster, he quit. A few months later, in England, a lung X ray showed a suspicious shadow.

When Alan called from London, I suggested that he come to MSK. He asked if there were another hospital he could go to because Memorial brought back sad memories of his father's many operations and death. However, I persuaded him that there was no better place for his problems.

Within a few days, the diagnosis of lung cancer was established and the cancer found to be too far advanced for surgery. It was also of a type notoriously resistant to chemotherapy. As his cancer advanced, he developed pneumonia, and his breathing became more labored, Alan was admitted to MSK's intensive-care unit. These units care for seriously ill patients who need the constant monitoring that cannot be provided by routine nursing care. It has, therefore, an air of seriousness and foreboding. As a consequence, it is rare to find any smiling moments there. One morning, while the night nurse in charge was giving her report, she interrupted its medical details by saying that during the night, a young nurse hurried into the nurses' station and said, "I know that this Mr. Lerner is very sick—but now I think he's hallucinating!"

The senior nurse asked why.

"Because he says he wrote *My Fair Lady*."

When I told him this story straight from the generation gap, Alan roared with laughter.

But his confinement was less amusing. While ill, Alan became a member of People for a Smokefree Indoors, a volunteer group whose mission was to persuade New York's City Council to ban smoking in public places. One day, as Alan and I were discussing the campaign, he sat bolt upright in bed and through his oxygen mask yelled, "Stop those tobacco bastards from killing people! Look what they've done to me. Stop them before it's too late."

Nurses and doctors came running to the glass-walled cubicle, alarmed at the outburst, only to see him sink back exhausted.

Within a week, as a result of antibiotics, Alan miraculously went from being in an intensive-care unit to dining out in a restaurant, laughing with friends. All those who were aware of his condition were amazed. Even I, knowing that the serpent still lurked, forgot its presence for those few hours and joined in the give-and-take.

When Alan's final admission to the hospital occurred a few weeks later, all of us had to make a quick shift from our wishful illusion that all would be well. Alan died surrounded by his wife and children, with a sip from a glass of champagne that all of those present also sipped.

Three years after Alan's death, MSK gave a gala fund-raising event at Lincoln Center, called *An Evening with Alan Jay Lerner.* As I heard song after song, splendid examples of Alan's genius, I was at the point of tears, particularly when Liz Robertson, his widow, sang some of his romantic ballads.

And once more, as I sat listening, I grew infuriated and depressed that Alan and so many other artists had had their creative lives aborted by smoking.

As Liz sang, I remember Alan telling how in his last few days out of the hospital, they had walked to Central Park and lain down on the grass. They looked up at the sky and clouds; they talked of their love for each other, and of his impending doom.

Alan's memorial service, like Yul's, was also held at the Shubert Theater. Outside, a small group of young people stood with signs reading LENNY, WE LOVE YOU. PLEASE STOP SMOKING. They knew that Leonard Bernstein was to be one of the eulogists. When Alan became sick, he told me he had called Lenny frequently, hoping that by using himself as an example, he could persuade Lenny to quit. I, too, had tried. I heard Lenny cough constantly and talk with a gravelly voice at a dinner we both attended. "You seem intent on killing yourself." He was hoarse and looked haggard, so, once more, I implored him to stop.

It was hard to believe that this highly disciplined conductor, composer, and musician could not liberate himself. He mentioned the op-ed article I had written for *The New York Times,* about child abuse by smoking. A pregnant woman who smokes a pack a day and averages five puffs per cigarette delivers 270,000 insults to her fetus before it is born. When Lenny read this, he figured out that in his lifetime, he had smoked over a million cigarettes. As we talked, I kept being haunted by the ghosts of Aline Saarinen, Alan, and others.

Five years later, the *Times* described Lenny conducting a Tanglewood concert*: His face looked worn and as he conducted, he had to stop from time to time to expectorate into a handkerchief. He was forced to cancel future engagements. I was horrified and wrote him a note urging him to have a lung X ray and get his sputum analyzed, concluding: "Please quit. All of us can't bear to think of life without you." A few days later, this extraordinary artist was dead.

November 20, 1990.

I hate funerals that are symbols and expressions of defeat, when the deceased was a victim of treachery and died a preventable death.

On November 4, 1990, as I sat in Carnegie Hall at the memorial service of Leonard Bernstein, I thought to myself: So they got Lenny, too, those patrons of the arts. To see him now reduced to dust by two lousy packs of cigarettes a day and all that musical leadership, extraordinary memory, and teaching destroyed desolates me.

Tobacco interests are a metaphor for the constant battle between good and evil, ethics and amorality. As a nation, we cannot allow this scourge to continue: It is bad medicine, bad economics, and bad morality. I cannot remain abstracted, inactive, passive, and still live with myself, nor can I rest easy while this holocaust of our own making continues unabated. I am haunted not only by the tobacco dead I see but by lungless, voiceless, bladderless, gulletless, tongueless patients and those close to them who must also suffer.

Knowing this, as they must, how can our legislators endorse such lethal activities by indifference? What cynical fancy foot-work, double-talk, politico-speak, can countenance those child molesters, rapists, indiscriminate killers?

---

* Beethoven's *Seventh Symphony,* the one Morton gave me when I went to war. The symphony's third movement is a funereal march.

CHAPTER XXII

"Communists Get Cancer, Too"

In the summer of 1973, I was invited to give a series of lectures on lung cancer and cryosurgery in Moscow. At the Moscow airport, I ran into problems. The Cold War tension between Russia and the United States was still flourishing, although at that time it had moderated somewhat. I had brought a collection of slides to illustrate the lecture. When the customs man spied them, he held each one up to the light while I tried to explain what it represented. This was a formidable task, and the biology lesson might have gone on for hours had not a Russian physician who had been delegated to meet us come to my rescue, and cut it short.

Grace's and my friends Piero and Maria Laura Vinci, the Italian ambassador and his wife, had invited us to stay with them, sparing us the Russian hotel offered by our scientific hosts.

The next day my lecture was to be held at the All-Union Cancer Research Center in Moscow. The center's hospital was reminiscent of Bellevue in my student days: huge, musty, and, by our later standards, primitive. Its vast wards were filled with patients who were barely separated by the width of narrow bedside tables.

Before my lecture on lung cancer, I was taken to a board room and introduced to a group of surgeons. We sat around a long table. To my astonishment, I and the others were each handed (at eleven A.M.!) a glass half filled with brandy. It was clear that, as a gesture of comradeship, I was expected to drink it. And I did.

My interpreter spoke fluent English; he quietly mentioned that he was a Jewish dermatologist, and, as we made our way to the lecture hall, he asked surreptitiously how difficult it would be to set up a practice in the United States. I felt that, for his sake, I should be guarded in answering and suggested, sotto voce, that we meet again to discuss this question and how I might help. But we never did.

The lecture went well. I said that I felt an ancestral tug being there because my father had been born in Russia (applause). As I talked, I had to pause after each sentence while my interpreter translated it. This would have doubled my lecture time, so I shortened the presentation. Afterward, I made rounds with attending surgeons to see cancer patients. At each bedside, I was asked how that particular condition would be treated at MSK.

I was driven to the Hospital for Lung Diseases, where I gave another talk on radical lobectomy and multiple primary cancers.

After that lecture, I was tendered a stag luncheon at the Hotel Moscow Restaurant, a large room on the second floor, overlooking Red Square. With its paneled walls and brass fixtures, it resembled the dignified dining room of New York City's University Club. A well-established caveat for foreign diplomats and military personnel: Beware; Russians will make several toasts before meals. Warned, I fortified my very low threshold for vodka by consuming large quantities of oily fish and the wonderful caviar before lunch. Oil delays the absorption of alcohol from one's innards, so I felt it would get me through unscathed. However, there were ten surgeons at the table, and after the ninth vodka toast, it was my turn. Oil barrier or not, the eleven A.M. brandy and the multiple vodkas were beginning to penetrate my alimentary Maginot Line.

As I stood to make my toast, my boisterous colleagues applauded and cheered, then became silent. So did the other diners in the restaurant. I recall being moved, touched, inspired! There I was, in a not-so-friendly nation, but that seemed of minor importance compared to the universal brotherhood of surgeons. This fraternal feeling was warmed further by, as someone wrote, the "small, blue, jet-like flame" of the vodkas. As a result, in a voice louder than I had intended, I said, "Let us drink to that which unites us, not divides us!" When translated, it was greeted by cheers from my table and, a few minutes later, a second wave of cheers from the other diners.

With my host, Nikolai Trapeznikov, I was driven back to the Italian embassy by one of the surgeons, who followed an invisible-weaving pattern all the way. Nicolai said that arrangements had been made for us to be taken to the Bolshoi Ballet that night. The surgeon would call for us later.

After profuse thanks to him (and, silently, to St. Christopher, patron saint of travelers), I left them and just managed to reach my bedroom when suddenly I was not feeling, as they say, "too marvelous." The protective coating of oil was fully breached. In my bed of pain, I kept thinking that if my luncheon companions were in a similar condition and any surgery had to be done in Moscow that afternoon, God help the patients.

While I was lecturing and lunching, Grace was taken on a tour of the fashion departments of Moscow's department stores. She returned to the embassy to find me anesthetized.

Later, when the surgeon delegated to take us to the Bolshoi arrived and introduced himself to Grace, he swayed back and forth so much that Grace felt she would have to reach out to prevent him from toppling over. Much as I loved ballet and would have been delighted to see the Bolshoi, it was impossible for me to go. I begged off—and I think I detected fires of gratitude in my would-be host's eyes before he left us.

Before leaving Russia the next day, I extended invitations to my new colleagues to visit MSK. Some months later, by arrangement with the Soviet-American Medical Bridge (a group sponsored by both governments) they arrived. Grace and I gave a cocktail party for them and invited Russian-speaking friends, among whom were Tatiana and Alexander Liberman. Alex, an internationally renowned artist and editorial director of Condé Nast Publications, had been born in czarist Russia in 1912 and had left just before the Revolution. At one point, I noticed that Alex, speaking Russian, was the center of a very attentive ring of listeners. Curious, I asked Nikolai Trapeznikov what Alex was saying that was so captivating. Nicolai replied that it wasn't *what* Alex was saying, but *how* he was saying it. My Russian guests had never heard prerevolutionary Russian spoken, and were charmed by its elegant accents and poetic flavor.

Much more up-to-date, and on my mind, was my hostess, Grace.

Our courtship was clearly prospering. Mutual friends, who thought we were a perfect fit, speculated about when we would marry. Some hinted that our courtship had been going on "long enough" and slyly asked the equivalent of what my intentions were.

Although I was almost always in Grace's company, on occasion, I would be asked to fill in as an extra man to squire a widow or a divorcée. When this happened, Grace-and-Bill watchers immediately felt obligated to step up their unsolicited advice. A major force—and when I say "major" I mean no small matter—was Estée Lauder. By intellect and sheer force of personality, Estée had built a great cosmetics empire. Having done all that, as well as having reared a family, she felt supremely confident that she could serve as Grace's adviser. No one, but no one, could repress Estée when she made up her mind. And so, one day, she invited Grace to lunch, ostensibly to talk business. The subject quickly changed to a campaign strategy for courtship. Estée told Grace that one of the best ways to nail a nice Jewish doctor was to ply him with good food. Grace did not need this generous or stereotypical advice, but was grateful for the good intentions. Estée went into details—in particular, how to make good chicken soup, for which she supplied the recipe, then and there.

Medicine knows no panaceas, but chicken soup may be as close to one as can be found, having been credited with healing everything from the common cold to infertility. In this case, it became a powerful love potion. With Grace, Estée, and chicken soup combined, what mortal could resist? I knew my goose was cooked, basted in you-know-what-kind of broth.

I was haunted by an unthinkable scenario: Grace turns me down because, as a Catholic, she cannot marry a divorced man. Now, she finds someone else and I am invited to their church wedding. As the happy couple comes down the aisle, I think: "There but for the God of Grace go I."

On June 14, 1974, I presented a Cartier watch to Grace, with a birthday card on which I had written, "Let's spend the rest of time together."

Grace studied the card, then said, "Does this mean what I think it means?"

That evening, we went first to the Nathan Cummingses' apartment for a drink and then to Ballato's, a favorite trattoria of ours on Houston Street, where I had laid on a surprise party to make our announcement.

Grace's seventy-six-year-old mother sat at my right. After hearing the news, she said: "Well, I hope you bring up any children as Catholics."

"I don't mind their being Catholic," I said, "as long as they vote Democratic."

I must confess that in the days that followed, I felt uneasy about my unresolved marital status, as columnists were making references to the forthcoming Mirabella-Cahan wedding. Sisi and I finally agreed on the terms of a divorce and, with her lawyer, I appeared before a judge in New York's Supreme Court Building, where it was made final.

I gave Anthony my old car and, one day in early September, Grace and I stood outside our rented house in Bedford as Anthony, with all his belongings, drove off to college. He said later, "As I looked back at the two of you, I suddenly felt terribly alone, not knowing what lay before me. But I knew it was a good idea."

And another loss was to come.

Doctors are not supposed to advertise, but there is no rule against family members doing so. My father had always boasted inordinately about me to anyone who made the mistake of seeming to listen. For some years, my mother had been working as a volunteer at the candy stand in MSK's outpatient building. My father made a practice of picking her up at day's end. While he waited for her to finish, he was content to sit in the patients' waiting area. But not quietly. Anyone who sat down next to him would be regaled at length about my accomplishments—Nobel prize–winning at least, as my father saw them.

Occasionally, he took to wandering into the clinic working area by himself and, after he had settled in, nurses or attendants would let me know that he was in residence. I would go down, kiss him, and shake the hand of the hapless stranger next to him, to whom he had extolled my virtues. Then, contented, he would get up and go home.

But I was soon to lose my best P.R. man.

In his eighty-eighth year, my father was doomed to progressive confusion and ever increasing isolation. Even then, as his world contracted to a few friends and his family, he was still able to draw and paint. Undoubtedly his love of beauty and his desire to record it was at the core of his being, for his talent lay undisturbed in the deeper recess of remembrance. My mother patiently cared for someone who had become a sad, pale sketch of his former self.

One cold night in early October, wearing little clothing, this gentle man walked out of his apartment building. When he failed to reappear after several hours, my mother called me and I telephoned hospitals and police stations. A few hours later, probably through some homing instinct, he returned, blue from exposure. After warming him, I got him to Memorial, where he developed pneumonia.

My father's walk into the cold reminded me of what a friend, Jim Houston, an expert on Eskimos, had said. Aging Eskimos, when they feel their time has come, leave the igloo and wander out into the Arctic night. Those remaining in the igloo know what is happening, and no one interferes. The next morning the old person is found, having committed frigid suicide, his dignity intact.

Although my father lay ill, I had been scheduled, months in advance, to deliver an important paper at a prestigious medical meeting in Florence. I was torn between going and remaining at my father's bedside. When I mentioned this to my mother, she asked gently if I wouldn't mind staying. She felt worried and alone. That was all I had to hear; I asked a colleague to deliver the paper in my stead.

It was a good decision, for I was with my father when, a few days later, he suddenly, instead of looking *at* me, looked beyond me, and stopped breathing. I closed his eyes, removed the ring that I had seen all my life, and went down the hall to tell my mother.

She, always quick to tears, seemed stunned. I knew by her quiet, dry-eyed acceptance that she realized how hollowed-out her husband had become and how his life had been a shell.

In my eulogy, I said, "Both in his art and to those who knew him, my father leaves a legacy of beauty and joy. More than that, we have seen demonstrated in him that, in this frantic world, there is strength in modesty, power in gentleness."

My father wished to be cremated. I scattered his dust in his Lower East Side, where the World Building stood; in the backyard of my house; at my birthplace; and, years later, on my mother's grave.

Wedding arrangements for Grace and me had been made months in advance. When my father died, we asked my mother whether we should postpone the ceremony. She said no; my father would have wanted us to go through with it.

Four weeks later, on November 24, Grace and I were married at Joanne and Nathan Cummings' apartment. The apartment was filled with art treasures, including fine examples of the leading

impressionists. Grace and I felt that my father should be represented by one of his paintings, and Nate Cummings agreed. The
wedding ceremony was to take place before the fireplace in a huge
dining room, so Nate removed a splendid Picasso from over the
mantelpiece and in its stead hung my father's painting "The Tulip
Tree." Later, I heard that one of the guests, the art dealer Richard
Feigen, had whispered to his wife, Sandra, "I didn't know Nate
had bought a new Pissarro."

It was a fitting and final eulogy.

My mother was delighted with her new daughter-in-law and
made one allusion to my father at the ceremony: "If only Dad
could have been here to see Grace and his painting among all this
great art!"

Although the wedding was not a religious one, I decided to
follow an ancient Hebraic tradition. As soon as we had been pro-
nounced man and wife, I crushed a glass that had been wrapped
in a napkin. As those guests familiar with the ritual wished Grace
and me "Mazel tov!" Nate scooped up the napkin and the glass
fragments. A few months later, he sent us a framed "still life,"
consisting of all the glass fragments spread out and mounted on
the Waldorf–Astoria napkin that had wrapped them. It looked like
a prize-winning collage.

RICHARD AVEDON

Photographer Richard Avedon's wedding gift to the Cahans—a series
of photographs of Grace Mirabella and Bill Cahan, 1975.

CHAPTER XXIII

Curbstone Diagnoses

Shortly after we were married, our brownstone was burglarized. I called the police station and Detective Molinari soon arrived. As he came up the front steps, I caught sight of a dark-pigmented spot on his right cheek that looked very much like a melanoma.

After he had questioned Grace and me about the burglary, I took him to one side and, pointing to his cheek, asked: "How long have you had that mark?"

"As long as I can remember." He said that it used to be brown and small and he had nicked it several times while shaving. Recently, he had noticed that it had darkened.

"Well, if I were you, I'd have it taken off promptly." And I explained why.

Later, he told me that his knees buckled and, for several minutes, he forgot everything else, including the burglary he had come to investigate. Soon, however, he regained control and asked with which hospital I was affiliated and whether I would remove the spot.

"I'd prefer you went to a colleague, Dr. Man E. Shiu, who is an expert on this condition."

It was a melanoma.

Dr. Shiu excised it and through the years it has not reappeared or caused any trouble. Sixteen years later, Detective Molinari is retired and well. Every year, after his follow-up exam, Molinari comes into my office and never seems to tire of telling the story of how we met and what I did, which was little enough. This tough officer, who has won medals for bravery, becomes teary when he goes into detail about how I caught the spot on his cheek in time.

Cancer-haters are like crime-fighters, constantly on the prowl, looking for trouble and ways to prevent it. I had risked curbstone diagnoses earlier. Seated next to Fifi (Mrs. John) Fell (now Schiff) at a dinner party, I noticed, as she reached for a roll, the long sleeve of her dress fell back, revealing a suspicious black spot on her forearm. When I asked her about it, she said that a mole she had for years had darkened recently and seemed to be irritated by friction from her clothes.

I said, gently but urgently: "It must come off as soon as possible."

She protested that she was going to the Bahamas the next day, but I persuaded her to delay the trip.

It, too, was a melanoma and twenty-eight years later has not recurred.

When I see a suspicious skin lesion, for example on a fellow passenger in an elevator or some other confined public place, what should I, a cancer specialist, do? Ignore it? Physicians pledge "do no harm"; to turn away from those who need help, *does* harm. So I will sometimes say, "Pardon me, but I'm a physician and I'd have that spot on your cheek looked into if I were you." Then, lest they think I'm drumming up trade, I quickly move away.

Apparently, some of my medical brethren feel this to be an invasion of privacy and refrain from offering unsolicited advice. I don't agree. It is a physician's responsibility to alert anyone to a life-threatening situation. In spite of others' disapproval, I do not intend to pass by, to look the other way, but to continue drawing the attention of strangers to conditions that might jeopardize their lives. By the same token, I cannot drive on past the scene of an automobile accident or a street emergency without seeing if I can be of assistance. Malpractice suits be damned.

Playing the Good Samaritan comes in different forms at different moments. In 1976, while watching Jimmy Carter on television during his campaign for the presidential nomination, I saw a suspicious area on his right cheek. He has a fair complexion. Such skin is notoriously sensitive to the sun's carcinogenic rays and, as a Southern peanut farmer, he probably had been exposed to excessive amounts of sunlight.

At the time, my friend Henry Brandon, a British journalist with the London *Sunday Times,* was covering Carter's campaign. I asked him to call Carter's attention to the lesion.

Weeks later, I went to a campaign breakfast for Carter at the Waldorf-Astoria, curious to see if the lesion was gone. I could only view it from the edge of a large crowd who were shaking hands with Carter, but I thought I saw a pale pink spot on his cheek where it had been. I still scrutinize photographs of him to be sure.

In one case, my diagnosis was anything but accurate. As former New York City mayor Fiorello La Guardia once said about a flawed appointment to the bench (the judge proved to be scandal-ridden): "When I make a mistake, it's a beaut!" In my zest to be helpful, I committed a beaut of a miscalculation—and in full public view.

One Sunday afternoon in August 1989, Grace and I were watching a New York Mets baseball game on our forty-five-inch television. During an interval between innings, a camera focused on baseball commissioner A. Bartlett Giamatti. I noticed what seemed to be his left forearm and hand resting on the back of an empty seat next to him. I said, "Good God, Grace, look at those fingers. They're four-plus clubbing." ("Four-plus" in medical jargon denotes a condition that is far advanced.) Grace asked what I meant and I outlined the clubbed end of the fingers with my own. As I did so, Giamatti took a long drag on a cigarette and exhaled slowly. In its entirety, the episode lasted six to seven seconds.

Clubbing is a mysterious condition in which the ends of the fingers and fingernails are enlarged and rounded like drumsticks. It can be a sign of lung cancer, heart disease, chronic pulmonary disease, psoriasis, or certain heart infections. It can also be congenital. I was so preoccupied with delineating the clubbing for Grace that when Giamatti smoked, I did not notice that it was not a hand with clubbed fingers that held the cigarette. What was unmistakable was that the way he took a drag was typical of one who smoked heavily.

I assumed that the combination of smoking and clubbed fingers could reflect a serious, perhaps undetected, lung condition. In which case, Giamatti should be alerted.

How to contact him? I remembered that the author Gay Talese had written a book about the Yankees, so I called him for advice. Gay suggested that I get in touch with Dr. Robert Brown, a third baseman for the late-1940s Yankees, now president of the American League, who was also a cardiologist.

The next day I called Dr. Brown. We discussed what I had seen on TV. Dr. Brown confirmed that Giamatti was a heavy smoker and said that for years he had tried to get the commissioner to quit. Brown suggested that I write a letter to him and he would bring it to Giamatti's attention. In it, I expressed my concern regarding the possibility that the clubbing could be a sign of emphysema or even lung cancer and suggested a chest X ray and pulmonary-function studies. Since Giamatti was a former president of Yale, I closed, "Tell him that although I am a Harvard man, I like to keep good Yalies alive."

Dr. Brown showed my letter to Giamatti, who promised he would look into it.

Twelve days after I had seen him on television, Giamatti suddenly died of a heart attack at his summer home in Martha's Vineyard.

Gay Talese, a former reporter, thought the warning, and Giamatti's death soon afterward, was newsworthy. He called a reporter friend at the New York *Daily News*. The next day the *News* had a front-page headline with a story inside.

Immediately, I was besieged with requests for television interviews. On some of these, to illustrate clubbing, I showed a still picture I had in my files of clubbed fingers. I asked Channel 9, the "Mets Channel," for a tape of the episode so I could review it, but it was late in arriving. However, a medical reporter for Channel 5, who was a physician, was enterprising enough to call the pathologist who did Giamatti's autopsy. The physician said that he had not noticed any clubbing.

I spoke with him and he confirmed it. What now?

When Channel 5's reporter got the news, she asked if I would review those moments of the Mets game while I was on camera. As soon as those few seconds were replayed I saw, to my enormous embarrassment, that the markedly clubbed fingers were not Giamatti's, but probably those of a man sitting behind him.

Soon afterward, I wrote to Dr. Brown explaining my mistake, concluding: "I think our main aim now is to find *that* man so that he might benefit from this information."

The man was found: He was Giamatti's bodyguard. Indeed, he had markedly clubbed fingers—but they were congenital.

For a time, friends would tease me by approaching with their fingers bent into a fist as if to hide their clubbing. I often thought afterward: No good turn is left unpunished.

As senseless as this episode made me appear, it had some unexpected value. The day after my TV appearances, several strangers, recognizing me on the street, told me that after seeing the clubbing, they had decided to quit smoking. In my letter to Mrs. Giamatti, I apologized for any additional burden I might have created for her and her family, but said that at least *some* had benefited from my mistaken diagnosis.

A reporter for *The Boston Globe* used this episode to ask several physicians what they would do if they were to see someone with what they considered to be a life-threatening condition. Most replied that they would do as I had done—warn the person about it. However, one who dissented was Dr. Arnold Relman, editor of the *New England Journal of Medicine*. The *Globe* article stated:

> Doctors are entirely divided on the issue, but . . . in [Relman's] opinion, in the absence of immediate life-threatening risk, "You ought to keep your silence." He said Cahan had "jumped the gun" in the Giamatti case and shouldn't have said anything even if seated next to the Commissioner at dinner because "he had no right to draw conclusions that there was something wrong."

I wonder if Dr. Relman would remain silent were he to see a suspicious lesion on someone's hand or cheek. It does not have to be an *acute* emergency to be life-threatening. In the cases cited by the *Boston Globe* reporter, other physicians said that those patients who had been alerted to a problem were grateful to the physician who, they felt, saved their lives. I found Relman's attitude impersonal, suggesting as it does a certain aloofness and detachment, a posture for which physicians today are being condemned more and more. I'd rather fail by making an error of commission than allow someone to go on to an incurable state.

On television, I once watched Yuri Andropov review troops in Moscow's Red Square. He had the typical look of someone with emphysema: barrel-chested, taking frequent shallow breaths through his open mouth. I learned from Pam and Averell Harriman that they were going to Moscow as representatives of President Carter. I told them of my suspicion and asked that they observe whether Andropov seemed to take breaths at short intervals, especially whether he interrupted long sentences to do so.

When they returned, Pam told me that Andropov spoke in short sentences, but this could have been attributed to having to wait for them to be translated. However, she noticed one thing: Each time he fed the interpreter a new phrase, he took a sip of water. My guess is that he may have used this device to allow himself to sneak a short breath before completing the sentence. It is typical of those with advanced emphysema who, when asked to count to ten, will do so by saying, one, two, three (pause), four, five (breath)—and never quite make ten unless they take longer and longer pauses between the numbers.

Several months later, *Pravda* reported that Andropov had died —from emphysema. It added that he had been a heavy cigarette smoker.

In Kosygin's case, I had been at the distance of a photograph when making a diagnosis; in Carter's, Giamatti's, and Andropov's, at the distance of a TV image. These are not feats of observation; any physician is capable of spotting pathological conditions and all have undoubtedly done so. In fact, medical professionals sometimes amuse themselves by detecting pathology in works of art. The *Journal of the American Medical Association* used to feature such examples from art on its front cover.

As an incorrigible collector of curiosities, when I first saw Michelangelo's statue of *Dawn,* which reclines on the top of a Medici tomb in Florence, I noticed what looked like a classic sign of breast cancer: dimpling of the skin of the lower outer quadrant of her right breast.

At the National Museum in Tarquinia, Italy, the left upper area of the abdomens of the life-sized Etruscan statues was uniformly enlarged. Historians have long been puzzled by the disappearance of the Etruscan nation two and a half thousand years ago. It had been a powerful force in the Roman empire. I was aware that malaria was commonly found on Italy's west coast, the area occupied by Etruscans. (The U.S. Army Corps of Engineers helped clean out malaria breeding in the Pontine marshes after World War II). As chronic malarial infection can enlarge the spleen, an organ that occupies the left upper corner of the abdomen, I wondered whether a virulent form of malaria, perhaps the quartan variety, could have done the Etruscans in. Archeologists, please note.

◆ ◆ ◆

Medicine has led me to many byways, sometimes as physician, sometimes merely as observer. When, in 1977, newspapers, radio, and television carried news of the death of Anthony Eden, a former prime minister of England and, during the Second World War, first secretary under Winston Churchill, I recalled an extraordinary bit of dialogue I had been lucky enough to hear.

In the late winter of 1976, Pamela and Averell Harriman invited Grace and me for a weekend in Hobe Sound, Florida. Pam was particularly anxious for me to be there because the former prime minister and his wife, Clarissa, would also be there. Eden was suffering from uncontrolled prostate cancer, and Pam thought that perhaps, in discussions with Clarissa, I might be able to come up with something helpful.

Henry Brandon, the star Washington correspondent for the *Sunday Times* of London, whom I had contacted about Jimmy Carter, was a fellow house-guest.

Averell was a true patrician, educated at Groton and Yale, tall, wealthy, handsome, aristocratic, witty, and wise. A lifelong Democrat, he served as President Franklin Roosevelt's adviser and envoy to England in 1941 and as special adviser during World War II. He became ambassador to the U.S.S.R. in 1943 and accompanied FDR to the historic 1945 Yalta meeting with Churchill and Stalin, at which the three leaders discussed the strategy of the war and future peace plans. From 1955 to 1959, he was governor of New York State. In later life, as a statesman in the grand tradition, he kept up his political activities, serving four presidents as adviser and special envoy to various countries.

Later, in his nineties, chair-bound and with diminishing eyesight and hearing, he would have his attendant wheel him to the edge of the croquet field that Pamela had given him as a birthday present. There this upright, elegant man would sit while the attendant described each shot of the contest in high decibels, and beamed if Pam's team won.

Pamela, born Lady Digby, was first married to Randolph Churchill, son of Winston Churchill. After a divorce, Pam had many prominent gentlemen admirers who found her superb complexion, honey-colored hair, and beguiling charm irresistible. She married producer Leland Hayward and after his death married her World War II beau, the newly widowed Averell.

One side of Pam not generally known is that each summer, she would invite me to be present when thirty to forty physically

deformed children and their attendants spent a day at her West-
chester estate. Pam provided them with a lavish picnic and went
from one to another to talk and play games with them. Averell
and I were the only outsiders, and could tell that these kids were
having an unforgettable experience.

Pam inherited her devotion to the Democratic party from her
husband, and since his death at ninety-four has continued as an
adviser and fund-raiser for them. Her reputation as a gracious
hostess is without equal, and invitations to her star-studded dinner parties are coveted by everyone in and out of politics. Recently, in late 1991, she held two huge parties to commemorate
the hundredth anniversary of Averell's birth.

During the 1976 weekend at Hobe Sound, Clarissa Eden and I
had many private conversations about her husband's condition. I
called my urological colleagues at Memorial and others around
the country to discuss the treatment he had had so far and ask for
suggestions. At the time, work was being done on a drug called
Flutamide, which was in short supply, but reported to have been
beneficial.

Eden and Averell Harriman used to sit around in the relaxed
and sunny atmosphere of that secluded island and talk over current events as well as political situations, past and present. And
then one time, the journalist, Henry Brandon and I heard Eden
say, out of the blue, to Averell:

"Why didn't you and Franklin tell Winston and me that you
were going to demand an unconditional surrender from Germany?"

Averell thought for a moment, then said: "Because we didn't
think you and Winston would agree to it."

Brandon and I looked at each other wide-eyed, feeling privy to
a footnote to history. It was awe-inspiring. It also had an element
of shock, as I had always believed that these two great allies
worked in harmony and would certainly have settled between
them the major question of the surrender terms.

A few months later, in a gracious letter thanking me for sending
her further details on Flutamide, Clarissa stated that "Anthony
has been having trouble with his breathing which is tiresome. He
has been X-ray'd, scanned and EKG'd with nothing to be seen—
so we are a bit stumped." Several months later, Anthony Eden
died, and Henry Brandon called me to ask about the wording of
that exchange between Eden and Averell. He wanted to include it
in his obituary, written for the *Sunday Times*.

◆ ◆ ◆

While at Hampshire College, Anthony had designed a course of studies that he had kept secret from me. He was well into his third year when, during a holiday recess, he said, "Dad, I've got something to tell you."

Now when a teenager begins a discussion that way, it usually means trouble—pregnancy, VD, or worse.

Anthony said: "I've decided to become a doctor."

Flabbergasted with joy, all I could think of saying at that time was "Wonderful, dear Antonio! Full speed ahead." Then I hugged him, hoping this gesture would say all that I wanted it to.

Apparently, Anthony had worked out a pre-medical curriculum and had not wanted to divulge his plan until he was satisfied that he had a good chance of getting into a medical school. He had been taking the required courses—biology, chemistry, physics, and so forth—at Smith, Amherst, and Mount Holyoke, so that he would receive standardized grades instead of Hampshire's written reports. Medical-school admission committees, he felt, would probably be more interested in grades than in opinions. He had been getting high marks in these subjects and hoped to do well with his MCATs—the nationwide aptitude tests for those who want to study medicine.

Afterward, I thought back to six years earlier, when, after watching me operate, he had said: "Dad, that was a trip!"

My exaltation was matched only by that of my mother, who kept recalling the day when I had announced a similar decision. Grace was quietly, deeply enthusiastic; she had the utmost confidence that Anthony would be a fine physician. Friends kept telling me how complimented I should feel that a son had chosen to follow my profession. I did.

I also felt complimented that Grace, who was skittish about anything to do with illness, overcame her fear to attend some of the medical lectures I gave. She always sat as far back in the lecture hall as possible and closed her eyes when the lantern slides of surgical specimens were shown. But, squeamish though she was, she stuck it out.

If Grace was hesitant, even phobic, about entering a hospital's doorway, I was anything but that when she invited me to designers' fashion shows, complete with music, runways, cameras, and a bouquet of long-stemmed models. Now I rarely go, but when I do, they remind me of the openings of Broadway shows, complete with the excitement, music, beautiful girls, applause, and critics—fashion editors and buyers. Grace is always given a choice seat, and sometimes I am lucky enough to be seated next to her, like being seated on the fifty-yard line in a football game. Shortly after we were married, I went to Paris with Grace to see the couture collections. I was told that at a Dior showing I would not be seated next to Grace, but, nevertheless, would have a reserved seat with my name on it. Once Grace was seated, I began searching for my chair—and there it was, clearly labeled: DR. MIRABELLA.

What Grace diagnoses in a collection and what I see are quite different. Her professional eye focuses on the way the clothes hang, on their length, color, cut, and movement, as she decides what will "work" at that particular period of time and what to use in her magazine. I, on the other hand, preoccupied with derrière pensées, am busy figuring out how the models' femurs articulate with their pelvises to produce the swivel in their caboose. I am fascinated by the graceful way models walk and hold themselves so elegantly erect. I concluded that it's a by-product of the precise way they place their feet—one in front of the other—plus the engineering and architectural features mentioned above. Once again, nature's wisdom cannot be denied—such seductive movements and structures do foster procreation. That summer, at one of Yves St. Laurent's collections, the models wore sheer, see-through blouses. I couldn't resist whispering to Grace: "I feel I am on a bust man's holiday." She, as does almost everyone hearing puns, winced. Just why puns produce winces instead of smiles is an unsolved mystery.

In May 1978, four years after we were married, my own dear Grace entered Memorial Sloan-Kettering to have a hysterectomy. Although the operation was considered routine, I knew how apprehensive it would make her, so I withheld the possibility that although her condition was most probably benign, it could have unpleasant surprises.

As she registered in MSK's admissions office, I said, "Noblesse oblige. As my wife, now you'll be treated royally." The wonders of modern medicine would be hers.

That evening, as I sat at her bedside, Grace told me that her patient identification wristlet listed her age as 74 instead of 47; that her blood chemistries had been lost; and that, although she was supposed to have had dinner, she had not been given any although the other patients had already been fed. "Bill," said Grace, "what happens to those who are not treated royally?"

Grace Mirabella, *Vogue* editor-in-chief for seventeen years, and whose
name, taste, and talents made *Mirabella* into one of the most impressive
and successful magazine startups in modern history.

At home that night, I found short "Grace notes" left for me in nooks and crannies. Alone, I looked around at the many mementos of her presence—photographs, shoes, her cluttered desk—and wrote: "My love, I miss you already and can't wait for this to be over so we can re-begin our glorious life together."

At seven the next morning, I was in Grace's hospital room dressed in my O.R. scrub suit, as I was scheduled to operate. Those who have been through such a situation know that the wait before going to the operating room can seem eternal. As I watched Grace doze from the effects of the preoperative medication, I went through the typical rigors of a doctor when someone close is about to have surgery. It is an occupational disease—physicians imagine all the *ifs*—and I was no exception.

Such thoughts were curtailed when her stretcher arrived. I walked beside her to the operating room door. There, I greeted her surgeon and anesthetist and, as I leaned down and kissed her, Grace handed me an envelope, which I placed unopened in the pocket of my scrub-suit shirt. Then I went down the hall, three operating rooms away, to see my patient before he was anesthetized.

A half-hour later, the surgeon thoughtfully sent a bulletin to me: All was going well. Two hours after that, I completed my operation and was surprised to see that Grace's was still in progress. I resisted calling the surgeon by intercom, not wanting to interfere with his concentration. Instead, like other mortals, I paced and imagined.

While waiting, I opened the envelope that Grace had given me. In it was a single sheet of paper.

Dear Billy:
Natural history by E. B. White—and from Me to You!

> The spider dropping down from twig
> unwinds a thread of his devising
> a thin, premeditated rig
> to use in rising.
>
> And all the journey down through space
> in cool descent, and loyal-hearted
> he builds a ladder to the place
> from which he started.

Thus I, gone forth, as spiders do,
in spider's web a truth discerning,
attach one silken strand to you
for my returning.

xxx
G.

When the surgeon emerged, he told me that he had found free fluid in the peritoneum and had been concerned that a malignant degeneration of the fibroid had occurred or that an unsuspected cancer was present. However, his exploration of the rest of her abdomen was negative and the pathologist had examined the operation specimen and found it to be benign. I thanked him and went to the recovery room to see my patient and to be there as Grace emerged from anesthesia. Although she was still groggy, I leaned over to kiss her and to say that all was fine.

Both Grace and my patient did well, and left the hospital on the same day. To this day, each time I read of spiders and silken strands, I am swept into tears.

Goddard Lieberson, president of the Columbia Records division of CBS, was also a fine composer. He had brought Columbia Records to preeminence in the industry by his early advocacy of the LP record, among other wise decisions. Grace and I had known Goddard and his wife, Brigitta (the dancer Vera Zorina) for several years and often played tennis together.

One evening, while Brigitta was visiting relatives in Norway, we invited Goddard to join us for dinner at a restaurant. Instead of being his charming, outgoing self, Goddard appeared unusually somber and haggard. Instinctively, I became alarmed and when he ordered and barely touched a cup of clear soup, and kept clutching his abdomen, grew even more so. When I asked him about this, he said that for several days he had had a steady upper-abdominal pain that London physicians had said was probably due to a peptic ulcer. They had prescribed antacids, which had not relieved him. Intuitively, I felt that his ashen color and drawn features suggested something more serious. For some reason, my first thought was that he might have cancer of the pancreas—an organ in the mid-abdomen that secretes both digestive juices and insulin. The next day I called Jack Nelson, Goddard's physician, and told him of my suspicion. Immediately, Jack took Goddard to University Hospital where, along with other diagnostic procedures, a needle biopsy of his enlarged liver showed it to contain cancer that had metastasized there from his pancreas.

When Goddard came under my care, once again I felt frustrated and appalled that I could not offer a close friend any treatment that had even the remotest chance of being curative. In the months that followed, his abdomen swelled from the fluid caused by cancer cells in the peritoneum. As Goddard insisted on remaining at home, I repeatedly tapped his abdomen in the outpatient clinic. The intervals between the tappings became shorter. It was painfully evident that he was being consumed by his cancer.

As his face became more drawn, his ribs grew more prominent, his abdomen swelled, and his leg muscles shrank, he described himself as looking like an unripe pear held up by two toothpicks. As ill as he was, Goddard maintained his sense of humor. He told me that every day he and Babe Paley, who was also being treated then, called each other to have a "cancer klatsch." Brigitta said that she would often hear Goddard laughing uproariously—and Babe, she was sure, was laughing just as hard at the other end.

When Goddard could no longer come to the hospital, I visited him at home. On one occasion, Grace accompanied me, and while we were chatting with Brigitta, Goddard suddenly said: "How sick am I?" Brigitta and Grace stared straight ahead, not knowing what else to do. All I could say was, "It's a tough situation, Goddard, but perhaps something will come along that will reverse it."

He listened attentively, then looked out of the window at the East River below. I could imagine what was going on in his mind, for his musician's sensitivity to nuances and inflections must have caught my tone of false optimism. When he looked back at Brigitta, Grace, and me, I could tell that he was resigned to his mortality.

Later I thought: Goddard's question was one I would never ask myself were I in his condition.

In his last days Goddard became even more handsome as his fine bone structure grew more prominent. Fortunately, medications controlled his pain and intravenous liquids helped slake his thirst. His faculties remained intact up to his last few days. Just two and a half months after our meeting in the restaurant, he died where he wanted to be, at home. At his funeral, which was attended by hordes of people and at which some of his music was played, some of his eulogists lightened the proceedings with touches of Goddard's humor. At its end, those assembled filed out of the synagogue, past Brigitta and her two sons. As I leaned over to kiss her cheek and offer a few words of condolence, she whispered, "We tried. God knows, we tried."

So Goddard joined those whose cancers flouted my boyhood vow not to stand by helplessly while someone close to me was in desperate straits. Although in my lifetime there have been many winners, for the losers I console myself that everything that could possibly be done had been tried. Still, Goddard's death left me feeling tormented, frustrated, and overpowered once more by the "enemy," which had so many times before reduced talent, joy, hope, and beauty to dust.

Recognizing how often we have to admit defeat and what it must mean to deal with so much tragedy, Grace asked: "How can you stand it? Doesn't the suffering, the failures, the pain and heartbreak get to you? Isn't your personality eroded?" And: "What happens when there is an extra burden of failing with those who are close to you?"

CHAPTER XXIV

How Can You Stand It?

I'm often asked "How can you stand it?" Meaning the defeats, the frustrations and heartbreak, the pain, the dying. The most serviceable answer is that, instead of wringing my hands, I do something with them. In other words, I instantly sublimate my initial reactions of sympathy, concern, or even horror, into thinking of what could be done to lessen or rectify the problems before me.

But there is more to being able to "stand it": to cope; in fact, to survive repeated heartrending experiences, particularly the extra burden of failing with those close to me; to understand. For me, this may have had its earliest beginnings in childhood, learning the meaning, the feel of pain from many injuries and burns. Ultimately, fascination overcame revulsion when I made the first incision on a cadaver and watched my first autopsy. As one grows in the profession, you become, to a certain extent, conditioned by exposure to repeated injuries, illnesses, operations, pain, and death. In time, in order not to be emotionally traumatized and spiritually depleted, one develops a tolerance of—never indifference to—suffering and learns, by disciplining oneself, not to overreact, to maintain equanimity. There *are* cures, many times, and there are always techniques to help.

However hardened I may be by constant exposures, I'm never left unscathed, particularly with cancer patients, so that I am no stranger to tears, others' or my own. Almost always, I keep mine from public view, and when confronted with what is clearly a tragic or hopeless situation, I instinctively move to reassure, aid, and comfort.

Professionals who work with cancer patients are only one group who must learn to adapt and reconcile their own emotional reactions in order to care for those who are chronically ill. The same exposure to pain and sorrow that coarsens the mind and calluses the soul of one may give to another a power of compassion, understanding, and humility without which mere achievement remains primitive. This certainly is true for those who are dedicated to the care of retarded or deformed children, the senile, elderly, Alzheimers disease, paraplegics, the severely burned. Those working with these problems must form a protective layer lest they be drowned in a sea of troubles.

I can stand it because I feel more fulfilled than depressed and realize how, to a large extent, these challenges, like a religion, fill my life. Loving people, puzzles, beauty in any form, I become deeply involved in the counterpoint and fugue of many lives. No question: I am enriched by patients, who give me as much as I give them.

In a world filled with frills and inconsequentials, dealing with such problems never leaves one feeling useless or unwanted. Only those who have been through some painful personal experience with cancer can understand and sympathize with my obsession with this disease. From family, close friends, and many patients, I've learned what terror strikes the moment cancer touches one's life and how it changes that life forever.

So cancer is a burning city within me. Its omnipresence stalks me constantly whether I am walking the hospital corridors, lamenting the cynical seduction of innocents by tobacco giants, listening to the anxieties of those seeking guidance for someone close to them or for themselves. Although death is a physician's silent partner, one who will inevitably inherit the business, I struggle to prevent, to heal, to delay, to relieve. This is competition at the highest level and it appeals to the competitor within me. What greater contest is there than to try to overcome, such a devious, malicious, guile-ridden, untrustworthy, unsentimental, ancient enemy?

In the middle of the dark night of suffering and despondency, I am able to draw on, and be sustained by, a full and deep reservoir of caring as well as by peace of mind in my personal life. It also helps to feel confident that what I am doing is in the best interests of the patient.

And there are flashes of soaring moments, great rewards. Nothing can match the exhilaration I feel on observing the elation and relief of those whose anxieties are almost palpable and who, at the end of an examination, are told they do not have cancer, or that their cancer has not recurred, that they are going to live.

Then, there are grateful looks or words. And the letters:

November 4, 1982

Dear Dr. Cahan:

I hope you will be operating on my father soon.
He is a humble, kind, simple man, loved by many people. He is a man who has lived with dignity and respect. I love him unashamedly. Please treat my Dad special and help him as much as you can.

And one from a saint:

March 2, 1981

Dear Dr. Cahan:

Your love and care for my brother, your anxiety to share his pain by lessening it—it is one of those beautiful gifts of God to have people like you sharing the joy of loving Christ in the suffering brother.
My gratitude is my prayer for you that you may grow in holiness by sharing the passion of Christ and the suffering.
God bless you.

Mother Teresa
From the Missionary of Charity
Old Circular Road, Calcutta, India.

So I can stand it because there is so much left to do, so many dragons to slay, and, despite many failed dreams, so many "miles to go before I sleep."

❖

CHAPTER XXV

"Cornell!"

In his second year at Hampshire, while eating lunch in the Smith College cafeteria, Anthony saw a young woman get in line at the counter. Anthony said to himself: "That's the woman I'm going to marry."

During a spring recess, Anthony brought Karen Gellerman to meet Grace and me. Karen, tall, willowy, auburn-haired, hazel-eyed, had been a runner-up for Miss Teenage America. She was a political science major at Smith, a strong feminist, and had a keen interest in interior decoration and fashion.

Some time later, Anthony called from Hampshire and suggested I read the front page of that morning's *New York Times* "carefully." Naturally, I suspected a trick. Not until I had read the entire page did I finally spy in tiny print at the bottom of a column: "Karen G. Will you marry me? Anthony C."

Their wedding took place on June 25, 1978, in the walled garden of our Sixty-second Street house, where Anthony and Chris had romped as kids. My mother was there in a wheelchair, along with some of Anthony's, Sisi's, Grace's, and my friends. Chris was Anthony's best man. To those who witnessed the ceremony, it seemed that only good things could come to such a handsome pair.

That fall, Anthony applied to several medical schools, including Harvard, NYU, and Cornell. His first choice was Cornell. I secretly hoped he would be accepted there as it was not only an excellent school, but was across York Avenue from MSK.

Walking with him on the way to his admission interview at Cornell, I recalled my own long walk, nearly forty years before, at P&S. "Unlike yours," I told Anthony, "my academic record was not brilliant, but I did have a strong recommendation from my faculty adviser at Harvard, who mentioned something about 'an investigative mind.'" My interviewers—several faculty members—had begun with routine questions: Why did I want to study medicine? What other interests did I have besides science? To the first question, I gave a sincere, if unoriginal answer: I wanted to help the sick. To answer the second, I mentioned my interests in the arts, particularly in music, pointing out that I had studied harmony and composition. One interviewer (later my anatomy preceptor) asked, "Do you think you could compose in medicine?"

"I intend to," I said. "But I don't know enough about the fundamentals yet."

I could tell by the way they looked at me and then at one another that this response was okay. To this day, I am convinced that it made a difference.

Anyone who has applied to special schools knows the agony of waiting that follows: weeks of anxious mailbox-watching for the telltale envelope with *the* answer. We waited.

Early in 1978, I saw John Cazale, a gifted actor from Joseph Papp's Shakespeare company, who consulted me about his far-advanced lung cancer. (He had smoked a pack a day for twenty-plus years.) The cancer had metastasized to his bones and he was looking for straws to grasp.

He was accompanied by a young woman whose blue eyes, set deep in prominent cheekbones, and pouting lips somehow made her look vulnerable and kissable. Her face was so striking that, while examining him, I had to comment on it. John agreed that hers was a remarkable display of nature at its finest and added, "One that I hope to keep seeing as long as possible."

Unhappily, several months later, at the age of forty-two, John died and was mourned by his beloved friend, Meryl Streep.

And so, friend after friend kept falling. Doubly mourned are those who had given so much, who still had so much more to give, to the quality of our civilization—and who would have continued to do so had they not been lured as adolescents into a self-annihilating addiction. These senseless killings enraged me: There *had* to be more that I could do to stop these killings.

◆ ◆ ◆

Anthony was at Hampshire, so any mailed notice from medical school would be delayed two days in reaching him. Therefore, he had given my name and address. One morning, Phyllis Atkinson, my secretary, rushed into the office with an envelope from Cornell. She said, "I think you'll want to open this yourself." With shaking fingers, I tore open the envelope.

My sheer, unadulterated delight could not be described. I immediately called Anthony. Karen answered the phone and suspected that it was something important, for instead of chatting, as we usually did, I asked for Anthony. When he got on the phone, I read the letter with no preliminaries. There were shouts and laughter at both ends.

Unable to contain my enthusiasm, I called Grace, who was lunching, and asked the maitre d' to call her to the phone. When she picked up, all I said was "Cornell." She was ecstatic.

Funny, how overjoyed we are when a young man or woman has just had the door opened to a life of extraordinarily demanding work, risk, and fatigue. Perhaps because a life in medicine carries the promise of becoming a force for good.

In 1978, commemorative stamps honoring George Papanicolaou were issued both in the United States and in Greece. In light of my friendship with Pap, I thought it fitting to pay tribute to him by having a memorial plaque made and placed at the base of the Hippocratic tree, which was now about thirty feet tall:

TREE FROM HIPPOCRATIC ISLAND OF KOS PLANTED IN MEMORY OF
GEORGE N. PAPANICOLAOU, M.D.,
CANCER CYTOLOGIST, CORNELL UNIVERSITY MEDICAL COLLEGE, 1914–1962,
AND MEMORIAL HOSPITAL, 1976.

Often, I would visit the tree, which became like a member of my family and a part of the Medical College's tradition. I was unprepared for a sad, strange event that occurred twelve years later.

CHAPTER XXVI

Sketches on a Tablecloth

Disraeli described that period of life when the urge to recall one's past becomes irresistible as one's "anecdotage" and a time to retire. I am no exception. For years, I have been a cross between a diarist and an archivist.

My father could not resist sketching a face that interested him anywhere, anytime, on anything. Backs of envelopes, blank spaces in newspaper ads, table linen. As a boy, I would sit at a restaurant table squirming with embarrassment as my father used the tablecloth to draw the face of someone at another table. Usually, the subject would feel his constant gaze and, out of curiosity, come over to see what he had done. Invariably he or she was pleased, and some even offered to buy the tablecloth from the proprietor. One restaurant owner was impressed enough to cut out and frame my father's sketch.

Not having his talent, but nudged by his genes, I have felt compelled to record my reactions to people and ideas that intrigued, depressed, delighted, or inspired me. So when Anthony entered medical school forty years after me, it provided me with a splendid opportunity to compare his medical-school days with mine.

I thought it best not to tell him what I was doing lest it make him self-conscious.

In what follows, I refer to Anthony as "A."

Thursday, September 7, 1978.
    The moment I had been waiting for came today: I ran into A. in his short white coat. While leaving Memorial, I spied him across

York Avenue talking with a classmate. He didn't see me at first so I gave the family whistle. His head snapped around and he grinned: He knew what I must be feeling. Then he left his friend and I walked with him to the school entrance. He was bubbling with enthusiasm for his new life. As we separated, he looked at me with an expression I'd never seen before. "I feel a new, different thing with you, Dad . . . now that we're going to be talking the same language."

That same October, 1978, former vice president Hubert Humphrey, who had been a patient at MSK, died of bladder cancer.

While he was at MSK, he was his usual exuberant, optimistic, irrepressible, effusive self. Even after surgery and throughout the enervating period when he received chemotherapy, he would delight other patients on his floor by introducing himself and any eminent visitors such as Henry Kissinger, ex-president Gerald Ford, and Senator Walter Mondale.

A touching scene: A few days after Hubert's surgery, Averell Harriman told me that he had attended a reception for presidential candidate Jimmy Carter at the Foreign Policy Association. Before Carter was introduced, a speaker paid tribute to Hubert. This, Averell said, was greeted by a standing ovation that was longer and more enthusiastic than that shown for the candidate. Averell asked me to relay this to Hubert.

When I went to his room to do so, Humphrey was lying in bed with a plastic tube in his nostril to suction his stomach. When I finished telling him what had transpired, he thanked me . . . and then, tearfully, stared straight ahead with such a plaintive look that I left quickly.

At the time of Hubert's cancer, chemotherapy—the use of a drug or combination of drugs to treat cancer—was in its early, formative stages. The basic principle of chemotherapy is to give chemicals strong enough to kill cancer cells while, at the same time, stopping short of destroying normal cells as well. However, it is virtually impossible not to damage these cells to some degree. Therefore, patients usually face the prospect of uncomfortable side effects—nausea, gastrointestinal disturbances, loss of appetite, hair loss, depleted energy, and bone-marrow depression. The intensity of these reactions varies from drug to drug and individual to individual. Some can be severe enough to necessitate the patient's admittance to a hospital to tide him over acute reactions; others are not upsetting at all.

Hubert had to endure hair loss, weight loss, nausea, and anorexia.

A month after this ex–vice president died, Henry Kissinger asked me how long Hubert's life had been prolonged by chemotherapy. Hadn't it really been a pointless exercise? I explained that Hubert and his wife, Muriel, knowing that further surgery and radiation therapy would be ineffective, had entered this therapeutic regimen with no illusions. Even though they were advised that there was only the remotest chance of success, Hubert said that he was willing to suffer any debilitating side effects as he was "reluctant" to relinquish his hold on life. He and Muriel felt that, at least, chemotherapy afforded some hope and, as was typical of Hubert's style, he preferred that to just sitting by passively, waiting to die. As to whether his life had been prolonged, chemotherapy may have added a few months at best.

Henry asked, "What do a few extra months of survival mean if you have to suffer from all those side effects? Wasn't the quality of his remaining days ruined?"

He was right to be skeptical. However, when patients realize they soon may die, they can use even such an allotment of borrowed time to wind up their affairs, gather their families around them, and seek religious counsel.

Kissinger's questions reminded me that in earlier days, when surgery and radiation failed, physicians had nothing left to offer patients dying from cancer. Since Hubert's time, chemotherapy has worked very effectively against certain cancers such as seminoma of the testicle, Hodgkin's disease, acute leukemia in children, Wilms's tumor of the kidney, and bone sarcoma.

In others, although falling short of being curative, it has slowed the cancer's growth. What is encouraging is that the debilitating side effects have been reduced.

It takes a strong-willed patient not to be eager to embrace a reasonable medical regimen, particularly if the cancer has spread. Patients feel that although it is a long-shot gamble, they may be one of the lucky ones who respond dramatically and even make medical history. And sometimes they do, too. When they read or hear of new discoveries, they feel that the name of the game in cancer is to stay alive, for tomorrow some radical breakthrough might make all the difference.

Inevitably, in spite of a wide variety of measures used to relieve pain, such as stronger medications and neurosurgical procedures, some cancer patients die a slow, painful death. Probably, there is no physician who has not been tempted to abbreviate this painful, often undignified, economically draining phase of a person's life. Some physicians, acting purely out of conscience, give lethal injections and are brought to trial.

The ethics of euthanasia (from the Greek, it means easy or good death) are a constantly recurring dilemma, and legislators frequently introduce bills so that it can be legally carried out. The pros and cons of euthanasia are too well known to be repeated here. However, Zinsser in his book *As I Remember Him,*★ said:

> To put hopeless sufferers deliberately out of their agonies with lethal drugs may often be desirable. But to admit even a consideration of this implies the exercise of judgment that will inevitably be fallible in a small percentage of cases. It might be worked out under reliable boards and a limited number of conditions. It will open the doors for dreadful possibilities.
>
> The average integrity of the medical profession is, perhaps, a little higher than the population as a whole, but not high enough for euthanasia.
>
> It is quite another question, however, whether doctors should continue to keep a hopeless case alive for a few weeks or months when judicious inactivity would bring rest to the patient and peaceful resignation to his family and friends.

Although I am careful to work within the limits of the law, once the patient has become irreversibly comatose, I have reduced life-sustaining measures such as intravenous fluids, although I confess I am unable to turn off the oxygen supply.

Such unconditional surrender usually comes at a point when the patient, the relatives, and I recognize that the limit of trying has been reached. Les Samuels, a philanthropist who made major donations to opera, said to me after a long siege, "Let me go, Bill, I've had enough." Putting such a person through further treatment such as vitamins or blood transfusions is both pointless and inhumane. Fortunately, with judiciously administered drugs, the majority of hopeless cancer patients die in peace and

---

★ Hans Zinsser was a scientist at the Rockefeller Institute who made a major contribution to our understanding of typhus and whose book *Rats, Lice and History* was a best-seller. *As I Remember Him: the Biography of R. S.* is, in fact, his autobiography; R. S. stands for "romantic self." (Little, Brown & Co., 1940)

without pain. To their everlasting credit, hospices have made this an art, a great contribution to the dying and those around them.

Wednesday, October 11, 1978.

A. invited me to the anatomy lab to see his dissection. As I entered, I was greeted by a strong odor of Formalin that recalled my anatomy classes of forty-three years ago. A.'s lab is well lit, the cadavers neatly wrapped, everything antiseptic-seeming, white, and super-efficient. Quite an advance over the murky anatomy lab we had as students.

A. had lamented beforehand that the body of his cadaver whom he calls "Lazy Jane" was petite: her muscles like ribbons, her organs especially small, thus making fine structures hard to distinguish. A. said he had no trepidation about making his first incision in human flesh. But, I reminded him, there's quite a difference between the quiet, unfeeling cadaver and the live bodies of the future. No need to worry now about pulsating arteries, vital organs, or anxious relatives in the waiting room. His anatomy instructor had bluntly assured the class to start with: "You may be apprehensive now, but soon you'll be having your lunch with your stiff."

As Anthony peeled back the layers, I saw that Lazy Jane's arteries and veins had not been injected with red and blue dyes in order to preserve them. Probably this technique is not necessary with to-day's methods of embalming. A. pointed out her tiny uterus, her normal liver and spleen, and a gallbladder with gallstones. However, there were no anatomical clues as to what caused her death. In an earlier day, many cadavers had gross evidence of advanced tuberculosis, pneumonia, or peritonitis.

A. was proud of the abdominal viscera he could name, and began reeling off the Latin names of muscles, vessels, bones, and so forth. His recitation sounded to me like a Bach cantata. I thought: *There is democracy in anatomy*.

Thursday, November 9, 1978.

I got a kick out of hearing Anthony using the mnemonics we had as anatomy students: "*Never Loosen Tilly's Pants, Mother Might Come Home*" (bones of the wrist); "*On Old Olympus Topmost Top, A Fat Assed German Viewed Some Hop*" (cranial nerves). To this day, these help me remember the anatomy of areas that I might otherwise have forgotten.

December 18, 1978.

My father's illustration of the touching Christmas story, O. Henry's "Gift of the Magi," came to mind when, at Christmastime, a grateful Lebanese patient of mine gave a dinner party at his suite in the Waldorf-Astoria to express his gratitude to those who had attended him in the hospital. Because of the holiday season, Grace and I felt it appropriate to bring along two bottles of champagne as a gift.

The dinner table was covered with a number of Near Eastern dishes that surrounded an entire roast lamb. The entrée made Grace uncomfortable: She recalled that the eyes were often presented to honored guests for privileged consumption. Fortunately, this was not done.

When dinner was over, the son of the patient toasted my colleagues and me with a glass of fruit juice. Then he presented me with a small gift in a wrapped box. "A Christmas present," he said. In turn, Grace and I gave our host and his son the gift-wrapped bottles of champagne.

When I opened the box, I found (much to the amusement of my colleagues) a gold-plated cigarette lighter. On the other hand, in our ignorance, we hadn't realized that religious Arabs who are Muslims do not drink alcoholic beverages. Nevertheless, all of us were effusive in our thanks.

One of those I subjected to antismoking prodding was Abe Rosenthal, then editor-in-chief of *The New York Times* (now one of its op-ed columnists). I told Abe one day that he was the newest recipient of the Yellow Palm Award. This meant that when I entered a room, Abe would guiltily turn the lighted cigarette he held between his fingers so that the burning end was cupped in his hand; hence the yellow palm.

On a New Year's morning, TV movie reviewer Gene Shalit assembled a group of his friends, including Abe, Beverly Sills, Grace, and me, to appear on NBC's *Today Show*. Gene asked about our expectations and resolutions for the coming year. After Abe had commented on some of the situations he expected would make major stories, he said, "On the subject of New Year's resolutions, I want to tell Bill that I so hated feeling guilty each time he caught me smoking, that I have given it up." Although eight A.M. on New Year's morning was hardly prime time, to say that before a national television audience *was* a commitment, and one to which Abe has religiously adhered ever since.

Although my special interest in cancer was in what can be called the northern hemisphere of the body, a friend had a unique reaction in her southern hemisphere.

When she received radiation therapy in her pelvic area following an operation for uterine cancer, the skin and mucous membrane of the area became inflamed—and she developed symptoms simulating hypereroticism. Although I had seen this symptom in women who had received male hormone for breast-cancer metastases, this result of radiation therapy was new to me and, more significantly, to her. Apparently, the radiation-induced inflammation increased sensitivity in the vaginal and clitoral sector to such a degree that when she took warm tepid baths, prescribed to relieve the inflammation, just getting into the tub triggered an orgasm. As she took several baths a day, she naively wondered why she felt so lethargic when evening came around.

In a few weeks, both her inflammation and hyperexcitation subsided. However, as high doses of radiation can reduce normal vaginal lubrication and desensitize nerve endings, her multiple orgasms could well have been among her last. Further sexual delights would probably rely more on the psychological than the physiological aspects of lovemaking.

Dealing with the lovemaking problems of patients is not solely the province of psychiatrists. Many studies have been done on the effect on one's sex life produced by a mastectomy, or other operative procedures that distort one's anatomy. Under the heading of "You're never too old to yearn," a ninety-four-year-old man with a large cancer of his lower lip walked into my consultation room spry, bow-tied, and frisky, and said, "Doc, I want this damn thing removed because it's cuttin' down on my kissin'."

He had been offered radiation therapy, but was told that the size of his cancer would make this only palliative. He disliked the idea, perferring instead to have the cancer removed and "over with." Surgeons whom he had consulted had turned him down because of the cancer's size and his age. It was immediately apparent to me that regardless of chronology he was a spirited candidate for surgery. A few days later, under local anesthesia, his cancer was removed and his lip reconstructed.

The night of his operation, I ordered a special nurse because an elderly person can fall out of bed or wander about confused, disoriented by unfamiliar surroundings.

The next day, as I came off the elevator, the patient's solidly built nurse stood facing me with arms crossed below a baleful stare. "I'm signing off this case, Doctor. The patient made improper advances to me all night long!"

After apologizing, I went to see my patient and, feigning anger, told him to behave himself. Although he was recovering well, he had to remain yet another day and night in the hospital, so I ordered another night nurse, this time specifying that it be a male. The next day, as I came off the elevator, there was the male nurse, arms crossed, wearing his version of the same baleful stare. He was quitting. Why? "The patient made passes at me all night long!"

Fortunately, I was able to discharge my elderly satyromaniac that day. Apparently, at a vigorous ninety-four and under cover of darkness, one grabs at anyone or anything that moves.

Patients can leave scars that haunt you long after they have departed. Certain patients stay with me forever: those whose pains were unrelieved before they died; those who maintained great dignity through their prolonged suffering; and, doubly lacerating to my conscience, those rebukes to my skill who died postoperatively as a result of some technical mistake or flaw in diagnosis or treatment. Curiously, although many linger in memory because of their strong, colorful personalities, it is the meek who affect me most, their quiet despair creating an extra dimension to tragedy.

Max Bloch left a deep scar. He was forty, a former concentration-camp inmate, an ex-Israeli who had been a U.S. citizen for one year. He was in the import-export business and had an adoring wife, a son, and a daughter.

Max was ruggedly good-looking; he had dark hair, and brown eyes with crow's feet, which deepened frequently as he exercised his suave and sardonic sense of humor. He had first been treated at another institution for cancer of his left lung that had been considered inoperable. After receiving chemotherapy there, for a while he felt encouraged because his left shoulder pain had lessened. But it soon returned and intensified. Comparison of a new lung X ray with previous ones showed that the original shadow had increased in size. Also, a new shadow had appeared in the opposite lung that could either be a metastasis or a new primary lung cancer.

To relieve his pain, we operated on his left chest and, to our surprise, managed to remove the cancerous lung as well as a section of the phrenic nerve that the cancer involved. Postoperatively, his shoulder pain disappeared. Then, after a month's convalescence, we discussed the shadow in the right lung and he insisted, "I want *all* the cancer out of me." Using a pie-shaped excision, we removed what proved to be a new primary cancer in his right lung. Within a few weeks, this stalwart fellow was back at work.

One day ten months' later, his wife phoned. She thought his old Ménière's disease had returned, for he was having bouts of vertigo and dizziness. I immediately became suspicious; a CAT scan showed that the cancer had spread to the cerebellum, at the base of his brain.

After he received cortisone followed by radiation therapy, his symptoms rapidly subsided. He remained asymptomatic for four months. Although the radiation caused him to lose his hair, he made light of it by sporting colored berets and once appeared for a follow-up examination in an outrageous beanie, complete with pinwheel.

As outwardly bright and cheery as he was, he called one day and asked if I could see him alone in the privacy of my consulta-tion room. When the door was closed, he insisted that I discuss his cancer situation candidly. I told him that he was doing well, but that his future was unclear. He said that he had been putting on a good show but that inside he was being overwhelmed by the enormity of the disease. At which point he began to cry. I had a difficult time holding my tears back. This somber scene lasted only a few minutes; then, drying his eyes, he got up to leave and we shook hands firmly. Fully composed, he joined his wife in the waiting room. On his way out, he stopped to banter with my secretary and I heard the three of them laughing.

On his last follow-up visit, he walked steadily and told me he was eating well and had regained his strength. He asked me for permission to go south for a few weeks' vacation, then to London and Paris for business.

Grace, Anthony, Karen, and I were at Ballato's restaurant on Houston Street celebrating the end of Anthony's first-year med-school examinations. The owner came to the table to say that I had a telephone call. He led me to a wall phone in the bustling kitchen. My answering service said to call Elsa Bloch immedi-ately. She told me—in a voice that broke from her usual wonder-fully composed manner—that Max had just began to cough up bright red blood.

Instantly I knew what was happening. The cancer was eroding

a large blood vessel in his chest. "Elsa, as soon as I hang up, call an ambulance. But first turn Max right side up and keep his head low so that he won't aspirate blood into his only functioning lung" (and drown). As I spoke, I heard, in the background, a high-pitched scream from his daughter. Elsa dropped the phone. The son picked it up, said, "Please forgive us," and hung up.

I could imagine what had happened. The pulmonary artery had ruptured into Max's windpipe and he had died in seconds.

At the moment, I was struck by the juxtaposition, the counterpoint, of death with the hustle and bustle of life, the food preparation going on about me. When I returned to the table, Anthony caught the meaning of the look on my face, but I was able to disguise it from Grace and Karen. Later, I called Elsa and told her that I knew what had happened and expressed my sympathy. She managed to thank me "for everything" and hung up.

That night I asked myself whether "everything"—the numerous efforts to keep Max alive—had been worthwhile.

I felt they had. Max had had a year of comfortable living, free of pain, and been able to return to life.

For whatever consolation it might afford, Max Bloch died in private, with the family he loved at his side. He was not buried in a mass grave with thousands of pathetic anonymous bodies, as he would have been in the Holocaust. One virtue of freedom, I thought, is to be able to live and die privately and with dignity. One last consolation: although the terminal event was gruesome and would haunt his family for the rest of their lives, it was mercifully brief.

So, together, patients and I have weathered many battles, some of which ended in glorious victories; others in tragic defeats. In time, most winners may fade from memory, but I can never forget those who, like Max Bloch, had so desperately and trustingly reached for my outstretched hand; and, try though I had to sustain them, I felt their grip loosen and was forced to watch in horror as they fell to their deaths.

Not all medical problems on the telephone are serious or shrouded in black crepe. Occasionally, in the middle of the night, the phone will ring and I, being on that side of the bed, will pick up the phone and hear a "breather." Such calls are usually of pornographic intent. However, in my world, the breather could well be a dyspneic patient desperately trying to catch his or her breath. As a result, I say, "Please try to give me your name and phone number and I'll get an ambulance to pick you up. I'll meet you at the hospital." There is a pause, then a sharp click at the other end.

The means of saving lives can take unexpected forms, and the telephone, in at least one instance, was one of them. Joe Bushkin, the great jazz pianist, a friend of *Winged Victory* days, called me at 2:00 A.M. because his wife's aunt, Rosie Dolly, one of the generation ago's famous singing Dolly Sisters, had locked herself in the bathroom and threatened to commit suicide. Joe wanted me to coax her out of it as he held the phone close to the keyhole. Such an assignment snapped my eyes open and set me bolt upright in bed. As Joe held the phone, I shouted loud enough, I hoped, to be heard in the bathroom: "Rosie, these crises will soon pass. Tomorrow will be a beautiful day. The toughest problems will be looked at in a different light. Think how beautiful life can be with flowers, beautiful skies—and *Variety!*"

By then, my wife Sisi, who had been fast asleep, woke up saying: "What the hell are you talking about?"

After a while, I ran out of steam and asked Joe if I should continue. I envisaged Rosie taking an overdose of pills or slashing her wrists, and thought it was time to dial the emergency police number. He said, "Wait a minute more, Doc, I'll try to get her to say something." When he returned, he said, "Give it a few more minutes. It's still silent in there." I re-began the litany, this time dredging up every possible incentive plus those I'd already used. A few minutes later, Joe interrupted me, saying, "Wait, Doc, she's turning the key. Here she is! Thanks, Doc."

Click.

Click, indeed!

April 12, 1979.

Today, for the first time, A. assisted me in the O.R. We shared a locker since he doesn't have one of his own. He was at my side as I stood by a middle-aged woman, holding her hand, as she was being anesthetized.

When my two assistants and I went to scrub, A. came with us and copied every move. After carefully drying his hands and forearms he was asked by the nurse for his glove size. He looked at me; I whispered, "Seven and a half—the same as mine."

Gowned and gloved, we assembled at the patient's side, my chief resident and I on her left, the assistant resident and Anthony across the table on her right. While performing a modified radical mastec-

ERICH HARTMAN

The doctors Cahan. The author (left) and his son Anthony
talk it over while scrubbing up for the operating room.

tomy, I questioned A. about the anatomy involved, particularly the
nerves that innervate the shoulder muscles. As low man on the
totem pole, he was given a retractor to hold from time to time,
which he did as if he were made of stone. His big moment came
when I allowed him to tie three of the knots used to close the skin.
While my assistant and I stood quietly by, all of us smiling behind
our masks, he awkwardly but accurately completed them. He realized, as do all novices, that there is a vast difference between
practicing with thread on objects in the privacy of one's own room
and doing the real thing. As A. finished the last knot, in unconscious echo he sighed and made a remark I had made years before:
"Well, I guess it's back to bedposts."

As we finished the procedure, for some reason I felt compelled
to reach across the table and shake Anthony's gloved hand.

June 15, 1979.

A. is finishing his first year. Today, I invited him to meet me
and make teaching rounds at Memorial.

In our lifetime, like any parent and child, he and I have experienced many firsts: his first steps; the first time he threw and caught
a ball, made an unassisted bike ride, swam the entire length of the
pool, tied his shoelaces, whistled, crossed the street by himself.

He has not begun clinical studies, so when I showed him a chart
with the patient's history and physical-examination results, A. immediately ran into confusing medicalese: *PI, WD. W.N. ♀ of 49 who*

2 wks PTA, gives a HX of acute onset of pain in her CVA. (Translation: present illness, a well-developed, well-nourished woman of forty-nine, who two weeks prior to admission, gives a history of acute onset of pain in her right costrovertebral angle.) Soon A. will use such medical shorthand, docspeak, without thinking—IV, ICU, ō, c̄., s̄., t.i.d., OR, LP, KJ, BX (intravenous, intensive care unit, no, with, without, three times a day, operating room, lumbar puncture, knee jerk, biopsy). They speed note-making, which with most physicians is indecipherable in any event.

Now I show him conditions he has never seen before: cyanosis, jaundice, clubbing of the fingers, enlarged livers. His wonderment at each new discovery is touching: He's like a sponge.

Wednesday, June 27, 1979.

Pulled an old trick on A. today. I took him to the bedside of a man (who was in on the ruse), handed him a flashlight, and asked him to examine the pupillary reflexes, etc. Anthony flashed the light into each eye and noted that the right pupil did not contract. Then he remarked that the distance between the lids was slightly smaller on the right. I covered the right eye and asked Mr. X if he could see my son's red ID badge. He said he could. But when I covered the left eye, he said he could not. Anthony said, "He's blind in that eye." Then I asked Mr. X to look from side to side; while the left eye moved freely, the right was limited in its range. Finally, it dawned on A: The right eye was false. The color of both eyes matched remarkably well, and the false eye's movement was possible because of the attachment of some of the eye muscles to the replacement for the original.

This joke has been played on countless students; it teaches them to sharpen their powers of observation. It also warns them to avoid the pitfalls of hasty, thoughtless examination.

July 1, 1979.

Nothing better expresses A.'s and my relationship than our joint effort to solve the London *Times*'s "World's Most Difficult Crossword Puzzle." Working together, Anthony and I follow a system. We begin solving separately, usually over the phone. Then, if I've hit upon some particularly difficult word before Anthony has, I don't reveal it right away, but give him hints instead. He almost always gets the word after a minute or two. He does the same with me. Working together, we usually complete about 90 percent of the puzzle; separately, about 60 percent.

This teamwork is something we hope to bring to medicine. At the moment we're working together to determine whether women have a greater susceptibility than men to the damaging effects of smoking. The project began as an hypothesis based on the precipitous rise in the incidence of lung cancer among women. Although this increase can undoubtedly be accounted for by women's increased use of cigarettes in the last thirty years, the astonishing *rate* of the rise makes one wonder whether, in fact, women are somehow more vulnerable to the carcinogens in tobacco. For one thing, the female chest is, on average, smaller than that of the male. Therefore, a pack a day concentrated and confined in the smaller space of a woman's lungs could be the equivalent of two packs a day for a man.

A.'s gathering the data for this, and together we will analyze it. As with solving other puzzles, each will fill in the spaces that the other cannot.

August 2, 1979.

When I came home, on my sixty-fifth birthday, Grace asked me to go upstairs and not come down until she called. Two hours later, when I was permitted downstairs, the backyard of our brownstone had been converted into a paradise of fountains, Chinese lanterns, and tropical plants and was filled with thirty close friends.

At dessert time, when I thanked and toasted Grace, I said that one experiences a sense of disbelief on occasion; you win a big promotion or a rich legacy, you fall in love, you become a parent, you have a dread disease, you are *really* in Europe—and you get to be sixty-five.

For some reason, sixty-five has come to be a landmark age. True, it is Medicare and geriatric benefits time: half-fare on buses, movie theaters at reduced rates, added tax deductions, monthly Social Security checks, and mandatory retirement.

But anticipate it though one may, passing over the razor's edge that separates yesterday—August 1—from today—August 2—is like crossing a mystical boundary. One can huddle under a shawl draped around the shoulders, sit on a rocker on a porch, or resolve to stay active rather than passive, contentious rather than acquiescent. One thing is certain: I won't let sixty-five amputate my youth. To me it merely separates the first part of my life from the second, and I will continue to run without slackening or looking over my shoulder to see if time is gaining on me.

The fact that I was now five years away from MSK's mandatory retirement did not enter my mind. I was lulled by a recent New York State law that had done away with the original mandatory retirement age of sixty-five; MSK had had to amend its by-laws accordingly and extended retirement to seventy. I felt carefree celebrating this birthday. Retirement seemed far, far off.

September 12, 1979.

Anthony, in his second year, was beginning to study physical diagnosis: the use of a physician's senses to help make a diagnosis. As we were getting dressed to play squash, I said, "Feel my neck and see if you find anything unusual or abnormal." At first he palpated too tentatively, so I gently placed his fingertips directly over the large lymph nodes on either side of my neck just above my collarbones. When he felt the firm, mobile, almond-sized swellings, he knew enough to be alarmed: "Could they be malignant?"

Anxious, he asked all the right questions: "How long have you had them? Were they always this size? Are there others in the axillae (armpits) or elsewhere? Have you had a chest X ray? Why were they never biopsied?"

Anthony was absolutely right not to consider the enlarged nodes alone but in the context of a history and a physical examination. I had been aware of these nodes for some time; so far they hadn't changed in size. I had no other symptoms to go with them, so their nature remained a mystery. As for the need for biopsy, the fact that they have not increased in size and are symmetrically placed is somewhat reassuring. I promised Anthony that I would check them myself now and then and should they change, he'd be the first to know.

He was not wholly convinced. "I hope it never comes to that," he said. "But *I* am going to keep an eye on them."

While looking at the sky one day, I suddenly noticed vague shadows in my visual field. Alarmed, I asked myself: Could these be a sequel to the eye injury I had when a tennis ball hit by Grace accidentally struck me in the eye? Or—a question consistent with my physician's morbid outlook—could it be a detached retina, or even a malignant tumor such as a melanoma?

Immediately taking the worst-case scenario, I assumed the shadows to be a melanoma, and a dismal scenario unfolded. First, the eye would have to be removed—and, even so, the chances for cure were not good. Then, one-eyed surgeons are of questionable value, so this would probably end my career. No, maybe not entirely: I tested my depth perception by closing my left eye and was able to put a cap on a pen. I avoided the usual self-catechism of "Why me?" "Why there?" for I knew well that I was in an age group where this diagnosis is a possibility. Besides, I didn't have to look far for causes, as I had undoubtedly stared directly into the sun on frequent occasions, so that whatever oncogenes lurked within my retina could have been activated.

Then, as I became more and more enveloped in this shroud of my own making, my next thought was how to shield Grace from this news as long as possible—although, sooner or later, if my eye were removed, she would have to know why. In my journal I wrote, "As I move my eye again, the shadow now seems to undulate, expand, and contract. Maybe it is only a retinal detachment or a blood-vessel problem."

The next day, Dr. Virginia Lubkin dilated my pupils and, knowing me as well as she does, after looking in my eye with an ophthalmoscope, immediately informed me that it was *not* a melanoma. Instead, it was a "floater"—a piece of floccular material that appears with aging.

Once more, I had experienced what it must be like for someone to wait for a life sentence—or one announcing the end of life.

September 14, 1979.

A. relishes the admiration and respect with which the first-year students treat "experienced" upperclassmen. To a first-year student, those just a class ahead seem infinitely older and wiser. In like manner, each class reveres the one above it—and so it goes in stages, to such celestial bodies as interns and residents, finally reaching the gods themselves: the professors or "attendings."

A. has begun his course in pathology and asked me to define the difference between a carcinoma and a sarcoma. Before answering, I thought: *This is the last time he'll ask me that question—soon the distinction will be indelibly engraved on his mind.* (A carcinoma is a cancer of the skin or of the lining of the organs that communicate directly or indirectly with the surface of the body, such as the lungs, stomach, colon, uterus, bladder, pancreas, testicles. A sarcoma is a connective-tissue cancer of the bone, muscle, cartilage, fat, nerve, blood, or lymph tissues.)

September 15, 1979.

Med students use one another to learn how to draw blood. I remember vividly how we dreaded jabbing the vein of a classmate who would be sticking one's own arm next. The kindest thing, A. says, is for the victim to look away so that he or she doesn't make the sticker feel self-conscious. A. had experienced puncturing fine vessels in laboratory mice this summer, so much larger human veins posed no great challenge. Happily, his partner didn't have too much trouble either, but there were several women in the class with small veins who had to endure the torture of repeated attempts. Lots of wincing and an occasional gasp could be heard.

Learning how to draw blood is students' first invasive procedure involving a live human. Once they learn how to do so, they are eager to master the technique because they know that they are going to insert countless needles for intravenous fluids, transfusions, emergency measures ("Get an I.V. line going quickly!") and to administer medications. For patients to say "I hardly felt it at all" is music to a student's ear and a boost to self-confidence.

Students will also learn to do spinal taps. Even more than sticking a vein, a spinal tap fills one with apprehension. One has nightmares that the spinal cord will be damaged, or that the needle will break off if the patients suddenly squirm. Such disasters rarely occur.

January 11, 1980.

Tunnel vision can be dangerous. The case history of a thirty-eight-year-old woman was presented to an audience of students and faculty members at a conference on bacteriology. She had symptoms of headache, lethargy, and neck muscle spasm. A chest X ray showed multiple shadows in both lungs. Although her skin tests were negative, her sedimentation rate was high, and she was assumed to have pulmonary tuberculosis and TB meningitis. She was being unsuccessfully treated with specific anti-TB drugs and was being offered as an example of the resistance of TB to the usually effective drug regimen.

During a pause, Anthony raised his hand. "Couldn't this be cancer instead?" he asked.

A thoughtful silence followed; then a Memorial bacteriologist seated nearby leaned over and whispered, "I think you've got the answer."

To avoid such tunnel vision and, in particular, to emphasize cancer's ever presence, I thought students should spend more time on the subject. With the help of Cornell's assistant dean, Dr. Laird Myers, we convened several faculty meetings to discuss doing more than the Cancer Teaching Day once a year.

A cliché: To change a medical-school curriculum is like trying to move a cemetery. Nevertheless, we arranged it so that Cornell students could elect to spend more clinical time at MSK. Not only would this enable them to come into contact with different forms of cancer, but, as important, it would sensitize them to cancer's omnipresence. They would be imbued with such a heightened index of suspicions, that it would be second nature for them to think of cancer as a diagnosis *earlier* than they might otherwise have done.

One personal reward of this new arrangement between the institutions was that Anthony, in his third year, came to MSK.

January 30, 1980.

Anthony is suffering through mid-year exams, some of which are three to four hours long. "Exams, exams!" he sighs. "Remember," I said, "every day's an exam, every patient's an exam."

To celebrate the end of the ordeal, I took him to lunch—spaghetti *con burro* and sympathy. We talked about the enormous increase in his vocabulary—the thousands of words that had to be learned. Anatomy, physiology, chemistry, pharmacology, pathology, psychiatry, neurology and more—each of them has its own vocabulary. Back in my office, Anthony wanted to see some of my published articles. This was the first time he had asked.

I gave him the article on radiation-induced bone sarcoma from the premier issue of *Cancer.* I told him that, at the time, it was a radical concept that outraged radiation therapists but since then has been universally accepted.

When he finished reading, I was surprised to see him looking at me with an expression of unmistakable pride, like my feelings each time I saw my father's signature on one of his illustrations in the *New York World.*

Tomorrow Anthony is off to join Karen for a much-needed rest in Florida. He has had little sleep this past week: No surprise, medical school is a tough, demanding grind. No wonder that three out of four medical students seek psychological help before they graduate. It's what's called the BMSS: battered medical-student syndrome.

February 21, 1980 (A.'s twenty-fifth birthday).

Image: Anthony, white coat flapping, racing down the hall with a tray of specimen slides to be studied in pathology lab. I joined him and thought: His family's specimens have been examined in this very lab—his mother's, stepmother's, brother's, grandparents', and my own. He reeled off a list of conditions he had seen, some for the first time. Together we looked down the twin barrels of a teaching microscope at multicolored cancer-cell nuclei that were malevolent eyes staring back at us. We wondered how and why those tiny, black chromosomes were so capable of such treachery and destruction.

I tell Anthony that one has to have lived through the experience to understand the unease patients and their families must endure while waiting for a biopsy report. Instead of prolonging this painful period by waiting for results to arrive by mail two or three days later, I shorten it by calling the pathology lab for the answer.

May 7, 1980.

While I was riding Memorial's elevator, the door opened, and a woman standing outside pointed at me and said, "Jew?" Somehow, I sensed she was Italian. In Italian, the word giù means "down." I knew enough to say, "Sì, avanti." And she entered the elevator and exited on the main floor.

Afterward, I thought how fortunate she had asked me instead of one of our Hasidic patients or yarmulke-capped M.D.'s.

June 6, 1980.

At long last, we took my mother to see the Hippocratic-Papanicolaou Tree outside New York Hospital. This fulfilled a much-delayed promise. It was the first time my mother had been outside for two years. We bundled her in a wheelchair and with Grace and me as convoy, she sailed out of her apartment house, her lap covered by a blue-and-white quilted comforter Grace's mother made for her.

August 20, 1980.

A. has been working in a surgical research lab during the summer. He invited me to see his experiment on the effects of high temperatures (hyperthermia) on cancer. I watched him insert a plastic bag into a rat's cancerous abdomen. Tubes attached to the bag led out through openings in the abdomen through which hot, not scalding, liquid would be introduced from time to time. To facilitate this work A. had invented a variety of devices, for which he received the ultimate compliment from his mentor, Dr. Man E. Shiu: "Why didn't I think of that?" I was impressed by the meticulously conducted experiment from incision to final suturing. To my pleasure, I saw Anthony operate with either hand.

He worked all day Saturday and part of Sunday. His schedule was about to become even more demanding. Any day now he was going to be a father.

August 30, 1980.

Anthony called at two A.M. about Karen's beginning labor. At about eight A.M., a jubilant Anthony calls: "Guess what? Nicholas Sykes Cahan's here!"

I was so elated and charged with excitement that I kept walking from room to room, hardly able to believe our good fortune. Anthony told me that he was in the delivery room through it all and was moved to tears. Some case-hardened surgeon.

Chris called from Vienna, sounding excited and very involved in this family business. I told him that he had to take Nick to Randalls Island to teach him football and to Shea Stadium to see the Mets.

Sisi visited the hospital while Grace and I were there. She and I congratulated each other and stared through the same windows through which we had peered at Chris and Anthony twenty-seven and twenty-five years before. When my mother heard the news, she suddenly looked ten years younger, repeating, "Nicholas, Nicholas," again and again.

October 17, 1980

The arrival of Nicholas has halved the already far-too-little time Anthony can spend with us. He's now in psychiatry, attending to the anxious, the depressed, the suicidal, and the psychotic. Karen complains good-humoredly about how Anthony says he'll be home in a half-hour and does not appear until several hours later. Recently, he had to subdue a screaming teenager, outline his care, reassure his family.

November 12, 1980.

I got to hold Nicholas on my lap for the first time yesterday. I studied his adorable face: the deep blue eyes, the tiny but distinctly blond eyebrows, the perfect mouth, his mother's red-gold hair. And then I saw the lump on the left side of his neck! Alarmed, I palpated it: a firm 2.5-cm semi-mobile mass. No corresponding swelling on the right.

When I asked her, Karen told me that Anthony had discovered it and had anxiously taken him to the emergency room. Conjectures by residents there varied from a "cyst" to a "bone." They covered the baby's tiny body with a lead apron and took X rays of his head and neck. Nothing abnormal. A pediatrician told them it was a hematoma (collection of blood) in a major neck muscle that not uncommonly follows a forceps delivery like Nicky's.

Karen and Anthony had shielded me, not wanting me to worry. I wish they had not done so, as I probably would have advised against taking X rays to avoid exposure to radiation at so tender an age.

October 26 1980.

Yesterday, her nurse-companion called to say that my mother, who is ninety, had suddenly gone pale and had a gurgling noise in her chest. Within minutes I was at her side. Mother was making a harsh, rasping sound with each breath. At first her pulse was not palpable, but when I told her to take deep breaths, it came back, faintly.

As I tried to reassure her, I reached for the phone and called an ambulance. By now Anthony, whom Grace had alerted, arrived out of breath and with his brown bag and stethoscope. He listened to the loud systolic heart murmur and the noisy moisture-laden lungs—fluids backing up in her lungs because her heart was beginning to fail.

By the time the ambulance arrived, Mother had picked up a bit, although she still labored to breathe. Oxygen was begun and she was carried on a stretcher to the ambulance. When we arrived at Memorial, my mother still looked extremely anxious and unable to catch her breath. In the emergency room, an intravenous was started and she was attached to a running electrocardiogram machine. Because of her "wet lung"—secondary to the backup of circulation from her heart—she was given a diuretic and, to relieve her apprehension, intravenous morphine. Within seconds, I saw her sag as it took effect.

Before leaving the apartment I had called my thoracic resident, who intubated my mother's trachea to facilitate artificial respiration. At this point, there was no audible heartbeat so external cardiac massage was begun.

The operator on the PA system repeatedly called, "Code: Urgent Care Unit." Within minutes, a team composed of an anesthesiologist, chief medical resident, medical fellow and intern, the assistant director of nursing, and a respiratory therapist converged from different parts of the hospital. The emergency cart with medicines and instruments for cardiac resuscitation was already there.

Anthony and I stood to one side as the team made every effort to start my mother's heart. Blood was taken for analysis of oxygen content, and sodium bicarbonate was given to overcome the acidosis (the buildup of acidic chemicals in the blood) that accompanies declining circulation. Cardiac stimulants were injected directly into her heart. As a last resort, electric paddles were applied in an attempt to shock her heart back to activity and a normal rhythm.

Although each shock registered a momentary blip on the running electrocardiogram, the recording immediately returned to a straight line. I soon knew the team's efforts were futile. To be certain, I allowed them to persist.

Shades of the same frustration I had felt when my grandmother was dying kept entering my mind, and I put my arms around Anthony's shoulders and said, "This is unreal."

The chief resident, who had been directing the cardiac team, looked at me. "I don't think she's responding." I replied quietly, "Let's not try any further." In a louder voice, I thanked everyone.

I went to the head of the bed; my mother looked like a tiny, broken doll, and I closed her eyes.

November 20, 1980.

A. began dog surgery yesterday, assisting in a kidney transplant. He fairly gushes questions: "What is the best way to close the abdomen?" "Is it easier to suture the ureter in a human than in a dog?" Et cetera, et cetera.

It has not yet been determined whether A. will operate right- or left-handed. Although he writes with his left hand, he can suture with either hand. (Chris is a switch-hitter in baseball, but is predominantly right-handed.)

Though he's practiced a lot under my guidance, A. still feels awkward tying knots and releasing clamps. He says he does not want to fall into bad habits simply because dogs, rather than humans, are involved. He feels conscience-bound to treat animals with the same care and respect he would patients.

He asked me to come to the lab to see the closure of an abdominal incision he had done, some days before. It was a fine job and I noticed, particularly, that the stitches were buried to prevent the "patient" from nibbling them. Although A. was proud of his workmanship, he is determined to do better. I know that he'll keep practicing until he gets it right.

While Anthony was on student rotation at Memorial, I took him to meet Sir Peter Medawar. Medawar was awarded the 1960 Nobel prize in physiology and medicine (together with Macfarlane Burnet) for the discovery of acquired immune tolerance. He was also the author of several charming books, including one I adored particularly: *Advice to a Young Scientist*. After a beguiling lecture by Peter at MSK on immunology, we had been introduced by Bob Good, then head of Sloan-Kettering Institute. We chatted for a while. A few days later, Bob called to say that Peter had had a small stroke and had been admitted to Memorial. Would I look in on him?

When I did so, his wife, Lady Medawar, was in constant attendance, sleeping on a cot in his room at night.

I told Peter about Anthony's work in the immunology lab doing research with mice on killer cells (white blood cells that kill tumors). And he asked to meet him. From the first, they chatted amicably as equals. It was a touching scene: A. leaning over to catch Peter's blurred words, and Peter, in spite of his condition, addressing A., a fellow professional, often with humor. At one point Anthony helped move Peter to a more comfortable position. As he did so, Lady Medawar took a photograph of the two of them together.

Anthony told Peter of an idea he had while working in the immunology lab and Peter encouraged him to pursue it. As I watched the two exchange ideas, their dialogue seemed symbolic of the extraordinary continuity of science—the unseen, but nevertheless tangible ceremony of torch-passing. Anthony will never forget it.

A day or two later, Lady Medawar dropped by my office to give me the roll of photographs she had taken of the two of them to be developed. In our conversation, she told me of a line the dignified Peter sometimes uses in lectures at medical meetings: "If you can't dazzle them with brilliance, blind them with bullshit." The combination of my diminished hearing and her soft-spoken delivery made me uncertain as to her last word; for some reason, I thought it had been "poetry." So I asked her to repeat it. This genteel lady then repeated the phrase with such strength that it was heard outside in the corridor.

Once, as he was coming out of anesthesia after a brain operation, she asked, anxiously, "Can you hear me or see me, Peter?"

He had opened his eyes and whispered, "Entire visual field pleasantly occupied."

As long as Anthony was assigned to Memorial, in 1980, I kept a lookout for interesting patient cases to bring to his attention. I told the nurses to alert me if they knew of any, and one suggested that I see a patient who had an odd manifestation of Kaposi's sarcoma.

Kaposi's disease, or sarcoma, was named after the Hungarian pathologist who first described it in 1886. It is a cancer in which purplish, malignant nodules appear on the skin and eventually overwhelm the patient. I had seen a number of examples of Kaposi's disease over the years; in its earlier phases, the cancer usually began on the feet and legs of men, many of whom emigrated from countries that bordered the Mediterranean Sea: Italy, Turkey, Israel, Egypt, Greece. However, the patient that A. and I saw did not fit that profile at all. For one thing, he was a Nordic American with blue eyes and blond hair. For another, the skin nodules were not on his feet or legs, but covered his abdomen, thighs, and chest. This *was* odd.

At the time, the fact that the patient seemed effeminate both in speech and gesture did not seem significant. However, when I discussed the patient with his dermatologist, Dr. Bijan Safai, he said that he had seen Kaposi's sarcoma take this form in several homosexuals and wondered why.

When I told this to Anthony, he speculated whether some homosexuals have a disturbed glandular function, perhaps a hormonal imbalance, that predisposed them to Kaposi's disease.

The next year, 1981, AIDS was identified, and it was found that not only Kaposi's but lymphomas also occurred with some frequency in AIDS patients and became rampant because of their diminished immune responses.

John Borowski, a forty-five-year-old construction worker, married with three teenage children, was a good-natured, handsome, square-rigged man whose family doted on him.

At the age of sixteen, and continuing through his adult life, he had smoked two packs of cigarettes and drunk three to six beers a day. Such a combination is notorious as a major cause of cancer of the esophagus.

Because we could find no evidence that his cancer had spread, I first explored his abdomen and then, through a leaf in the diaphragm, removed his cancer from the involved lower part of the esophagus. To restore his ability to swallow, I joined the top part of the stomach to the remnant of the esophagus. To John's family, immediately after finishing the surgery, I explained that he was doing well and that all the cancer we found was removed. I refrained from telling them, at the time, that at best, patients with esophageal cancer have a poor prognosis: only 3–8 percent survival more than five years after treatment.

Subsequently, John's pathology report gave every indication of a bleak future, because the cancer had spread to local lymph nodes and invaded blood vessels. In all likelihood, silent, as-yet-undetected metastases were present at other sites.

John was doing well, out of bed and walking soon. On his third postoperative day, when he reached for a newspaper on his bedside table, he fell out of bed. He was immediately examined and seemed unscathed. However, that night he began having difficulty breathing and a chest X ray showed fluid in his right chest, suggesting that a leak had occurred at the point where the stomach was joined to the esophagus. This was confirmed by fluoroscopy. If the leak was not immediately repaired it could be fatal, for the stomach juices and those of the upper intestinal tract that were draining into the right chest could irritate and destroy normal tissue such as the lung.

In surgery, a temporary feeding source was made by inserting a catheter into his jejunum (small intestine). Once the abdomen was closed, we entered his right chest to find, as expected, the opening. Using fine steel wire, I repaired the leak.

At first, John did well, but then developed one complication after another. As a result, he wound up with ten tubes: one through his nostril to his stomach, two tubes in his right chest and one on his left (for drainage), a feeding tube in his small intestine, a catheter in his bladder, intravenous in both right and left arms and one in his neck vein to be used for supplemental nutrition, plus a tracheotomy tube to suction secretions from his windpipe. Pasted to his chest he had plastic skin patches that led by wires to an EKG monitor, as well as small cups on his fingertips that gave continuous blood-pressure readings. All in all, he was a remarkable display of bottles, bags, monitors, lights, beepers, and recordings.

Some may question the advisability of prolonging life this way. But as the patient improves, each contrivance is removed and, if the patient survives, will be forgotten in time.

It might also be asked whether it is worth the huge effort, discomfort, and enormous expense to keep a patient like John alive, whose grim pathology report portends such a poor prognosis. Frankly, it never entered my mind at the time to do anything else. My job was clearly defined: Get John over this setback and use as many measures as necessary. His family adored him. His wife said, "We want him with us as long as possible for whatever time is left." In any event, no matter how bleak John's future seemed to be, no one, as I've said, could be certain about the length of his survival, and judgments of this complexity certainly cannot be made while a crisis is going on.

Five weeks later, I wrote in my journal: "Borowski lives! We have reduced his tubes to three: Both left chest tubes have been removed, while those on the right are still in. Also discontinued are the urinary catheter, the tracheotomy, and the nasogastric tubes. The jejunostomy feeding tube remains, through which he is receiving food in liquid form. So we discontinued intravenous feedings."

For those five weeks, John had not been able to talk because of the tracheotomy and nasogastric tubes. His eyes and facial movements expressed a lot. When his hands were free of I.V.'s, he wrote brief notes on a Magic Slate, repeatedly expressing his appreciation for "all that you are doing." When he was able to speak, his first words were: "What plans do you have for me?"

If given a chance, what secret subtle, silent services Nature provides: Six weeks after the operation, John Borowski left the hospital with only the intestinal feeding tube still in place. I did not want to risk his taking food by mouth until we were certain that the hookup of his stomach to his esophagus had completely healed.

Surrounded by a convoy of his wife and children and wearing a beaming, triumphant look, he was wheeled by a nurse out of the hospital to a waiting car.

Six months later, John's cancer overwhelmed him by metastasizing to his liver. But, his family told me later, even so short a time was filled with precious memories for which they were grateful.

Patients like John Borowski, or those whose futures seem to be very much in doubt because of the extent of their cancer, often make me ask myself: Am I persisting too long in their treatment? Does being such a competitor blind me to realities? As in playing tennis, do I chase every drop shot, strive for every point, to the detriment of the patient? Am I really benefiting them—or am I gratifying my urgent ego?

I think not. A major force behind my persevering in those with cancers more lethal than John's is that I am mindful of past Improbable Cures, when, against all odds and by using every possible measure, we are able to bring in winners.

At no time do I persist recklessly to prolong a painful, pathetic situation, for no one more than I loathes inhumane kindness. There is a time for judicious inactivity that, as Zinsser wrote, "brings rest to the patient, and peace and resignation to his family and friends."

As the decade came to a close, I became aware of a disturbing phenomenon: a deepening distrust between physicians and patients. I had, from time to time, heard friends' complaints about their physicians' indifference, but dismissed them as anecdotal. But after a visit to a friend who had just had cardiac bypass surgery, I began to wonder. This bright, buoyant woman, when asked for her surgeon's name, had trouble remembering it; he had not seen her the night before surgery and had not seen her during her stormy postoperative course, during which she had had a cardiac arrest. No wonder she had difficulty in remembering the name: He would also have difficulty remembering hers.

Such behavior is inexcusable and cannot be justified by claiming the pressure of so many other demands. I began hearing similar complaints about this surgeon from others. Yet, given his prestigious reputation, patients were apparently willing to accept his notorious absenteeism so long as the results were good.

Is it because I am a member of the old school that I consider that the complete surgeon is not just a good technician but an artist in humanity as well?

As friends used me increasingly as a sounding board for grievances, I was forced to assume that a pattern of indifference was not confined to one surgeon, but seemed to be all too prevalent. There is an old saying that butchers and surgeons are latent sadists. From what I was hearing, in some surgeons, the sadism is less than latent.

The more grumbling I heard, the more I suspected that a major, worrisome trend was on its way: that compassion, the important element that warms our beloved profession, was cooling.

CHAPTER XXVII

The Half-Clad Truth

One of our family's best-kept secrets was that my mother eventually had not one but two cancers. I never told my father at all and I kept a curtain between reality and my mother's illusion that all was well. Shading the truth in her case enabled her to function without being burdened, as I knew she would be, by constant dread.

Fortunately, my mother's cancers never spread, so we never had to deal with her as terminal. However, such shielding occurs with less frequency in this generation as patients become knowledgeable about disease. Today's patients insist on being informed about what treatment is planned. Fine. But should they be hopelessly sick, there are variations in the opinions of physicians as to what is the best approach. Some insist upon being totally candid at all times, with all patients; this can be tantamount to pursuing the "sadism of unvarnished truth." Those physicians who support such a method claim that total candor keeps the dying patient's confidence in the physician and does away with the need for those around them to use subterfuge. Besides, patients can get their business affairs in order, gather their family about them, and seek religious guidance. In addition, patients are made to feel like participants in their management and care, rather than like outsiders. Those advocating this approach maintain that when patients are white-lied to, it makes them feel they are out of control. *Whose Life Is It Anyway?* was a play that used this as its main theme. Now, with the recent openness about ways to commit suicide, some feel that at least they would like to be provided with that option.

However, I have seen what hope does for patients too often to force them to abandon it by telling them how hopelessly sick they are. Putting myself in their place, I can imagine how I would react were I to be burdened with the news that I was doomed, that I had no future, that "nothing more can be done; go home and die" or "you've got six months to live."

Maya Pines in *The New York Times* described it well:

Physicians and psychologists are horrified by what they view as heartless "truth dumping." Brutal announcements such as "your cancer has spread" can send patients into a tailspin, older doctors maintain, and the anxiety can make them much more ill or sap their will to live when the situation is far from hopeless.

I agree with those who maintain that doctors tell the truth to make it easier for themselves, letting the patient handle it, and, instead of taking responsibility in facing the pain with the patient, abdicate the situation.

Maya Pines concludes: "A graceful, more gentle approach to the truth may be the best prescription for patients—and for lovers, too." Amen.

Physicians who dogmatically insist upon "truth dumping" meet Oscar Wilde's definition of a cynic·as one "who knows the price of everything, and the value of nothing." Using candor indiscriminately rapes all hope and can be so shattering to some sensitive individuals that the time left to them becomes a continuous nightmare.

My policy is that unless strict orders are given by the patient to do so, I cannot bring myself to be that blunt. I will convey such tragic information without flinging it like acid into patients' eyes. So I plead guilty to sustaining dying patients with pretended optimism while, at the same time, gently conveying the improbabilities of cure and the advisability of making plans for any eventuality. I feel that if physicians cannot cure, they should at least comfort, and their duty extends beyond the mere direct care of the body.

There are no two cases alike; judgment, tact, and compassion can be the only guides; and external circumstances must be taken into account. In some, the cold truth may bring panic and serve no useful end whatsoever. In others, the certainty of impending death may clear the mind for the resigned tenderness of the precious remaining days, which lend dignity and gentleness to death itself. One must pick one's situation and one's cases and adjust the truth to the judgment of wise kindness.

My mother was a classic example of the value of the school of shielding the truth. However, some patients insist on being told the truth: no double talk, euphemisms, half-truths. One patient, a successful writer, made me promise that, following surgery for her lung cancer, I would tell her exactly what was found. She was single, highly intelligent, and told me that she wanted to finish writing a book and make plans for distribution of her estate if she were going to die.

She had hardly emerged from anesthesia when she sent word for me to visit her. I told her as gently as possible that her cancer was too advanced to be removed.

She took this news calmly and remained silent for a moment or two, looking straight ahead. Then, with a rather bemused smile, she said: "Dying—now *this* is going to be a fascinating experience." And for her, it was. As she grew steadily weaker, I offered her chemotherapy, which was then in its infancy. She thanked me saying, "I've got to do this my own way. I hope you won't be angry with me for refusing, but I've got to get it over with as soon as possible. Will you come to visit me nevertheless?"

She finished her book, part of which chronicled her dying.

Experiences like this enrich my life and I never stop marveling at what a privilege it is to be an intimate part of so many lives. Some collect books; I collect people, whole libraries full. To glimpse their tender, inner selves, to see hopes and fears laid bare devoid of sham and artifice, can be heart-warming or heart-wrenching, for a doctor must project himself into others' feelings, and even be part of their dying.

I can't help identifying closely with patients, and I partake of their reactions in so many ways that sometimes I feel I almost become them. When they are dying, I imagine that they are experiencing a heightened appreciation of small things previously taken for granted: the crunch of snow underfoot, the crackle of log fires, stars, smiles, moonlight, music, a blade of grass, chocolate, children, clouds, fragrances. They may think: I see you; I love, I appreciate you and, God knows, I'll miss you.

Another example of those who partook of the processes of

dying: An Italian restaurateur was robust, hearty, barrel-chested, and loaded with lung-cancer metastases. His restaurant in Greenwich Village was famous for having as customers many opera singers, who, to the delight of the other diners, would occasionally burst into song.

He was memorable because of his remarkable, forthright approach. When he was told as gently as possible about his condition, he, too, refused chemotherapy and asked that he just be kept as comfortable as possible. One day I came upon his wife crying quietly in the corridor. It seemed that he had refused to see his children: "Why let them see me like this? They should remember me as I remember them now when I think of them by name. I see them at their best; let them remember me that way, too."

Shortly afterward, he asked, "What forms do I sign to give my spare parts away to those who need them—eyes, kidneys, blood vessels, cartilage?"

After he became comatose, one son came to his bedside to support his mother; his daughters came only to his funeral. He died silently, suddenly, and at ease.

Which brings us once more to the subject of hope. What is this thing called hope, this "thing with feathers," as Emily Dickinson described it, that is very much a part of the quality of life with cancer, particularly in its advanced stages? The U.S. bishops' meeting on war and peace in 1983 stated, "Hope is the capacity to live with danger without being overwhelmed by it; hope is the will to struggle against obstacles even when they appear insufferable." For hopelessly sick cancer patients it is all this and more for they keep dreaming that something miraculous will occur that will change the course of their disease and their future. I do not find it sinful or unprincipled to let them persist in such a hope. And once in a while, once in a *great* while, what they hope for comes true.

CHAPTER XXVIII

A String of Pearls

May 5, 1981.

Anthony says he is beginning to feel a coming together of all he's learned so far. He is also feeling more confident and less awkward with patients and, in particular, less worried that his inexperience might show. He had made up a "bastard" word, of Greek *and* Latin derivation: *Ignophobia*—the fear of not knowing. It expresses what young medical students dread most. (Bill Safire: please note.)

One can see him maturing as he adds clinical experience to basic knowledge. A well-designed medical school curriculum balances the two. These formative years, however arduous, will be recalled with affection years from now, after countless intravenouses have been started, hearts oscultated, abdomens and pelves examined, and innumerable complaints—and thanks—heard.

As he and I walk the corridors, stopping to see "interesting" problems, it offers opportunities for then-and-nowing. I stop these reminiscences well short of his MEGO ("my eyes glaze over") threshold.

But this threshold is high. He likes bits of medical history. Besides it provides him with a feeling of superiority at a time of great vulnerability—not unlike what we felt when told of horse-and-buggy doctors with their little black bags.

When I recalled that, "in my day," we had to get along without measures now taken for granted—blood banks, antibiotics, I.V.'s, recovery rooms, air-conditioning—Anthony turned and said: "My God, Dad, that sounds like the Dark Ages."

One night I wrote a list. It did *not* include many advances in specialties of which I was ignorant. Here are a few:

heart surgery
replacement of bone and joints by prostheses
arterial grafts for clogged arteries and aneurysms
ultrasound for kidney and ureteral stones
chemotherapy for cancer
dialysis for kidney failure
antihistamines for allergies
cortisone
microsurgery
retinal surgery with laser
recovery rooms
the Heimlich maneuver
test-tube babies
artificial insemination
psychopharmacology
organ transplants (kidney, heart, lung, liver)
neonatal care
early ambulation after surgery

And, just for fun, I listed maladies and terms A. probably never sees or hears of:

St. Vitus's dance
death rattle
apoplexy (stroke)
catarrh
fever blisters
"ingrown hair"
sciatica
scarlatina
gleet
blue balls
"going under the knife" (being operated on)
a "strain" (penile discharge)
tongue-tied
trench mouth
devil's grip (pleurisy)
pinkeye
chilblains
gumboil
consumption
get the pip
hunchback
croup

Diseases Anthony never sees:

paratyphoid
scarlet fever
rheumatic fever
mastoiditis
polio
smallpox
CNS lues (syphilis)
rabies
syphilitic aneurysms
"blood poisoning"
erysipelas
melancholia
milk fever
housemaid's knee (prepatella bursitis)

Yet, although I welcome the amazing advances made in forty years, I lament the passing of a few picturesque ones: nurses' caps, for example. These toppers, rarely if ever seen today, identified each nurse's training school. They came, like the nurses, in many sizes and shapes: Some looked like elegant eclair containers (University of Pennsylvania) perched precariously on top of the head (held there by invisible pins). Some were small, white, oval gauze containers (NYU). By far the most impressive were those, worn by a certain order of nuns, that looked like enormous swans' wings. I was told that these caps were a nuisance, just another thing to keep clean; they were phased out along with the dark blue capes nurses wore over their uniforms when they went outside.

May 17, 1981.
What a recurring, unmitigated delight it is to walk from Sixty-eighth to Seventieth Street on York Avenue, particularly in spring and early fall, like a scene out of Breughel. I observe swarms of students in short white coats, interns and nurses dressed mostly in white, and an occasional one in a lavender scrub suit, flowing in and out of Cornell's Gothic-cathedrallike entrance. Sometimes, when I watch from a high floor at MSK, they seem like a stream of milk, puddling on corners waiting for lights to change, then flowing across York Avenue to pool as they wait to enter the medical school's revolving door.

Such a sight never fails to rejuvenate me. Occasionally, as I walk on York Avenue I spot other graybeards, professors in long white

coats, looking grave, dignified, and abstracted, as if deeply involved in important thoughts. They may nod briefly to the respectful glances and greetings of students. When I see the familiar face
of one of my students, we smile like old friends as, sooner or later,
we are.

Once in a while, serendipitously, I run into Karen pushing Nicky
in a baby carriage amidst a fleet of other baby carriages—medical
students do breed!

Each time I observe this scene, I glow with the beauty and the
promise of it. And I resolve to pass on to them, A. especially, the
knowledge and technique hard won by my patients and me.

Making rounds with Anthony along my familiar hospital corridors, I ache with nostalgia: Almost every room has held an unforgettable patient. Invariably, as we pass patients in the corridors, I
know that A. feels as I do, that there is something sweetly sad and
touching about the worn bedroom slippers, the faded dressing
gowns or bathrobes. Somehow, these garments seem to symbolize
the patients' vulnerability.

When my mother would see an old, impoverished, or crippled
person, she murmured an ancestral German or Dutch phrase: "Ach
Gott!" I tell Anthony that I, too, say the same thing to myself as I
imagine their pain, their anxiety, their longing to survive.

Serious illnesses can often bring out unadorned feelings and the
finer qualities and even a rush of poetry in people. When an ancient,
weather-beaten Irish patient was once asked if he had coughed up
bloody sputum, he thought for a moment and with felicitous ease
said, "No. There's no maroon in my mucus." As a medical student
I asked a woman to describe her abdominal pain. "What is your
pain like? Is it dull, sharp, constant, cramplike?" The patient, an
elderly, soft-spoken black woman, said, "Doctor, it feels as if
something just crawled up inside of me and died." What more
powerful way to describe inner aching? At times, someone is funny
or touching in her childlike simplicity and expression.

A patient from Texas, just before being anesthetized for a breast
biopsy, said: "Doctor, please don't take off one of my play-pretties
unless you absolutely *have* to."

I didn't.

June 12, 1981.

A. carries a little black leather looseleaf notebook, which he calls
his brains. It is titled *Do No Harm* and he describes, the entries as
"Pearls and Other Good Things to Know"; in it he jots down
advice, experiences, observations. He'd suggested many times that
I write down my advice for future doctors like himself. So, part

father, part pedagogue, I started, in no particular order—except number one:

• The first principle was set down a long time ago: It is the Golden Rule.

• The second, and equally valuable rule: Always think of patients as friends in trouble. Don't just take care of them, care *for* them. Care *about* them. Clutch compassion to you.

• At the first meeting with patients, the bonding between you begins. Welcome them with a handshake, warm words, and a smile. By making such simple gestures, within minutes you become no longer physician and stranger, but friend and friend. Soon you will be privy to some of their most intimate concerns and well-kept secrets—a person's *real* age, for example. Remember, patients are healed not just by science and skill alone, but by encouragement and reassurance as well.

• Wash your hands before examining. Preferably with warm water and in front of them. Also, warm your stethoscope bell in the palm of your hand before using. ("Warm for friends, cold for enemies.")

Father and son at Anthony's medical school graduation.

• Keep your white coat clean and change it if it's bloodstained. Be careful with garlic.

• Have a nurse nearby or, preferably, in attendance when examining women.

• As a surgical assistant, learn when and when not to be helpful. Anticipate your surgeon's needs even by such small gestures as adjusting the overhead light to focus on the operating field, cutting sutures without being asked, setting retractors for better exposure, keeping the operative field clear of blood. Know also when being too helpful gets in the surgeon's way.

• When presenting patients at a medical conference, don't refer to them as "cases"—for example, "This is a case of pneumonia." Instead, use "patient with pneumonia." Remembering this simple detail, not reducing patients to abstractions, indicates how sensitive you are to the importance of personalizing care.

• Do not discuss a patient while riding in hospital elevators or in places where visitors might be present. People overhearing you assume (sometimes rightly) that you are talking about their kin. Also, be careful when talking outside patients' rooms, for although you may be discussing someone else, the patient inside assumes he or she is the one being discussed. Avoid talking freely about patients' conditions while they are being anesthetized. You may assume they are asleep when they are not.

• A breast examination is a large responsibility. One of the leading causes of malpractice suits involving gynecologists is an inadequate, sketchy, superficial breast examination. As gynecologists focus on and are preoccupied with regions below the navel, many tend to examine a woman's breasts hurriedly and can forget to order a mammogram. If, in time, that patient develops a far-advanced breast cancer, she may claim that it reached this stage because she had an inadequate examination. *Any examination less complete than what follows risks missing a cancer.*

Begin by relaxing the patient (again, say a few friendly words and wash your hands in warm water). Then use an outline drawing of both breasts on the patient's chart. Seat her in a well-lit room and *look* before palpating. With her hands on her waist, tell her to squeeze and, as she does so, look for swellings or dimpling of the nipple or skin that could indicate an underlying cancer. Do the same with her hands held over her head. Feel above the clavicles for any enlarged lymph nodes. Place your fingers alongside her trachea and have her swallow as you feel for a thyroid abnormality.

Holding first one of her forearms, then the other, reach into each armpit in search of enlarged lymph nodes.

With the patient lying supine (face up) have her make a half-turn so that the upper breast lies flat on her chest wall. (Some place a pillow to help her do this, but it is unnecessary.) This automatically occurs when she places her hand on her forehead.

Palpate gently. Examine the *entire* breast: collarbone to fold beneath the breast, then from the breastbone to armpit. Some begin at the nipple and examine in ever-widening circles; others prefer the up and down "strip" technique. Whichever method is used, be sure that every area is covered.

Use your fingertips as sensing antennae, first with up-and-down motions as if playing the piano, then with two or three fingers together. Remember, too much pressure desensitizes your touch and defeats your purpose. Probe deeper-lying tissues firmly but not roughly: Squeezing, or pressing too hard is not only painful but will alienate the patient.

When finished with one side, have the patient turn to a mirror-image position and repeat the examination.

• Almost all women have some breast thickening. With experience and good teaching, you will learn to distinguish what is and what is not abnormal and worrisome. Mammograms are invaluable aids in detecting breast cancers and sonograms help distinguish a cyst from a solid tumor. However, 10–15 percent of the time mammograms are falsely negative, so they must always be supplemented by physical examination.

• Don't be too quick to dismiss symptoms that could conceivably be cancer. Avoid what I call the "only" or "just" school of misdiagnosis:

a chronic cough: *just* too many cigarettes
a shadow in a lung X ray: *only* "walking pneumonia"
a dark-pigmented mole: *only* a birthmark
blood in stool: *just* hemorrhoids
persistent abdominal pain: *only* nerves or indigestion
postmenopausal vaginal bleeding: *just* hormone effects
persistent shoulder pain: *only* bursitis
painful breast lump: *just* an inflamed milk gland

• Nature has provided a valuable aid in physical diagnosis: symmetry. Learn to compare one side of the body with the other. Although asymmetry can be normal as, for example, the almost universal differences in the size of feet, hands, or women's breasts, nevertheless it can be a significant clue. For example, one side of the mouth, or an eyelid, droops; one ankle or knee is larger than the other; one pupil is larger or smaller than the other. Wonder why.

• Avoid describing tumors in terms of fruits and vegetables. Instead of a "lemon-sized mass" or a "lung shadow the size of a grapefruit," it is clearer by far to use a ruler. A "4–cm" nodule is better than a "plum-sized" one. For convenience, use your own built-in anatomic rulers: I found that from the tip of my forefinger to the first crease on my knuckles is exactly eight centimeters. The distance between two creases in my palm measures one centimeter.

• Greet and be courteous to all hospital personnel, professional as well as nonprofessional. Nurses deserve respect: They are your patients' and your best friends.

• Don't be late for operations. Nurses say they spend half their time waiting *on* surgeons, and the other half waiting *for* them. Plan your day. Get up early enough to leave room for unpredictables that could delay you. Promising young surgeons wait for their attendings in the O.R., and don't have to be the subject of a frantic search.

• Never apply adhesive tape used for dressing directly on hair-bearing areas. I warn residents that if they should be so thoughtless, I'll do the same to them so they will know how it feels when it is removed.

• Keep physically fit. For a doctor, especially a surgeon, this is a must. Early in my practice, I did not follow this advice and was exhausted after long procedures and dragged myself around for two or three days afterward. When I took up tennis, the difference in my stamina was striking.

• Other than AIDS, cancer is the most feared disease; be gentle when telling patients they have cancer—you are about to change their lives. They will go through phases of shock, fright, anger ("Why me?"), depression, determination, optimism. Comfort them throughout by describing what needs to be done; answer their questions and, in doing so, avoid medical jargon and encourage them to call when others arise. One explanation may not suffice and probably reflects your not having been clear the first time.

• Use vocal as well as local anesthesia to reassure patients who are awake while being operated on.

• Return all telephone calls from patients and/or their relatives. The vast majority are justified, for most patients hesitate to disturb a physician on or off hours without a good reason. Many a life has been saved and many a fear allayed by the prompt return of calls.

• "Defeatism" is one of the worst words. Defeatism immediately lies down and plays dead before adversity. It has no place in medicine, particularly in treating cancer, where hope is so closely linked to the quality of survival. Therefore, make every effort to sustain patients with optimism, particularly those with advanced cancer.

One day, you will be rewarded by an unanticipated, rare, wonderful experience: Someone will be victorious.

• Discuss a patient's condition only with those designated by the patient; they may not always be the next of kin.

• Follow cancer patients at regular intervals for their lifetime and yours. The "safe" period of five years is only an arbitrary estimate of cure as cancer can recur at any time.

• Should complications occur, offer to get consultants—and choose them because of their expertise, not because they will second your opinion.

• Never lose your temper either in or out of the operating room, or criticize subordinates in front of others. If they have erred, take them aside and tell them so in private.

• Remember: A surgeon's responsibility does not end with a patient's discharge from the hospital. Patients should be advised that if any concerns arise—uncontrolled pain, fever, or other worrisome symptoms—the surgeon must be called.

• A simple act that requires little time or energy and is enormously appreciated is for surgeons to make an unsolicited phone call to their patients. Sometimes surgeons' intuition that something might be wrong prompts them to do so. Such a gesture invariably gladdens the patient and helps solidify the relationship between the two.

• Fees for service usually fall within a standard range and are preferably discussed before surgery. Don't hesitate to reduce them if they represent a financial hardship. Yes, Anthony, even cancel the bill as an act of charity, which occurs all too rarely these days.

• Write daily progress notes on a patient's chart and make them legible! Besides keeping others concerned with the case informed, they serve as testimony to your care and continued interest should there ever be a malpractice suit.

• Keep your scalpel for the operating room, not for colleagues. Although physicians, like brothers, have traditionally been reluctant to testify against each other, this custom is slowly breaking down. At some social gathering, you may hear a physician criticized for a misjudgment or misconduct, after which the complainant may look to you for reactions. Avoid giving an opinion, not just out of loyalty but because you do not know the entire story. Such tales reeling off the teller's tongue are often distorted.

• Even the simplest surgical procedures can take unpredicted turns. Therefore, be prepared to have unexpected postoperative complications and deaths. Other than those attributable to faulty judgment or poor technique, sooner or later these occur even to the most fastidious and skillful surgeons. They may take the form of an acute coronary, stroke, hemorrhage, or embolus.

Knowing you to be well-trained, skilled, and careful about details, I believe such bitter experiences will rarely happen. However, I know how shocked you will be when something goes wrong, and no words of mine can prepare you for the self-recrimination and the remorse you will feel. Nor can I prevent you from reliving these nightmares during the sleepless nights that follow. Console yourself by knowing that you have done your utmost to bring about a successful outcome, that whatever caused the disaster, you could not be faulted for being negligent or unavailable when needed.

• For your and their delight, ask grandmothers who are patients about their grandchildren. Immediately, all self-concern vanishes and you will be rewarded by the loveliest, most radiant looks that nature can provide.

• Be generous with your praise of nurses and other physicians, particularly younger ones.

• Avoid the weak, self-indulgent pseudo-apology "I haven't got time." Make time. Time is not fixed in concrete and can be expanded and contracted like an accordion. Decide what *is* important and what has to be done, then deal with it. Lose sleep, but finish it!

• And again, in the end as in the beginning: Never forget that patients are friends in trouble . . . and I know you value friendship highly.

Along with the practical and philosophical advice were a few words of warning on less momentous subjects, none of them life-and-death, unless you are a turkey or a cow:

Undoubtedly you will be faced with a dinnertime dilemma when a turkey or roast beef needs to be carved. The hostess will turn to you and say brightly, "You're a surgeon. Please do the honors." At that moment, all conversation will stop and all eyes will focus on your performance.

Avoid this trap at all costs! First, the knife is bound to be dull, so you will end up hacking (and swearing). Second, the "patient" may be slippery and tough, and you won't be able to find the damn leg joint. Third, in your struggle, a piece of meat or a glob of gravy will invariably slide off the plate, at which point some guest will remark, "Glad you're not operating on *me!*"

In refusing your hostess, take refuge in some gentle aside, such as "I can't operate without my anesthetist." Or "This turkey hasn't got Blue Shield."

If you are foolish enough to succumb, try lightening the situation by saying, "Okay, if you insist; I've done many of these operations and haven't lost a turkey yet." If you give in, my guess is that (a) either way you will not be asked to perform again; and (b) no one at the table will ever come to you as a patient.

At one dinner party (where fortunately, I was not asked to carve), the architect I. M. Pei said to me, "I don't know how you can stand doing surgery. I can't even look at a scratch or even a slight bruise without shuddering." This is, of course, an understandable, common reaction.

Many people become horrified, paralyzed, or repelled by the spectacle of another's injury or acute distress. Attempting to put I.M., a friend, at ease, I quoted a line attributed to Shaw: "The difference between surgeons and architects is that surgeons bury their mistakes; architects have to look at them all day long."

Pei's smile seemed a bit wan to me. I didn't know that only a few weeks before, during a severe windstorm, many windows had blown out of one of his skyscrapers in Boston.

No fault of the architecture but embarrassing nonetheless.

Back to medicine.

• When speaking to a much younger companion of an elderly patient, never refer to the patient as "your father" or "your mother"; he or she may be a spouse or lover.

• Learn the word for "pain" in Spanish, French, Italian, Greek, and Yiddish. It will be of help in taking histories and doing physical exams.

• No patient should be made to feel that he is imposing on you. If you are in a hurry, explain that you'll be glad to discuss the problem when you have a little extra time to do so.

• Do not defer to the rich, the famous, or the mighty. Treat all patients the same: affectionately and skillfully.

• The intimacy between patient and physician is sacred. The media's thirst for information about a prominent individual will prompt them to call. Although tempted to talk to them, resist doing so. A simple "No comment" will suffice. (This also applies to a patient's sincerely concerned friends, who can be gently turned aside by reminding them that such information can only be given by the patient or those close to him or her.) Let others gain the dubious reward or dispensing information instead of discretion.

March 15, 1982.

Wonderful news! Anthony has been accepted for a surgical residency at New York Hospital, thus accomplishing what I had not. This means that for at least five more years he will receive first-rate training and be living and working nearby, a perfect arrangement in every way.

And for Anthony to have chosen to be a surgeon is for me what in Yiddish is called *naches,* meaning intense pleasure or joy.

As part of his residency, Anthony will eventually be doing a rotation at Memorial, but not for another three years. Unfortunately, by that time I will have reached the Hospital's mandatory retirement age, which means that the longed-for moment when we might operate together may never come to pass.

May 26, 1982.

Today, Anthony became an M.D. The graduation ceremony was held at Lincoln Center in Avery Fisher Hall. Sisi, Grace, Karen, and I were there. Anthony won a $100 prize for "Efficiency in Medicine" and has been elected to AOA, the Phi Beta Kappa of medical schools.

Grace and I gave a graduation party in our home, with two special gifts: one a leaf from the Hippocratic tree; the other, an engraved brass shingle: ANTHONY C. CAHAN, M.D.

Anthony once remarked: "Dad, you're going to be a hard act to follow." Now I told him what one of his professors recently remarked: "You're beginning to be known around here as Tony Cahan's father."

Several classmates had asked Anthony what I thought about the way President Reagan was treated after the shooting. Naturally, I could only guess, but one thing was clear: He is in good hands. I had a few minor reservations: For example, as long as Reagan had a fever, I would have maintained him on antibiotics and kept his drainage tubes in place until his temperature became normal.

A few weeks later, I happened to be talking to Muffie Brandon, social secretary to the White House. She mentioned that the President was suffering chest pain in the region of his operation and, because he was scheduled to address Congress the next day, everyone was concerned that the effort might aggravate the pain and handicap his delivery. Muffie asked if I would call the President's personal physician, Chad Ruge, with any advice I might have. I did so immediately and suggested that a six-inch Ace bandage be firmly wrapped around the President's chest. By restricting the motion of his rib cage, it would reduce the pain each time he breathed. His physician thanked me for the "good idea." Later, I watched the President on TV and was relieved to see him speak without hesitation or wincing.

Twice during the Reagan years, Grace and I were invited to the

White House. We declined the first invitation, a dinner for Ferdinand Marcos and his wife, Imelda, because I felt strongly that I hadn't risked my neck in the Philippines during World War II only to see that beautiful country fall under the heel—or do I mean shoes?—of tyrants. We did accept the second invitation, a state dinner honoring President Rudolf Kirchsläger of Austria, largely out of curiosity, for we'd heard that the pomp and circumstance of the White House in full regalia had to be experienced.

Before dinner, Grace and I talked with Vice President George Bush and his wife. I had known Barbara Bush when she was a volunteer at Memorial and I had met her husband when we took care of his father, Senator Prescott Bush, who died there of lung cancer.

The Bushes' attachment to Memorial began when their three-year-old daughter was treated, almost forty years before, for acute leukemia. For nine months, the hospital staff had fought a losing battle to keep the little girl alive. Later, Mrs. Bush wrote: "We felt that we were not alone. We felt we were part of a team—surrounded by doctors and nurses who were all working to save our child and all of whom loved her, too."

CHAPTER XXIX

The Democracy of Illness

Someone* said, or should have, "Illness doth make commoners of us all." No truer words express the disrespect and indifference viruses, excessive sunlight, and cigarette smoking have for those of high rank, wealth, and power, who are otherwise fortified by bodyguards, bulletproof vests, limos, filter tips, and royal heritage. A mouse may look at a king; a virus can certainly attack one. There is democracy in anatomy, illness, and death.

History contains many examples of how the mighty are disarmed by disease; how an illness at a critical time has altered the course of world history. At my request, Valerian, the great-great-great-grandson of Wellington (the "Iron Duke"), traced for me the movements of the French troops as they converged on Waterloo from different parts of Europe. He said that in the crucial battle, Napoleon was too ill to command his troops. History is not clear as to what illness necessitated his remaining far behind the battle lines, but chronicles suggest that Napoleon either had cystitis (bladder inflammation) that forced him to void frequently, or was agonized by a gastric ulcer. Facetiously, I could not resist saying that I would lay this mystery or enigma to rest once and for all: Napoleon must have had cystitis, not an ulcer, for he had to go to his Waterloo.

Less momentous, perhaps, but nonetheless important to millions of Americans, the Boston Red Sox pitcher Roger Clemons

---

* Me.

almost didn't make it to his Waterloo, the battlefield of the 1987 World Series. Clemons was traveling on the plane carrying the team and had an asthmatic attack precipitated by others' cigarette smoke.

There is an adage—or did I make it up?—that several categories of patients, in addition to the poor, get inefficient, inadequate care: the very rich (surprise!), the very beautiful, the very famous, the very old, other physicians, and physicians' own families.

What this means is that each category carries an extra "presence" that can cloud judgment and reduce aggressive treatment when needed, causing a physician to lose objectivity and become tentative rather than forthright.

The very famous ("My God, it's the President of the United States!" or "Frank Sinatra!" or "Madonna!") can receive an extra dimension of concern and caution and delay. The same is true for the very rich (and the powerful) who can be arrogant, demanding, or intimidating, causing those around them to run scared and stumble in the effort to please.

The very beautiful may cause some surgeons to minimize scarring, thereby reducing the margin of safety, for example, around a skin cancer, thereby risking a local recurrence.

Physicians are probably the most difficult patients of all. (I know: I was one.) They want to participate in decisions, they see the pitfalls in each treatment, and are certain that there will be complications (such as an allergy to medications or mismatched blood transfusions). They can become paranoid, assuming that the truth about their condition is being withheld (again, I did). Some secretly feel that they could do a better job than those in charge and are not above trying to modify their medications or trying to persuade the hapless nurses to do so for them.

As for the physician's own family—well, remember the shoemaker's children? Just try to find an aspirin or a Band-Aid in my house.

To be sure, these are half-jests and half-truths. Most physicians are secure enough not to allow themselves to be snowed by a unique personality. They know that both great and small are subject to similar diseases and that bacteria couldn't care less about fame, beauty, or fortune.

When I operate on someone prominent, or on a physician or close friend, once they are anesthetized and covered by surgical drapes, they assume an anonymity that enables me to maintain perspective as to what has to be done. Shylock said, "If you prick us, do we not bleed?" Sympathetic, skilled care is universally appreciated no matter who the patient is.

Alfred DeLiagre, Jr. (Delly), had been a very successful Broadway producer of plays such as *The Voice of the Turtle* and *The Madwoman of Challiot*. In 1984, on his eightieth birthday, many friends paid tribute to him at dinner at New York's Century Association. The birthday boy and his wife, Mary, stood on the receiving line shaking hands with the guests. Only the three of us knew that he was to have lung surgery within a few weeks.

As I congratulated him, I said, "Happy returns of the day." Delly looked searchingly at me for a moment and said, "Will there be?"

I said, "You bet."

It was true. He had three full years to live.

Mrs. William Rhinelander Stewart was possibly *the* greatest beauty of the 1930s and 1940s. Her first operation was a radical mastectomy. At the time, she smoked two packs per day and, like another beauty, Babe Paley, scoffed at the idea of quitting, claiming that she would put on weight.

In 1969, she had developed a shadow in her lung X ray which some considered to be a metastasis from the breast cancer but which proved to be a separate lung cancer. This combination of both a breast and a lung cancer in the same woman was relatively rare at the time. Years later, when I reported on sixty-five of these in an article, Janet was "a beautiful statistic."

With the precipitous rise in the incidence of lung cancer in women and the prevalence of breast cancer (one in every ten women in America), this combination is being seen with increasing frequency (150 at MSK to date).

Janet quit smoking following her lung operation. However, the damage to her lungs was done. Years later, she died not from breast or lung cancer, but from emphysema.

Each time Andy Warhol and I met, he would place a tape recorder on a table or hold it in his hand. I always felt that I was "on." But I didn't let it impede our conversations, which usually centered around Candy Darling, one of his Factory habitués. Candy had undergone a transsexual operation, following which she/he took many hormones to help develop female characteristics (such as breasts), to achieve a high-pitched voice, and stop the necessity of shaving, etc.

A friend asked me to see Candy because she had a lymphoma and needed to be directed to a specialist. In retrospect, I wonder if her lymphoma was actually secondary to AIDS, which at that time was unrecognized. (Lymphoma is sometimes associated with AIDS.) It is also possible that the megadoses of feminizing hormones Candy took may have been carcinogenic.

Within a year Candy died. I recalled her at an exhibition of Richard Avedon's photographs, one of which was a life-sized nude portrait of male Factory members, all of whom were facing the camera. Candy, yes, beautiful Candy, was one of them.

On another occasion, I told Andy about one of his recent portrait subjects, a thirty-two-year-old Venezuelan mother of three who smoked incessantly even though she knew that her heavy-smoking father had died of lung cancer. Her mother pleaded with her to quit many times and she finally did so—after an inoperable lung cancer was found. I sent her mother the latest chemicals used for lung cancer chemotherapy, but her daughter refused to take them and died soon thereafter.

Andy agreed with me that there was something surrealistic about such juxtapositions of illusion and reality: While he was painting this beautiful young woman's portrait, a lethal cancer had begun its insidious growth within her that, a few months after the portrait was finished, caused her death.

As can be seen, cancer is an unsentimental disease. It rides rough-shod over plans, hopes, dreams. In 1978 Nicholas Ray, a well-regarded movie producer/director best known for his film *Rebel Without a Cause,* lay dying of lung cancer. An unusual conflict developed between his desire to be done with life, to "get it over with" and his scheduled appearance to play himself in a documentary, *Lightning Over Water,* that was in progress.

A tug-of-war began between satisfying this one last appearance and his advancing cancer. He realized that this would be his last hurrah, his swan song, yet, like an old trooper, he felt that the show must go on.

"All we ask," the film's producer said to me, "is that he be sustained for five more days of shooting." Lest it be considered cold-blooded, I should say that Nick desperately wanted this. However, in spite of vitamin shots, stimulants, exhortations to eat, he kept steadily wasting away. In his late stages, he had completely lost his appetite, and his esophagus was so narrowed by the cancer that it was impossible for him to swallow. To delay this race with death, we fed him food concentrates intravenously. On this routine, the reverse of a crash diet, he gained a pound a day and, for a short time, renewed vigor.

Poetic justice was served when, just before he became mentally disengaged from all bodily controls and reality, the movie was finished.

Many years later, turning on the television, I saw Nick playing a most effective and touching role—himself. Once more, I relived those days of creative life yielding to corrosive disease, days when he struggled so that the show could go on and death was held, waiting in the wings, so that *he* could go on.

Musicians' ears prick up when they hear some novel or interesting melody; artists constantly see subjects or scenes they must record. By training and instinct, I react reflexively to abnormal signs and symptoms. My curiosity is triggered when someone I know—or for that matter, don't know (as you've seen)—looks not quite "right."

New York's longtime leading liberal senator, Jacob Javits, and a group of us were playing tennis doubles. Jack was playing his usually enthusiastic, aggressive game when suddenly, across the net, I saw him bend over, clutching his abdomen. All play stopped and I ran to him.

"No," he said, "I'm not in any pain; I just seemed to lose my ability to stand up for a moment . . . so I hunched over." He refused to let me examine him.

In a few minutes, he seemed fine, insisting that it was a "big nothing," and resumed play. The next time we played, a few months later, his racket flew from his hand as he went to make a forehand. He said that he had noticed a little weakness in his right hand for some time, but had dismissed it as part of "getting older." (He was then seventy-five.) This time I wouldn't let him shrug it off and persuaded him to see a neurologist, particularly as I noticed a slight atrophy of the muscles between his right thumb and forefinger. Also, when I asked him to grasp both my hands, his grip was weaker on that side.

Jack went through a series of tests and was scheduled to have an operation for a "pinched nerve" in his neck. I was skeptical about the diagnosis and prevailed upon him to get a second opinion from Dr. Jerome Posner at MSK. Posner spotted the real culprit—Jack had early evidence of Lou Gehrig's disease, amyotrophic lateral sclerosis. This disease, of unknown origin, is marked by a gradual deterioration of nerves that, secondarily, causes muscles to waste away. Death can occur from respiratory failure, which follows paralysis of the diaphragm and chest-wall muscles and usually occurs within two years of the onset of symptoms.

Jack did better than that; he lived four more years, an exceptionally long period for this disease. In his last months, to assist his breathing, he had a tracheostomy tube connected to an electrically driven oxygen pump.

Throughout his ordeal, although his muscles were wasting away, he retained his amazing spirit, was uncomplaining, wrote his memoirs, saw a daughter marry and his son begin law practice, and had a library and convention center named after him. He was consulted by government officials, including the President. He lectured to college students on government, and to Cornell medical students on how it feels to live with, and adapt to, his disease.

When Douglas Fairbanks, Jr., Grace, and I went to visit him in Palm Beach, he was in a wheelchair. I knew he liked to discuss matters other than his health, so I asked his advice on how to mount an effective legal attack against the tobacco giants. I told him that up to then, no successful lawsuit had been brought by lung-cancer patients or their survivors. He suggested that juries might be convinced that tobacco companies *knew* that their products were addictive, but failed to adequately warn customers about this hazard. As we left, he gave us his usual broad smile and said he hoped to see us soon. We wished it could have been so.

In 1988, at a reception to launch the Strang Clinic's High Risk Clinic, Carmen Dell'Orefice, a beautiful model, described how, as a volunteer to be examined while cameras rolled, she had a heart-warming experience. Before the assembled group, she described how a "young M.D.—Dr. Cahoon" (one of the more bizarre variations on the pronunciation of our name), had been so knowledgeable, and gentle when taking her history, and so thorough examining her, that when he found an unsuspected lump

and advised her to have it removed, she said she would go anywhere as long as he was her surgeon. Although her mammograms
were negative, the surgeon thought the lump "was suspicious
enough to be biopsied."

Thirty-five years before, the American Cancer Society had
asked me to help make an instructional film on breast examination. I helped with the script and also performed as the examining
physician. Dr. Arthur Holleb, later vice president of the society,
had the not-too-difficult task of selecting bosoms for the occasion
from a string of candidates. He screened them initially from their
photographs in bathing suits (some had been retouched). The field
narrowed and live auditions were held discreetly. The winner and
I met for the first time in one of MSK's examining rooms, where
the movie cameras were set up.

As the cameras ground away, I went through the basic steps of
a thorough breast examination. On the finished film, I pause at
one area, clearly concentrating on a finding of some sort. As I was
palpating, I felt a lump!

I waited until we finished filming to tell her what I had discovered. A week later, it was removed, and, like Carmen's, it was
benign.

Pat Tanner was dying of pancreatic cancer and refused to go to a
hospital to do so. As "Patrick Dennis"—Dennis was a family
name—he wrote books under several pseudonyms, one of which
was Virginia Rowans, after his favorite cigarette, Virginia
Rounds. He leaped to fame and fortune with his best-seller *Auntie
Mame,* which was made into *Mame,* a memorable Broadway musical starring Angela Lansbury, and a movie with Rosalind Russell
in the title role. Pat also wrote a "photo-novel," *Little Me,* in
which many of his friends appear under hilarious pseudonyms,
dressed in flamboyant costumes, as characters who peopled the
life of its heroine, Belle Poitrine. In 1962 it, too, became a musical
comedy, starring Sid Caesar.

Pat had spent his last years in Mexico squandering a great deal
of the wealth he had accumulated. When he realized he was mor-
tally ill, he strode, not crawled, home to be near his wife and
children to die.

Each time I visited him, I found him sitting cross-legged on his
bed, a gaunt, bearded figure resembling an El Greco Christ. I
greeted him and he berated me. "Stop all this nonsense and let me
go. Snuff me out."

Pat dying was as unique as Pat living. As he rocked back and forth in pain, he would make outrageous, often witty remarks. Then, pausing after a string of sardonicisms, he would say: "I'd just as soon get it over with. I hate leaving a mess. Besides, I can't shoot straight and I can't use the window because heights make me dizzy. Why not leave me some pills, and this time I'll do a better job." He was referring to an incident, years before, when I had revived him after he had attempted suicide. Now, he told me, the very least I could do was give him enough pills and, this time, not interfere.

I wouldn't do that, of course, but, after every visit, I did leave some pills to alleviate the pain.

My guess is that he saved them up until he had enough to finish the job.

An episode that could be called *Pumping Irony:*

One night, at a dinner party, Henry Ford II began choking on some food. I took him to the bathroom until he caught his breath. My God! When I think back to the first Henry Ford, his grandfather, and his loathsome newspaper, *The Dearborn Independent,* with its anti-Semitic articles on the *Protocols of the Elders of Zion,* I am weary with the incongruity of it all.

Again, I had a similar reaction when asked to treat Baron von Krupp, the scion of the German munitions manufacturer that supplied German armies during World War I and II. He was gay and was dying of advanced cancer of the jaw that had persisted and spread despite heavy radiation therapy. For some reason, he felt that I could be of assistance; I convinced him to come to MSK to be seen by Dr. Elliot Strong to determine if there were any possibility that surgery might help. The baron arrived (with two companions) dressed in an ankle-length blond mink coat with Rita Hayworth shoulders. Unfortunately, there was nothing to offer and he died soon after his return to Germany.

We hear much about the lives of the rich and famous, less about their deaths.

CHAPTER XXX

"You've Come the *Wrong* Way, Baby"

During the Roaring Twenties and the 1930s, my grandmother thought that if a girl smoked, it was a sure sign that she was "fast." Smoking by women then was considered to be a sign of sophistication. This image was magnified by the movies in which glamorous stars were always seen smoking in elegant drawing rooms and at that unforgettable romantic moment when, in *Now Voyager,* Paul Henreid lit two cigarettes and passed one to Bette Davis.

During World War II, as Rosie the Riveter replaced men in the workplace, women took to smoking at work. After the war, they did not confine their smoking to the workplace but began smoking at home, in restaurants, anywhere. Cigarette companies used seductive advertisements in which society personalities and film stars gave testimonials implying that to be like them, "you, too, should smoke Brand X." Adolescent girls, anxious to look older, were led to believe that a cigarette would give them poise ("Be nonchalant, light a Murad") and that they could stay thin by smoking Luckies. To boys and girls, smoking made them appear grown up and was a rite of passage into adulthood. They were willing to go through the nausea, bleary eyes, and coughing that beset a virgin smoker so that eventually they could proudly display their prowess—to inhale deeply, then blow smoke rings.

These seductive lures, combined with peer pressure, caused cigarette sales to soar as smoking became rampant in high schools, colleges, homes, places of entertainment, and offices and factories.

However, after the Surgeon General's report in 1964 stating that smoking was hazardous to one's health and a law was passed that made it mandatory to print a warning on cigarette packages and in advertisements, cigarette sales fell.

To counteract this, the tobacco industry went into high gear, plotting to confuse the public by sophisticated smokescreens that employed innuendo, half-truths, and unscientific "data." The industry deliberately ignored over thirty thousand scientific articles that demonstrated smoking's role in the etiology of a variety of malignant and non-malignant diseases. Anyone who has ever battled tobacco companies knows not to underestimate the devious methods they, and their Madison Avenue cohorts, employ to get their lethal messages across. This behavior follows the tradition of an industry that a generation before had maintained that in smoking Old Golds, there was "not a cough in a carload"; that Chesterfields were kind to your "T Zone," etc. — all patent lies or distortions.

I first met the devoted, caring philanthropist Mary Lasker in the late 1950s. Asked by friends to tell Mary about my smoking research, as she had been remarkably effective in lobbying Congress to appropriate funds for cancer research, I said that from what we knew about the latent, or incubation, period of smoking, the full impact of the effects of smoking on the current rash of female smokers would become evident in twenty-five to thirty years, and be of epidemic proportions.

Mary remained silent. She looked thoughtful, then said, "My husband, Albert, was an advertising executive and it was he who coined the slogan 'Reach for a Lucky instead of a sweet!' He must have started millions of women smoking. Poor Albert must be turning over in his grave." This beloved lady then looked so wistful that I immediately changed the subject.

Soon afterward, I met CBS president William Paley's elegant, soignée wife, Babe Paley. Babe was a striking beauty and a strong personality. I watched with dismay as she chain-smoked before and during dinner. I gently chided her by reminding her of the hazards involved and even invoked her late father, the world-renowned neurosurgeon Harvey Cushing. "As a doctor's daughter, you must realize how dangerous smoking is more than anyone else." She smiled and gave the same excuse I've heard so often: "If I quit, I'll get fat." With that, she lit another cigarette.

Twenty-five years later, Babe was in Memorial's recovery room, having had the lower half of her right lung removed. As she sat upright in bed, an oxygen tube in her nostril and chest drainage tubes running to a container beside her, I told her that even after surgery, and with all those contraptions, she still looked beautiful. She smiled, then frowned and whispered the words that I was hearing over and over again from others: "Why in hell didn't I listen to you?"

Babe had her wish: Smoking kept her weight down all right, but what price vanity! Within a year, she developed painful metastases that reduced her to skin and bones. I'm told that her beauty became even more haunting as her cheekbones were accentuated and her dark eyes shone luminously through her pallor, until they were dulled by narcotics—and death.*

Through the decades, I often thought back on those meetings with Mary Lasker and Babe. Those concerned about women smoking get no satisfaction in seeing our dire predictions realized: smoking-related diseases in women were rising precipitiously. Sadly, ruefully, we said, "Women who smoke like men die like men": Death from lung cancer in women rose 300 percent in twenty-five years.

At MSK, the epidemic of smoking-related cancers resulted in a marked increase not only in lung-cancer patients, but also in patients with cancers of the oral cavity, larynx, esophagus, and urinary bladder. Incredibly, 30 percent of the hospital's adult population would not be there had they not smoked. What is more, the ratio of lung cancers, which in men and women was ten to one in 1960, had become six to one a decade later. Currently, the ratio between the sexes is about even and women are edging ahead.

The more smoking-related tragedies I observed, the more passionate I became about their prevention. Feeling uniquely qualified as a lung-cancer surgeon to speak out and even dramatize the Surgeon General's warnings, I joined those Davids who were taking on the Goliath tobacco industry. Our only weapons: words and principles; theirs, all the power and influence that billions can buy.

The American Cancer Society, aware of my interest, asked me to lecture and appear on radio and television. During the eighties

---

* Her daughter, Amanda Burden, told me that Babe was always carefully made up, including the night before she died.

I debated representatives of the tobacco industry and each time I did so, I seized on the opportunity to mention the name I had given our operating room ("Marlboro Country"), hoping that Philip Morris would sue me. But it never did, sensing, I'm sure, that a suit could become a front-page story.

Let me confess at this point that writing this chapter has been most difficult, for each time I try to remain abstracted and distill my feelings about tobacco interests, I become so incensed that I have difficulty finding words adequate to convey my rage.

For any of those who have fought so hard, so many times, to save one life, to know that hundreds of thousands are being destroyed overwhelms any restraint. Nevertheless, the crusade against them has been so much a part of my life that any memoir would be incomplete without a description, however inflamed, of those whom I've grown to detest and who are my sworn enemies.

Each time I was about to bank the fires of indignation and fury with the tobacco industry and our government's all-too-slow, inertia-ridden measures to restrict smoking, I would lose yet another close friend. Melanie Kahane, a heavy smoker, a renowned interior decorator, widow of the broadcast journalist Ben Grauer, was a bundle of energy, constantly bubbling with laughter and joie de vivre. She was reduced to a thin, dry-lipped pathetic soul, pleading to be released from pain.

Even the one group that should know better—the physicians and nurses in my hospital—many smoked heavily on the premises.

October 25, 1976, was a day that had been too long in coming to MSK. Prior to that date, in perhaps the most prestigious cancer hospital in the world, smoking was permitted everywhere except in elevators and operating rooms. Not only did this seem incomprehensible and profane, but, until three years before, the hospital's gift shop had sold cigarettes. It had taken six years for some of us to get *that* stopped. Perhaps my repeated unsubtle cry to those who ran the shop—"You're causing lung cancers down here faster than we can cure them upstairs"—may have helped.

I had repeatedly tried to have an official in-hospital total ban on smoking. Finally, after much frowning and head-wagging by skeptics about how such a dictate could be enforced, plus the concern that nurses who smoked would threaten to quit if this were instituted, I was able to say to a small group that gathered for the occasion, "Welcome to the first Memorial Hospital floor dedicated to *non smoking*. It is unnecessary to state why this is being done; the evidence is unfortunately all around us. [Almost all patients on that floor had lung or esophageal cancer.] This is one floor down and we've got nineteen more to go."

The nurses on that floor who smoked did not quit their jobs, but several did quit smoking, partly because they had to go elsewhere to do so, thereby breaking their accustomed ritual of lighting up anywhere at any time.

Twelve years later, a state law was passed that forbade smoking in all hospitals. Now Memorial has a sign on its entrance: MSK IS A NON-SMOKING ENVIRONMENT. Those who must smoke do so on the sidewalk in front of the hospital. As I pass through the stench of their cigarettes and the revolting litter of the stamped-out butts on the sidewalk, I am often tempted to say, "If you smoke on the outside, you'll wind up on the inside."

Dr. Cahan (third from left) testifies before a Congressional committee on why he calls his operating room "Marlboro County."

A more contemporary promotion strategy of the tobacco industry is to use attractive images in advertisements that shrewdly exploit the rise of feminism. Thus, the Virginia Slims slogan, "You've come a long way, Baby." Although cigarette advertising on television was banned in 1970, Philip Morris circumvented the problem by craftily posting huge billboards in sports stadiums so that the Marlboro ad would be easily visible each time a home run was hit, a play was made at first base, a point was scored after touchdown, or a field goal was kicked. The mandatory warning was so small that it was illegible on a TV screen or, for that matter, anywhere in the stadium except for the bleachers.

Another diabolical method used to dodge the TV ban was the Virginia Slims tennis tournaments. This not only got the name of the cigarette on television but, by associating it with professional athletes, suggested that smoking, athletic success, and women's athleticism were compatible. It mattered little, of course, that professional athletes who rely on endurance would not smoke.

Sadly, when some professional women tennis players were asked by antitobacco forces to refuse to play in these tournaments, they demurred, saying, "Look at what they've done for women's tennis," and preferring to ignore what was being done to women's lungs.

In spite of the veneer of respectability that advertising and public relations agencies tried to put on the reputations of tobacco companies, the public gradually began to recognize them for what they were: greedy, health-destroying organizations. The companies smarted under an increasing number of criticisms and newspaper reports of smoking's unsuspected ill effects. As a result, to launder their nicotine-stained reputation, tobacco companies linked themselves to prestigious organizations and events supported by charity, giving them ready cash. To return this favor, fund-starved institutions listed them as sponsors and gave tobacco executives testimonial dinners at which their praises were sung, all the while closing their eyes to the fact that the funds they were receiving were at the expense of hundreds of thousands of American lives. Thus, some of the citadels of our culture, some of the major forces for good in our civilization—the Metropolitan Museum, the Metropolitan Opera, the Brooklyn Academy of Music, the Dance Theater of Harlem, the Anti-Defamation League, the National Urban League, New York University Hospital, the Whitney Museum—abandoned principle and, full of gratitude, made bold public announcements of their benefactors. This seemed to them a reasonable compromise with principle. As further justification, they pointed out that tobacco companies are "after all, in a legal business."

I often brought this last point up on my radio and TV appearances, (and later in my correspondence with John Brademas about the renaming of University Hospital after Lawrence and Preston Robert Tisch), that tobacco companies use the term "legal" as a license to kill. The Ku Klux Klan and neo-Nazi organizations are also "legal" and, repulsive as they are, are not mass killers.

When the American Ballet Theatre solicited me for funds, I wrote to its chairperson:

> I sincerely regret not having joined you to celebrate ABT's 50th Anniversary. Worthy as this cause is, and aware as I am how ABT has enriched my life and those of many others, I could not participate in a program that has Mr. Hamish Maxwell as its corporate chairman and his company, Philip Morris, as a major sponsor.
>
> Undoubtedly ABT's Anniversary was memorable. However, had I been present, I would have been haunted by Mr. Maxwell and his company's choreography: a danse macabre . . .

And to the Anti-Defamation League:

> At a time when integrity and principled behavior are in short supply, it is distressing to see the ADL, one of the major guardians of our social conscience, "honor with pride" the "civic commitment" of Philip Morris Companies, Inc.

I continued:

> One wonders just how many of Philip Morris's dollars will be needed to erase, cover up, or atone for the millions who died as a result of smoking its cigarettes or for its seduction of children, young women and minorities into a lifetime addiction and premature death.

And then Philip Morris pulled off probably the most cynical trick of all: They bought our sacred Bill of Rights. Apparently, when the head of the National Archives, where the Bill of Rights is on display, was approached, she was elated to receive $600,000 from Philip Morris to help pay for the Bills of Rights' two hundredth anniversary celebration. In return for which, Philip Morris could use the Bill of Rights in an advertising campaign.

Almost immediately, on TV, with great pomp and circumstance, the Bill of Rights was first displayed reposing in its case at the Archives. Then, a handwritten line taken from the original copy was shown; it read: "Freedom of Speech." The TV segment ends with the logo of Philip Morris "Companies."

Broadcasters, eager for revenue, justified accepting this spot in the face of restrictions on TV cigarette advertising, claiming that after all, cigarettes are only one part of Philip Morris's "family of products," which includes Kraft Foods, Oscar Mayer meats, and so on. Their stated motives fooled no one, for everyone knows well that when one thinks of Philip Morris "Companies," cheese and meat do not come to mind.

Not just content to use pretended patriotism to flag-wave their way into the hearts (and lungs) of Americans, they hope to make the public resent any reduction in P.M.'s freedom to advertise, or of smokers' "right" to smoke at any time, anywhere.

Philip Morris issued yet another commercial. This one showed the interior of a synagogue, of a church, and of a mosque. As each appeared, it was accompanied by music appropriate to the faith. The spot ended with the phrase "Freedom of Religion"—and, of course, Philip Morris's logo.

Larry White★ and I wrote an article for the *New York Observer* of December 11, 1989, called "Marlboro Man Lassos the Founding Fathers." In it, we describe Philip Morris's exploitation of the Bill of Rights and its TV "religion" spot. In condemning the latter, we wrote: ". . . and at the end, we see Philip Morris's 'Companies' logo. An unintended image comes to mind: funerals. After all, there are 340,000 of these a year, courtesy of their cigarettes."

I followed with a note to *The New York Times,* expressing the hope that the "Companies" would not buy the Ten Commandments next. Perhaps they might be deterred only because of the Sixth: Thou shalt not kill.

Add to the deadly ironies: While much of civilization is caught up in the struggle to raise the status of women and minorities, to improve the quality of their lives and strive for justice and fair play, the tobacco marketers continue to target them.

Speaking of freedom, the Tobcos (as I sometimes call them), feel free to target children, young women, and African-Ameri-

---

★ Author of *Merchants of Death,* a book that describes the cynical practices of the tobacco industry (Beech Tree Books-William Morrow, 1988).

cans. Once hooked, young people may become enslaved for a lifetime. All the while the Tobcos disclaim any responsibility for continuing the practice, saying: "After all, the warnings are there," and deliberately ignore the fact that nicotine addiction is stronger than that to heroin or cocaine.

Concerned about the falling rate of smoking due to death from cigarettes as well as people quitting, the Tobcos aimed to replace these losses with children. Well aware of how addictive nicotine can be, tobacco companies use a variety of cynical tricks to seduce those at a tender age with free handouts on streets, at rock concerts and athletic contests, and vending machines placed where youngsters can easily get at them.

One reason why Tobcos have become "families" of companies, in addition to the fashionableness of conglomerates, is that when the antitobacco groups began to score gains, the companies must have felt the heat and the long-term threat. So they moved into food and other related and unrelated businesses, storing up nuts against what might become a long winter or a gathering storm of public outrage. Then, with the loss of customers due to those who stop smoking, never start, or die, they went for the true, long-term, far-in-future customer, the child.

The huge, lucrative children's market was targeted by Camel in its current cigarette campaign. The ads feature a caricature of a camel performing all sorts of gung-ho activities such as motorcycle racing, skiing, and playing the piano while dressed in a tuxedo. In each cartoon, the camel smokes and leers lasciviously. It takes little imagination to see that the camel's face resembles male genitalia. Children in particular identify with cartoon characters and are most willing to accept free handouts, which can take the form not only of cigarettes but sweatshirts, comic books, and so on.

Sales figures show that this campaign has been eminently successful. So, butt-to-butt, Philip Morris and Camels compete to launch children on a life-shortening addiction and premature death. And, sadly, they have succeeded: In America, every day, four thousand to five thousand children light up for the first time.

One of the Tobcos' favorite ploys is to try to call smoking a "habit" instead of an addiction. Make no mistake about it, it *is* a powerful addiction and one that the vast majority of the fifty million Americans who smoke would like to overcome. Yet I saw one patient, who had a permanent opening in his neck after removal of his larynx, devise a gadget to hold a cigarette that fitted the opening. I've seen those dying from emphysema, or who have had a lung removed or several acute coronaries, unable to break the heavy shackles of nicotine addiction.

Knowing all this, it is hard not to sound strident, or be considered a wild-eyed zealot* when one reads that Gerald Long, an executive of R. J. Reynolds Company, has said: "If I thought in my heart of hearts that smoking was bad for one, I would resign." Or the cynicism of Philip Morris, which offers a free facsimile of the Bill of Rights—knowing full well that one major segment of our population actively studies it: children.

By emphasizing freedom of speech in the Bill of Rights commercials and advertisements, Philip Morris hopes to gain public support for their lobbying against legislation that would restrict the placement of their ads on billboards and make them use "tombstone" displays—descriptions without pictures.

Naturally, they deliberately ignore their own efforts to restrict freedom. For example, when Philip Morris bought General Foods Corporation, signs that had been posted on bulletin boards, indicating where stop-smoking sessions would be held, were taken down.

One day my friend and patient Jay Weinberg called from the offices of his Corporate Angel Network to say that General Foods had notified CAN that their planes would no longer be available. Apparently, when Philip Morris took them over, some executive decided that it was probably bad for their image to be associated with planes carrying cancer patients.

I immediately called the editors of the New York *Daily News,* which along with its parent company, the *Chicago Tribune,* published an article about the withdrawal. An immediate retraction was made by Philip Morris and, to cover their embarrassment, they added planes to CAN's fleet.

On one TV talk show, I asked a pro-tobacco adversary†: "Have you ever seen cancer? Seen what it does? Have you ever had cancer in your family or among your close friends? Do you

---

* Each time I appear in public, I say how flattered I feel to be included with such wild-eyed zealots as four surgeons general, the former and present secretaries of health and human services, all American medical societies, public-health officials, et al.

† Talk-show hosts have more and more difficulty getting pro-tobacco speakers to face any of us on camera or radio.

know firsthand what it's like? If you have, you won't question its virulence, its capacity to destroy families, hopes, and dreams. If you haven't, you probably will one day, and let me tell you: It is an awesome, shattering experience, the awfulness of which you are not likely to forget.

"In any event, how can you possibly defend and justify promoting a product that is so clearly responsible for mass destruction? Does this mean you are indifferent to the suffering you cause? With you, business, I suppose, is business and so-called business ethics are 'special.' . . ."

Yet, as I say these words, I see their eyes glaze over and hear the usual devious replies as they take refuge behind walls of indifference.

Recently, the former chief executive officer of Philip Morris had to have a coronary bypass operation. Prior to this, he had been known to boast "I smoked all of my life and look at me, I'm fine." One wonders now whether he has taken up smoking again.

As I lost friend after friend and kept seeing so many suffer and die cigarette-related deaths, I could not restrain myself when I saw somebody smoke at close range. At the risk of being a bore, I feel obligated to tell those I meet socially that they are in jeopardy. (Grace says, "Bill and I are invited to the best of houses—once!")

Partly out of consideration for my strong feelings, and because some share them, hostesses remove cigarettes and ashtrays from dinner tables when I am their guest. Some seat me as far from smokers as possible; others concerned about an inveterate woman smoker will put me next to her, hoping I can persuade her to quit.

What usually transpires is a tragicomic psychodrama in which the hapless smoker, trapped by my presence, squirms and fidgets nervously during the meal while restraining herself from lighting up. Usually, around dessert time, she will excuse herself, ostensibly to use the bathroom.

When she returns, she has the telltale naughty-girl smile I've seen so often (see Babe Paley) and exudes the unmistakable aromas of tobacco smoke from her breath and clothes. Instead of chiding her, I compliment her on having gone almost the entire meal without smoking, and suggest that perhaps this could be the beginning of her quitting altogether. To lighten the moment, I say something like "If women's lungs were on the outside instead of where they are, they would never smoke."

At the time, I'm never certain whether I have been effective. However, at times someone will tell me: "After I sat next to you at dinner and heard you talk about smoking, I quit."

One hundred and fifty years ago, John Quincy Adams wrote to Reverend Samuel H. Cox in Brooklyn, who was preparing an introduction to a book on *Tobacco and Its Mysteries:*

> I have often wished that every individual afflicted with this arti-ficial passion can force himself to try but for three months the experiment which I made. [Adams did quit.] I'm sure that it would turn every tobacco land into a wheat field and add five years to the average human life.

The phrase "artificial passion" became part of the title of a book on nicotine addiction by David Krogh, *Smoking: The Artificial Passion,* for which I wrote the foreword.

Having heard endless confessions, I got to know what it is like to be a priest who hears penitents describe what they think is an offbeat form of sin. Smokers, like sinners, shift from being defensive to uttering such clichés as "We all have to die someday of something," or: "I enjoy it. After all, it's the only pleasure that's not illegal, immoral, or fattening." Other sophistries include:

"Half a pack a day can't hurt me."
"Filters and low-tar cigarettes prevent cancer."
"One always gains weight after quitting."
"Traffic fumes and city air are more dangerous than smoking."
"If I quit, I can take an occasional puff and stay quits."
"I can't possibly function or think without my friend at my finger-
   tips."
"I'm too old," or "It's too late to stop after X years of smoking;
   the damage is already done."

These myths are familiar, dangerous, and false. I take particular exception to the last: Too old? Damage already done? No one knows at which moment in time normal cells that have been repeatedly damaged by smoking reach the point of no return and become cancerous. However, if a carcinogen is stopped short of this razor's edge, damaged cells can recuperate to a major degree. Therefore, the sooner you stop smoking, the more likely it is that you will fall short of that critical moment when normal cells undergo irreversible malignant transformation: the point of no return.

Grace's cousin, Florence, was one who confessed that she had used some of these myths as refuges against quitting. I remember driving her to the airport for her return to Florida. As we drove north along the FDR Drive on a cloudless autumn day, the city was in one of those beautiful moods in which the East River, at dead calm, looks like a polished pewter mirror, faithfully reflecting wheeling gulls and the buildings along its banks.

To pass the time, I kept pointing out landmarks and other sights along the way. Florence sat next to me, holding an envelope containing her X rays. Just over a week before, I had explored her left chest and found that her lung cancer had invaded the phrenic nerve, the cable that controls the left side of the diaphragm along with the nerve that controls her left vocal cord.

Like many others who cannot stop smoking beforehand, Florence quit as soon as she saw the telltale shadow in her lung. Shaking her head in remorse, she vehemently vowed, "Never again."

During the operation, because I was unable to remove the cancer, I placed metal clips around its periphery to serve as targets for radiation therapy. I supplemented these by drawing on her lung X rays an outline of what I had found at surgery, so that the radiation therapist in Florida would know where to direct cobalt treatments.

As we rode along, I noticed that each time she questioned me about her condition and future prospects, she grasped and then released the envelope containing her X rays. I carefully avoided suggesting, by voice or gesture, that such cancer, at that stage, was rarely curable. However, I did tell her about Nellie, who survived her cancer against overwhelming odds, and that, even more than Nellie, she would be having chemotherapy added to her radiation therapy. As further encouragement, I said that new cancer treatments were surfacing all the time, so—who knows?—some extraordinary breakthrough could occur at any moment. She quietly stared ahead for a moment and then said: "I hope I have time."

Looking out on that beautiful day with that tragedy-to-be at my side, I recalled the last chapter of Hans Zinsser's autobiography, *As I Remember Him,* in which he describes his reaction immediately after being told he had leukemia. At the time, this distinguished scientist was standing in his doctor's office looking out at the Charles River Basin in Boston. He saw, as if for the first time, "clouds, leaves of grass, bricks, small boats. I savored every detail as never before." So Florence must have felt. She never saw New York again.

In 1982, I wrote an article, "You've Come the *Wrong* Way, Baby," ★ first published in a physicians' newsmagazine, *The Medical Tribune,* then in the *Reader's Digest.* Senator Claiborne Pell read it into the *Congressional Record* on December 18, 1982; saying:

> Dr. Cahan alerts us to some alarming facts about women. Lung cancer deaths increased by 353% from 1950 to 1977, and death from larynx cancer increased by 333%. These increases directly parallel a dramatic increase in smoking by women in the past 30 years, and Dr. Cahan's discussion of the problems and his warning to all smokers deserve sober study.

In the article, I had written:

> The rapid climb in these grim statistics fulfills the prophesies made a generation ago when women began smoking in earnest. As there is a huge unheard-from reservoir of over 25 million female smokers, they will probably continue for some time.

After indicating the influence of the tobacco advertising campaigns that seem to capitalize on the rise in feminism, I said:

> These seductive measures and influences are patently synthetic, transparent and cynical. As a consequence, it puzzles those who admire and are impressed by the idealism and accomplishments of the contemporary women's movement, to observe how they, who are often in the forefront of concerns about health and good causes and who militantly resist being exploited, should also readily embrace and persist in such man-made lethal habits as tobacco and alcohol.

I pointed out how women are particularly vulnerable to cigarette smoking. Beside tobaccogenic cancers and cardiovascular diseases, when smoking is combined with the Pill, it markedly

★ Through the years, it had been gratifying to hear "*wrong* way" used by others to ridicule the ad.

increases the chance of phlebitis, stroke, and heart disease. Pregnant women who smoke during pregnancy endanger their embryos and have increased numbers of miscarriages, newborns with lower birth weight, cleft palate and harelip, and children who, as they grow older, are more susceptible to respiratory diseases.

A nice letter arrived from a woman with an unusual occupation, one that I thought had been practiced only in biblical times:

October 29, 1984

Dear Dr. Cahan,
    . . . I thought you might be interested to know what impact your article . . . had on me.
    I am a shepherdess in Maryland. I smoked one and a half packs a day from the time I was fourteen until I read your article. I am now thirty-nine. The minute I read about the thirty-nine-year-old mother of three who was told she had lung cancer, I threw my cigarettes out. I have never once had an urge to smoke since, you put such a fear into me.
    I could feel the cold terror and I have so much to live for I wouldn't dare follow her . . .

By the early eighties, the government-mandated warning on cigarette packages and advertising ("The Surgeon General has determined that smoking may be hazardous to your health") was considered to have lost its punch. Although its initial impact in 1966 caused cigarette sales to fall, sales soon began to climb again (as did the death rate from smoking-caused diseases). In large part, this was due to the tobacco industry's vigorous campaign, as described, to neutralize the vague, mild warning about smoking's dangers. Antitobacco forces felt that the warning was a mere wrist slap when an uppercut punch was needed.

Although all public-health agencies can be said to be on the side of the angels, they usually keep their activities independent of each other. However, for the first time, the American Cancer Society, the American Lung Association, and the American Heart Association joined forces to persuade Congress to pass a law requiring stronger and more disease-specific warning labels.

The American Cancer Society asked me to represent it on March 8, 1983, at hearings before a House subcommittee on health and environment chaired by Congressman Henry Waxman of California. Others asked to testify were Luther B. Terry, a former surgeon general, who in 1964 was responsible for the first government report that linked smoking and cancer; Amanda Blake of TV's *Gunsmoke,* who had smoked until she developed a cancer of the jaw; Bob Keeshan, aka Captain Kangaroo, who for years hosted many children's TV programs; and, to my delight, my old friend from *Winged Victory,* John Forsythe. John's good looks and talent, along with those of many future stars of stage and screen, had been buried in the show's crowd scenes. Through the years, it had been gratifying to see his steady rise to stardom in plays, movies, and successful TV shows such as *Bachelor Father* and *Dynasty.* I hadn't seen him for many years. The last time we met, I was able to convince him to quit. He had been asked to testify because of his much-publicized militant stand against smoking.

After Luther Terry, Amanda Blake told the subcommittee that, had she seen the warning label when she was a young woman, she never would have started smoking and probably would not be in her present predicament. Captain Kangaroo talked about how, out of concern for children, he wanted to do everything possible on his TV program to stop them from starting. He felt that more-visible warnings would help.

John Forsythe addressed the subcommittee members. "My brother and sister died of smoking-related diseases," he said. "If it had not been for Dr. Cahan, I would still be smoking."

Before the hearing, I had self-consciously gone to a drugstore and bought two different brands of cigarettes. Strange sensation. I felt as guilty as a bachelor used to feel, years before, when buying condoms. I also bought a bottle of tincture of iodine. Now I brought them out.

I challenged the subcommittee: "Where does the warning appear on a cigarette package? The front, back, top, bottom?" None of them knew. Then holding the pack aloft, I said, "It's on its side . . . so that when holding the pack in the usual way, one's hand and fingers cover it. Besides, the warning is printed in such tiny, pale letters that it is all but invisible."

Next, I brought out the tincture of iodine and covered its label with my hand. "Can you remember from your childhood what the label looks like?" Although for years tincture of iodine had rarely been used, each remembered that the label had the word "poison" along with a skull-and-crossbones.

John Forsythe *(Dynasty)*, and Dr. Cahan, old friends, after speaking
out against smoking at a House subcommittee hearing

"You see," I said, "if there's a strong enough message on the
label, you remember it for the rest of your life."

In May 1983, I appeared before Senator Orrin Hatch's Labor-
Human Resources Committee. At the hearing, I showed the chest
X ray of a fifty-nine-year-old "wife, mother, grandmother" who
had lung cancer. In spite of her family's pleading with her to stop
smoking her two packs a day, she couldn't do so. Then one day,
she coughed up blood, and when she saw the shadow in her lung
X ray, she quit—too late.

As might be expected, not all the committee members were
sympathetic, particularly those from tobacco states. One Southern senator asked, "Well, what *laboratory* proof do you have, Doctor?" I then described, among others, the dog experiments I had
done. Alan Davis, an American Cancer Society official who was
sitting in the closely packed audience, overheard a nearby to-
bacco-company lobbyist's groan: "Oh my God, he's bringing up
the smoking dogs!" ★

★ Because of my antismoking activities, the American Cancer Society gave me
its Distinguished Service Award in 1982.

When we emerged from the committee hearings, I was asked by a television reporter how I could be so sure *smoking* caused cancer if science hasn't discovered what really causes it.

I answered that "scientists may not know the minute reasons why overexposure to radiation causes cancer, but it does; why excessive sunlight, inhalation of asbestos cause cancer, but they do; so it is with smoking: If everyone were to quit tomorrow, in time there would be four hundred thousand fewer deaths a year in America."

Two years later, in 1985, Congress passed a new warning-label act, stipulating that four different warnings be displayed in rotation on cigarette packages and advertisements. These were more powerful than the previous ones and more specific:

SURGEON GENERAL'S WARNING: Smoking Causes Lung Cancer, Heart Disease, Emphysema, And May Complicate Pregnancy.

SURGEON GENERAL'S WARNING: Quitting Smoking Now Greatly Reduces Serious Risk To Your Health.

SURGEON GENERAL'S WARNING: Smoking By Pregnant Women May Result In Fetal Injury, Premature Birth and Low Birth Weight.

SURGEON GENERAL'S WARNING: Cigarette Smoke Contains Carbon Monoxide.

Although the act was a victory of sorts, the tobacco industry managed to lobby out references to death and addiction. Little did we appreciate at the time that, ironically, the new warnings would be used years later as a legal barricade behind which tobacco interests could hide when sued by smoking-related-cancer victims or their families. Juries were told that the patients had known about the warnings and had assumed the risk by continuing to smoke.

In the early days, when investigators first began to see the smoking–lung cancer connection, other side effects of smoking were little suspected. In time, its effects on the pulmonary and cardiovascular systems became apparent, and cancers not just of the lung, but of other organs over which inhaled smoke flowed (such as the larynx, oral cavity, and esophagus—especially when the smoke is combined with alcohol) were linked to smoking. Later, smoking was found to contribute to cancer formation in distant organs such as the urinary bladder, the kidney, the pancreas, and the cervix. It was also the common denominator in a variety of nonmalignant conditions: bronchitis, emphysema, and chronic obstructive pulmonary disease.

However, what even specialists could not have imagined is that smoking plays a role in certain cataracts of the eye, male impotence, delayed conception in women, and a predisposition for male smokers' offspring to develop brain tumors because of smoking-induced defective genes in the parent's sperm: the sins of the fathers.

When I learned from obstetrical colleagues and from reading medical literature that women who smoke while pregnant were more likely to miscarry as well as compromise their newborn child, in March 1985 I wrote an op-ed piece for *The New York Times* called "Abusing Children by Smoking." In it, I pointed out that pregnant women who smoke increase the risk of spontaneous abortion. What is more, their newborns have lower birth weight and are more prone to neonatal diseases such as sudden infant death syndrome, cleft palate, and harelip. Pediatricians have recorded that physical and intellectual development were adversely affected in these children.

The article served as a complement to a dramatic TV spot in which a simulated fetus (in utero) slowly raises a cigarette to its lips and, as it exhales smoke, a voice-over says: "Mothers, please don't smoke."

The *Newark Star-Ledger* picked up on this and headed its interview with me: CANCER FOE FOREWARNS MOMS-TO-BE AGAINST SMOKING.

When then–vice president Bush's wife, Barbara, read the op-ed article, she wrote: "I'm a fanatic on the subject of smoking— George, who has never smoked, says I'm a bore. I'm sending your article to two of my daughters-in-law; they need it!"

It turned out that Mrs. Bush, the First Lady, owed a debt to another—an unknown—lady.

She said, in a talk to nurses:

> I was in the hospital just having had minor surgery and awakened in the middle of the night. I was a smoker in those days (two packs a day maybe). Because George didn't smoke and I had a rule that I never smoked in bed, when I awakened the second time, alone and half drugged, I longed for a cigarette and struggled out of bed— not easy with my arm tied to a board and an intravenous feeding going on. I was having a cigarette when a nurse, a feisty little lady in white, charged in, scolded me harshly, put me back to bed and told me she'd see me in the morning.

She did return, waited until after she was relieved from duty, and came in on her own time. She minced *no words*. She said I was addicted to nicotine and I'd better do something about it.

Although I'd tried to give up smoking for years, this little nurse did it. She was the trigger that stopped me from smoking and never ever knew it!

One more occasion, from uncounted others, for Barbara and all of us to be grateful for unknown, unnamed nurses.

CHAPTER XXXI

Not a Very Retiring Person

Mandatory retirement, which at one time seemed so remote and improbable, came closer. For years I could subconsciously feel its foreboding, ominous presence, which became more sharply focused in 1984, the year of my seventieth birthday. MSK's by-laws originally had it that one must retire at sixty-five, but had been amended as a result of a state law to the age of seventy. Nevertheless, as with Christmas, there seemed plenty of time left to do something about it—then, suddenly: My God, Christmas is only two weeks away!

As it is well-nigh impossible to be objective about one's own aging, I thought that seventy was a good time to take physiological, psychological, and neurological inventory of myself. Although all systems seemed fine, to avoid any bias I had an internist do a work-up complete with blood pressure, EKG, blood counts and chemistries, urinalysis and chest X ray. All were normal.

However, I have always promised myself never to hang onto surgery by my rubber-gloved fingertips if there were the slightest evidence of an age-imposed error.

Certainly, judging by the results, I was able to carry out ongoing commitments: teaching, research, antitobacco strategies. As my capacity for productive activity seemed unaltered and undiminished, why then must I be forced to surrender to restrictions imposed by the calendar? There must be a better yardstick than numerical age to measure capability.

As reasonable as this seemed to me, I began encountering inflexible policies and attitudes. About a year before hospital rules would force me to retire, I brought up the issue with Dr. Jerome DeCosse, then chairman of the department of surgery (and a former resident of mine). His attitude was disquieting. "After all, Bill," he said, "seventy is seventy and we have to make room at the bottom for younger surgeons. If you continue, you'll be taking operating time from them. Don't forget, we have to build up stratas. Besides, seventy years of age is a time that you might well begin making mistakes in surgery, and your judgment might not be as clear."

"At Memorial," I wrote back, "we are careful to deal with patients as individuals. Shouldn't the same approach apply to staff members? In which case, wouldn't it be wise to be less concerned with a particular surgeon's chronological age and more with his performance? How old I am is unimportant; how *able* I am is." Half-seriously, I boasted, "I'd be willing to retire if one of the powers-that-be can beat me at tennis," adding: "Singles."

I got nowhere with DeCosse. I asked to go a step higher on the ladder, to Samuel Hellman, physician-in-chief, and, if necessary, to Paul Marks, president of MSK. When I did so, both Hellman and Marks gave me an outwardly friendly but essentially cool—that is, bureaucratic—reception.

On September 12, 1984, with nine months to go, I wrote to Marks pointing out that a New York State law prohibiting arbitrary mandatory retirement was to become effective in January 1986. Six months later, I received a two-paragraph letter from Hellman. In language reminiscent of military orders, it informed me that, "you will be unable to admit patients, operate on patients, or maintain a consultation or follow-up clinic." He, like DeCosse, stressed that "the institution has a regular mechanism for staff and faculty renewal. This is essential not only at this institution, but at all other academic centers."

His last statement prompted me to make inquiries at other prestigious teaching hospitals in New York City, including New York Hospital, Roosevelt, Lenox Hill, University, and Presbyterian. None had mandatory retirement policies. Hellman's former hospital, Massachusetts General in Boston, also did not impose retirement on surgeons on the basis of age alone.

As for the need for staff renewal: No one was more sensitive to the necessity of making room for young staff members than I. After all, Anthony would soon be trying to join a hospital staff.

However, at the time, the thoracic service was not fully staffed. Besides, I was willing to relinquish my "prime" operating time and adapt my operating schedule to the priorities of younger surgeons. More important, I thought, was that during many years of experience, I had acquired valuable information to impart to younger men and women. Besides, I had several major research projects to complete. By cutting me from the active surgical staff, MSK would lose these, too.

In a letter to Hellman, I said as much and added what was perhaps an even more telling point: MSK was one of the first hospitals to disregard race, creed, color, and sex in selecting its staff. Now the hospital had a chance to rise above yet another prejudice: ageism. If it conquered that, it would demonstrate that it valued talented, innovative scientists and their ideas above lesser considerations such as calendar years.

Time passed. Then came what appeared to be the first tiny crack in the bureaucratic façade.

Paul Marks informed me that I would be appointed a "consultant," an honorary position that carried no fringe benefits. I could continue several projects I had propounded and would have an office in the new Cummings Building.

This last concession was made possible because of the foresight of a friend. Years before, Nathan Cummings had called. "Instead of giving myself an eighty-fifth birthday party," he said, "I have decided to give five million dollars to your hospital." The terms of the gift stipulated that I should have an office in Nate's new building for the rest of my professional affiliation with MSK. "Thank heavens," I said. "Otherwise I'd be practicing in a phone booth on First Avenue."

Although granting this much, Paul Marks made it quite clear: I could not continue seeing patients.

Perhaps I should have been content with such a setup. But I still believed these attitudes to be arbitrary. It reminded me of doctors who will tell an otherwise healthy seventy-five-year-old cancer patient that he or she is "too old" to have a life-saving major operation. Such thinking is not at all uncommon. A UCLA study shows that older women get less vigorous treatment for breast cancer solely because of their age.

Ten years before, I had given a lecture, "Age and Cancer Surgery," during which I described how well patients over seventy withstood even physiologically demanding operations such as lung removal. I had been convinced of this for years and, in the 1960s, when I asked the chief of the thoracic service permission to report the results with a group of these septuagenarians, he said it was "too radical an idea" and refused. Now, major surgery for those in their seventies and eighties is commonplace, and there are more and more reports of successful cancer surgery for those in their nineties and hundreds.

Another graphic expression of changing attitudes about age occurs in case presentations made by residents at surgical conferences. When they begin by stating the patient's age, they say "seventy-six. However, he or she is a *young* seventy-six." And everyone understands what is implied. Today septua-, octo-, and nonagenarians are often more vigorous and in better physical condition than those of previous generations and should not be deprived of the chance to be cured. Such an "aggressive" approach reflects, too, the extraordinary advances made in preoperative, operative, and postoperative care, which have markedly reduced the risks of surgery and have made numerical age alone less of a consideration.

The oldest patient on whom I performed a lobectomy for lung cancer was eighty-three. In spite of the physiological strain this placed on his heart and lungs, he was up walking the first postoperative day and went home a week later.

Today, this is no longer considered to be a radical geriatric surgical feat. Years ago, a ninety-four-year-old woman was brought to see me with a large, weeping breast cancer that she had neglected over the years. Because of its size and the fact it had ulcerated, nothing short of a radical mastectomy could rid her of this grotesque tumor. Radiation therapy as an alternative would probably have aggravated the ulceration and would not have controlled a tumor of such monstrous proportions.

She had all her faculties; there was no evidence that her cancer had spread; and a medical consultant had found her to be an "acceptable risk." I performed a radical mastectomy.

She was out of bed the next day and soon walking the corridors. Four days after the operation, we celebrated her ninety-fifth birthday. The nurses made a big fuss over her, doing her makeup and putting ribbons in her hair. They pinned a corsage on her gown and filled her room with balloons, streamers, and cards. I sent her a bouquet. As we assembled about the foot of her bed, a cake was brought in with a single lighted candle, and we sang

"Happy Birthday." When she read my card out ("To my teenage girlfriend, [from] Her Doc"), she cried and smiled, and so did we. Seven days later, she was discharged and went home, where she resumed keeping house for herself. She lived more than a year.

"Was it worth it?"

We didn't have to ask her.

Hearing nothing further from Hellman, I assumed that I would have to give up my practice. At the end of each scheduled office hour, I had a disturbing, poignant task: telling my patients that I would no longer be able to take care of them. I was touched by their disappointment when they heard that "circumstances beyond my control" were forcing me to end my practice. Several tearfully recalled that as long as they could remember, they had entrusted their lives (or at least their health) to me. I assured them that I would find them a worthy substitute. Nevertheless, many said they felt abandoned. So did I.

During one of our last office hours, there seemed to be curious restiveness among some patients I had just seen. Glancing into the waiting room I saw them huddled with those waiting to see me, looking agitated and talking excitedly among themselves. This seemed odd: Few of them knew each other. No longer able to contain my curiosity, I walked over and asked what was going on. They fell silent and seemed reluctant to say anything, but I finally pried it out of them.

"We're hatching a plan," one woman said. "Yes," said a middle-aged man. "We've decided to picket the hospital. We're not going to take your retirement lying down."

Stunned and touched, in part by the precision of their language, I managed to calm them and convince them to abandon their plot. Disappointed, they said that, in any event, they were going to write to the authorities.

Paul Marks called me to his office one day and, clearly in high dudgeon, paced back and forth behind his huge desk. "I'm sick and tired of getting letters and sitting next to friends of yours who keep after me about this retirement business. I wish to hell they'd quit!"

"Cool it, Paul. I have no control over what my friends say. I certainly didn't put them up to it."

"Well, I'm always being asked, 'Why are you doing this to Bill Cahan?' "

"Paul, I had *nothing* to do with it. But you know—they're right."

Soon afterward, I talked to Sam Hellman once more to remind him that if MSK rigidly adhered to its by-laws, I'd miss qualifying by just six months for the new state law that prohibited mandatory retirement for reasons of age. I had been at MSK for forty-three years; I told him I didn't believe that the great institution would be small enough to adhere stubbornly to a technicality, thus depriving me of hospital privileges. This was unjust and unfair, and I planned to distribute a letter to that effect to the board of managers.

The letter must have had done some good, for the board decided that I could continue seeing outpatients. *But* I could not do surgery.

As grateful as I was about having at least won a skirmish, the restrictions on surgery were particularly painful, for just at that time Anthony had begun his rotation at MSK. This meant that I would have another failed dream: I would never assist him. I'd have to content myself with just watching.

Operation (Phase III)

The surgeon was approaching the more intricate part of the operation: dissecting the tissue in the armpit that contained lymph nodes. This phase requires particularly delicate handling, as the lymph nodes lie in close proximity both to a large vein and to two nerves that control the muscles of the upper arm and shoulder.

I remained as unobtrusive as possible. However, from time to time, I adjusted the overhead lights to focus on a particular area that needed illumination. The surgeon seemed unmindful of my presence and limited his conversation to brief requests for various instruments or to ask his assistant to hold this or tie that.

Halfway through the operation, he told the rotating nurse to call the waiting relatives and say that all was going fine.

As the lymph nodes were being removed, he paused, and without looking up, the surgeon said: "Is this the way you used to do it?"

"Yes, pretty much. However, instead of cauterizing the intercostal nerves together with their nearby blood vessels in one bundle, I'd isolate the nerves and cut them: This will help reduce postoperative pain."

Then I added, half-seriously: "As you surgeons use so much cautery these days, I'd suction away its fumes—it can't be good for you. Besides, it would be too ironic if surgeons got lung cancer from their own second-hand smoke."

He said nothing, but proceeded to do just that.

When the specimen had been removed and handed to the rotating nurse to send to the pathology laboratory, and preparations had been made to close the incision, the instrument nurse said, "Sponge and needle count correct, Doctor."

Just before bringing the skin edges together, two plastic tubes are inserted beneath the lower skin edge to drain secretions that always occur.

As this point, the surgeon turned and said: "Here's a trick to eliminate the annoying pain caused by these tubes." I knew what he meant, for mastectomy patients will often complain more of the annoying pain from the drainage tubes, and the stitches used to anchor them in place, than about the incision itself.

He went on, "There's always an area of anesthesia at the lower outer margin of the incision and about two inches below it. I place the drains and their sutures there and I've done it on about thirty patients and no one complains of pain."

I smiled again—and recalled that I had been concerned that this doctor, no longer a student, would not be interested in innovation.

❖

CHAPTER XXXII

"Who's in O.R. Six?"

For six months after June 30, 1985, I continued to see patients in
follow-up and others in consultation. Try though I might to be
philosophical and count my blessings, being shut out of surgery
rankled. Once more I wrote to Sam Hellman saying that I didn't
want to seem ungrateful, but I saw no reason not to be allowed
to operate. If there were any doubts, I was willing to subject
myself to tests to help judge my competence.

Sam said he understood how I felt, but made no further
moves. As a result, I felt that I had exhausted every avenue, and
I resigned myself to the unhappy fact that my surgical days were
over.

Then a hint, sharp as a scalpel's edge . . . David Mahoney, a
handsome, dynamic man, former head of the Norton Simon Corporation, has for years supported a neurological-research institute
that bears his name. Every other year he gives a dinner party to
describe the institute's progress to his many friends. At one of
these, David had Mrs. Milton Petrie as his dinner partner. The
Petries, among many other philanthropists, are very generous
benefactors of MSK. David, a great man for coming to the point,
said: "Carol, women don't always use the power they have in
higher echelons. You're on the board at Memorial, and your
friend Bill Cahan is being discriminated against because of his age.
He's no longer allowed to do surgery. Why don't you pitch in for
him?" After dinner, Carol came to my table and said she would
like to help. The board would be meeting the next morning. "It's

at nine fifteen, so why don't we meet in the hospital lobby at nine so you can fill me in?"

The next morning we talked. I walked Carol to the elevator after I explained the situation and, just before the door closed, she waved to me cheerfully.

Later that day, my secretary, Beatrice Arbaiza, went to New York Hospital to return some X rays. When she returned, she said, in tones usually used to break the news of a tragedy in the family, that, as she was walking to the main entrance of New York Hospital, she saw a hole where the Hippocratic-Papanicolaou tree had stood: It had been taken down to make room for a new biomedical-research building.

Shocked, hurt, outraged as if a friend had been murdered, I immediately called New York Hospital's administrators, who told me that, faced with a decision about the tree, they had thought about transplanting it, but it would have cost $20,000 and the tree's chances of survival were only 10 percent. They had, however, kept the plaque.

After I had recovered somewhat, I called a friend in Athens, who told me that I could count on getting a new sapling from Kos. This time, I would insist that the tree be planted on the pathway to New York Hospital where no building would ever displace it.

That was the bad news of that day. Other news came later.

Walking over to see the site where the tree had stood, I met Benno Schmidt, Laurance Rockefeller, and Barbara Harbach who, as head of MSK's Women's Society, was present at the board meetings. Barbara knew of my campaign, so she could not contain herself: "You've made it! The board just approved your return to surgery."

Jubilant, ecstatic, I shook hands all around and thanked them, then flew, not walked, to the nearest telephone to call Grace.

When I was asked to leave the thoracic service, and accept assignment to the breast service, I did not contest the decision, for it was time for me to reduce the load of very demanding lung operations. Besides, to confine myself to breast surgery was an excellent compromise. Breast surgery is less intricate than lung-cancer surgery, yet it gave me the opportunity, literally, to keep my hand in and continue with research, teaching, scolding, and crusading.

I was also asked to surrender the office where so many sad or happy poignant scenes with patients and their relatives had been played out. Still, I was content to move to the tiny one that Nate Cummings's foresight had made available, and managed to squeeze secretary, files, desks, chairs and me into the ten-foot-by-ten-foot space. At its entrance, I hung a sign resembling the official ones issued by New York's buildings commissioner: OCCUPANCY BY MORE THAN 480 PERSONS IS DANGEROUS AND UNLAWFUL.

In December 1986, Sam Hellman confirmed the changes in MSK's rules and regulations: "In accordance with the New York State and federal statutes, MSK prohibits mandatory retirement on the basis of age. A voluntary program with options for individualization has been designed to permit clinicians to reduce their clinical activity."

Eureka. Or that's what I should have said, were it not such an old-fashioned expression.

Although I'd won a victory over ageism, there were, nevertheless, other nonnegotiable reminders of the "silent footfall of time." No longer was I asked for an ID card to get a reduced rate on buses or at movie theaters. Tennis pros seemed reluctant to teach new ways to improve my game. Why teach new tricks to an old dog?

The unkindest cut of all for this aging surgeon (appropriate for an aging surgeon) was when a young man watching me play singles with a pro said, with evident admiration when I'd finished: "Sir, do you mind if I ask your age?" When I told him, out came the crusher: "Well, God bless you!"

I may never forgive him.

August 30, 1989.

Yesterday, for whatever it's worth, I became the oldest surgeon ever to operate at MSK. Hubris perhaps, but it is a triumph of sorts to overcome bureaucratic resistance to surgeons who were anxious, willing, and capable of doing surgery after the age of seventy.

As I entered the surgeons' locker room, I had, along with a sense of déjà vu, the first of several poignant moments: eighteen months after I had first used it, I was able to recall the combination of the lock on my locker (now shared with a resident).

Then followed a cascade of remembered acts: putting on a scrub suit, donning the paper O.R. cap and shoe coverings, tying the strings of the face mask behind my head and neck with automatic, not-thought-about gestures. What was particularly touching occurred as I entered the O.R.: I was greeted warmly by the anesthetists and nurses and could see behind their masks broad smiles that had "welcome back" written all over them.

Once more, standing by the patient's side, I patted and reassured her before she was anesthetized.

Then followed the familiar ritual of scrubbing with the resident, backing into the O.R., hands held aloft and, after drying them, being gowned and gloved by the instrument nurse.

The operation was routine: the removal of a suspicious breast tumor. Even so, I automatically fell back into my old pattern of teaching fine points as I worked.

After the specimen was sent to pathology, once again I heard over the intercom the pathologist's metallic-sounding pronouncement: "Dr. Cahan, the biopsy of your patient, Mrs. Alice Jones, is benign."

When we had put on the dressing, I stripped off my gloves and gown, gave post-op orders to the resident, thanked everyone, and left the O.R. to dictate the details of the procedure on the phone to be typed for the patient's chart. Then, after I dressed, I went to the visitors' waiting room to give the patient's husband the good news and, jubilant, went to my office.

Emily Dickinson came to mind:

> Long Years apart—can make no
> Breach a second cannot fill—

In a way, I was a lover returning at long last to his former love.

In due course, the dire predictions that looked so logical and inevitable to hospital authorities never came to pass. My presence did not block or interfere with the addition of younger staff members; nor was there ever a conflict with other surgeons about operating time. Most important, in the four years following my return to surgery, there were no mishaps. What is more, hospital officials not only learned to accommodate gracefully to the staff members over seventy who wished to continue, but also discovered how best to use their talents for teaching and fund-raising. Finally, those in charge came to realize that a staff is not renewed simply by pumping in young blood, but can be equally vitalized by the still-hot blood of seasoned veterans; new, valuable ideas know no age.

What delighted me most was that my reprieve had come just in time for my long-delayed dream to be realized. As Anthony was scheduled to come to MSK on rotation, perhaps there was still time for me to operate with him.

And indeed, there was! Anthony was the surgeon and I his first assistant when he removed a soft-tissue sarcoma from a patient's shoulder. As Anthony gingerly dissected and carefully identified and spared nearby major arteries and nerves, I felt completely relaxed. Nothing he did worried me. At one time, I suggested that he use the tip of his scalpel instead of its heel ("Just as your grandfather used the tip of a pencil to sketch fine lines, rather than its flat surface, for shading"). For one particularly ticklish area, I felt using curved scissors instead of a knife would facilitate the dissection. Anthony gently demurred: "I'd rather stay with a knife, if you don't mind, Dad." So, once again, I was content to play a supportive role, like the times when he had asked me to steady a board while he sawed. Now he handed me hemostats or retractors to hold.

In two hours, the banana-shaped, banana-sized specimen was cleanly removed, the drains placed, the skin closed. Later, after the patient awakened, together we tested the circulation and nerve function of his arm and found them intact. Should his sarcoma recur, Anthony would be the one to remove it—and probably without me.

Grace, who knew what this day meant to me, asked at dinner that night: "How did it go?" In particular, she wanted to know if Anthony felt apprehensive or distracted by my presence. I said, "I don't think so." Later, when she called Anthony, he confirmed that my being there seemed "natural"; that he felt no difference from when we worked on other projects. "Honestly," he said, "in concentrating, I almost forgot that Dad was there."

But I would never forget.

Just before going to sleep that night, I relived the day's experience. I was proud of how well Anthony had conducted himself. I couldn't help smiling when I recalled how an anesthetist who happened to be standing outside the operating room while the operation was going on told me she had overheard two nurses talking.

One said, "Who is in O.R. Six?"

The other replied, "The Cahans."

October 18, 1986.

Today, Anthony and I had another chance to work together side by side, this time to keep a close friend of ours alive. A few weeks before, this man, in his seventies, had an operation for throat cancer that required a tracheotomy. The tube had been removed a week later and skin healed over the opening in his neck. However, at home he developed a cough that became more persistent and intensive. Suddenly one morning, he found it difficult to move air in and out of his windpipe. When his frantic wife called, I told her to take him by ambulance to New York Hospital's emergency room. Then I alerted the E.R. staff and called Anthony and told him to meet me there.

As our friend was carried by stretcher out of the ambulance, we could see that he was making a considerable effort to breathe. Both of us felt that a plug of mucus or a nubbin of "proud flesh," probably at the former site of the tracheotomy tube, was obstructing his trachea. We suctioned the back of his throat, but because he was becoming cyanotic (blue), an endotracheal tube was quickly inserted through his mouth and into his windpipe. Once it was in place, we suctioned out more mucus and, as he took deep breaths, his color improved. At one point, he gave a vigorous cough and expelled a plug of tissue through the tube: the fleshy plug was probably sheared off by the passage of the endotracheal tube. Had the tube not been inserted, he would soon have died much in the same manner as someone with a "café coronary," when a piece of inhaled food lodges in and occludes the opening of a windpipe. In him, the Heimlich maneuver would not have dislodged this plug, because it was fixed to the trachea. No question, this was a close call: For at least forty-five minutes, he had had an inadequate supply of oxygen, and since his heart was scarred from a previous heart attack, prolonged, inadequate oxygenation could have precipitated another attack.

During these hectic activities, I deferred to Anthony, not only because it was *his* hospital and *his* emergency room, but because I was confident that he would do the right thing.

The patient's wife remained at the door to the cubicle, watching. Afterward, she said that in the midst of her anxiety, she knew that Anthony would make the right moves. She also said that the sight of the two heads—one white-haired, one brown—bent over her husband, helping him survive, was unforgettable.

Not all emergency efforts are successful. While Anthony was assisting a surgeon to perform a liver resection, the patient hemorrhaged. In spite of repeated, rapid transfusions, her blood pressure fell and her heart stopped. Immediately, open-heart massage and cardiac stimulants were given, but to no avail.

Later, I could see that this was a bruising psychological blow to Anthony. He said wistfully: "I worked her up on admission and got to know her. This was like losing a close friend. What a lovely lady.''

From experience I know he will become one of her mourners and will be haunted by this experience. And relive it in nightmares.

We talked about how a family should be given the news. This encounter is one that surgeons dread more than any other. Although it was not his responsibility in this case, I was curious about how he would face such a problem.

"First," he said, "take the relatives to a private area. Then quietly and sympathetically tell them exactly what happened."

"Fine," I told him. "And remember, too, that surgeons whose patients face what is undoubtedly a risky procedure should prepare families by explaining to them beforehand that an operation of this magnitude is bound to be dangerous, but that it is worth the risk if it gives the patient his or her only chance.

"Once their acute shock and grief have subsided somewhat, they are bound to question you. Be sure to take time to answer as many questions as you can—and honestly. On leaving, reassure them once more that every measure was taken to help the patient survive. Say that you will always be available to answer any further questions they may have."

I added one further suggestion: Explain once again that the radical surgery was done because every other reliable treatment had failed and the patient would have been doomed to a slow, painful death. Although it's scant consolation at the time, the survivors need such thoughts to take away with them.

January 30, 1983.
  To everyone's delight, Devon Julia (my mother's middle name) was born today. . . . Finally, we have a girl in the family.

What I and all those who knew them had considered to be an idyllic domestic life—attractive wife, up-and-coming surgeon, and two fine children—was apparently an illusion. Karen and Anthony had managed to keep their conflicts from those around them. He told me, "I felt I couldn't go on with Karen any longer."

The situation seemed irremediable, although for the sake of the children I tried to make some sort of reconciliation.

Some time later, after Karen and the children moved to other living quarters, Anthony introduced me to Mary Beth. As she emerged from her apartment on East Eighty-eighth Street, I saw a very pretty young woman of medium height, brown hair, a turned-up nose, blue eyes, and a good figure. She had been a nurse at MSK for several years.

The three of us walked to Central Park and sat down at a bench to talk. After polite conversation, Mary Beth suddenly blurted out through tears: "I want you to know, Dr. Cahan, I am very much in love with your son."

When Karen and Anthony's divorce became final, Karen took the two children to live in Florida near her parents. Anthony entered the five-year residency program at New York Hospital.

Part of the program included not only time spent at MSK, but also at Jamaica Hospital in Queens. Jamaica Hospital provided valuable experience with trauma patients because of the troubled neighborhoods around it, and a soberingly active ambulance service.

While Anthony was on emergency duty, a young woman was admitted by ambulance who had been badly burned in a gas-station explosion. Besides being burned, she had inhaled hot gasoline fumes that caused her vocal cords to swell; the swelling was beginning to obstruct her breathing. Within minutes, she would suffocate. Anthony could tell by the sound of her breathing what was happening, and immediately inserted an endotracheal tube through her vocal cords into her windpipe.

From the extent of her burns, she clearly needed specialized care —and soon. As Jamaica Hospital had no burn unit, Anthony decided to transfer her to the one at New York Hospital. However, it was rush hour and the roads to the city were choked with bumper-to-bumper traffic. Getting there, even by ambulance, would consume time that the patient could ill afford.

Anthony called the police, who cleared the hospital's parking lot of cars to land their helicopter. Soon, Anthony and his patient were flying over the East River to the Sixty-first Street heliport. Badly burned though she was, and having to breathe through an artificial airway, the woman later said she was even more alarmed by a very bumpy helicopter ride on a windy day. Fortunately, the ride was over in six minutes. As soon as they landed, an ambulance sped them the nine blocks to New York Hospital. Two weeks later, the patient was discharged, healed with only a few minor scars.

Once more, I couldn't help seeing the "then and now" aspects of this story. Had this accident occurred during my internship, the woman would have died. None of the things that worked for her survival existed then: endotracheal tubes, helicopters, burn units with sophisticated methods of treating severe cases. She was lucky that this occurred in Anthony's and not my generation. (For that matter, he had not existed back then, either.)

On September 16, 1987, in A.'s final year of residency, while reading a medical journal, he came across an article on the occurrence of larynx and lung cancers in the same patient, with bibliographic references to my articles. He photocopied it and sent it to me with a note:

"I guess you called this one years ago. Respectfully, Antonio."

But it wasn't all sweetness and enlightenment between Anthony and me—and understandably.

Recently, he told me that, for a while, he reacted to some of my advice with resentment tinged with skepticism. He was at a loss to know why, at this stage in his career, he felt that way. Perhaps, he thought, it was a hangover from the typical reaction to a son-father relationship in which, to declare his independence, the son resists authority and is reluctant to be influenced or to acknowledge a parent's advice. But he told me he abandoned that attitude when he found that he had automatically and subconsciously adopted any number of "pearls" of mine that had worked.

His underground resistance may have begun in medical school and during the days of his internship, when some of my ideas were at variance with those of his professors. After all, they were respected mentors, too, and he was reluctant, naturally, to doubt their teaching. I told him that I understood; it reminded me of the time-honored remark of Mark Twain's: As he grew older, Twain said it was remarkable how intelligent his parents had become.

Anthony finished his residency at New York Hospital at the end of June 1987. He opened an office in an apartment building just opposite Gracie Mansion (the residence of New York City's mayor) On July 11, he and Mary Beth were married in Sisi's apartment. Chris was Anthony's best man. Devon was the flower girl; Nicky was the ringbearer.

Anthony allotted me some of the announcements of his office to send to his friends.

Months before, we had a rare difference of opinion for, in addition to private practice, I had urged him to become attached to a teaching institution—like New York Hospital—in order to keep up with current medical advances and, if he felt so inclined, to do research. He felt that such a move would confine him to that hospital as a full-time staff member and, automatically made a faculty member of an affiliated medical college, he would be subject to control by his academic superiors.

He had been admitted to the staff of Doctors Hospital (now Beth Israel North), where Mary Beth was the nurse-in-charge of the outpatient surgery. His application to New York Hospital had been turned down for unspecified reasons. (I thought: This is the second mistake this hospital has made involving Cahans.) In a way, Anthony was relieved, because he would have had to become a full-time staff member of New York Hospital and automatically a faculty member of Cornell Medical College, both of which would have subjected him to control by his academic superiors.

Grace gave Anthony a telephone answering service for a year, his mother gave him office stationery, and I helped him defray some of the start-up expenses not covered by a bank loan he had taken. All was in readiness. Now if only he could have patients—*any* patients. He had lots of questions: "How much do you charge patients for their first visit? What kind of letter does one write to referring physicians?"

It is difficult to convey the mixture of trepidation, excitement, eagerness, and optimism that a young physician feels upon starting private practice. Overnight, he is transformed from a trainee in a short white coat, on constant call to take care of hordes of patients within the protective confines of a hospital and under his elders' supervision—to being his own boss and alone.

I was able to send two of my patients to Anthony. One had troublesome varicose veins; the other, an undiagnosed lump in the neck. It must be rare that a patient carries the surgical scars of both father and son. Weeks later, I kidded Anthony by saying that when I saw both patients in follow-up, my scars were finer and paler than his (this is to be expected, as mine were long-standing). Maybe from now on, we should keep a scar card.

January 3, 1988.
Anthony has removed his first acute, or "hot," appendix since starting practice. For some reason this operation has created more

excitement for him than any other, perhaps because an appendectomy is a classic example of the need for a general surgeon. Apparently, the diagnosis of appendicitis in this strapping nineteen-year-old was tricky, as it did not present classical symptoms. However, when exposed, "it was hot, all right, on the verge of rupturing."

So: four years of medical school, five years of residency, all focused one night on saving this young man's life. If Anthony never does anything else, this was worth it.

As I watched his practice grow, I warned Anthony to be careful not to let it overwhelm or enslave him. Physicians can become victims of their own success and get caught in a treadmill that so saps their energy and time, there is little of either left for kind, thoughtful care. Usually, physicians recognize this too late, consumed by the desire for more financial gains. Many are brought up short only when their patients repeatedly complain that they are getting depersonalized care. Rather than wait for this to happen, see it coming, and rather than being drowned by excessive numbers, be caring enough to refer some patients to equally capable colleagues. Or, if necessary, take on a trustworthy assistant.

Ah, the life of a surgeon who is on twenty-four-hour call, and for whom emergencies take precedence over everything else. One lovely winter's evening, Grace, Anthony, Mary Beth, Anthony's kids, and I were intently watching the second period of the Giants-Broncos Super Bowl game. Large logs burned in the fireplace, the chicken pot pie was almost ready and fragrantly delicious, and the score was 10–9 in favor of the Broncos. Just as Anthony was about to sit down to eat, his beeper went off. "It's the trauma number," he said, dialing the hospital.

Anthony knew then that for the rest of his professional life, he could be called any time, anywhere—during Super Bowls, at Christmas, while making love, during family squabbles. A good physician is never liberated from his patients—and despite grumbling, never wants to be.

I reached Anthony at the hospital just as he was about to operate on an automobile-accident victim. I quickly said: "Nineteen–ten Giants." He let out a loud "All right!" and hung up.

Grace sent Mary Beth and the kids home loaded with a generous portion of chicken pot pie, salad, and a slab of cake for Anthony. Both the patient and the Giants did well: The one survived nicely; the other won, 39–20.

November 26, 1987.

At our first family Thanksgiving in our new Bedford home, Chris clinked a glass for attention and announced his engagement to Vicki Sheff.

Vicki could be a Swedish movie star—high cheekbones, blond hair, sharp features, marvelous smile, and infectious laugh. She is on the staff of *People* magazine and, most important, devoted to Chris, for whom she has been a stabilizing influence. A son from her previous marriage spends five months of the year with Vicki and Chris and he is, I suspect, teaching Chris to be a father. Chris, now thirty-eight, will, I hope, father his own child. (I was thirty-eight when I had my first.) . . .

Vicki and Chris were married in the garden behind our brownstone on April 21, 1988. Anthony was the best man.

The day after they married, Chris and Vicki went to my mother's grave in a Brooklyn cemetery. Chris stood silently before it for a moment, then suddenly wrapped his arms around her tombstone and began to sob. He told her how much he missed her and how he wished she could have been at their wedding.

Then, taking the ring I had removed from my father's finger moments after he died and had given to Chris as a wedding present, he scratched a little notch on the tombstone.

Chris Cahan (left) on location and in action as a
TV producer for NBC News

When news of the San Francisco earthquake broke, the Financial News Network was anxious to determine what impact it had on the Pacific Stock Exchange. Chris volunteered to go as a field producer.

San Francisco's airport was closed. He flew to Stockton, California, where he gave an executive of San Francisco's Fairmont Hotel a ride in his rented car in exchange for the promise of a room. (He ended up sleeping on the floor.)

He got to the steps of the Pacific Stock Exchange, where he ran into the vice president who provided him with all the information he needed. Immediately after the earthquake, all lines of communication with the outside world were inactivated except the telephone. Chris used stacks of quarters to report his findings to FNN. As a result, he had a news scoop, supplying the only report on the structural condition of the Exchange and informed speculation on when it might reopen.

That night, I listened with pride to his reports of what he had seen. Perhaps the printer's ink flowed in his veins from my father, or wherever. He got his story.

March 25, 1988.

Three days ago, Anthony removed the gallbladder from the daughter of close friends, Beverly and Peter Greenough. Merideth ("Muffy"), their daughter, had been referred to Anthony by their internist. Peter, probably my oldest friend, called beforehand to tell me this and, I suspect, to be reassured. He knew me well enough to know that my relationship with Anthony would not stand in the way of an unprejudiced opinion. I said, "Anthony has the best hands I know."

Beverly Sills Greenough has played many roles superbly, whether as a brilliant soprano, director of the New York City Opera, or ebullient, effervescent mistress of ceremonies for major cultural events. Seeing her in action, one instinctively feels genuine sincerity and beauty reflected in her warm, smiling lovely face.

Perhaps her most difficult role, and one which she carries on with great affection and understanding, is as mother to Muffy, who has been deaf since birth. This is one of nature's raw deals: a great opera singer's child who has never heard her mother sing. But Muffy, a bright, pretty, sensitive girl, learned to read lips skillfully. A few nights after the operation, Beverly told me, "Just before Muffy was anesthetized, Anthony, seeing how apprehensive she was, held her hand and lowered his surgical mask so that he could carefully frame the words: 'Don't worry, I'll be right here with you all the way.' " When Beverly finished, she was on the verge of tears.

I had trouble with my own.

When one sees Beverly, Peter, and Muffy together, they give off a glow of such mutual affection and support that one cannot help but love that family.

June 21, 1990.

Anthony has succeeded where I had not: He was invited to join the staff of New York Hospital. This is both ironic and gratifying as the application he had submitted after completing his residency had been turned down.

Just why this offer was made at this time probably reflects the fine reputation he has made for himself, not only as a surgeon, but as an organizer and chief of the breast clinic at Doctors Hospital. He was also voted one of the five Physicians of the Year (1990) by the New York County Medical Society. So, though I have overweening paternal pride, others also recognize Anthony's talents.

Another more probable reason for New York Hospital's invitation is that, like other institutions, they are concerned about their falling census of patients. Anthony's burgeoning practice, therefore, was not lost upon the hospital's powers-that-be.

CHAPTER XXXIII

Smoke Gets in Your Eyes

James I, in the sixteenth century, bitterly complained:

> And for the vanities committed in this filthy costume, is it not both great vanity and uncleanness, that at the table, a place of respect, of cleanliness, of modesty, men should not be ashamed, to sit tossing off Tobacco pipes, and puffing of the smoke of Tobacco one to another, making the filthy smoke and stink thereof, to exhale athwart the dishes, and infect the air, when very often men that abhor it are at their repast? . . .
>
> It makes a kitchen, also often-times in the inward parts of men, soiling and infecting them, with an unctuous and oily kind of Soot, as hath been found in some great Tobacco takers, that after their death are opened.
>
> . . . Have you not reason then to be ashamed, and to forbear this filthy novelty . . . a custom loathsome to the eye, hateful to the nose, harmful to the brain, dangerous to the Lungs, and in the black stinking fume thereof, nearest resembling the Stygian smoke of the pit that is bottomless.

Until the early eighties, it was considered that smokers jeopardized only themselves. Although the fumes they exhaled, or that drift from a burning cigarette, were a nuisance, they were not thought to be hazardous. Then two published papers—one from Japan, the other from Greece—radically changed attitudes about secondhand (or "ambient") smoke. The authors described how nonsmoking wives of smoking husbands were two to three times more likely to develop lung cancer than the wives of nonsmokers.

At first, these articles were treated with skepticism by much of the American scientific community. Subsequent research determined that smokers' exhaled smoke—so-called mainstream smoke—and, particularly, the fumes arising from a lighted cigarette in an ashtray or held in a smoker's hand—"sidestream smoke"—contained forty-three cancer-forming chemicals. Suddenly, secondhand smoke became established as irritating to more than the likes of me or those whose nose and throat, food and clothing are contaminated. But ominously, innocent nonsmokers' health could be seriously threatened. Not only did secondhand smoke cause acute spasms of coughing and breathing difficulties in asthmatics and those with emphysema, but nonsmokers living or working in proximity to smokers, particularly in confined areas, could develop lung cancer even though they had never smoked.

This finding especially interested those who had been puzzled by the fact that 15 percent of those who developed lung cancer were nonsmokers. When they were questioned more closely, it was found that some had been exposed in childhood to the fumes of heavily smoking parents. Others had been chronically exposed in the workplace, as waitresses or airline hostesses. So nonsmokers had, in fact, been smoking—other people's smoke.

When the Environmental Protection Agency and the Centers for Disease Control published reports that over 3,500 nonsmokers died each year from cancers caused by passive smoking, this was new and strong ammunition for activists. The pro-tobacco people were maiming and destroying even those they hadn't hooked. Organizations, particularly those in California, working for nonsmokers' rights educated the public and mounted effective campaigns to limit smoking in the workplace, public areas, airplanes, hospitals, and restaurants. They were constantly supplied with ammunition. An increasing number of studies showed that children exposed to ambient smoke developed more frequent respiratory infections, risked having their lungs permanently scarred, and were at increased risk of developing lung cancer later in life. Subsequent surveys showed that not only lung cancer, but increased numbers of cases of cardiovascular diseases occurred in nonsmokers chronically exposed to somebody else's smoke. And more evidence appeared, showing that—to a lesser degree than if they themselves smoked—nonsmoking pregnant women whose husbands smoked had more complicated pregnancies, and their newborn babies were more liable to neonatal diseases.

Particularly shocking was that nicotine's by-product, cotinine, was found not only in the urine of breast-fed infants of cigarette-smoking mothers, but also in that of infants of nonsmoking mothers whose husbands smoked.

A landmark was achieved by Californians for Non-Smokers' Rights (now called Americans for Non-Smokers' Rights) along with ASH and DOC (Action for Smoking and Health, and Doctors Ought to Care). Their successful campaign for laws restricting smoking in specific areas such as public buildings and the workplace have since been adopted in many cities and states. Probably the most impressive, far-reaching victory was in San Francisco where, in 1980, in spite of the millions spent by the tobacco industry to defeat it, a referendum restricting smoking in the workplace was passed.

In light of such successes, and in response to a rising tide of concern, in January 1987, New York mayor Ed Koch and several members of the City Council initiated a proposal limiting public smoking. Hearings were held at City Hall at which opponents—tobacco interests, restaurateurs, certain union officials, bowling alley operators—and proponents—health associations, physicians, patients—testified.

Months before, I had been asked by Tony Schwartz, that extraordinary "Mogul of the Media," to join him and a few volunteers to form a group to rally New Yorkers behind the mayor's proposal. Tony's strong antismoking sentiments stemmed from his close friendship with Ken McFeely, a former head of the Police Benevolent Association, who had been a heavy smoker and was dying of lung cancer.

The four of us—Tony; Edith Everett, a financial expert; Chris Godek, deputy commissioner for communications for New York's fire department; and me—called ourselves People for a Smoke-Free Indoors.

We met regularly at Tony's remarkable studio, the walls of which are lined with hundreds of his tapes, awards, and trophies. Scattered everywhere were signed photos from Lyndon Johnson, Jimmy Carter, senators Ted Kennedy and Abraham Ribicoff, and other elected officials whom he had helped with his effective, often provocative radio and TV spots. Although our group was tiny, we felt that we could use what Tony called guerrilla tactics —shaming officials into action. One of Tony's most effective spots extracted remarks from a speech by Mayor Koch in which he justified closing gay bathhouses to slow the AIDS epidemic. In high decibels, Koch was heard saying that bathhouses were "selling death and we don't want this to go on."

Tony's commercial asked: "But I wonder, Mayor Koch, did you ever stop to think you can make the same statement about cigarette companies?"

Koch: "They are selling death."

"So why does the city allow cigarettes to be advertised on city bus shelters?"

Koch: "They are selling death."

"Why does the city allow cigarettes to be advertised on public property?"

Koch: "They are selling death."

"Why does the city allow cigarettes to be advertised on the city's radio stations' guides?"

Koch: "They are selling death."

"Why does the city allow cigarettes to be advertised on subway trains, buses and city-licensed cabs?"

Koch: "They are selling death."

"Mayor Koch, cigarette companies are selling death, and like you, we don't want them to go on."

To support the ordinance, I appeared as our group's representative at a hearing chaired by Joseph Califano, Jr., the secretary of health, education, and welfare under President Carter.

As expected, the tobacco companies raised specters: Such an ordinance would cause restaurants to fail. Their customers would not appear; the ordinance would pit smoker against nonsmoker; it would be extremely expensive to enforce and difficult for the city to monitor.

We were prepared for these and told the Council that although these same objections had been raised elsewhere, the predicted consequences had not come to pass. In fact, some restaurants had *increased* their business because parents now felt free to take their children with them without worrying. Also, the no-smoking rules were found to be virtually self-enforcing and inexpensive to monitor; and there had been very few conflicts between smokers and nonsmokers.

Some smokers organized groups to campaign against what they felt was abridging "smokers' rights." We said: "We are not against smokers—alas, some of our best friends smoke—we are against having to breathe their smoke. When a conflict arises between the right to smoke and the right to breathe fresh air, the latter must always prevail."

As an advocate for the ordinance, I was asked to debate Paul Screvane on several occasions. Screvane, a former head of the New York City Council, was chairman of an organization called the Committee for Common Courtesy. Its theme: All one had to do when someone nearby was smoking was to ask the smoker to stop. Screvane testified. Secretary Califano asked him point-blank: "Do you think smoking causes lung cancer, Mr. Screvane?" To which Screvane replied: "I don't know. I'm not a doctor."

In each confrontation before various organizations, chambers of commerce, labor groups, on television, I began by saying that if Mr. Screvane did not believe that smoking caused cancer, there was no point in continuing the discussion. It was like trying to talk geography with someone who believes the world is flat. During the time we shared the podium, Screvane would chain-smoke —until one chairman said: "Would *you* have the courtesy to stop smoking, please."

On one occasion, Screvane said smilingly that if the "good doctor" was correct and if he, Screvane, were to develop lung cancer, he hoped I would take care of him. I said that if he quit, this probably would never happen; but if I did operate on his lungs, I would find an ashtray.

Fortunately, radio station WMCA was willing to play the commercials that Tony had made; most of the other stations were reluctant to do so for fear of reprisals by tobacco interests withdrawing beer and food commercials.

Probably the most effective radio spot was one made by Tony's friend Ken McFeely, former head of the Patrolmen's Benevolent Association. Under Tony's direction, this leading, tough police officer made radio and TV spots in which he described tearfully what cigarettes had done to him and his family. Tony took a particularly effective section of tape and put it on to a telephone answering number; as many as three thousand callers a day were made to hear Ken, in a tremulous voice, make his plea. A special segment was played over police patrol-car radios throughout the city.

My name is Ken McFeely. Right now I am living under a death sentence. The doctors tell me that I have maybe five or six weeks to go because I have lung cancer caused by smoking.

You face more danger with the twenty cigarettes that are in your pocket than any six bullets in somebody's gun. Cigarettes are a time bomb that you plant in your own life that explodes twenty or thirty years later; and you know something, you can stop it if you stop smoking now.

The danger that threatened my life as a policeman was sitting in that radio car and lighting up that cigarette. I am forty-seven years old and I'll never see forty-eight.

When I met Ken, he was clearly deteriorating, and he died a few months later, killed not by criminals but by cigarettes.

Tony made an audiovisual record of the various stages in the progression of Ken's lung cancer; it concluded with Ken's funeral, attended by many uniformed policemen. The videotape, *If You Love Someone Who Smokes,* with its heart-tearing message, is a most persuasive document.

On May 16, 1989, the New York City Council voted the proposed ordinance into law—and, as we anticipated, none of its opponents' dire predictions came to pass. What is more, because smokers, instead of lighting up any place at any time, had to think about where they could do so now, many decided to quit—yet another example of the value of breaking the ingrained, customary pattern that helps keep smokers addicted.

By no means was the fight over. Cigarette companies still handed out free cigarettes in New York streets to anyone, including children. A startling fact emerged: Of the three thousand to four thousand American children who light up for the first time each day, two hundred to two hundred fifty do so in New York City, and thus join thousands of adolescents who have already been launched on a lifetime, life-shortening addiction. This had to stop. Hearings were scheduled in 1990 at City Hall at which evidence would be presented that showed how prevalent this practice was.

Once more I found myself testifying before the City Council. But my testimony was overshadowed by that of seven children, all below the age of twelve, who carried plastic bags each containing four to five packs of cigarettes. Each child testified that he or she had purchased these packages from vending machines at various sites around the city, the names of which they had written on the packages.

To their credit, the City Council ruled that the free handouts of cigarettes must stop, and later decided that cigarette vending machines should be limited to bars. Thus bartenders became responsible for restricting cigarette buying to those over sixteen, much as they are supposed to restrict drinking to those over twenty-one.

Clearly, the tide was turning against the amoral behavior of cigarette manufacturers. The same spirit that persuaded universities to divest themselves of stock in South African companies as long as apartheid was in force was applied to tobacco companies. One of our group, Edith Everett, a board member of the City University of New York, asked some of us to testify before the board. Subsequently, CUNY rid itself of tobacco stocks in university portfolios. Harvard, Columbia, and Johns Hopkins universities have also done so, and more are following suit.

Like surgeons general in the past, the new surgeon general, Dr. C. Everett Koop, fearlessly decried cigarette smoking as a major health hazard and an addiction. His successor, Dr. Antonia Novello, has continued this doctrine.

From City Hall to the halls of Congress. In 1990, I was asked to appear again before a congressional subcommittee headed by Henry Waxman of California. The purpose of the hearing was again to strengthen the warnings on cigarette packages and in advertisements; these warnings were still too mild and inconspicuous. A witness from Canada was most impressive, describing how Canadian health warnings took up 20 percent of the cigarette-pack space and a similar amount in advertisements. Since these large warnings were initiated in January of that year, smoking in Canada had fallen 12 percent.

My presentation took the usual form. I described the tragedies I saw every day at my hospital, and the impact that smoking had on the health of children in particular. When the formal presentations ended, one of our group whispered to me that one of the less sympathetic congressmen, Dr. J. Roy Rowland, of Georgia, was a doctor. He had expressed concern about jobs in the tobacco industry.

Dr. Cahan: Mr. Rowland, I understand you are a physician; is that true?

Mr. Rowland: That is true.

Dr. Cahan: Do you think smoking causes lung cancer?

[After a pause:] *Mr. Rowland:* Absolutely. I am supposed to be asking the questions, not you.

Dr. Cahan: One worries about things you feel so persuaded by

. . . that you may not want to talk freely about. Senator Richard Russell of Georgia, and his brother, Robert Russell—

Mr. Rowland: I am very familiar with Robert Russell.

Dr. Cahan: Both died of lung cancer.

Mr. Rowland: That is not the question I asked.

Dr. Cahan: Let me answer the question you are asking. Would
this be a concern . . . if because of this activity . . . people
were laid off from cigarette companies because the sales began
to fall? . . .

Mr. Rowland: I am concerned about people having jobs in the
district I represent.

Dr. Cahan: Are [we] talking in those terms? Are we concerned
about the poor people in Colombia being laid off because of the
lack of demand for cocaine?

Mr. Rowland: Are you doing anything to promote attention to the
fact that there may be jobs lost? You mentioned earlier in your
statement, you said let us not forget the human element in this.
That is a human element.

Dr. Cahan: The human element has to be balanced against other
human elements.

Mr. Rowland: Right. It does need to be balanced.

Dr. Cahan: You and I have seen too many lives destroyed by
[smoking] to think about . . . the fine point . . . whether
somebody's job is in jeopardy. That is a political statement . . .

Mr. Rowland: I don't debate the issue about the health hazards of
tobacco.

Dr. Cahan: I think your higher interest, the Hippocratic oath, is
to do no harm. As a physician to a physician, you and I are
both trying to keep people well and alive. That is our prime
consideration. I sympathize with the tobacco farmers . . . [but]
you and I are devoted to keeping people well.

Some months later, Willard DaSilva, a lawyer representing the
father of a six-year-old son in a custody case, called. He remembered my op-ed piece about child abuse through secondhand
smoke.

The father had custody of the child and the mother was suing
to regain custody. The father claimed that he had quit smoking
the year before to protect his child. The mother, however, continued to smoke a pack and a half a day and lived with her parents,
each of whom smoked heavily. I agreed to testify, and said that a

child's home would be a refuge, a haven, not a hazard. To rear a child in a smoke-laden environment is not unlike living in an asbestos-lined house or one built on radioactive soil. A child does not have to be beaten and bruised to be abused.

Mr. DaSilva believed that this was the first time that smoking had been raised as an issue in a custody case. The judge (himself a heavy smoker) decided in favor of the mother on the basis of other, strong, mitigating circumstances. Nevertheless, he acknowledged that this issue, like alcohol consumption, should be considered when measuring the suitability of a household environment in future custody cases.

Then, within months of each other, two great entertainers died of cigarette-caused diseases: Sammy Davis, Jr., and Sarah Vaughan. Both were symbols of the precipitous rise in cigarette-related deaths in the black community, a fact that a former resident of mine, Dr. Harold Freeman, chief surgeon of Harlem Hospital and past president of the American Cancer Society, has often stressed at hearings on the hazards of tobacco use.

The tobacco interests fund organizations such as the NAACP and the Dance Theater of Harlem, and also advertise heavily in black magazines and newspapers. Therefore, when I met a representative of *Essence,* a premier black magazine, I asked her whether in light of the recent deaths of Davis and Vaughan, *Essence* would consider publishing a strong piece about the rise in smoking-produced diseases in the black community. Such frightening statistics and sad deaths, when added to those of Nat "King" Cole, Johnny Hartman, and others, might persuade the magazine's editor of its value to the magazine's readership. I was certain that prominent black leaders would be available for interviews, including Dr. Louis Sullivan, the secretary of health and human services; Dr. Harold Freeman, chief of surgery at Harlem Hospital; Dr. Lasalle Leffal, Jr., professor and chairman of the department of surgery at Howard University Medical School in Washington; and the Reverend Calvin Butts of the Abyssinian Baptist Church, who fought tobacco-advertising billboards, particularly those near schools, by painting over them. Such an article would be a real coup for the magazine and would prove its independence and dedication to its readers.

The lady from *Essence* looked thoughtful for a few minutes, then shook her head sadly and said that the magazine so needed revenue, they didn't dare alienate tobacco companies, which might withdraw their ads. So much for cigarette companies, who tout "freedom of speech."

Pat Reynolds, the grandson of the founder of R. J. Reynolds, has become a staunch antitobacco advocate and, in his radio and TV appearances, talks bluntly. "My grandfather, R. J. Reynolds, the founder of the company, chewed tobacco and died of cancer. My father, R. J. Reynolds, Jr., smoked and died of emphysema. My mother smoked and had both emphysema and cancer. My two aunts have emphysema and cancer, and my three older brothers have emphysema, all of whom smoked."

It is not inconceivable that the Tobco executives might be made to feel like pariahs as the public reacts with indignation to their greed and chicanery.

It worked in Philadelphia, where R. J. Reynolds wanted to launch its campaign for its Uptown cigarette. However, when Reynolds announced its intention to base the launch in the black districts of Philadelphia, there were outcries. Uptown cigarettes were taken off the market.

In 1954, Sisi and I had attended the congressional hearings of Senator Joseph McCarthy as guests of Senator Henry (Scoop) Jackson of the State of Washington, a member of the panel. There was one particularly memorable moment when McCarthy slandered a young lawyer who was a member of lawyer Joseph Welch's firm in Boston. Welch, a dignified gentleman of the old school, listened patiently while McCarthy said that this young lawyer had been on the staff of a liberal newspaper while he was a student—an accusation that in McCarthyite days was tantamount to killing his reputation. Welch stood up and, with tears in his eyes, stared at McCarthy and said: "Have you no sense of *decency,* sir?" It was said by many that this was the beginning of the tide against McCarthy that finally drowned him.

How apt to apply Welch's phrase to tobacco executives and marketers who, although denying it, know full well how destructive their products are. Where, indeed, is their sense of decency, and how can they sleep at night knowing that they are personally responsible for causing so much pain and death?

At times I grew weary of trying to help put out a forest fire with a bucket; of extinguishing a burning building by spitting at it; of wanting to reduce a plague by stamping on it. For it is an epidemic, no doubt about it. The magazine *M* recently reported that in 1989, the dollar value of sales of antismoking products in

American grocery stores alone was $604,000; of cigarettes, $6,124,348,000.

A favorite ploy of those who've amassed great wealth by amoral or antisocial, inhuman means, is to become visibly philanthropic so that one's past is laundered by showers of cash. In their quest for respectability, they will be abetted by those who receive their largesse and are willing to close their eyes to the sources of the donations.

One expression of this cynical behavior begins with an article in *The New York Times* in January 1989 that stated that brothers Lawrence and Preston Robert Tisch had given $30 million to New York University, in gratitude for which NYU was renaming its university hospital after them. The article mentioned that the Tisch brothers were chairman and chief executive officer, respectively, of Loews Corporation, which owns insurance companies, real estate, and so on. However, no mention was made of the fact that Loews also owned P. Lorillard Tobacco Company, makers of Kent, Newport, True, and Winston cigarettes. This corporate member of the Loews "family" creates its greatest cash flow, accounting in some years for 60 percent of their profits. For twenty years, it was also the major source of the Tisches' fortune.

When I read this, my blood pressure moved into the danger range. Imagine naming a *hospital* after those who have been, and still are, in a business that maims and kills thousands of Americans and millions of others over the years!

I wrote to ex-congressman John Brademas, then president of New York University, who was a friend.

> Surely such an action raises questions as to the propriety of accepting funds from individuals whose wealth was, and is being, amassed at the expense of our country's health. My guess is that at least one out of six adult patients at University Hospital are there because they smoked. . . .
>
> This is not a personal diatribe against the Tisches. However, they are part of a system that enables those responsible for holocaust-sized slaughter to use cynical means to buy respectability. By association, those who accept their gifts, are tainted as well.

In reply, John Brademas said:

> We at New York University are deeply grateful to the Tisch family for this extraordinary gift and we are proud to have the name of Tisch on our hospital.

It would be wrong for the University knowingly to accept funds as the result of unlawful activities. This is not, of course, true of the instant case nor is your representation accurate that this gift is from "tobacco interests." Loews Corporation—and I am a director —is also an insurance, watch, hotel and shipping business and Lawrence A. Tish as you know is president and chief executive officer of CBS.

On February 28, 1989, I wrote back:

I do not intend to discuss the ethical question as to the morality of accepting huge donations from those engaged in questionable practices. What I feel is unequivocal, however, is that NYU's gratitude and affection for the Tisches has blinded it to the irony of naming NYU's hospital after two executives with a long and close relationship with cigarette manufacturing. As a fellow Loews board member, you know that it owns 100% of P. Lorillard Company. As Lorillard has 8% of the cigarette market, it probably contributes to some 31,000 of the 391,000 cigarette smoking–related deaths annually in this country.

You state that NYU would only accept donations only from legal sources. As an academic, as well as a former Congressman, you must realize that "legal" does not always stand for moral. In this case, there is no escaping the fact that, for profit, Lorillard and other tobacco giants are the chief cause of preventable deaths in America. . . .

If the Tisches are as public spirited as you suggest and sincerely interested in the health and welfare of the community, they could: 1) discontinue Loews cigarette business; and 2) subsidize youth antismoking campaigns. In terms of good being done for the largest numbers, these measures would be unmatched.

And, to keep this from being an abstract, academic argument:

Let me suggest that you visit your University Hospital's floors, or for that matter any hospital's floors, and see at first hand as physicians do, the enormous dimensions of the havoc created by cigarette smoking. Perhaps it would also bring home to you the sad travesty of one of Lorillard's slogans: "Alive with pleasure."

To which Brademas answered on March 6, 1989:

Thanks for your further letter. Apparently we must agree to disagree.

Needless to say, NYU went ahead and named it the Tisch Hospital.

Larry White, in an article he wrote for *Newsday*, said that it was "unique in the history of medical philanthropy that donors gave not only the hospital but the patients as well."

To the *Daily News*, I said, in May 1989: "Naming a hospital after tobacco men is just too ironic. Around town, the University Hospital is becoming known as Lorillard General." Tony Schwartz put on a radio spot that concluded, "So keep on smoking those cancer Newports. The Tisches have a hospital bed waiting for you."

My correspondence with John Brademas was published in its entirety in the now defunct New York journal *Seven Days*. A journalist with wide readership wrote:

11 May 1989

Dear Bill:

Thanks so much for your letter and the information on the Tisch brothers. The first thing that comes to mind is that the nurses could double as cigarette girls (short skirts of course), and stop by each room twice a day.

Bill, we live in a screwed up world and I have come to the conclusion that it is not easy to change it. . . .

Love and kisses,
Art [Buchwald]

Hoping that I could raise the indignation of University Hospital's medical staff, I sent each department head and trustee a letter. To the doctors I wrote:

Dear Doctor (name):

Your hospital is being renamed after the Tisch brothers as a tribute to their philanthropy and services to New York University. What is rarely mentioned in news releases and, therefore probably not appreciated by your staff, is that Lawrence and Preston Tisch are, respectively, Chairman of the Board, and President and co-CEO of Loews Corporation that, besides its interest in real estate, insurance, hotels, etc., owns 100% of P. Lorillard Tobacco Company. Lorillard makes Old Gold, Kent, True, Satin and Newport cigarettes. The Tischs have benefitted enormously from their 20-year association with it.

As Lorillard has an 8% share of the cigarette market, it is probably responsible for some 31,000 of the 390,000 Americans who die each year from tobacco use (or for 600,000 of the 8 million tobacco-related deaths since the first Surgeon General's report in 1964).

The ethics of accepting funds from such dubious sources is open to question ("taking the Devil's money to do the Lord's work"). However, it is indisputably ironic to name a major *medical* facility after those whose business lures minors, minorities and young women into a lifetime addiction and to premature death. To justify doing so by saying that these gifts are from "legal" sources is to avoid its moral implications. Perhaps if those who rationalize this way were to make rounds at University, or any other hospital, they would see ample evidence of the havoc created by smoking. It would also be apparent what a grim joke it is for Lorillard to use the slogan "Alive With Pleasure."

This might appear to be gratuitous advice from a non-staff member but, as a physician, I deeply resent replacing University Hospital's time-honored name with one that is tainted by cigarette manufacturers. The decision to do so can be reversed if you and your colleagues (and patients) were to make your feelings known to NYU's President and Board of Trustees. By so doing, such a principled act would not only be admired by your medical colleagues, it would also serve as a model of ethical behavior for others who may, one day, be faced with such an ill-conceived idea.

On April 14, 1989, a reply arrived from Dr. Joseph Ransohoff, professor and chairman, department of neurosurgery, NYU-Bellevue Medical Center. Dr. Ransohoff believed my allegations to be "inappropriate," that the financial interests of the "Tish family," he said, was a "matter of historical interest." He saw the renaming of the hospital as a "real honor." (I did, too—but what was being honored?) And he referred to situations at Johns Hopkins and Peter Bent Brigham as similar.

He thought my letter might be well meaning but urged me to desist. I did not.

Dear Doctor Ransohoff:

It is difficult to understand how you, a neurosurgeon, who must see many patients with brain metastases from cigarette-caused lung cancers, can feel it is an "honor" to name your hospital after those responsible for such tragedies, among many others.

Lest you continue to labor under the illusion that tobacco business is just "some aspect of their (Tishs) family's financial interests", I am enclosing a portion of Loews' 1988 financial statement that speaks for itself. The Tishs have been associated with Lorillard for over 20 years and, undoubtedly, tobacco has been, and *still is,* a major source of their wealth.

Although you do not find it inappropriate and tasteless to name a major health facility after those in a health-destructive business, such irony is not lost on other physicians and the public who see in it yet another example of the cynical use of tobacco interests buying respectability and immortality. Some speculate as to how many additional Tisch millions will be needed to change NYU's name as well. Sadly, one now hears your fine institution being referred to as "Lorillard General".

In reply to some other statements in your letter:

1. Johns Hopkins and Peter Bent Brigham, your examples of hospitals named after wealthy donors, were merchants. In their day, neither trafficked in drugs, unlike their 20th century counterparts in [the] tobacco business, who thrive on selling addictive, lethal products.

2. As a physician devoted to preventing disease, I am unable, as apparently you are, to absolve and ennoble those whose business has been, and still is, responsible for so much havoc. Consequently, I will not "desist" as you suggest I do, in publicizing the Tisch–tobacco connection, hoping thereby, to restore University Hospital's prestigious name.

3. "TISCH" is spelled with a "c." Do your hospital's *No Smoking* signs spell it correctly?

Sincerely yours,
William G. Cahan, M.D.

It is such common knowledge that Tobcos so cynically market their lethal products that one wonders what code of ethics those institutions devoted to education, medicine, and the arts can possibly obey to justify accepting funds from companies that continue to kill artists (some of whose works make up the beneficiaries' programs), leaving music unwritten, songs unsung, dances unseen, and to kill educators and doctors, leaving many untaught or unhealed.

Would they accept funds from Saddam Hussein, Qadaffi, or crack dealers? Would a church show its gratitude by putting in a stained-glass window featuring the generous madam of a brothel if she were willing to give enough money? It would seem that cash has been elevated from king to emperor and "accepting the devil's money to do the lord's work" has not only become rampant but has reached new depths of cynicism.

How much money can atone for the mass slaughter and the diabolical measures used to perpetuate smoking? Is the Tisch brothers' $30 million gift to NYU a large enough trade-off for the 18,000 Americans that Lorillard products kill every year? Are Philip Morris's funds given to cultural and charitable causes enough to exculpate them from their killing over 160,000 Americans and countless others around the world? Can these be forgotten any more than the bitter memories of Auschwitz and Buchenwald can be erased by the Berlin Symphony Orchestra playing Beethoven's Ninth Symphony?

As one newspaper put it: "Charitable organizations are in a precarious position, dependent on the good will of their donors. It would be a shame if this dependence prevents them from expressing their rightful moral choice of whose money to accept or refuse." The same article says that Philip Morris is admired for its generosity towards minority business and cultural organizations. But the company also markets extensively to minority groups: "We shudder at the perverse logic that prompts a company to donate millions of dollars for education and health programs for disadvantaged people—and then targets the same groups for its addictive and health-impairing products."

And so the battle goes on, and I cannot for the life of me—or, more to the point, of others—keep myself from being in the smoke and fire of it.

❖

CHAPTER XXXIV

On a Collision Course with Cancer

In a lifetime devoted to persuading people to quit smoking, I've had a fair share of triumphs. Probably some of this success is, in part, attributable to being a voice of authority: a white-haired lung-cancer surgeon, complete with long, white coat, working in a world-class cancer hospital. This carries weight and any pronouncement I make seems to come from on high. I assume the composite image of clergyman, doctor, teacher, and parent.

As a result, I'm approached by those who either want to give up smoking themselves, or who want someone close to them to quit. I invite smokers to my office to discuss possible approaches, and begin by reassuring them that I am aware of how powerful nicotine addiction is; I tell them that the fact that they've come to see me is already a good sign. But two things are certain: In order to stop, one has to want to. *Badly.* The second is that one *can* do so. Curiously, some quit easily, saying all they needed was a doctor to tell them to do so. Most, however, are shackled by their addiction and have already struggled, sometimes hard and long, to free themselves.

I begin by taking patients' smoking history. When I ask at what age they began smoking, all go through a rather touching series of facial expressions. They begin by looking up and wearing a bemused smile as they probably recall their first, surreptitious, forbidden smoke. Seconds later, their smile becomes a frown and their eyebrows dip as they stare into the future and envisage the specter of what it would be like to be "hit by cancer." But at some point, their eyes take on a look of panic as they think of what it would be like to give up their beloved cigarettes. Some are innately risk-takers; they seem bent on self-destruction and feel helpless to extricate themselves. Even so, they must be told it can be done.

I ask more questions: Has anyone in the family had lung cancer? What exposure have they had in a lifetime to secondhand smoke, either at home or in the workplace? Both of these could increase their risk. Then I ask if they have a "cigarette cough" and when they had their last chest X ray. Some say they cough; others say they don't; all know what I mean by a "cigarette cough": one that is usually dry and hacking and first appears following the early morning "wake-up" cigarette. In some, the cough produces white spittle. During the day, the cough recurs and becomes such a part of life that they do not realize they have it unless someone calls their attention to it.

Even though some have not begun to cough, I describe to them what often happens to those that do: The cough becomes more frequent, the white spittle gradually turns into thick yellow sputum. The more insistent the cough, the more sputum is raised until, one day, it is streaked with bright red: blood. I explain that this progression of coughing from dry to producing white to yellow to red reflects the changes going on in the lining of the windpipe as it goes through various stages before it finally becomes cancerous.

For completeness, I run through a laundry list of established, sometimes successful systems for quitting: Smokenders, hypnosis, acupuncture, audio and visual antismoking tapes (many of which I have at hand and let them borrow). We talk about how to break the well-grooved ritual, the accustomed pattern; for example, instead of lighting the first "wake-up" cigarette in the morning, do something different—take a shower or a short walk.

Whatever method is decided upon must be adhered to religiously for the first three or four weeks, during which they must avoid the land mines, situations in which they are accustomed to light up: bars and social occasions, getting down to work by lighting up. To this end, it has been recommended that a "quit smoking resolution" be instituted at the beginning of a holiday, or to avoid the tensions that business situations can produce.

As substitutes for oral gratification, I suggest chewing gum, celery stalks, pacifiers, pseudo cigarettes (and even their thumbs). Some find cold showers (shades of advice to young men for their unrequited passion), physical exercise, meditation, or drinking lots of water can overcome the acute urge.

Nicotine chewing gum * has helped many quit who have "tried everything" and failed. By chewing a piece slowly each time the desire to smoke occurs, enough nicotine is absorbed through the mucous membranes of the mouth to give the smoker the accustomed nicotine high that a cigarette would have produced. Those who have used this method—and the gum is a prescription drug—are advised not to take coffee, alcohol, or carbonated beverages immediately beforehand, as these reduce its effectiveness.

Usually, it takes a minimum of two or three months before those using gum can wean themselves from it. Some continue using it for over a year or more, obviously addicted to the nicotine in it. However, at least they are not exposed to the more lethal element of the smoke itself. Many who have succeeded this way attribute their doing so to the gum providing a much softer landing than quitting cold turkey. Although not reducing total addiction to nicotine, the gum helps reduce the often painful acute withdrawal symptoms that heavy smokers have to endure and breaks the accustomed ritual—taking out a pack, selecting a cigarette, lighting it, inhaling and exhaling smoke.

Scare tactics—specimens of lung cancers or photographs of people in the last stages of cancer—used to be persuasive. These days, however, they are less so because their shock effect has been blunted by the public's many exposures to gory TV and movie images.

Women in particular are apprehensive, as we've seen, about gaining weight and, about three out of four do add five to ten pounds in the first year after quitting. However, long-term weight gain is not inevitable, and some even lose weight because concurrently they change their life-styles, are careful about their diet, and exercise regularly.

To those who gain weight, I reassure them that once they get over the most pressing problem, we will deal with their weight problem. I'd rather a woman were a slightly plump live lady than a thin corpse. You can't be too thin or too rich, says the old slogan. But you can be too dead.

---

* Recently, a nicotine-containing skin patch has been devised that might be even more effective—and far less difficult to stomach than the gum. To be of *lasting* benefit, all methods need supplemental psychological support as well to override those later moments when the temptation to cave in is strongest.

When all else fails, some inveterate smokers have success using a technique in which a small intravenous dose of pentothal is given to enhance the patient's suggestibility to commands given by the psychiatrist administering it.

Usually, I wind up our session by saying, "I'll take quitting any way it comes. Most important, don't be discouraged if at first you don't succeed. Although I think the best way to quit is cold turkey, everyone will find their own way of doing so." I tell them that should they fail, they should not think of it as a sign of moral weakness or lack of character or discipline.

Just before leaving, some, as a gesture of resolution, reach in a pocket and hand me a pack, claiming it is the last one. I ask each one to sign and date it. I mail them the signed pack (empty) one year later and, if they have been successful, send them a gift: a navy blue tie for men, a scarf for women, dotted with tiny red no-smoking logos. One letter in response:

San Francisco—Aug. 8/91
   Didn't discover until very recently who sent me the splendid "no smoking" tie which I flaunt shamelessly in front of all bartenders, B-girls and other sinners. However, a sad fact about human beings considered as shrewd observers is that nobody notices!
                                        Gratefully,
                                        Alistair Cooke

With so much at stake, I explore new ways to help smokers quit. Some I take on a walk on MSK's fifteenth floor, which is occupied almost entirely by lung cancer patients, several of whom are walking the corridors, attached to their tubes and the containers used to drain their chests. Some smokers are so affected by this experience that it haunts them enough to quit. In a letter to an inveterate smoker, I described in detail a lung-cancer operation from beginning to end, as if making a formal operative report. I concluded by saying: "Norman—don't let your name be in the space left for that of the patient." It worked.

Another method I borrowed from the buddy system used by Alcoholics Anonymous: I introduced two women nicomaniacs (two to three packs per day), each of whom had tried a variety of methods but failed. The two women were instructed to call each other anytime they felt they were going to cave in and *had* to smoke. After at least a dozen phone calls back and forth for the first few months, both have gone over three years without a relapse.

On a brighter note, I have become a clearinghouse for those who have been able to quit and cannot wait to say how they did so. Averell Harriman told me that when he consulted his physician about a chronic cough, the physician told him it was from smoking and added: "But I don't think you have guts enough to quit." That did it. Averell quit then and there and lived to be ninety-four.

Other collector's items:

1. "If my play is a success on opening night, I'll stop." It was, and Howard Teichman never smoked again after the first performance of *The Solid Gold Cadillac*.
2. "I put a dollar in the jar every day that I feel the urge to buy a pack and buy my wife a present when it's full."
3. "I think of my friend Jill and of her last days with lung cancer each time I reach for a butt."
4. "Just as I'm about to light up, I hear your voice."
5. "My little granddaughter, age five, crawled onto my lap and said, 'Grandpa, please don't smoke; I don't want you to die.' "
6. "When I play tennis, jog, run, or even climb a flight of stairs, I get so winded I realize I'd better change."
7. "My husband's lung cancer [or larynx cancer, or emphysema, or heart disease] forced him to quit so I thought it only fair to do likewise."
8. "One day I hated myself for being hooked by such a puny weed."
9. "I had a revelation: I dreamed I was dying—and that did it."
10. "I woke up one morning and saw and smelled my unemptied ashtray."
11. "My yellow fingers, coated tongue, bad breath, burned holes in my clothes, tablecloths, and tabletops finally got to me."
12. "If the Americans beat the Russians in the 1984 Olympics, I'll quit." (They did, and he did.)

To the never-ending list of novel ways to desist, I add one theory based on the idea that, since smoking is a pleasure, another pleasure is needed to substitute for it. The most likely substitute: sex. Wow. Just think: It might work—for those who were smoking one to two packs a day, such a scheme could be so exhausting that by evening, they'd be too weak to strike a match.

CHAPTER XXXV

Compassion

Barbara Bush once referred me to a touching article in *The New York Times Magazine:* "The Victors . . . Patients Who Conquer Cancer," by Curtis Bill Pepper. It told the story of a young medical student with acute leukemia who believed that he was dying. He said:

> One evening, something tremendous happened. A young man came into my room; he had blond curly hair and was sort of smiling. I didn't know who he was. I *think* he was a resident but wasn't assigned to my case. He came over, grabbed my hand and said, "Don't give up. You have a curable disease." *Nobody* had said that to me. They were all taking care of this and that, but nobody told me I had a chance. This gave me the drive to go through that first period.

Some time before, I had written in my journal: "What a difference in personalities among residents! One holds a dying boy in his arms, comforting him with words of closeness; the other tells the nurse not to wake him up as the death forms were already signed."

Could this latter behavior be symbolic, another example of what seems to be a deteriorating patient-physician relationship? Have physicians become so involved and interested in the mechanics or the measures used to care *for* patients, that they forget to care *about* them?

This extra quality of individual, affectionate care seems to be in short supply with some of today's physicians. It saddens me to hear friends describe the breakdown of rapport with their physicians and how unapproachable and unavailable some physicians are to discuss their conditions with them. Just why some physicians distance themselves and remain callous, glacial, unsympathetic, when sympathy is so evidently needed, can only be guessed at. Perhaps those whose patients have advanced cancer feel frustrated and guilt-ridden at having failed as healers. I've heard some rationalize such aridity by saying that nonprofessional duties are so demanding that they would be emotionally burned out were they to surrender themselves unconditionally to patients. It is unfortunate that while they husband their energies, common courtesy, graciousness and warmth are extinguished.

Probably one of the most unfeeling expressions of this occurs in the case of those patients who are terminally ill and whose physicians are making rounds. These patients *thirst* for understanding. Some physicians are content merely to wave at them from the doorway and quickly move on, looking, as relatives have often said to me, as if they wore DO NOT DISTURB signs around their necks, or patientproof vests.

I teach residents to enter patients' rooms, find some encouraging words and, most important, *listen*. Individuals who are in advanced stages of dying yearn for someone with whom they can share their fears about pain or the loss of dignity, or the unknowns of death. It is so easy to brighten their last moments by simple gestures.

In all fairness, with all the criticism leveled at my profession, there is no question that the life of today's physicians is not an easy one. As never before, they are burdened by enormous amounts of bureaucratic demands that can sap the energy and strain the patience of even the most dedicated. An editorial in *The New York Times:* "Frustrated doctors are drowning in paper work. Medical groups say that every visit to the doctor generates at least ten pieces of paper. The American Medical Association estimates that the average doctor's office devotes 80 hours a month to pushing paper."

In addition, today's highly litigious climate makes many physicians feel that today's patients are more contentious and demanding and that for fear of malpractice suits, the physician must sacrifice principle and practice "defensive" medicine, ordering expensive, often unnecessary tests to protect themselves.

Yet in spite of frustrations, vexations, and tedious chores, many physicians accept these as necessary evils and remain compassionate and courteous.

Stung by patients' repeated complaints and criticisms, physicians and their organizations are taking measures to heal themselves. In searching for causes of the worsening patient-physician relationship, they have found, for one thing, that medical schools' admissions committees have overemphasized the importance of scientific, rather than cultural courses in judging candidates' qualifications. Now philosophy, music, history, literature, and religion classes are given increased weight.

On the theory that compassion can be taught, medical-school curricula lately include courses that stress the intrinsic value of ethical and humane behavior. Students learn that if a physician cannot heal, he can at least comfort.

However, lest it be thought that today's physicians are unusually difficult to approach and deal with, let me go back a generation or so ago. I remember the surgical prima donnas of yesteryear, some of whom even dressed in stylish, often garish versions of operating caps and gowns. Not only were these doctors autocratic, dictatorlike, and short-tempered, but they would rant and roar in the operating room when displeased; when their low threshold of anger was crossed, they would flail about, loudly berating their assistants for minor infractions of technique. They would mercilessly blame them first and then dismiss them from the operating table. Some accompanied their tirades by rapping the assistant's knuckles with an instrument, or in high dudgeon would fling a malfunctioning instrument across the operating room, following it with a string of invectives.

Needless to say, the victims of such sharp discipline felt it to be the stuff of nightmares and were haunted by the feeling of inadequacy. Their futures, they thought, were in jeopardy. Most weathered these storms.

For some reason, these personalities and their outrageous outbursts were tolerated—possibly because they were unleashed at a time when the influence of the traditional German and Austrian *Geheimrat* school of teaching was still influential.

Geheimrat professors were godlike physicians whose pronouncements were never questioned and whose word was law. These lofty ones always had a cluster of lesser mortals following them everywhere, willing to suffer any indignities just to catch a crumb of wisdom from the master's lips.

At Memorial, displays of this sort were extremely rare.

Medical-school faculty members have been cautioned about taking a harsh, unsympathetic tone when using patients for demonstrations before students. For that matter, they are not to treat students like "ciphers" or to seem to teach them begrudgingly. No wonder that some of those who enter the study of medicine filled with ideals can become disenchanted or even become imbued with the bad manners and cynical attitudes of their mentors, to whom they look for guidance.★

Hospitals now post the "Patients' Bill of Rights," and have committees to hear the complaints of patients who feel they have been treated disrespectfully.

Unquestionably, no easy or immediate solution to this problem can be expected, composed as it is of so many influences and elements. Like democracy, medicine is constantly adjusting itself to the times and improving. What must not be lost sight of is that individuals should be respected and compassion should be the overriding force.

Has it become old-fashioned to care? Is it passé, anachronistic, unsophisticated, to be generous and affectionate, to love one's fellow man, friend or stranger, unabashedly?

The "sophisticates" are wrong in implying that it is maudlin, eye-wateringly boring, nauseatingly sweet, to hold someone's hand, to hug or grin, to distribute good mornings and thankyous, to open doors, hold elevators, answer calls promptly.

Believe me, affection and respect are there, waiting. There are some early signs of a renaissance of the good feeling and trust that for all too long have been buried under the other news.

Promises made—promises kept; the haves will help the havenots or the have-littles overcome suspicion and doubt. My guess is that you will see the frost melt rapidly as the world warms.

★ One of the by-products, painful to me, of this disturbing climate is the reduction in medical-school applications. In particular, gifted college students who were originally anxious to become physicians now think twice when faced with medicine's long educational process that, following four years of college, requires four years of med school and two to five years of postgraduate training. Then they have the expense of setting up an office, paying malpractice-insurance premiums, and so forth. All of this puts them in considerable debt before they have even seen their first private patient. No small wonder that many elect instead to study law or engineering. Yet, in spite of these deterrents, many young and old physicians remain dedicated to their ideals and accept these annoyances in return for the glorious rewards, both human and economic, of practicing medicine.

CHAPTER XXXVI

Look Good—Feel Better

Compassion in medicine, as I've suggested, can take various forms. When a woman whose spirit is in tatters following the news that she has cancer, is told that she must also undergo chemo and/or radiation therapy, she can become even more despondent. Although her physician tells her what to expect from treatments, she often worries more about the cosmetic results, even if temporary, than physically debilitating side effects. "Will I lose my hair?" "How will it affect my skin?"

While she is under treatment, her fears are often justified by her reflection in the mirror, as she sees an image that is not her own. Her concern is magnified by those around her, who are not always successful at hiding how disturbed they are by the marked change in her appearance. As a result of these shocks to her self-confidence and vanity, she feels as if she has lost control of herself. Although men, too, are traumatized by the change as they lose their hair, it probably cuts deeper in women.

Into this very disturbing situation, what can only be described as a master stroke of compassion was initiated by the Cosmetics, Toiletries, and Fragrances Association (CTFA). Their "Look Good—Feel Better" plan was to provide free cosmetics and consultation to women undergoing cancer therapy. Because of this extraordinary idea, Lane Adams, former vice president of the American Cancer Society, asked me to attend a meeting that the Cancer Society was holding with the CTFA. Lane thought my association with the fashion world through Grace might be of value to such a project. When the formal presentations had been made, Lane suggested that I say a few words. On such short notice, I told them of the Lipstick sign, the first sign of real recovery, and from then on became one of their advisers.

The inaugural trial took place on MSK's eighteenth floor, one occupied by breast-cancer patients who have recently had surgery and/or radiation and chemotherapy. In a small room with a one-way mirror, I observed six women patients. Although clearly interested in what lay ahead, they looked dispirited and barely seemed able to drag themselves into the room. The nurse seated them at a long table with individual makeup mirrors, beside which was a package containing a variety of cosmetics. An instructress from a major cosmetics firm began telling them the fine points of a makeover. As they followed her instructions, I was, within minutes, delighted and touched to hear them talking excitedly amongst themselves and even giggling. Thirty minutes later, they stood up and, each carrying her own bag of cosmetics, emerged from the room smiling, radiant, buoyant. They strode instead of shuffled and I heard one say, "Wait until *they* see me!" And, indeed, their visitors, instead of showing their usual concern and sympathy, were full of admiration. Such reactions in others generates still more confidence in patients. One woman told me that she felt she had rejoined the land of the living.

As part of the makeup program, instruction is also given by volunteer cosmetologists on the selection, shaping, and tinting of wigs, how to apply artificial eyelashes and brows, and the cosmetic value of properly tied bandanas.

The more I see of this program—more than one thousand women have participated at Memorial to date (20,000 nationwide) the more I know what a wonderful example of compassion in action it is.

CTFA made a documentary in which several women who are receiving radiation and/or chemotherapy are being made up by experts and instructed on how to wear wigs, turbans, etc., to beautify themselves even while undergoing the duress of their stringent treatments. The film and its valuable message is widely distributed throughout America with the help of the American Cancer Society and, along with a "Look Good—Feel Better" campaign, will be shown in Europe when the program is inaugurated there.

In the film, Judith Garden is seen first arranging flowers and then putting on makeup. Judith had been a very successful florist in New York City. When she retired, she used her expertise and connections in the flower business to amass a huge daily supply of fresh flowers (wholesale) for our hospital. She made sure that each patient on admission would receive a flower in a small round brown medicine bottle. Judith inspired Enid Haupt (a sister of Walter Annenberg) to give a donation large enough so that the interest from it would ensure that there always would be flowers at Memorial. Judy attracted many assistants, who were usually ladies of wealth and social distinction. They would begin their day by sorting out the daily supply of fresh flowers that were in the "flower shop" that had been specially built for this purpose. They would then put these flowers in old champagne bottles that all of us had contributed. With Judy at its head, this "army" pushed carts that looked like floats in the Rose Bowl Parade. With majestic hand gestures, Judy would indicate where the flowers would be placed. These ladies had probably never been bossed around like this before, but they adored Judy and felt they were on a mission to help beautify the hospital and add to the quality of its care. Judy was probably the first in any hospital to inaugurate classes for patients in flower arranging.

When Judy herself was admitted to MSK with advanced cancer, I would visit her every day in her flower-bedecked room and try to amuse her with tidbits of hospital gossip. Without fail, she was beautifully made up and, when she walked down the corridor, displaying her cosmetic splendor, her nurse told me that other women patients would come to their doorways and, seeing her, quickly return to their mirrors and begin making themselves up as well.

On one of my visits, Judy said to me, "Bill, this is the last lap." Before I could utter any expressions of reassurance, she added, "Let's cut out the bullshit; my only kidney is shutting down and that will be that." Indeed, that is just what happened. It was unique in my experience with dying patients that Judith instructed her nurse to keep her makeup intact even after she became comatose.

In her memory, a stand of trees will be planted along Sixty-seventh Street in front of the new Enid Haupt Clinic Building.

Experiences like these taught me that cosmetics, like laughter, can be therapeutic; and although applied on the surface, have a deeper significance. As I saw how little it takes to make such a vast difference—an eyeshadow, a touch of powder here, a little blush on the cheeks there—I recognized what an enormous morale booster it was and how it helps draw some of the sting from the dread of contemplated chemo- or radiation therapy.

And perhaps it did more. Recovery is aided by hope and pride and belief in the benign future. Perhaps by looking good and feeling better, some might even *do* better. As one patient put it: "You've got to have a few things to keep you going—faith, humor, and mascara."

She was right: Another beneficial influence that has been introduced to help improve the quality of life not only for those with cancer, but also those who have other debilitating illnesses, is humor. For years, I searched for a phrase that would neatly define the medical equivalent of "foxhole humor" and I found it in W. B. Yeats's poem "Lapis Lazuli": "Gaiety transfiguring all that dread."

Humor is a restorative, a holiday for the spirit. Laughter, which someone once called "sudden glory," is a tension reliever. Without question, a deft, light touch is a welcome distraction from worry and gloom and, if those who are distraught and burdened by despair, such as cancer patients, can be made to laugh or even smile for a moment, they feel that things can't be all that bad and that all is not lost.

I call it *risotherapy,* a made-up word. The prefix *riso* is borrowed from the risorius muscles that are attached to the corners of the mouth and act to draw them up when one smiles. The word *risible* uses the same prefix.

Humor helps generate a feeling of empathy, a bridge between people and, in this instance, between patient and physician: Those who laugh (or cry) together feel an automatic kinship. Patients are quick to appreciate a physician's efforts to use humor, a light touch, and recognize it as a gesture of affectionate care used to relax them. Not everyone can carry it off, requiring as it does a nicety of judgment to prevent it from being ill-timed or heavy-handed. Conceivably, some of humor's basic elements can be learned so that, one day, medical school curricula might have a course called "Risotherapy-A" taught by professors Allen—Woody and Steve.

Norman Cousins, in his book *Anatomy of an Illness* (Norton, 1979), describes what a beneficial effect he felt humor had on his illness by its restoring harmony to a discordant body system.

Recently, clinics using humor therapy have been established in various medical centers. Conceivably, these could complement the mood-elevating "Look Good, Feel Better" program, and perhaps paraphrase that slogan by saying "Smile (or Laugh), Feel Better."

In the operating room, a place of dread, I try to lighten patients' apprehension by telling them how great they look in the cap they are forced to wear there. I may also say just as they are about to be anesthesized: "Don't forget to dream only about me—and in Technicolor." Anthony says, "The anesthetist is so good that she will take you to the island of your choice."

One major caveat: I try to be sensitive to a truly somber situation, in which any attempt at being amusing would be more resented than appreciated. The old dictum "When in doubt, leave it out" must be kept in mind.

CHAPTER XXXVII

Grace Under Pressure

Writing of truth, beauty, compassion, and love brings me to Grace. She is all of those, and the juxtaposition of our two lives has often produced interesting effects on our careers.

At a fund-raising event for the psychiatric department of New York Hospital, we were asked to appear to discuss the topic, "Are Fashion and Medicine Two Different Worlds?" Using our marriage as a metaphor, we demonstrated how our careers reinforce each other, and that health and fashion are not incompatible. The talk ended with a showing of the "Look Good, Feel Better" tape as a graphic example.

Many of our joint appearances are seen as social—and raise questions and sometimes eyebrows.

After columnists record our appearances at business, professional, charitable, and social events, someone asks how Grace can do all that and look—and be—so good, and how I can function as a surgeon and still "go out so much." First, "so much" may amount to one to two times a week, and what the papers do not record is that I always leave my whereabouts with an answering service, drink only an occasional sip of wine, I leave no later than ten-thirty P.M., and need only four or five hours' sleep.

Perhaps I should be concerned about my public image, but not having been one seeking "the bubble reputation," as Mr. Shakespeare said, or striving for the "smile of the crowd," I decided ages ago that as long as I fulfill my obligations to patients, I can in good conscience enjoy life and its many delights. This style is not antithetical to achievement.

Recently, while dancing furiously at a friend's wedding, I stopped and asked my partner half-seriously: "Do you think that those watching are wondering if a cancer surgeon should be so carefree and rambunctious?" (Three of my patients were there.)

She said, "Nonsense. C'mon, let's dance!"

All of which leads me to confess unashamedly: I am a man-child. Those close to me say, a romantic disguised as a realist. Although I deal daily with the stark reality of cancer, it is alien to my nature to assume the lofty mien that some may feel is appropriate for someone in my calling.

From what has gone before in this book, it should come as no surprise that I share the sentiments Lewis Thomas expresses in "A Doctor's Love Letter to Women:

> *I am, in short, swept off my feet by women, and I do not think they have yet been assigned the place in the world's affairs that they are biologically made for.*

A natural curiosity of laypersons, usually unspoken, is how physicians maintain their objectivity in their examinations, particularly of erogenous zones. Let us speak plainly. In my professional life, I have examined literally thousands of breasts. Yes, once in a while, *very* rarely, in the middle of an examination, an unannounced, unanticipated difference in my usual objective attitude insinuates itself. For an instant, I am diverted from detachment, from purely scientific considerations to those of another kind. Yet such a lapse is seldom brought on merely by the esthetics of a well-formed bosom. Rather, it comes from some indefinable something in that patient's appearance and manner, or personality, as if some chemical or atavistic reaction were set in motion.

In an instant, recognizing what is happening, I snap out of it. Outwardly, I remain at all times the cool professional, and follow established technique for breast examinations. Within seconds, the pulse-quickening moment has passed and my professionally palpating fingertips finish their work, tending strictly to business.

Examination completed, the patient dresses and we discuss the findings. Then she leaves, none the wiser, I think, that this transient, ephemeral, evanescent "bond" between us existed.

Am I wrong to say so, wrong to admit to these lapses into momentary reverie? It would be wrong, I think, to pretend they never happen.

Although never studied scientifically, probably such unannounced reactions occur particularly in male physicians upon beholding a great beauty. It is no sin to balance for a flickering moment on the razor's edge between esthetics and the scientific, just so long as you don't lose your equilibrium.

When confronted by a Brooke Shields or a Diane Sawyer at some social function, I am dissolved in sheer admiration, and the furthest thing from my mind is the substructure responsible for that serene brow, that glorious nose, or those cheekbones. Oscar Wilde said it: "Beauty is greater than genius, for genius has to be explained." Amen.

Enforced intimacy creates other problems. As a physician's practice grows, he encounters a new situation: recognizing some

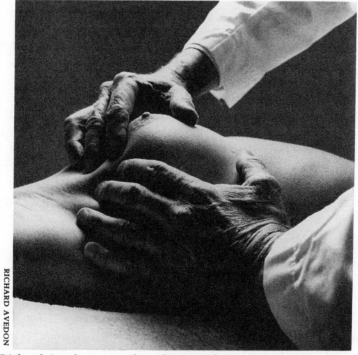

RICHARD AVEDON

Richard Avedon wanted to photograph "experienced hands" for an article on breast examination. Here the author shows the technique for palpation.

patients out of context. At social gatherings or in restaurants, someone will come over and say, "Hello, Dr. Cahan, remember me? You operated on me years ago." I manage to smile weakly through the first awkward moments as I try, usually futilely, to recall names. Seeing my confusion, they are thoughtful enough to take me off the hook. I make light of my lapse ("I may forget names, but I never forget a scar. Where's yours?") Just think, I say to myself: *This person entrusted me with her life.*

I have suggested ideas of medical interest to Grace from time to time that might amuse and benefit her readers. Because of my fervent involvement with breast cancer, she decided to do a major article on the subject.

She commissioned the photographer Richard Avedon. One day Grace called to say that Avedon needed a pair of "experienced hands" to pose as if examining a model's breast. I told Grace: "You're talking to a pair of experienced hands."

When the photograph appeared to illustrate the article in *Vogue,* it is not clear as to whether Grace used her editorial prerogative or there was an underlying conjugal motive. The photograph was only two inches in diameter.

Later, Avedon gave me a two-foot-by-two-foot enlargement of it; it is one of a kind, and undeniably a masterpiece.

Grace Mirabella worked at *Vogue* for twenty years before she became its editor-in-chief in 1972. Under her aegis, the magazine's circulation increased from 250,000 to 1,250,000 and its pages bulged with lucrative advertisements. But, in the late eighties, Grace was frequently depressed when she came home from work. Each time I questioned her, she said that she was increasingly frustrated: "I'm thinking of quitting. I just had another battle with Alex and I don't want to face yet another one. Life is too short."

These moods were serious, but usually ended when we agreed that personality problems as well as other kinds were to be expected in all jobs. But the conflicts at work occurred with regularity and mostly revolved around the all-important editorial director of the magazine, Alexander Liberman.

Liberman is a remarkable man: gray-haired, patrician in appearance, elegant in manner, a distinguished graphic designer, painter, sculptor, and photographer in his own right apart from his work on the Condé Nast magazines, of which *Vogue* is one. The ambi-

WILLIAM G. CAHAN

Alexander Liberman

guities of his position as "editorial director" of Condé Nast produced more than a little storm and strife, as well as some lively,
successful magazines.

For example, when Grace wanted to run the story on breast
cancer, Alex told her, "*Vogue* readers are more interested in fashion than breast cancer." As staffers who work for her know full
well, Grace can also be stubborn and tough. "Alex, I've been a
woman longer than you, and they're interested in *both*."

Months later, Alex called and, as if it had just occurred to him,
enthusiastically proposed doing an article on breast cancer.

But even occasional professional friction did not affect our
friendship. Grace and I spent many weekends with Alex and his
wife, Tatiana, at their home in Warren, Connecticut, where the
Libermans made us feel like part of their family. (That included
Tatiana's daughter, the writer Francine du Plessix Gray; Francine's husband, the painter Cleve Gray; and their sons.)

In light of subsequent events, it may seem incongruous that we
were also friends of Condé Nast's owner, Samuel I. Newhouse,
Jr. ("Si") and his wife, Victoria. From time to time, I had given

medical advice to Si's parents and to him. In 1985, Si and his brother, Donald, gave a handsome donation to the Cahan Chair in Surgery at MSK.

When gossip about Grace losing her job broke in the press, Grace asked Alex and Si about it. Each one reassured her that there was nothing to it, and both were quoted in *The New York Times,* saying as much. For my part, I could not believe the rumors. Grace was a unique, important, and beloved figure in the world of fashion, and *Vogue* had blossomed under her leadership.

Still, friends kept warning us about one Anna Wintour, who was known to be very ambitious. Anna had done well as the editor of British *Vogue*; later, as editor of *House and Garden,* she had made changes in its format and character that some readers found unappealing; she had been editor of *HG* for only a few months. She was thirty-eight.

Then, one day in June 1988, I had a phone call at home from Marie Fauth, a friend. "Turn on Channel Four immediately." When I did so, I heard the tail end of columnist-commentator Liz Smith's announcement: "The rumor is now confirmed. Anna Wintour is going to take Grace Mirabella's place at *Vogue.* Si, if it's not broken, why fix it?"

I thought: *For God's sake, Liz, you must be out of your mind to make such a ridiculous statement in public.* I called Grace at her office. Grace said, "I haven't heard a word, but let me speak to Alex and call you right back."

A few minutes later, she called: "It's true."

When Grace came home, she calmed me down and explained: "I think they were alarmed by the success of *Elle* magazine [which, although its U.S. edition was only a few years old, had had a meteoric rise in circulation]. I've been trying to tell them that *Vogue,* to compete with *Elle,* should go after a readership of younger women. But each time I wanted to do something about it, Alex blocked it."

Not only I, but many of Grace's professional and close friends, felt that Grace had been shabbily treated. Grace, on her part, remained calm through it all and handled herself with great dignity. Her widely admired quote was in *The New York Times* the next day—"For a magazine devoted to style, this was not a very stylish way of telling me."

Just before Grace made her final departure from *Vogue,* Si Newhouse called her to his office and invited her to lunch. She said to him, "Thank you very much. It's very gracious of you, Si, but I'd rather not."

This took two to three minutes, and after thirty-seven years, she left.

At no time was Grace deeply depressed by the incident. In fact, she seemed relieved. Beverly Sills called to console Grace, saying that when she resigned as head of the New York City Opera, all she could think of was Martin Luther King, Jr.'s phrase, borrowed from a spiritual: "Free at last, oh Lord, free at last!"

Given our busy lives, Grace and I rarely had lunch together. But the day after she got the news, I took her and one of our friends to the fashionable Four Seasons restaurant. A procession of well-wishers stopped by our table with remarks like, "They must be crazy!" or (Liz's phrase) "If it's not broken, why fix it?"

At a nearby table, Howard Kaminsky, once the publisher of Si Newhouse's Random House, was lunching with sex therapist Dr. Ruth Westheimer. When they finished, they came over to our table to chat. Dr. Ruth told us she was celebrating the publication of her third book with Howard, who had been responsible for publishing her first. Then, Dr. Ruth looked at me and said, "I know what you do, Doctor, and I hope I never have to see you."

I smiled, "I know what you do, Doctor, and I hope I never have to see *you!*"

Alex and Si, who were at the Four Seasons, dropped by on their way out to say hello and shake Grace's and my hand. Weeks later, Alex, was given a party to celebrate the opening of an exhibition of his work at the Museum of Modern Art. We went. Friendship is friendship and, I guess, business is business.

I've mentioned "Bedford." Early in our marriage, it was evident that we needed a refuge from the febrile pace of our lives. Grace and I had little time together during the week. As for summers, we hoped to have our own retreat somewhere to avoid the sadness of packing up each Labor Day, leaving a rented house behind. I had always yearned for a place with a view.

One day, a real estate agent suggested taking a look at a spot that, although a wilderness of sorts at the moment, might be what we were looking for. Anthony went with me. We saw a derelict, gray clapboard bungalow at the foot of a large field, densely overgrown with thickets that extended up a hill. Anthony and I made our way to its top where he climbed a tree to get a better view. He was silent for a moment. Then said, "Dad, this view's *magnificent*."

Grace converted the bungalow into a charming little country cottage, and we weekended there happily for a few years.

But we always longed for the spectacular view to be had from the top of the hill, so we decided to clear the thickets and build some sort of a house there.

We looked over several uninspiring architects' plans. Then, we met Alexander Gorlin, an architect in his early thirties, who had studied in Rome and lectured at Yale. He had never designed a home, but was sympathetic to the idea of a little villa reminiscent of those seen in Italian hill towns. As Grace and I admired the serene, symmetrical style of Palladio (who influenced Jefferson's Monticello), Alex's design reflected this.

(As an architect manqué, I learned a lot about the exquisite logic of good architecture and the importance of every detail, and became completely involved in every aspect of construction. Because of this, Grace expected that one day Alex would tell her to "get that manqué off my back.")

The result, which we named Cielo—Italian for "heaven"—has yellow stuccoed walls, an octagonal vestibule and octagonal living room. The latter has an eighteen-foot ceiling and huge windows looking out onto the extraordinary vista; it is flanked on one side by a dining room–library and on the other by a bedroom.

While we were building the house, Grace was building a new edifice of her own, *Mirabella*. Naturally that consumed most of her time and energy, but she was always available to say no at strategic times and to everyone's advantage. It's been said that the true test of a sound marriage is that it can withstand a husband's teaching a wife to drive or to swim, or the couple's building a house. Fortunately, Grace knew how to drive. The other two we went through together. Grace remarked: "It takes a solid marriage to survive a magazine's start up."

Grace had been fired on a Thursday. By Monday she was deluged by calls offering all kinds of opportunities. One evening, Grace was called by Rupert Murdoch, the Australian-born head of a considerable media empire. He invited Grace to lunch. He talked in vague terms about starting a new magazine about women, or "something like that," and wanted her views on the subject.

After they parted, Grace heard nothing further for three months. Just as she was about to sign a contract with another substantial media corporation, Rupert called and again invited her to lunch. When she told him that she was about to sign a contract that afternoon, he said, "It won't hurt to wait just one more day. Please lunch with me tomorrow."

Grace called the other people to apologize for the delay and the next day drove to New York. To avoid rumors, she met Rupert in an obscure restaurant. At the end of lunch, he said, "Please do me one more favor: Delay signing just one more day until you meet with John Evans, the president of my magazine section."

To maintain secrecy, she met Evans at the cozy Box Tree Restaurant in an upstairs room suitable mainly, I think, for an intimate meal or a still more intimate assignation. (Afterward, I said, "I hope nobody we knew saw the two of you go up there.")

As they talked, Evans said, almost as an aside, "In Rupert's plan for *Mirabella* he would like you to . . ."

Grace wasn't sure that she heard him correctly. "What did you say, John?"

"You mean Rupert didn't tell you? We're thinking of naming the new magazine after you."

When Grace came home, she said, "Wait until you hear *this*." However, she began to have some doubts. "I'm almost sixty [the newspapers said fifty-seven at the time] and I'm not sure I want to work that hard. Besides, the name 'Mirabella' will be meaningless on the newsstand." To me, the fact that *Mirabella* translated from the Italian as "beautiful vision" seemed like a natural.

As soon as I heard the idea, I recognized that this was a great opportunity for Grace to express her philosophy about style, fashion, women, and the world they inhabit. What is more, she could do so without having her ideas modified or restricted by others.

"Grace," I said, "you know how I feel about age in numbers. You're the best there is, you have a large public who knows what your name stands for. Now get going!" What might have been even more persuasive: "Just imagine how your mother will feel when she sees a magazine called *Mirabella*." No matter how busy she was, Grace always took time to visit her ninety-year-old mother three or four times a week.

When Grace told the other corporation that she had a more attractive offer, they offered to match it. She thanked them sincerely and declined, saying that there was one feature that they couldn't match, a detail she was not at liberty to divulge.

Grace organized offices, editors, editorial assistants, format, and photographers. All had to be interviewed, corraled, and inspired. And *Mirabella* came together with the first issue in June 1988, just six months after Grace's first meetings with Rupert Murdoch and John Evans. The cover had a half-face closeup of Diandra Douglas and inside, a caricature of Grace by Al Hirschfeld.

From the first, the magazine seemed to be a success. As Grace said it would, *Mirabella* dealt with the many interests of contemporary women. In short, pithy articles on beautifully designed pages, the magazine mixed politics, art, fashion, theater, movies, books, and, yes, health with touches of humor. Within a year, it had a circulation of more than 350,000.

An unexpected reward for me, and one I never tire of seeing, is the glowing look on women's faces as they tell Grace how much they enjoy her magazine and how much it has come to mean to them. Apparently it filled a niche for women who had been looking for a relevant voice, rather than one suggesting that their interests were limited to children, home, husband, cosmetics, and clothes. These women include a large and important segment of our population—volunteers, fighters for causes, social leaders, tradition and barrier breakers, voices of conscience, taste-makers, refiners of our culture. These are not women who will allow themselves to be ignored, overlooked, bypassed, and they recognize that *Mirabella* understood this.

Early in its inception, when Grace was asked to what age bracket *Mirabella* was directed, she said that style knows no age. And that fashion, important as it is to many women, is only one component of style. "There's more to women than concern about the length of a hem"—and Grace exemplifies this dictum.

Poor Doc Gooden, our favorite Mets pitcher, was being battered as we watched on television. When he was relieved in the fourth inning, I remarked that he had had a bad day. Grace suddenly said: "Do surgeons have good and bad days the way professional athletes or singers have off days now and then, when they are not in top form?"

The answer had to be yes. "If so," she asked, "are patients jeopardized if their surgeon doesn't feel up to par when operating? And should an operation be postponed, or another surgeon called in to operate instead?" I thought—even more pertinently to my constant inventory-taking in my seventh decade—*Does being seventy-plus mean that I will have more frequent off days?*

Fortunately, most operations are satisfactorily performed by capable surgeons, who do not always have to be in peak form. (A head cold is no deterrent to operating and, when I have one, I wear a double-thickness face mask.) As with actors' and musicians' performances, most surgical procedures follow established patterns and can be carried off safely and successfully without necessarily requiring a virtuoso performance ("Four Scars"— *Daily News*).

But other problems require other solutions. While I was playing unwilling host to a kidney stone, I transferred the care of patients needing surgery to a capable colleague. Some surgeons suffer from such acutely inflated egos that they will persist in operating in spite of physical disabilities. During my internship, one prominent orthopedic surgeon kept his fractured left arm (in a cast) tucked away beneath his operating-room gown while he operated with his right hand. His assistants took up the slack.

As a result of Grace's question, I felt it wise to review my own status at this time of my life. Although my energy, skill, and concentration have not flagged, the thought of giving up surgery occurred with increasing frequency. If, at an advanced age, artists continue to paint (Matisse, Picasso), writers to write (Alfred North Whitehead, Isaac Bashevis Singer), or musicians to play (Arthur Rubinstein, Vladimir Horowitz) and the result is not perfect, no harm is done except to their reputations. However, should an aging surgeon's fingers become all thumbs, others *are* affected.

Grace's questions raised all sorts of accessory considerations. Is it advantageous to be operated on early rather than late in the day? In some hospitals, the surgical load is so large that some operations begin as late as nine P.M. For a surgeon to begin at that hour, would he not be fatigued after a full day's activities, in and out of an operating room, and not be scalpel-sharp at its end? I told Grace that I knew of no serious repercussions resulting from this practice, and that it is not unusual for surgeons to have three or four operations on the same day.

Grace then said: "Is a patient handicapped by being the last one?" Here again, the analogy with musicians is apposite: Concert artists perform many works, the last of which can be the equal or even better than the first. Some baseball pitchers do not tire but actually improve in later innings.

What Grace did not ask was whether an "elderly" surgeon

would be able to make proper judgments at a critical time and perform exacting, technical feats if needed. I can only answer for myself and honestly say I've had no lapses in judgment nor rebukes to my skill.

Nevertheless, avoid them though one may, intimations of one's mortality begin to intrude. In spite of my stoutly disavowing age-by-the-numbers as an index of capability, more visible signs of the inexorability of growing older appear. To the silvering and diminishing of my hair was added an increase in wrinkles. I have to undergo a sobering experience each time I board a bus or enter a movie at reduced prices for "senior citizens": I am no longer asked for an ID card.

As a veteran observer of changes in anatomy and physiology, I am amused by those of my own attributable to age. I wonder if certain creaks and aches herald the onset of decay, and every forgotten name or misused word, or slight awkwardness, which in anyone younger would go unnoticed, signals "getting on." When I see my contemporaries' altered appearance—stooped, sometimes slack-jawed, walking hesitantly—I immediately straighten up, close my mouth, walk firmly, trying to appear as though I'm on some purposeful mission.

Recently, as a private test of memory and acuity, I sat down to the piano for the first time in over a year and was able to play many songs I had written fifty years before, plus other popular ballads. Although the piano needed tuning, and our dog, Cara, kept wailing, it was a rich, reassuring experience.

To that oft-used definition of growing old ("You're old when nuns and policemen look young") I've added personal ones: You're old when you lose hair where you want it and get it where you don't, and when your former surgical residents are not just professors, but deans of medical schools.

So, somewhat reluctantly, I kept flirting with retirement from surgery and would probably not have retired for some time had not a chance meeting focused my thinking.

While Grace and I were walking on Madison Avenue, we passed my former mentor at MSK, ninety-plus-year-old Dr. Frank Adair. We had walked a few steps beyond him before I realized who he was, because his advanced years had made such radical changes in his appearance. When I called his name, he stopped and smiled vaguely as he groped for mine. Supplying it, I heard him once again call me "Bill," but now in a quavering voice.

Standing there, it was hard to believe that this frail man, whose neck was tortoised and far too small for his collar, was once the jovial, ebullient, robust, eminently successful, silver-haired surgeon who was considered by many the finest breast specialist in America. Although he looked almost like a wizened caricature of his former self, he still retained an air of his former dignity and graciousness.

We chatted for a few minutes about old times and what was going on at MSK. Then he said good-bye (I instinctively knew it was probably "Farewell") and moved on, hesitating, as if unsure about where he was going.

I thought: Here is a man who once seemed indestructible, who strode confidently along hospital corridors and into operating rooms, whom we residents nicknamed the Great White Father. Now, heavy-handed time has changed all that and, like no other signal, our chance meeting gave me an insight, a preview, of what I might be like were I to survive into my nineties. Seeing Dr. Adair this way did more than any other experience to remind me that I, too, was vulnerable—the fragile man whom I had just seen was only sixteen years my senior. If he was not indispensable, neither was I.

Not long after, Dr. Adair died. At a memorial service at our hospital, he was eulogized by the few remaining staff members who knew him and by his son. One eulogist recalled that Dr. Adair was so wedded to his mission in life that he had to be, as one might say, dragged protesting from the operating room when he was told he no longer could operate. He grumbled about this for years.

A few months later, after forty-plus years of practice, I eased myself out of what had once been a consuming passion: I stopped operating.

The most compelling reason for doing so was not that I had an early menopause of spirit; but out of consideration for patients, I wanted to quit rather than wait for the first awkward gesture, the slightest flaw in technique or judgment, a moment's inattention that could be attributed to age. Such an experience would haunt me for the rest of my life.

Additional incentive for my surgical swan song was a letter I received from MSK's president, Dr. Paul Marks, stating that the institution would like to name a chair in surgery after me.

I felt honored, of course. However, a chair must bé funded by $1.25 million, to generate income used to support whoever occupies it. Gratifyingly, that sum was raised in a year from friends and patients of mine, and a search was begun for a surgeon to fill the chair. The new chief of thoracic surgery, Dr. Robert Ginsberg, was named to the William G. Cahan Chair. However, according to hospital policy, no one could occupy a surgical chair named for a staff member unless that member no longer practiced surgery. So, to my title of emeritus professor of surgery at Cornell University Medical College was added emeritus attending surgeon, Memorial Sloan-Kettering Cancer Center.

There is something cobwebbed about the title "emeritus" and the term "semi-retired," but there is no "emeritus" in my new status.

Unlike some surgeons—who, when they retire, heave a sigh of relief at first, then, after a while, find it difficult to fill their days —I do not find time hanging heavily on my ungloved hands. Besides being Grace's husband—a full-time job—being involved in promoting *Look Good, Feel Better* make-over programs and my running battle with tobacco interests; playing with grandchildren, and writing this book, I am accelerating rather than slowing down.* More than ever I have become a clearinghouse for those with cancer, or their friends and relatives, who seek my opinion or want to be referred to an appropriate specialist. I still dispense avuncular advice to youngsters contemplating medicine as a career and, as relentlessly as ever, try to convince smokers to quit. I have become increasingly involved in public-health measures that more than amply replace my previous one-on-one sermons.

From time to time, I feel a momentary urge to operate—in surgispeak to "get my hands wet"—but this is compensated for vicariously when Anthony describes to me his more interesting surgical experiences.

And I still see patients.

---

* Pat York's 1991 book *Going Strong* contains photographs and brief texts of seventy individuals who are seventy-five years or older and who are still immensely active. George Abbott, still producing plays at 104, like Abou Ben Adrem led all the rest. I, too, am in it, along with Kitty Carlisle Hart, Gene Kelly, Allistair Cook, Leo Castelli, et al. All of us have plans, none of which includes lying down and playing dead.

CHAPTER XXXVIII

Who Changes the Water?

Often called an art and a science, medicine might also be called religion in the sense that faith (or will) can play an important role in a patient's recovery from serious illness. Certainly a lot of things happen in treatment that are not fully understood today. Maybe they never will be. Darwin believed that complete comprehension of the laws of the universe is beyond the human intellect. Which reminds us of the goldfish who said to his bowl-buddy, "All right, wise guy, if there's no God, who changes the water?"

—NY COUNTY MEDICAL SOCIETY BULLETIN

The promise I made to myself as a teenager after my grandmother's death, that I would never stand by helplessly while someone I loved was in acute distress, has been fulfilled on many occasions. And like those who've placed their lives in my hands, I now place mine in yours.

As noted, I am no stranger to tears—others' or my own. Anthony has entered a world in which there will be torrents, floods.

Women weep unashamedly, more readily than men, perhaps because they are more vulnerable, and are not, as are men, supposed to maintain a stalwart image in the face of distress. Men apologize for crying, embarrassed that they do not seem strong enough to hide this "weakness" in public.

Children cry readily for many reasons. Even the strongest and most dignified adults weep as they recall mothers, pets, moments of supreme beauty or sorrow. I told Anthony: If you are like me, you will often witness tears as a result of sad tidings you bear. Obey your instinct and gently pour the balm of affection on those who are bruised, worried, anxious, and despairing.

When patients are in great distress, lying in a bed attached to all manner of tubes and wires, I feel like saying, "Come to me, weep in my arms; let me blunt your fright and set you down ever so gently. Know that despite the tubes, catheters, and such, we love you all the same."

It is painfully clear that, among other unfulfilled dreams, I will probably not live to see the longed-for conquest of cancer. There is some consolation in that battles have been won and that many promising starts have been made. In all probability, my grandchildren will not be haunted by the awesome, awful specter. Amen, amen.

I wonder, if at the end of a long medical lifetime, some physicians think: "I'm spiritually exhausted. There is a limit to compassion; the wellsprings of caring have dried up; I've reached the point where I no longer feel concerned."

I cannot believe it will happen to me for, barring the frosting of my arterial channels, it is unthinkable that I would ever feel indifferent or "too tired" to come to the aid of—whoever.

A friend recently called at night and began, as all do, with profuse apologies for having disturbed me. Then he used that ambiguous phrase, "I couldn't find anyone else." I kid him afterward by saying that I am obviously Dr. Faute de Mieux, whom one calls when it is impossible to reach anyone worthwhile—so "Let's try Bill."

For whatever reason, it's nice to know I'm still needed.

But is this memoir needed?

In looking in the rearview mirror, I have not succeeded in avoiding rose-colored contact lenses. For one who stoutly supports the warts-and-all school of autobiography, I've failed miserably by committing the unpardonable sin of conferring antemortem sainthood on myself: a dangerous practice. All too often, a halo has a way of slipping down to become a noose. (Oscar Wilde's "To love one's self is the beginning of a lifelong romance" applies here.)

Perhaps some will grant me absolution for the sin of self-canonization if I confess I have been both a hero and a coward, an idealist and a cynic, a Galahad and a sensualist.

It's this last trait that has stalked me most of my life, what with Russian-Jewish genes and an impressionist painter as a father. As a result, I have had all I could do to rein in the foam-flecked, wild-eyed emotions that threatened to trample the scientist in me underfoot.

I was somewhat less successful in disciplining my private life, for I have been guilty of peccadilloes in which women, sometimes wives not my own, played stellar roles. Virtue and the devil constantly competed within me and, I confess, I often had more fun when the devil was ahead, although I usually hated myself in the morning.

Hubris in me has been strong, humility far too weak. Other vices abound: I am quick to an unbecoming jealousy, and overly playful and antic, perhaps. But except for occasional puns, I hope that my overall Wince Index is low.

In summing up: Have I lived up to the Hippocratic oath "to do no harm"? Have I done good?

The records of patients whom I've saved—and lost—can be found in hospital files. What is immeasurable, pure speculation, is the ripple effect of various writings, lectures, and teachings, particularly those about prevention. What has been the impact of warning labels on cigarette packages and advertisements? Or helping to heighten public and professional awareness to the hazards of irradiation? One answer sounds like beautiful music: "You don't remember me, but I sat next to you at a dinner party [or, "saw you on television"] and afterward I gave up smoking."

When some realize their days are numbered, they intensify their vision of things about them so that the minutiae of everyday life, which they have taken for granted, are brought into sharp focus. As never before, a blade of grass, a child's smile, the various colors of objects assume a new importance.

Although not threatened by acute foreboding, nevertheless I am faced with the intimations of my own mortality these days; I savor beauty in any form as if it were my last chance to do so.

Now, more than ever, I am conscious of the simplest acts and experiences and find myself taking retinal snapshots of scenes I cherish and want to recall: Grace in repose, my grandchildren at play, moments of full-throated laughter.

More than ever, my mind seems alive, my sensitivities keener, my affections stronger. I love people more deeply and comprehensively and see my work in its proper relationship with science as a whole.

Alas, all will be erased when I depart, but one of my gene-bearers down the line will understand when I say that this morning, framed in Cielo's huge picture window, I am looking at flowers accented against the early morning pale-blue sky, which frames a few copper-colored clouds; I am luxuriating in the peace and beauty of this scene; my heart leaps at the sight of a hummingbird that, having discovered the pink geraniums, and stabbing the flowers, darts over to buzz the picture window, mistaking the flowers' image for the real ones. Then, frustrated, and with bruised beak, it darts back to the genuine ones. I am momentarily saddened and wonder if there is a lesson for the writer of a memoir, in mistaking reflections for reality.

All this delectable floor show was outlined against two huge willow trees I had planted years ago; they are now over thirty feet tall. For posterity's sake: Cerubi, our old tabby cat, lies buried beneath one of them and, each spring, tulips bloom over her grave. Some day, some of my dust will join hers.

October 18, 1988.
    A. called to tell me that my third grandchild, Samuel Crawford Cahan, was born. Minutes afterward, while Anthony was in the delivery room with Mary Beth and they were both congratulating each other, they noticed Sam's little hands grasping the clamp on his end of the umbilical cord.
    In unison, they exclaimed: "Oh my God! Another surgeon!"

July 10, 1990.
    Another grandson! James Bennet is named after Sisi's father. Anthony is so prolific. It's risky for his wife to hold hands with him.

"Even the weariest river winds somewhere safe to sea." Soon after my mother's death I wrote: "Sometime during the night atoms, weary of each other, let go: A string breaks and a picture falls; a leaf leaves its branch; rust dissolves a girder, and a heart stops." Lying in bed one night, feeling my own pulse, I had the morbid idea that just so many beats are left: hardly an expression of my usual zest for living.

Through my professional career, death has always hovered, a constant presence and adversary. Knowing how common sudden deaths are at my age, and having seen my parents die this way, I keep wondering how mine will present itself.

I can imagine myself on a tennis court, running as usual for a shot as if life depended upon it, suddenly clutching my abdomen (aneurysm), or my chest (cardiac arrest), or my head (stroke) and, for a split second before oblivion, recognizing what is happening. Others I have known have made sudden departures while doing surgery, climbing stairs, shoveling snow.

A traumatic end is not impossible, considering the way I drive. Like many colleagues, I may have a rendezvous with my mortal enemy, cancer, which, even as I write, may have begun its insidious treachery.

Whatever form death takes, I hope to depart in a graceful swan dive of an ending, rather than linger as a travesty, a poor imitation, a garbled version of my former self as the result of slow neurological deterioration.

I write to Anthony and Christopher: Grant me one last wish. My mother and father died when they should have and I would also prefer to do so rather than linger on. Therefore, when it is clearly time, and I am unable to orchestrate the coda myself: As a favor and a tribute, be my surrogates and don't let sentiment cloud your judgment. Just as you would for any helpless, hopelessly sick animal, make my end short and sweet. Be careful, however, not to rely entirely on drugs; to do so could subject you to legal complications. Instead, ample sedation and strict inanition should do it. I assure you that I will be most grateful.

Enough memories of me, both good and bad, are available for those who wish to retrieve them. I would hate becoming progressively pathetic and painful to gaze upon so that, in time, pity is replaced by resentment.

Therefore, with a clear conscience, consider it to be yet another privilege of this wonderful life of medicine to be able to ease me on my way. Miles down the road, one of you may ask Nicky, Devon, Sam, or Jimmy to do the same for you. Remember, sad as this event may be, "The heart does not stop when one thinks it should; we smile; there is tea and bread on the table." (Czesław Miłosz)

As I approach the age when one is said to be nearer one's Maker, let me be clear: I still do not believe in an omniscient, all-powerful deity who alternately smiles and frowns upon us, forgives our transgressions, and eventually welcomes us in a celestial embrace.

It has always seemed simplistic and even ingenuous to assign and explain all things in nature as the workings of a man-made god. Too much has been and continues to be discovered about phenomena of astonishing complexity and beauty that have long been considered as incontrovertible evidence of the workings of a supreme being. I take them for what they are: Nature's remarkable attention to detail.

In my teens, I read about pantheism, a romantic concept that God is present everywhere and in everything. In a sense, a residue of pantheism may still be with me.

My father was an ardent antireligionist, incensed that people are divided from each other by labels, rituals, and their own version of a deity. He was particularly infuriated by the tortures and killings done in the name of a particular religion to please a particular god.

At one point, I came close to praying when Chris was a few days old and thought to be hydrocephalic. It was a great blow and, as I kept it to myself, I clutched for any possible support. Some atavism suggested praying. But I found myself incapable of doing so. Instead, as I have done many times since, I converted despair and anxiety into constructive activity, intensifying my research and spending more time with patients and their problems until the acute anguish subsided.

I see no reason why medicine cannot be a religion; it certainly is mine. It is not blasphemous to say that its universal themes follow the precepts of Christ the Healer, and when practiced skillfully and compassionately, are a true expression of His teaching.

At my memorial service, I'd like it said: "He wanted less to be known as a skilled surgeon and more as one of the most caring."

After all, who *does* change the water?

January 4, 1992.
Leave-taking means many gestures: parting kisses, hugs, waved farewells. Today, I took leave of my stethoscope.

For my medical lifetime, I have carried a stethoscope like a side-arm in my long white coat. As medical students, we longed to display them in public in our outside pockets so that everyone would know we were doctors. Since then, countless lungs have whooshed and wheezed, hearts thumped, and abdomens gurgled through its tubes. Now, like old soldiers who put their weapons away in an attic, or artists who store their paints and brushes and canvases in some closet, I put my stethoscope in a bottom desk drawer to gather dust. However, it is always at the ready should a cry come in the night that, at that moment, only I can answer.

One day, I stopped reading medical journals. I still scan them cover to cover, however—less with a thought of improving my patients' care, and more to bring important articles to Anthony's attention. However, I still keep on the prowl for some bright spark of an idea that could set off a string of fireworks.

No longer operating, I notice a new feeling of being unburdened. Now, when Grace and I go out, instead of being shadowed by a patient's condition, or thinking of tomorrow's O.R. schedule, I enjoy myself fully. Gone, too, is the ever-present feeling of responsibility that shortened our weekends in Bedford when, each Sunday afternoon, I would have to leave for New York early enough to see patients who were scheduled for Monday morning surgery. Having done that for so many years, I now catch myself on Sunday afternoons still thinking I have to cut short the end of that day. Then, with a sigh, I realize I no longer have to do so.

There is yet another reminder of the gathering dusk. At the end of office hours, I give patients a return date, usually six months hence. I realize that when I see them next, I'll be hearing the strains of "September Song": It is:

a long, long while from May to December . . . and the days do grow short when you reach September.

Or, in my case, October or November.

On the morning of my seventy-fifth birthday, Grace handed me a letter confirming her gift to MSK: a research laboratory in surgery in my name.

Shortly after that, I learned that Ann and Herb Siegel, long-standing friends, had donated a new conference room, also in my name, on the same floor of the Rockefeller Laboratory Building.

(Herb, a philanthropist, is president of Chris Craft Corporation and a major stockholder in Time-Warner Corporation.) At a reception held to observe these two inspired gifts, I said:

I can think of no greater birthday present than to have been given the gift of hope by the one I love. Grace's laboratory is just that: a symbol of hope—for in it, fine minds are working so that many may live. The ultimate dream, the cure for cancer, will emerge from just such units of basic research.

One of the important elements of research is for researchers to mingle and exchange ideas and discoveries. This will be done in the

conference room that Ann and Herb Siegel so generously donated.
They have given a gift not just to me but to us all.

Honors are often built on ironies. On January 1, 1992, I had been
on MSK's staff for fifty years. The Center planned to commemorate a milestone—the first staff member in its 108-year history
to do so. I decided to attend. It would be a first in my history,
too.

◆

POSTLUDE

———————

Recently, when Anthony asked if I wanted to watch him operate, I jumped at the opportunity. Once more, I found myself looking over his shoulder.

Misty-eyed . . . were these dexterous hands the grubby ones that I struggled to get into mittens, that used to reach for mine as we crossed the street, that I taught to tie shoelaces?

As Anthony kept working away, unmindful of me, I thought: This golden moment might not have come to pass had my grandmother not died in my arms. Who else was in that room rejoicing? What forebears' shadows, ghosts, specters, genes, were working harmoniously in him, contributing to this young surgeon's striving to cure this patient and comfort him afterward?

At one point, I glanced down and was amused to see my specially constructed operating shoes, which I had handed down to him when I gave up surgery, beneath Anthony's O.R. shoe covers. Now, when patients tell me how pleased and proud I must be to have a son follow in my footsteps, I add: "He's not just in my footsteps, he's in my shoes."

When Anthony and I talk medicine, I notice, wistfully, that my reservoir of suggestions has dwindled down to a precious few. In fact, the tutor is now being tutored by the "tutee," for Anthony tells *me* about advances and discoveries.

At last, contented, I can sit back and rest easy.

Or can I?

E. J. CAMP

Three generations—and counting

INDEX

❖

ABOUT THE AUTHOR

DR. WILLIAM G. CAHAN was born in New York City. He took his undergraduate degree at Harvard and went to medical school at Columbia's College of Physicians and Surgeons. He was a resident at Presbyterian Hospital and then at Memorial Sloan-Kettering, where he became a staff member and practiced for over fifty years.

ABOUT THE TYPE

This book was set in Bembo, a typeface based on an old-style Roman face that was used for Cardinal Bembo's tract *De Actua* in 1495. Bembo was cut by Francisco Griffo in the early sixteenth century. The Lanston Monotype Machine Company of Philadelphia brought the well-proportioned letter forms of Bembo to the United States in the 1930s.